# Landmarks

## Twentieth Century in Pictures

# Landmarks

## Twentieth Century in Pictures

AMMONITE PRESS

PRESS ASSOCIATION Images

First Published 2009 by
Ammonite Press
an imprint of AE Publications Ltd,
166 High Street, Lewes, East Sussex BN7 1XU

Text copyright Ammonite Press
Images copyright Press Association Images
Copyright in the work Ammonite Press

ISBN 978-1-906672-30-0

British Cataloguing in Publication Data. A catalogue
record of this book is available from the British Library.

Editor: Richard Wiles
Series Editor: Paul Richardson
Picture research: Press Association Images
Design: Gravemaker + Scott

Colour reproduction by GMC Reprographics
Printed by Kyodo Nation Printing Services Co., Ltd.

Page 2: Searchlights
frame St Paul's Cathedral
in spectacular fashion in
celebration of VJ Day.
**15th August, 1945**

Page 5: One of the most
iconic landmarks in Britain,
the White Cliffs of Dover on
the south coast of England
where the English Channel
is at its narrowest.
**4th June, 1975**

Page 6: Dryburgh Abbey,
on the banks of the River
*Tweed* in the Scottish
borders, was founded in
1150 by Premonstratensian
canons from Alnwick Abbey,
Northumberland after an
agreement with the Lord
High Constable of Scotland.
Surviving generations of
strife it was finally destroyed
in 1544. Sir Walter Scott,
prolific Scottish historical
novelist and poet, was buried
there in 1832.
**7th March, 2009**

# Introduction

What visual image can claim to encapsulate the nature of Britain? A strong candidate is undoubtedly the rugged beauty of the White Cliffs of Dover, a sight that has both inspired song and spelled 'home' to countless travellers returning to their native shores, as well as troops returning from battle overseas. Britain boasts a unique set of landmarks that make it stand out from the global crowd, instantly recognisable to many.

From Land's End to John O'Groats, mountains, valleys and rivers define the contours of the country, but most of its true landmarks are man-made. From primitive depictions of horses and figures such as Dorset's Cerne Abbas Giant, etched into chalk hillsides, to statues and monuments such as London's Nelson's Column erected to celebrate a historical event or figure, and monolithic skyscrapers that thrust upward, they are all the products of the ingenuity and skill of artists and architects, engineers and builders. Their edifices – reflecting the styles of the eras in which they were built – determine the character of the nation's towns and cities. As with every major conurbation, London's skyline is instantly recognisable by its classic landmarks: the clock tower that houses Big Ben, the Houses of Parliament, Tower Bridge, St Paul's Cathedral and others, which exist in harmony with modern icons such as the London Eye, the 'Gherkin', and the lofty tower blocks of Canary Wharf.

The inescapable march of time, destruction brought about by war and the results of changing fashions or obsolescence have seen many of the nation's historic landmarks disappear while others stand defiant. Testament to the long, rich heritage of the British Isles, many of these architectural relics date back thousands of years. Among them are ancient and beautiful priories established by missionaries, the cavernous, spired cathedrals that were hundreds of years in construction, and mighty castles that withstood siege and assault during feudal times eventually to be undone by gunpowder, great age, the climate or simple neglect.

Many landmarks may have been lost but they need not be forgotten, thanks to the diligence of the photographers of the Press Association who, for more than 100 years, have captured these architectural icons on film. Their intentions may have been to record a news story to which the landmark was an incidental backdrop, or perhaps to mark the unveiling of a statue or the opening of a new building, but now the images in this book, selected from the vast archives of the Association, record the development of Britain's built environment and preserve it forever.

**Landmarks** • Twentieth Century in Pictures

Facing page: St Paul's
Cathedral seen from Fleet
Street, a view that was restored
in 1990 by the removal of the
railway viaduct at Ludgate
Circus, between Blackfriars
and Holborn Viaduct, which
had obscured the landmark
since 1866.
**1890**

The new Hammersmith Workhouse, London, pictured in
the early years of the 20th century. The site still serves
as Hammersmith Hospital, although many of the original
buildings have now been replaced or much altered. Of the
workhouse, only the administrative block survives.
**1900**

The original Bank underground station near Mansion House, London. The first station opened on the 25th of February, 1900 when the City & South London Railway (now part of the Northern Line) opened an extension from Borough to Moorgate.

**1st August, 1901**

The ornate pavilion of Fratton Park, complete with
clocktower, at the home of Southern League Division One
club, Portsmouth FC, was designed by renowned football
architect Archibald Leitch. The distinctive structure was
removed with the later expansion of the ground.
**30th September, 1905**

The broad façade of the
London Hospital on the south
side of Whitechapel Road in
the East End. It was founded
in 1740, becoming The Royal
London Hospital on its 250th
anniversary in 1990.
**1906**

The 68,000 seat White City stadium was built to the north of Shepherd's Bush, London for the Franco-British exhibition and the Summer Olympics of 1908 by George Wimpey for the sum of £60,000. It closed in 1983 and was demolished two years later to make way for the buildings of BBC White City.
**24th July, 1908**

Facing page: A night scene at the Indian 'stand'; a Mughal-style palace complete with lake, at the Franco-British Exhibition, White City, London.
**1908**

The official residence of the Prime Minister of the United Kingdom, 10 Downing Street, London (C). One of the most recognisable houses in the world, 'Number 10' was originally three houses built around 1683 by Sir George Downing, formerly a spy for Oliver Cromwell. The subject of much deterioration and renovation, the building had been constructed cheaply on shallow foundations. Former Prime Minister Winston Churchill wrote that the Downing Street buildings were *"shaky and lightly built by the profiteering contractor whose name they bear."*
**1909**

People enjoying the sun on the Leas, the cliffs above the beach at Folkestone in Kent, with Victoria pier jutting out into the sea beyond.
**1st July, 1909**

An Edwardian view of Caernarfon castle in North Wales, part of the chain of fortifications built by Edward I in the 13th century to subdue the rebellious Welsh. The architecture was influenced by the double line of crenellated Theodosian walls of Constantinople, modern Istanbul, Turkey.
**1910**

The elegant west façade of Chatsworth House, in Derbyshire, seat of the Duke of Devonshire – with James Paine's bridge spanning the River *Derwent*, foreground. The house has been home to the Cavendish family since Bess of Hardwick built a Tudor mansion and settled there in 1549. Rebuilt in its present form between 1687 and 1707, the house is set in expansive parkland backed by wooded hills. Early in the 20th century burdensome taxes and debts saw the estate's fortunes dwindle.

**1st August, 1910**

The imposing west frontage of York Minster, one of the largest Gothic cathedrals in Northern Europe, the construction of which began around 1230 and was completed in 1472. The twin west towers and the central tower are each 200ft high, and the Minster's 128 stained glass windows contain about two million individual pieces of glass.

**1911**

King George V unveils the memorial to his grandmother,
Queen Victoria, outside Buckingham Palace, London.
**1911**

The Royal procession during the Coronation of King George V passes down Fleet Street, London. The bustling street was home to the British press from around 1500 when William Caxton's apprentice, Wynkyn de Worde, set up a printing shop nearby, and Richard Pynson began publishing in the street, until the 1980s.

**22nd June, 1911**

Old Waterloo Bridge, spanning the River Thames, London, was named to commemorate the British victory at the Battle of Waterloo in 1815, and opened in 1817 as a toll crossing. After its nationalisation in 1878 serious defects were highlighted and during the 1920s it was decided to replace it with the present structure, which opened in 1942.
**1911**

The Old Curiosity Shop, Portugal Street, London, dates from the 16th century and was thought by some to have been the inspiration for Charles Dickens' description of the odds and ends shop in his novel of the same title, although the name was added only after the book had been published in 1841.
**1911**

A Royal garden party in the
Palace Gardens, overlooked
by the Bath stone west
façade of Buckingham
Palace, London.
**1911**

The Grand Stand at Royal Ascot, a landmark no longer
existing after a £185m redevelopment in 2004.
**23rd June, 1911**

Facing page: The new quadriga (a chariot and four horses), on the Wellington Arch at Constitution Hill, Hyde Park Corner, London.
**April, 1912**

A view of Nelson's Column in Trafalgar Square, London, from the top of the Duke of York's Column.
**1912**

The new Admiralty Arch,
designed by Sir Aston
Webb, constructed by John
Mowlem & Co.
**June, 1912**

The Crystal Palace, south east London. The mainly glass structure was built to house the Great Exhibition of 1851. Originally located in Hyde Park, it was moved to Sydenham Hill after the exhibition.

**1913**

Unloading tobacco at Royal Victoria Docks, London. The docks were built on Plaistow Marshes, and opened in 1855, the first London dock designed to accommodate large steam ships.
**1913**

The onion-shaped dome and tent-like roofs of the Royal Pavilion at Brighton were added by designer John Nash when he rebuilt the original structure in 1815 as a seaside retreat for the Prince Regent.

**1st June, 1913**

Nash's redesigned Royal Pavilion, replacing the one built by
Henry Holland for the Prince of Wales in 1787, introduces an
eastern flavour to Brighton's architecture, with minarets on
the exterior and a strong Chinese influence inside.

**1st June, 1913**

Ye Olde Cogers' Discussion Hall at Salisbury Square. The Society of Cogers is a free speech society, established in 1755. Still running today, it is the oldest debating society in the world.
**1913**

Boulter's Lock on the River *Thames* near Cookham, Berkshire
was a popular venue for boating parties, and attracted the
wealthy and famous on the Sunday after Royal Ascot.
**1913**

The view north over the top of Tower Bridge's upper walkway
into the City of London, and the Tower of London.
**June, 1913**

New recruits drilling on
the terrace of The Crystal
Palace, then requisitioned
as a naval training
establishment.
**June, 1914**

A Royal Naval Unit of
12-oared Cutters at the
Thames Pageant passes by
the Houses of Parliament.
**1919**

The exterior of the Olympia
exhibition centre in West
Kensington, London built in
1886, pictured in 1920.
**1st August, 1920**

The main pedestrian entrance to London Waterloo station, the Victory Arch, was built as a memorial to company staff who died during the First World War, and opens onto an 880ft long concourse with 21 platforms after extensive reconstruction between 1900 and 1922.

**25th April, 1922**

Facing page: After extensive rebuilding, London Waterloo station was reopened on the 21st of March, 1922, rationalising the station's notoriously confusing layout, which had earned it scorn from music hall comics and writers such as Jerome K Jerome, who wrote about the difficulty in finding a platform, departure time or destination in *Three Men in a Boat*.
**1925**

King George V and Queen Mary in the grounds of the Royal Observatory, Greenwich, during a visit.
**23rd July, 1925**

Facing page: An aerial view of Wembley Stadium during the FA Cup
Final between Arsenal and eventual winners Cardiff City, the first to
be broadcast live on BBC radio. The landmark, which opened in 1923,
was instantly recognisable for its distinctive twin towers, until it was
demolished in 2003 to be replaced by a new 90,000 capacity stadium.
**23rd April, 1927**

Traffic on London Bridge.
**1st May, 1929**

The Gaiety Theatre on Aldwych at the eastern end of the Strand, in the West End of London was known for its successful musicals, notably the 1929 run of *Love Lies* by Stanley Lupino and Arthur Rigby, which starred Cyril Ritchard and Madge Elliot. The building was demolished in 1956 and replaced by an office development.

**11th October, 1929**

Dense traffic in central London around Mansion House (C), the official residence of the Lord Mayor of London. Built between 1739 and 1752, it is notable for its Palladian style portico with six Corinthian columns. The building contains its own court of law and 11 holding cells: 10 for men and one, the 'birdcage', for women. The famous Suffragette Emmeline Pankhurst had been an inmate in the early 20th century.

**1st May, 1929**

Covent Garden Market, central London, showing the traffic congestion that would force its relocation to Nine Elms, south of the *Thames* in the 1960s. The market was created by English architect Inigo Jones along the lines of an Italian piazza. The Great Fire of 1666 destroyed rival markets and left Covent Garden as the premier market in England. The original site became one of the most visited tourist areas in the UK.
**10th May, 1929**

The Forth Railway Bridge connecting Edinburgh with Fife, the first cantilever bridge in the UK to be built entirely in steel, was constructed between 1883 and 1890. Designed by Sir John Fowler and Sir Benjamin Baker it was built by Sir William Arrol's company.

**1st January, 1930**

Crowds flock to the All England Lawn Tennis and Croquet Club, Wimbledon, in the annual pilgrimage to the most famous tennis tournament in the world.
**25th June, 1930**

The Old Vic Theatre on the corner of The Cut and Waterloo Road, south London. Founded in 1818 by actor William Barrymore as the Royal Coburg Theatre, becoming The Royal Victoria Hall and Coffee Tavern, with strict temperance principals, in 1880. In 1929 The Old Vic repertory company was established at the theatre, led by John Gielgud.

**1st October, 1930**

The Leather Bottle Inn, in Cobham, Kent, was a favourite watering hole of Charles Dickens, who also refers to it in his novel *Pickwick Papers*. Built in 1629, during the reign of Charles I, the attractive half-timbered inn was given its name when a leather bottle containing gold sovereigns was found there in 1720.
**13th May, 1931**

An aerial view of the Royal Exchange in the City of London.
**18th June, 1931**

The Clock Tower of
St Stephens, known as Big
Ben after the bell that it
houses, trying out its new
floodlights for the Triennial
International Illumination
Congress, taking place in
London.
**21st July, 1931**

St Michael's Mount, *Carrack Looz en Cooz* in Cornish, is
a tidal island located 400yd off the Cornish coast opposite
Penzance, and connected to the village of Marazion by a
man-made causeway that is passable at low tide.
**4th August, 1931**

HMS *Victory*, launched in 1765 and the sixth ship to bear the name, gained fame as Lord Nelson's flagship at the Battle of Trafalgar, and was located in her present dry dock at Portsmouth in 1922. Although officially the oldest naval ship still in commission, the *Victory* functions as a museum.

**7th August, 1936**

The *Graf Zeppelin* flies over
St Paul's Cathedral on its
24-hour cruise around the
British Isles.
**18th August, 1931**

The newly built BBC Broadcasting House. Eric Gill's controversial statuary is still a work in progress; the major pieces, *Prospero* and *Ariel*, are absent from above the front door. Gill's scaffolding is set up to work on a smaller bas-relief (L).
**13th August, 1931**

Thames River Police headquarters at Wapping, London, still a working police station, now houses a museum that traces the history of the marine police force from its inception in 1798 to the present day.

**7th September, 1934**

St George's Hospital, London, was founded in 1733 as a teaching hospital, a role it has fulfilled continuously to the present day, although relocated to Tooting since the 1970s. The original hospital was opened in Lanesborough House, Hyde Park, built between 1827 and 1844, now a luxury hotel.
**26th September, 1935**

A landmark destroyed: the ruins of The Crystal Palace, Sydenham Hill, London after it was burned down, leaving only two water towers standing. Winston Churchill, returning home from the House of Commons remarked of the tragedy, *"This is the end of an age."*
**30th November, 1936**

The Embankment from Hungerford Bridge showing the Art Deco Shell Mex House, built between 1930 and 1931 between the Savoy and Adelphi hotels on the Strand as the headquarters of a joint venture between Shell and British Petroleum.
**1st February, 1937**

The Poldhu Wireless Station Monument at the Cornish cliff-top site of the first transatlantic radio message in 1901. Three clicks in morse code, forming the letter 'S', were transmitted from Poldhu to Guglielmo Marconi in Newfoundland.

**22nd September, 1937**

London's Piccadilly Circus just before the start of the Second World War. The famous Shaftesbury Memorial with its winged statue (not actually *Eros*, but his brother *Anteros*) has been covered prior to being removed for the duration of the conflict.

**August, 1939**

The ruins of Burlington Arcade during the 57 consecutive night-bombings of London known as the Blitz. Britain's first shopping arcade, opened in 1819, it was later restored, as was its ethos to *'epitomise impeccable service, specialist knowledge and elegant surroundings'*. The arcade is patrolled by Beadles wearing Edwardian frock coats and gold braided top hats, members of the smallest private police force in the world.
**1st May, 1940**

The ruins of Coventry Cathedral, West Midlands, after the medieval building was destroyed by Luftwaffe bombs during air raids. Only the tower, spire, the outer wall with its bronze effigy, and the tomb of its first bishop survived, remaining hallowed ground alongside Basil Spence's new cathedral that was built between 1956 and 1962.

**14th November, 1940**

St Paul's Cathedral stands amid the destruction of London as work begins on the rebuilding of the city, which has been left devastated by six years of bombing.
**1st June, 1945**

A floodlit Buckingham
Palace with the crowd
cheering King George VI
and Queen Elizabeth after
his speech on VJ Day.
**15th August, 1945**

Facing page: Fifty one
flags of the United Nations
flying outside Central Hall,
Westminster.
**10th October, 1945**

St Clement Danes Church, London, with the Law Courts in the distance, was completed in 1682 by Sir Christopher Wren and now functions as the central church of the Royal Air Force.
**5th April, 1946**

The clubhouse of The Royal and Ancient Golf Club of St Andrews, a famed Scottish institution dating back to 1754, where the game is thought by many to have originated during the 12th century.

**10th April, 1946**

Huge crowds around
Nelson's Column, Trafalgar
Square, which has been
adorned with flags, to watch
the fly-over after the Victory
Parade from Marble Arch.
**8th June, 1946**

Market traders use handcarts to pull their produce through Covent Garden market, which traces its origins back to the reign of King John in the 17th century, when it was known as 'Convent Garden'.
**29th November, 1946**

The Pool of London with
Tower Bridge in the distance.
Its various docks once
comprised the largest port in
the world.
**1st June, 1948**

Blackpool sheds its wartime status as an evacuation destination and resumes its role as a holiday resort, its famous tower rising above a packed beach. The tower, inspired by the Eiffel Tower in Paris, is 158m tall, and was opened as a tourist attraction on the 14th of May, 1894.
**26th July, 1948**

Kensington Palace, a 17th century royal residence improved
and extended by Sir Christopher Wren, is bathed in sunshine
amid Kensington Gardens.
**23rd June, 1949**

The Ritz Hotel in London's Piccadilly, opened by Swiss hotelier César Ritz on the 24th of May, 1906, is synonymous with style.
**3rd August, 1949**

Situated in the heart of the
capital with the Foreign
Office visible in the distance,
St James's Park provides an
oasis of tranquility.
**7th August, 1949**

King George VI, accompanied by Princess Elizabeth and the Duke of Gloucester, leads the nation's homage to the dead of two World Wars in a solemn ceremony at the Cenotaph in London's Whitehall.

**6th November, 1949**

Kenilworth Castle in Warwickshire is a 12th century Norman fortification situated in the Forest of Arden. Its defensive strength was increased by the addition of a man-made lake protecting three sides of the castle.
**1950**

Alnwick Castle, the residence of the Duke of Northumberland, was built soon after the Norman Conquest and overlooks extensive riverside meadows that were originally used for jousting competitions. From 1945 to 1975 the castle was used as a teacher training college.
**12th March, 1950**

A quintessentially English spring scene as people watch a cricket match on the green in the Gloucestershire village of Frenchay. Fine period houses overlook the green adjacent to the Anglican church of John the Baptist.
**26th April, 1950**

Blackpool Tower and annual illuminations shed their brilliance over the seafront and beach of the Lancashire resort.
**16th September, 1950**

An aerial view in crisp winter sunshine picks out the detail of Salford Docks and adjacent railway sidings. The docks, also called Manchester Docks, were located at the east end of the Manchester Ship Canal, built as two triangles of four docks, which met at one corner, and a single separate dock. The docks closed in 1982 and the area developed with office blocks and residential apartments.

**1st January, 1951**

The 300ft tall Skylon being constructed at the Festival of Britain site on the south bank of the River *Thames*. From a distance its supporting wires will no longer be visible so that the futuristic cigar-shaped structure will appear to float above the ground. Although popular with the public, sceptics joked that, like the British economy in the post-war years, the tower had *"no visible means of support."*
**6th March, 1951**

The Royal Festival Hall opens as the most up to date concert venue in Britain. Here, some of the Hall's modernistic boxes appear to be floating in mid-air.
**27th April, 1951**

A view from Westminster Bridge, after the opening of the
Festival of Britain by King George VI, picks out the distinctive
and apparently free-floating Skylon, the Royal Festival Hall
and the Dome of Discovery.
**4th May, 1951**

Windsor Castle photographed from a BOAC airliner, featuring
the round tower (L) with the State Apartments looking out
over the central lawn beyond it.
**11th February, 1952**

Windsor Castle's Round Tower occupies the oldest part of the castle complex and sits on the artificial hill of the original motte and bailey timber fort constructed around 1080 by William the Conqueror.
**1st May, 1952**

Britain's biggest cruiser, the 11,000 ton HMS *Belfast*, returns to a hero's welcome at Chatham Docks following her second tour of duty in the Korean war zone. On being decommissioned in 1963 she has been maintained as a museum ship since 1971, and has become a famous landmark in the Pool of London, near City Hall.

**4th November, 1952**

HMS *Victory*, Admiral Nelson's flagship at the Battle of Trafalgar, lies covered in snow at her berth in Portsmouth Dockyard.
**26th January, 1954**

An aerial view of Stonehenge, the UK's most famous
prehistoric monument, which dates back over 3,500 years
and is constructed from bluestone blocks transported from
the Preseli mountains in south-west Wales.
**1st June, 1955**

Facing page: Christmas
decorations in Regent Street.
**2nd December, 1955**

The British Museum contains the world's largest library
reading-room, with bookshelves totalling 80 miles in length.
At any one time nearly 400 readers can be accommodated
at the reading desks, which have been used by countless
famous people including both Marx and Lenin.
**2nd May, 1957**

The *Cutty Sark*, a clipper ship built in 1869, cuts a proud figure at her permanent berth near the National Maritime Museum at Greenwich, London. The ship was badly damaged by fire on the 21st of May, 2007, although she had been partly dismantled during extensive restoration. An estimate for fully restoring the ship was set at £35 million.

**27th May, 1957**

The Orangery in the Royal Botanic Gardens at Kew, in south west London, was built by Sir William Chambers in 1761 for Princess Augusta, the Dowager Princess of Wales.

**1st June, 1958**

The half-timbered Guildhall at Lavenham, Suffolk, was
built around 1530 with money raised by affluent local
cloth merchants. When guilds were abolished during the
Reformation, it served as a prison and a workhouse before
being restored as a meeting place for local merchants.
**12th June, 1958**

The vast circular building that forms the main block of
the British Broadcasting Corporation's Television Centre
in Wood Lane. When finished the building, shaped like a
giant question mark, and designed by Mr Graham Dawbarn
FRIBA, was to be Europe's biggest TV centre.
**14th July, 1959**

Facing page: Graham Sutherland's tapestry of Christ
dominates the scene inside the new Coventry Cathedral
during its consecration service. The building, designed by
Sir Basil Spence, replaces the medieval cathedral that was
destroyed by German bombing in 1940.
**25th May, 1962**

On the far bank of the River Avon stands the Shakespeare Theatre, formerly the Shakespeare Memorial Theatre, opened in 1932 by the Duke of Windsor.
**29th May, 1962**

The new Wembley Stadium. Improvements include an electric scoreboard and the all-encircling roof.
**3rd May, 1963**

Lower Green at Guiting Power, a small Cotswold village in Gloucestershire built in local stone. Nearby lie the excavated foundations of the original Anglo-Saxon church and a round barrow burial site.
**10th June, 1964**

Facing page: Walkers in single file along Hadrian's Wall at Winshields Crag, Northumberland, highest point of the landmark. Named after Emperor Hadrian, the wall formed the northern frontier of the Roman Empire.
**21st April, 1964**

Facing page: Set in the Weald of Kent, amid picturesque countryside and ancient parkland near Tonbridge, Penshurst Place is a medieval gem. The ancestral home of the Sidney family since 1552, the seat of Lord De L'isle and Dudley, at the heart of the original manor house is the Baron's Hall, built in 1341, with a magnificent 60ft high chestnut roof. The first recorded owner, Sir Stephen de Penchester, is buried in nearby Penshurst Church.
**31st July, 1964**

A fortnight before it is due to be officially opened by the Queen, the nearly completed Forth Road Bridge with its 3,300ft central span looms over houses on the shore. The bridge is to connect Scotland's capital city Edinburgh at South Queensferry to Fife at North Queensferry.
**17 August, 1964**

Facing page: The main train shed of St Pancras station, London, completed in 1868 by the engineer William Henry Barlow, was the largest single-span structure built at that time. In the 1960s the station served the rail network connecting the capital with the Midlands and the North of England, but in the 2000s it was enlarged, renovated and reopened as St Pancras International, providing Eurostar trains to continental Europe via the Channel Tunnel.
**11th May, 1965**

The neoclassical façade of Kenwood House, beside Hampstead Heath in north London. The house was transformed by Robert Adam during the 18th century and its richly decorated library is said to be one of his greatest achievements.
**13th June, 1967**

The ward of Caernarfon
Castle, which dates
from 1283, is host to the
investiture of Charles, the
Prince of Wales, at which he
was presented with a sword
to defend his land, a ring to
represent his responsibility
and a rod as a symbol of
governance.
**1st July, 1969**

Eton College boys sit on high to watch the Wall Game, contested by the 'Collegers' and the 'Oppidans' in a tradition dating back to 1766. Similar to modern rugby and football, the game is played on a strip of ground five metres wide and 110 metres long alongside the slightly curved brick wall, which was erected in 1717.

**29th November, 1969**

Arnos Grove tube station, designed by Charles Holden, is a distinctive landmark of suburban London. Opened in 1932 to serve the Piccadilly Line, the station was built in a modern style from brick, glass and reinforced concrete, and includes a distinctive circular drum-like ticket hall rising from a low, single storey building.
**3rd February, 1970**

Facing page: Mist rises from the River *Wye* beyond the ruins of Tintern Abbey in Monmouthshire, founded by Cistercian monks in the 12th century.
**1st September, 1971**

A long queue shelters beneath umbrellas outside the British Museum where the exhibition of treasures from Tutankhamun's tomb has opened to the public for the first time. Built to Sir Robert Smirke's neoclassical design between 1825 and 1850, the Greek Revival façade facing Great Russell Street features 44 Ionic columns, 45ft high.

**30th March, 1972**

A new motorway junction at Gravelly Hill in Birmingham is destined to become the country's best-known and most wryly-named transport feature, Spaghetti Junction.
**18th May, 1972**

The Church of St Mary and All Saints, in Chesterfield, Derbyshire, with its famous 15th century crooked spire, undergoes restoration to return its smoke-blackened sandstone to its original buff colour. The 220ft spire's 9ft 6in lean is attributed to the use of unseasoned 'green' timber, the absence of cross bracing, and the lack of skilled craftsmen at the time of its construction due to the Black Death. The 45 degree spiral twist, however, is thought to be by design.
**12th July, 1973**

The Queen, with Baroness
Spencer-Churchill and Mr
Winston Churchill MP, after
the unveiling of a statue
of Sir Winston Churchill in
Parliament Square.
**1st November, 1973**

Newcastle upon Tyne's
famed river crossings over
the River *Tyne*, seen from
the high level bridge looking
over the Swing Bridge
toward the arched Tyne
Bridge.
**5th November, 1976**

HMS *Belfast*, the last of the Royal Navy's great cruisers, moored in the Pool of London opposite the Tower, where she has become one of the city's most popular landmarks as a floating museum.
**21st April, 1977**

The Palace of
Holyroodhouse, official
government-owned
residence of the Monarch
of the United Kingdom in
Scotland, stands at the end
of the Royal Mile, opposite
Edinburgh Castle.
**24th May, 1977**

Christopher Milne, son of A A Milne who wrote the tales of *Winnie-the-Pooh*, stands on Pooh Bridge in the Ashdown Forest in Sussex, which features in his father's books. The stream beneath the bridge is supposedly where *Winnie-the-Pooh, Piglet* and friends played the game of Pooh Sticks.
**15th May, 1979**

Canterbury Cathedral is the seat of the Archbishop of Canterbury, leader of the Church of England and the worldwide Anglican Communion. The Cathedral's history can be traced back to 597 when St Augustine established himself in the town. It has been a site of pilgrimage since Archbishop Thomas Becket was murdered there in 1170.

**3rd March, 1980**

With a central span of 4,626ft and a total length of 7,283ft, the Humber Bridge, near Kingston upon Hull, was the world's longest single-span suspension bridge when construction was finished, a record it would hold for 16 years.
**21st March, 1980**

The southern façade of Sir Christopher Wren's Baroque wing of Hampton Court Palace, which was built alongside, and connected to the Tudor building. The unlikely pairing succeeds thanks to the use of similar pink coloured bricks.
**1st April, 1980**

Facing page: Hampton Court Palace, in the London Borough of Richmond upon Thames in south west London, is an unusual marriage of two disparate architectural styles. The Tudor palace, developed by Cardinal Wolsey and later Henry VIII, sits adjacent to a Baroque palace built by William III and Mary II.
**1st April, 1980**

Broadlands, situated on the banks of the River *Test* on the outskirts of Romsey in Hampshire, was the home of the late Lord Mountbatten.
**1st July, 1981**

Largely unchanged since the days of smugglers and ship wreckers, the First and Last House at Land's End, Cornwall, has been a popular refreshment stop with visitors arriving at the headland before venturing on the final stage to England's most westerly tip of the southern mainland on horseback or foot.
**19th November, 1981**

Overlooking the River *Mersey* with its ferry crossing, Pier
Head is an enduring image of Liverpool, location of the
'Three Graces', built during the 1900s: (L–R) the Royal Liver
Building, the Cunard Building, and the Port of Liverpool
Building. One of the first buildings to adopt the use of
reinforced concrete, the 295ft tall Liver Building is topped by
two mythical 'Liver Birds'. Legend holds that if the birds were
to fly away the city would cease to exist.
**1st January, 1982**

The outline of a naked man etched into the chalk downs of Dorset, called the Cerne Abbas Giant after the village nearby. Of uncertain origin, but first referred to in 1694, the figure is 180ft in length and is brandishing a 120ft knobbled club. The National Trust acquired the site in 1920, and in addition to keeping the grass trimmed, re-chalks the figure every 25 years.

**2nd August, 1983**

Cranes of the Harland & Wolff Shipyard, Belfast, where RMS *Titanic* was built for the White Star Line in 1909. Nationalised in 1977, H&W suffered mounting losses, being labelled a "lame duck" by the Heath government. In the 1980s it launched a line of Single Oil Well Production System (SWOPS) ships, which processed oil en route from oil fields to their destination, using the gas byproduct to fuel the ship's engines, and in 1984 delivered the largest bulk carrier, the *British Steel*.

**7th January, 1984**

The grave of Karl Marx at Highgate Cemetery in north London. The man credited as the founder of Communism had lived in relative obscurity and poverty on Dean Street, Soho, until his death in 1883. The tombstone, topped with a bust by Laurence Bradshaw, was erected in 1954 by the Communist Party of Great Britain, and survived an attempt by vandals to blow it up with a home made bomb in 1970.
**1st December, 1984**

Hampton Court Palace with smoke still rising from the damaged roof of the South Wing (L) following a fire in which one person died. The palace housed 50 grace and favour residences given to esteemed servants and subjects of the Crown, and it was in one of these apartments that the fire started, spreading to the King's Apartments and requiring repairs that were not completed until 1995.

**31st March, 1986**

The Centre Point building in central London has achieved fame not so much for its architecture but because it remained empty for the first 15 years after its construction, when property tycoon Harry Hyams preferred to realise his single asking price of £1,250,000 rather than allow tenants to rent single floors.
**1st March, 1990**

A cyclist climbs Monsal Head in the Peak District of Derbyshire, with Headstone Viaduct beyond. The 300ft long, five arch viaduct is considered elegant today, but when it was built in 1863 writer John Ruskin wrote: *"The valley is gone, and the Gods with it; and now, every fool in Buxton can be in Bakewell in half an hour, and every fool in Bakewell at Buxton; which you think a lucrative process of exchange – you Fools everywhere".*
**14th October, 1990**

The 800ft Canary Wharf Tower under construction in the London Docklands. The 50 storey structure contains 27,000 tonnes of British steel fastened by 500,000 bolts.
**6th November, 1990**

Facing page: Tunnelling teams from Britain and France celebrate the breaking through of the final underground section of the Channel Tunnel, creating the first ground-based connection to the continent since the Ice Age.
**20th November, 1990**

The completed Queen Elizabeth II Bridge over the River *Thames* at Dartford. The 137m high, 812m long cable stayed bridge forms the southbound element of the Dartford Crossing. It was only the second bridge downstream of London Bridge to built in more than 1,000 years: bridges denied large vessels access to the Pool of London until the construction of taller bridges became feasible.
**9th June, 1991**

The Dounreay nuclear power station complex on the north coast of Scotland consists of three reactors operated by the UK Atomic Energy Authority and two operated by the Ministry of Defence. The first reactor to be built is the one housed in the 60m giant steel sphere (R).

**5th December, 1991**

St Bartholomew's Hospital
in London is the oldest
surviving hospital in
England, having been
founded in 1123.
**31st October, 1992**

The Cenotaph in Whitehall, London, was designed by Sir Edwin Lutyens and is the setting for the country's main Remembrance Day ceremony.
**26th May, 1993**

Street entertainers at Covent Garden get members of the audience to participate. The area is now a focus for culture, its 300 year old market having been moved to a new location three miles away.

**8th July, 1993**

Farmer Mitch Atkinson tending his sheep under the shadow of the huge 'Golf Ball' radomes, at the Fylingdales US early warning base, in North Yorkshire.
**21st April, 1994**

Of the eight Coastguard Cottages built by the Admiralty in 1878, only six remain intact as coastal erosion affects cliffs at Birling Gap on the Sussex coast.
**1st January, 1995**

Land's End, the most westerly tip of the southern mainland, goes on sale in a package deal with John O'Groats, the most northerly settlement of mainland Great Britain, at a combined asking price of £5.5m, which means the fourth potential change of ownership of Land's End in 15 years.

**8th January, 1996**

Workmen reconstructing the Globe Theatre in London close
to its original site on the South Bank of the *Thames*. The Arts
Council comes under fire for giving the bulk of its National
Lottery handout to just two London venues, with £12.4m
going to the Globe project and nearly £30m going to the
Sadler's Wells dance theatre.
**16th October, 1995**

The Royal Albert Hall, in the City of Westminster, London, is one of the nation's most distinctive buildings, home to the annual summer Proms since 1941 and an almost daily programme of cultural events for the rest of the year. The hall was designed by Captain Francis Fowke and Major-General Henry Y D Scott of the Royal Engineers, with a glass and steel dome designed by Rowland Mason Ordish, and built by Lucas Brothers in 1867.

**14th May, 1996**

Britain's longest flight of locks, on the Kennet and Avon canal at Devizes in Wiltshire, opens again for the first time in 45 years following a £1m restoration project. The main flight of 16 locks at Caen Hill is part of a series of 29 with a rise of 237ft in two miles, a 1 in 44 gradient.

**1st August, 1996**

A procession escorts the Stone of Scone over Coldstream Bridge linking the Scottish Borders with Cornhill-on-Tweed, Northumberland. The ceremonial stone, used in the coronation of Scottish monarchs until 1296 when Edward I took it to Westminster Abbey, was returned to Scotland to be kept in Edinburgh Castle. The 18th century bridge over the River *Tweed* bears a plaque commemorating a visit in 1787 by poet Robert Burns, while the toll house on the Scottish side was infamous for conducting runaway marriages.

**15th November, 1996**

The city walls and ramparts of York are supported by an earth bank which is full of daffodils in spring.
**10th April, 1997**

Carlsberg-Tetley's brewery
at Burton upon Trent, a town
with a long history of brewing
beer.
**25th September, 1997**

Bordered on three sides by woodland colour, Balmoral Castle
is the large estate house deep in the Scottish highlands where
the Royal Family traditionally spend their summer holidays.
The foundation stone was laid by Queen Victoria on the 28th of
September, 1853 and is situated at the foot of the wall adjacent
to the West face of the entrance porch.

**22nd October, 1997**

The East Terrace and garden at Windsor Castle are opened to the public for the first time.

**6th August, 1998**

Shaw's Corner at Ayot St Lawrence in Hertfordshire, the former home of Irish playwright George Bernard Shaw, now owned by the National Trust and open to the public. The rooms remain much as Shaw left them, and the garden and Shaw's revolving writing hut can also be visited. Built as a rectory in 1902, the Arts and Crafts influenced house was home to the playwright from 1906 until his death in 1950.

**26th August, 1998**

The *Matthew*, replica of a caravel sailed by John Cabot from Bristol to North America in 1497, passes SS *Great Britain*, the Atlantic liner designed by Isambard Kingdom Brunel for the Great Western Steamship Company's Bristol-New York service. Launched in 1843, she was retired in 1970 to Bristol dry dock as a visitor attraction. A 1998 survey found her iron hull was corroding, and a glass air seal installed at her waterline to ensure the correct level of humidity below to preserve the material.

**12th September, 1998**

The figure of Prince Albert, centrepiece to the Albert Memorial in London's Kensington Gardens, following a four-year restoration project. The memorial, commissioned by Queen Victoria in memory of her husband, who died in 1861, consists of an ornate pavilion 176ft tall, which took more than a decade to complete. Opened in 1872, the statue was not ceremonially 'seated' until three years later.
**21st October, 1998**

Several hundred spotlights illuminate a one and a half mile woodland trail through Westonbirt Arboretum near Tetbury, Gloucestershire. The trail features some of the oldest, tallest and rarest trees in Britain, including giant African cedars and South American monkey puzzle trees.

**5th December, 1998**

The Blind Beggar public house in London's Whitechapel was closely associated with notorious gangster twins Ronnie and Reggie Kray, and where Ronnie Kray shot and killed rival mobster George Cornell on the 9th of March, 1966.
**17th January, 1999**

The *Angel of the North* in Newcastle with sculptor Antony Gormley. The sculptor won an award for visual arts at the 1999 ITV *South Bank Show* awards.
**21st January, 1999**

The Hoover Building, on Western Avenue, Perivale in Middlesex, is a classic example of Art Deco architecture. Designed by Wallis, Gilbert & Partners, it was built in 1932 as the main manufacturing centre for Hoover's vacuum cleaners. The Tesco supermarket chain purchased the building in 1989 and converted the original production area into a superstore, with the front section of the Grade II listed Hoover Building largely self contained.
**22nd February, 1999**

The stately home of Castle Howard in Yorkshire, designed by Sir John Vanbrugh, was severely damaged by fire in 1940 but has gradually been restored and now receives 200,000 visitors a year. It was the location for the fictional 'Brideshead' in TV and cinema adaptations of Evelyn Waugh's *Brideshead Revisited*.
**24th May, 1999**

Greenham Common near Aldermaston, Berkshire, was home to a US airbase, and the location of the Greenham Common Women's Peace Camp between 1981 and 2000. Thousands of women protested against Cruise nuclear missiles being sited at the base, and their disruptive actions were instrumental in the decision in 1991 to remove the weapons from the site. In 2000 a commemorative and historic memorial was established on the land the camp had occupied.

**21st July, 1999**

A signpost at John O'Groats, northernmost tip of mainland Scotland, which points to Land's End to the south and the islands of Pentland Skerries to the north.
**19th October, 1999**

A Virgin light airship over the still horizontal Millennium Wheel (London Eye) in central London. The wheel is sponsored by British Airways. Virgin boss Richard Branson is taunting rivals BA with the 'British Airways Can't Get It Up' slogan. The Millennium Wheel was supposed to be lifted to its full 450ft height – three times taller than Tower Bridge – earlier that month but when the anchor clips holding the support cables started to buckle under the weight, the mission was aborted.

**28th September, 1999**

The beauty of the West Front of York Minster was revealed for the first time in 10 years, as the final scaffolding covering the façade was removed on the completion of conservation work and the replacement of 3,000 stones.
**21st December, 1999**

A laser fired from the north side of the River *Thames* by the Prime Minister hits the Millennium Wheel at the start of New Year's Eve celebrations. Plans for passengers to use the new attraction had been scrapped after a last-minute safety hitch.
**31st December, 1999**

Facing page: A remarkable 4,500 year old legacy of mankind was discovered at Jarlshof in the Shetland Islands, Scotland in the 1800s, when a storm washed away shoreline and revealed evidence of habitation covering Neolithic, Bronze Age, Iron Age, Pictish, Norse and Medieval eras. Subsequent excavations since the 1920s revealed Jarlshof to be one of the most valued archaeological discoveries in the British Isles.
**25th January, 2000**

Fireworks explode over one of London's most recognisable landmarks, the Clock Tower of St Stephens (Big Ben) at the stroke of midnight, announcing the dawn of a new millennium.
**1st January, 2000**

Facing page: The archaeological site of Jarlshof in the Shetland Islands, with remains of an Iron Age village in the foreground and the Old House of Sumburgh beyond.
**25th January, 2000**

The entrance to Clouds Hill, Wareham, Dorset – now a National Trust property – the isolated cottage that was a retreat used by T E Lawrence, 'Lawrence of Arabia'. He died following a motorcycle accident nearby.
**21st May, 2000**

One of the finest examples of Elizabethan architecture in Britain, Lord Bath's stately home at Longleat, Wiltshire, is set within landscaped gardens and parkland designed by Capability Brown, and is also the site of the first drive-through safari park outside Africa. The current, seventh, Marquess, the eccentric artist Alexander Thynn, created various mazes and labyrinths on the property.
**30th May, 2000**

The Lloyd's Building, headquarters of the insurance institution Lloyd's of London, located at One Lime Street in the City of London, was designed by architect Richard Rogers and built between 1978 and 1986. Its innovative design places all the building's services – glass walled lifts, staircases, electrical power conduits and water pipes – on the outside, leaving uncluttered space within.
**6th June, 2000**

The SS *Great Britain* sits in dry dock at Bristol's Great Western Dockyard awaiting restoration funded by a £7m lottery grant.
**3rd August, 2000**

St Pancras mainline
railway station in London is
renowned for its Victorian
architecture.
**27th August, 2000**

The distinctive Radcliffe Camera Building in Oxford was built in the mid-18th century to house the Radcliffe Science Library. It is named after Royal Physician John Radcliffe who bequeathed the funds for its construction and *"one hundred and fifty pounds per annum for ever to the Library Keeper thereof."*
**6th March, 2001**

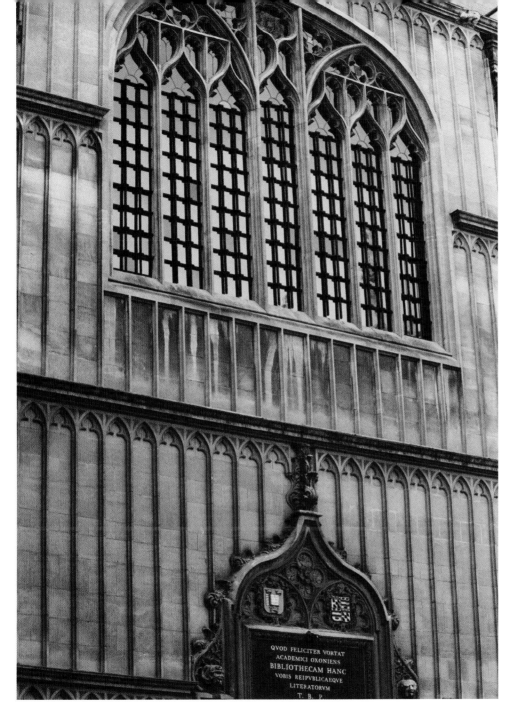

A window above the courtyard entrance to the Bodleian Library, Oxford, founded by Sir Thomas Bodley in the early 17th century.
**6th March, 2001**

The ruins of Urquhart Castle on the banks of Loch Ness in the Highlands, once one of Scotland's largest strongholds, is now a popular viewing point for those hoping to catch a glimpse of the loch's mythical monster.
**17th April, 2001**

Waddesdon Manor, a National Trust-owned stately home near Aylesbury in Buckinghamshire, was designed by architect Gabriel-Hippolyte Destailleur in a lavish Neo-Renaissance style reminiscent of a French château, and built between 1874 and 1889 for Baron Ferdinand de Rothschild, of the banking dynasty.

**11th June, 2001**

The National Space Centre in Leicester, one of two landmark science centres that have received extensive grant aid from the Millennium Commission. The 140ft tall Rocket Tower, designed by architect Nicholas Grimshaw, is clad with high-tech semi-transparent polythene 'pillows', and contains the American *Thor Able* and British *Blue Streak* rockets.

**21st June, 2001**

Finishing touches are made to the steam cleaning by English Heritage of the Westbury White Horse in Wiltshire. The equine carving, one of several in Wiltshire, is believed to date in its present form back to 1778.

**4th October, 2001**

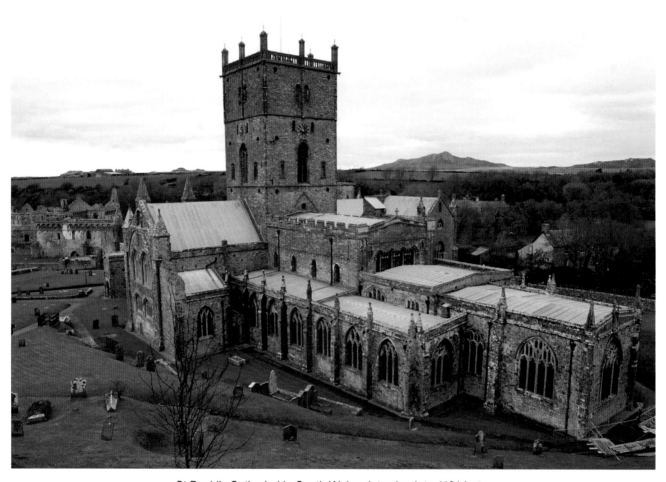

St David's Cathedral in South Wales dates back to 1181 but suffered a tower collapse in 1220, earthquake damage around 1247 and destruction at the hands of Cromwell's forces during the 17th century. Several periods of restoration have succeeded in preserving the Cathedral until the present day.

**22nd November, 2001**

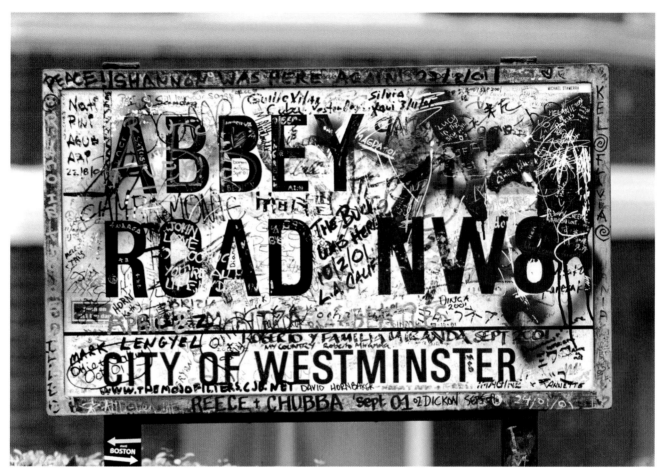

The tin street sign on the corner of Grove End Road and Abbey Road adorned with fan graffiti on the day tributes to the late George Harrison are laid outside the recording studios where The Beatles recorded their LP *Abbey Road*. A new sign was later fixed high on the wall of the corner building to save council expenses in cleaning and replacing the iconic symbol, which was frequently defaced or stolen.

**30th November, 2001**

Fountains Abbey near Ripon, North Yorkshire, a ruined Cistercian monastery founded in 1132, operated for more than 400 years until the Dissolution of the Monasteries by Henry VIII. The largest monastic ruins in Britain, the Abbey was designated a UNESCO World Heritage Site in 1978, and in 2002 the National Trust announced a 30-year, £10m management and conservation plan.

**5th February, 2002**

Facing page: Pedestrians cross the Millennium Bridge over the River *Thames* in London, following a £5m modification. The £18.2m bridge earned the nickname the 'wobbly bridge' when it opened on the 10th of June, 2000 as thousands of people making the crossing felt the structure sway disconcertingly. After just three days the 1,066ft long structure, which runs from St Paul's Cathedral on the north bank to the Tate Modern on the south bank, was closed, and special dampers retrofitted to cure the problem.

**22nd February, 2002**

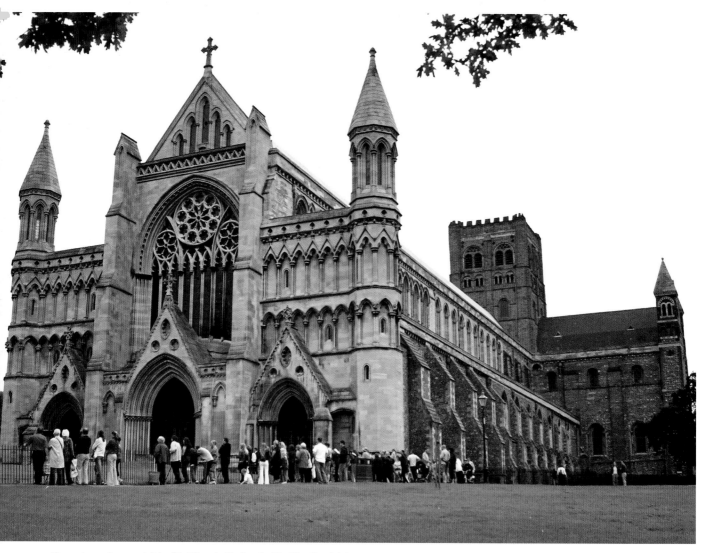

Crowds gather outside St Alban's Cathedral in Hertfordshire
for a celebrity wedding. At 275ft, its nave is the longest of
any cathedral in England.
**10th August, 2002**

The Great Court of the British Museum in London, a two acre square enclosed by a spectacular glass and steel roof, designed by Norman Foster, containing 3,312 uniquely shaped panes of glass, making it the largest covered public square in Europe. At the centre of the square is the 19th century Round Reading Room designed by Syndey Smirke, which formerly contained the British Library.

**24th October, 2002**

The Royal Observatory in Greenwich, east London is the home of Greenwich Mean Time (GMT) and the Prime Meridian of the world – Longitude 0° – the north-south line from which every place on Earth is measured in terms of its distance east or west of the line.
**29th October, 2002**

The futuristic design of architect Daniel Libeskind's Imperial
War Museum North, at The Quays, Greater Manchester, was
inspired by the concept of a globe shattered by conflict and
the shards reassembled. One of five branches, opened on the
5th of July, 2002 and the first located outside the south east of
England, the museum *"tells the story of how war has shaped
the lives of British and Commonwealth citizens since 1914"*.
**19th February, 2003**

The Lovell Radio Telescope
at Jodrell Bank observatory
in Cheshire, first used in
1957.
**28th April, 2003**

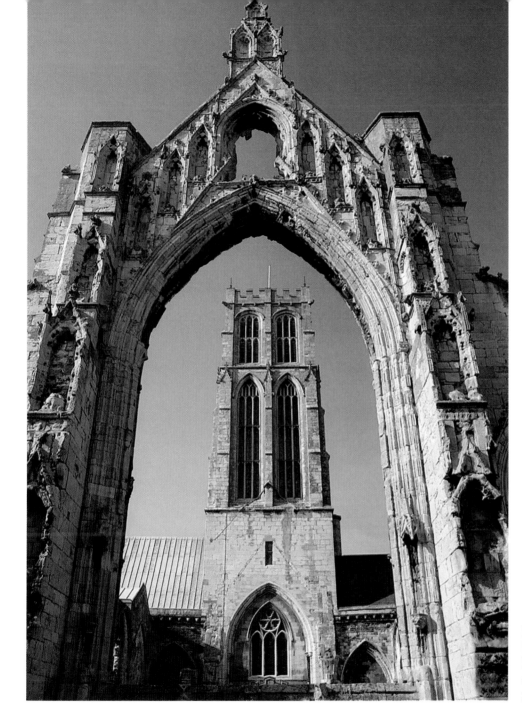

Howden Minster, a Grade I Listed Building in the Diocese of York, has its origins in Saxon times.
**3rd October, 2003**

Commuters take the
advantage of a temporary
road closure to walk home
across the traffic deck of
London's Tower Bridge.
**4th November, 2003**

The Wallace Monument, standing 220ft high on Abbey Craig
two miles north of Stirling, Scotland as snow arrives on the
Ochil Mountains beyond. It was from this prominent hilltop in
1297 that William Wallace watched the English army approach
across Stirling Bridge before leading the Scots into battle.
**7th February, 2004**

Towering above St Pancras Station, London, is the former Midland Grand Hotel, designed by Sir George Gilbert Scott, built in 1868-73 and opened in 1874. It was the first hotel in London to have lifts, then called 'ascending rooms'.

**2nd April, 2004**

The harbour entrance of the
fishing port of Whitby, North
Yorkshire.
**30th May, 2004**

Facing page: Leeds Castle is built on two adjacent islands in the River *Len* in the heart of Kent and was constructed in 1119 by Robert de Crevecoeur, a descendant of one of the Norman lords of William the Conqueror.
**10th September, 2004**

The remains of Whitby Abbey, founded in AD 657 by a Saxon king, stand on a cliff overlooking the Yorkshire coastal town and River *Esk*.
**30th May, 2004**

The village green and Plough Inn (R) in Kingham, Oxfordshire, was named in *Country Life* magazine as England's favourite village due to its particular mix of charm, practicality, community and spirit.
**10th November, 2004**

A *Routemaster* double-decker bus arrives at Buckingham Palace, where it joined other design classics for an exhibition showcasing British excellence hosted by The Queen.

**22nd November, 2004**

The restored façade, steps and ceremonial entrance of
St Paul's Cathedral are finally unveiled after 18 months of work
costing £5m, part of a long term project to restore the entire
central London cathedral in time for its 300th anniversary
in 2008.
**6th December, 2004**

With a backdrop of the
capital at dusk, the
Millennium Dome is
illuminated in support of
London's 2012 Olympics bid.
**16th February, 2005**

The Eden Project, near St Austell in Cornwall, is comprised of several self-supporting geodesic domes, each of which replicates different climatic conditions so that plant species from around the world can be cultivated. The landmark hosted a Live 8 concert dubbed 'Africa Calling', one of a series of benefit events in the UK's 'Make Poverty History' campaign designed to precede the G8 Conference and summit.
**2nd July, 2005**

The illuminated 550ft tall Spinnaker Tower in Portsmouth harbour finally opens to the public as a viewing platform, six years after its intended completion date – planned to coincide with the millennium celebrations.
**16th October, 2005**

The Diana, Princess of Wales Memorial Fountain in Hyde Park, London, celebrates the life and charitable work of the late Princess. It is made from 545 pieces of Cornish granite and flows from the highest point, cascading, swirling and bubbling before coming to rest in a calm pool at the base.
**12th June, 2006**

The Thames Barrier,
London's main flood
defence, situated to
the east of the city.
**7th September, 2006**

Facing page: The Giant's Causeway in Country Antrim, Northern Ireland, consists of about 40,000 interlocking basalt columns resulting from an ancient volcanic eruption. Most columns are hexagonal and the tallest 36ft high. The Causeway was declared a World Heritage Site by UNESCO in 1986.
**16th October, 2006**

The ruins of Tynemouth Benedictine Priory, burial place of St Oswin, King of Deira, is silhouetted against an autumn sunrise.
**25th October, 2006**

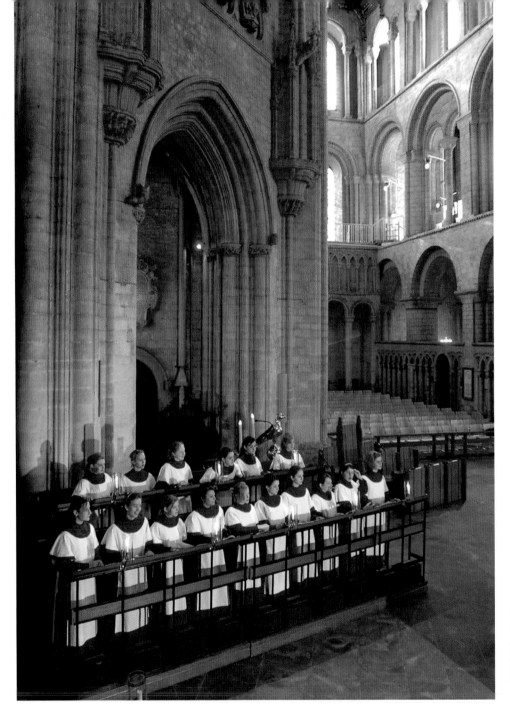

Ely Cathedral with its Girls' Choir during a rehearsal, the first all-female choir in the Cathedral's 1,000 year history.
**6th November, 2006**

A walkway leads from the organic form of Selfridge's department store at the Bullring Shopping Centre in Birmingham. Built in 2003, the 260,000sq ft store, designed by Future Systems in 'blobitecture' style, is clad with 15,000 spun aluminium discs, and was based on the female silhouette and a famous Paco Rabanne chainmail dress from the 1960s.
**18th November, 2006**

Facing page: The world's first cast-iron bridge in Coalbrookdale, Shropshire, crosses the River *Severn* at a point now known as Ironbridge Gorge. It was built in 1779 to improve the transportation of locally mined coal.
**1st December, 2006**

At the centre of Trafalgar Square in London stands Nelson's Column, guarded by four lion statues at its base. Designed by architect William Railton in 1838 and built by Peto & Grissell between 1840 and 1843, the monument commemorates Admiral Horatio Nelson's death at the Battle of Trafalgar in 1805. The 151ft granite Corinthian column supports the 18ft statue, which faces south towards the Admiralty.
**21st January, 2007**

An oil and gas installation at Waterston near Milford Haven looms over the village of Llanstadwell on Pembrokeshire's coast.
**28th April, 2007**

Blenheim Palace in
Oxfordshire, birthplace
and ancestral home of Sir
Winston Churchill.
**2nd May, 2007**

The Saracens Head Hotel in Southwell, a picturesque market town near Newark, Nottinghamshire. Once known as the King's Arms, the hotel has been visited by no fewer than 10 different monarchs in its 800 year history.
**5th June, 2007**

Facing page: City Hall and Royal Avenue in Belfast city centre.
**1st June, 2007**

Newark Castle, strategically
located on the banks of the
River *Trent*, Nottinghamshire,
was established as a mint
during the 12th century and
was where King John died
on the 19th of October, 1216.
**5th June, 2007**

**Landmarks** • Twentieth Century in Pictures

As part of the regeneration of Belfast's waterfront, Lagan Weir was built across the River *Lagan* in 1994 to artificially maintain the level of the tidal river. With developments underway, the Laganside Corporation set up to supervise the project had reached its £1 billion investment mark and handed over responsibility to the Department of Social Development.
**7th June, 2007**

Created by British sculptor Antony Gormley, *Another Place* is composed of 100 cast iron, full size statues spread out along two miles of foreshore, facing out to sea, on Crosby Beach, Merseyside. Each 1,400lb cast of the artist's body is set on a 6ft steel pile, and depending on the fall of the land, the state of the tide, and the weather conditions is more or less visible.
**9th June, 2007**

The commanding hilltop position and structure of Dover Castle in Kent made it one the most impregnable fortresses in Europe. A series of tunnels beneath the castle, created in the Napoleonic era as a barracks for more than 2,000 men, were used as air raid shelters during the Second World War, and later as a military command centre and hospital.
**20th June, 2007**

The 76th edition of the J P Morgan Round the Island Race, an annual 55 mile, anti-clockwise circumnavigation of the Isle of Wight – the largest of its kind in the world with 1,800 competing boats – passes two of the three rugged chalk stacks known as The Needles, which rise abruptly out of the sea off the western extremity of the island, guarded by a lighthouse built in 1859.

**23rd June, 2007**

A statue of Robert the Bruce at the site of the Battle of Bannockburn near Stirling, Scotland.
**26th June, 2007**

Stirling Castle sits high on a volcanic plug, guarding a vital crossing point on the River *Forth*.
**26th June, 2007**

A baronial mansion rather than a fortress, Stormont Castle in east Belfast served as an official residence of the Prime Minister of Northern Ireland until 1972 and now fulfils the same function for the Northern Ireland Secretary of State.
**19th July, 2007**

Hundreds of walkers make the most of a rare opportunity to cross the Ribblehead Viaduct on the Settle to Carlisle railway, which runs through the Yorkshire Dales National Park. Rail services were suspended for two weeks while restoration work took place along the line.
**22nd July, 2007**

The replica Globe Theatre in Bankside, London, built 750ft from the site of the Elizabethan original established by the 'Lord Chamberlain's Men', the company of actors where the bard worked as actor and playwright. Built by the Shakespeare Globe Trust, founded by American actor and director Sam Wanamaker, construction began in 1987 and was completed 10 years later.

**1st August, 2007**

Marble Arch was originally erected as a gateway to Buckingham Palace before being moved to its present location, opposite Speakers' Corner at the junction of Oxford Street and Park Lane, London, in 1851.

**1st August, 2007**

Royal York Crescent in the desirable Clifton area of Bristol. In a prominent position overlooking the docks, the Grade II* listed terrace of 46 houses, built between 1791 and 1820, is a distinctive landmark visible from much of the city.

**7th August, 2007**

The present day Belfast
Castle was built in the 19th
century within a deer park. It
was presented to the City of
Belfast in 1934 by the Earl
of Shaftesbury and, after
extensive refurbishment,
opened to the public.
**13th August, 2007**

Facing page: The natural
limestone arch of Durdle
Door at West Lulworth,
Dorset.
**13th August, 2007**

Iona Abbey on the Isle of Iona, just off the Isle of Mull on
the West Coast of Scotland, was the site where St Columba
founded a monastic community in AD 563, which eventually
became one of the largest religious centres in western Europe.
**22nd September, 2007**

Gateshead window cleaners
are faced with an immense task
at The Sage music and arts
centre by the River *Tyne*.
**25th September, 2007**

Scotland's new Parliament Building at the foot of Edinburgh's Royal Mile is an innovative design inspired by the surrounding landscape, the flower paintings by Charles Rennie Mackintosh, and upturned boats on a seashore. Combining steel, oak and granite, the building, according to Spanish architect Enric Miralles was to appear to be *"growing out of the land"*.
**29th September, 2007**

The south façade of the British Broadcasting Corporation's Broadcasting House in Portland Place, London. Designed by George Val Myer and M T Tudsbery, it was opened on the 14th of May, 1932. Above the main entrance are statues of the magician *Prospero* and spirit of the air *Ariel* from Shakespeare's *The Tempest*, by sculptor Eric Gill.

**18th October, 2007**

FLVM'N' · VINC'LA · P°SV'T

SIR JOSEPH BAZALGETTE
ENGINEER OF THE LONDON MAIN DRAINAGE
AND OF THE EMBANKMENT

A memorial on London's Victoria Embankment to engineer Joseph Bazalgette (1819-1891), chief engineer of London's Metropolitan Board of Works and architect of central London's sewer network.

**2nd November, 2007**

At 11am on the 11th November, Armistice Day, a ray of sunlight hits the altar at the National Memorial Arboretum at Alrewas, Staffordshire.

**11th November, 2007**

The new Wembley Stadium, built on the site of the original stadium, has a capacity of 90,000 with every seat under cover beneath a partially enclosing sliding roof. The 1,030ft span lattice arch supports the weight of the north roof and 60 per cent of the weight of the retractable roof on the south side.

**21st November, 2007**

An unmistakeable London skyline at dusk from Waterloo Bridge, capturing the London Eye, the Clock Tower of St Stephens (Big Ben) and Westminster in silhouette.

**16th January, 2008**

Whitby Lifeboat Station, North Yorkshire, with the town's ancient abbey on top of East Cliff towering above the houses.
**4th March, 2008**

Waves build up around the North Pier in Blackpool, oldest and largest of the town's three coastal piers. The cast iron screw piles that support the structure were twisted into the sand until they lodged in bedrock.
**12th March, 2008**

The Palm House at the Royal Botanic Gardens, Kew in Surrey, the first large scale structural use of wrought iron, was built between 1844 and 1848 by Richard Turner to Decimus Burton's designs. Restorations in the 1950s and 1980s saw the glasshouse emptied for the first time in its history, and the original hand-blown panes replaced with toughened safety glass and 10 miles of glazing bars, ensuring the elegant structure would remain a landmark in the 21st century.
**1st April, 2008**

Scotland's Gothic style Melrose Abbey, which dates from 1136, enshrouded by fog. The embalmed heart of Robert the Bruce is rumoured to have been laid to rest in the abbey's grounds.
**11th April, 2008**

On top of the 67ft high dome of the Old Bailey courthouse in London stands a 12ft tall gold leaf 'lady of justice' statue holding a sword in one hand and the scales of justice in the other; she is not, as is conventional with such figures, blindfolded.
**15th April, 2008**

The entrance to the Ritz
Hotel on Piccadilly, London.
**17th April, 2008**

A lighthouse on the Farne Islands off the Northumberland coast. The 7th century home of St Cuthbert and now owned by the National Trust, the islands are a summer home for 100,000 pairs of nesting seabirds including puffins and guillemots.
**4th May, 2008**

Workers add the top section to the Aspire tower on the Jubilee Campus of Nottingham University, making it Britain's tallest freestanding work of public art. The 197ft landmark is more than 26ft taller than London's Nelson's Column, and was commissioned by the University as part of the institution's 60th anniversary celebrations of the granting of its Royal Charter.

**23rd June, 2008**

Rising to an elevation of 518ft from a plain, Glastonbury Tor, with the roofless St Michael's Tower at the summit, dominates the town of Glastonbury, in Somerset. The *tor* is steeped in mythology, and the discovery of Neolithic flint tools suggest that the site may have been occupied throughout human prehistory.

**28th July, 2008**

A state of the art facility opened in 2005, University College Hospital on Euston Road in London works closely with University College London to facilitate innovation, teaching and biomedical research.
**29th July, 2008**

30 St Mary Axe, affectionately known by its nickname the *Gherkin*, is one of the London's most eye-catching structures. Designed by Norman Foster and partner Ken Shuttleworth the building features energy saving innovations and a natural ventilation system that insulates the office space inside. On the top floor a bar for tenants offers a 360 degree view of London.
**8th August, 2008**

The iconic landmark used as a symbol of Bristol, the Clifton Suspension Bridge spans the Avon Gorge, between Clifton and Leigh Woods. The result of a competition in 1830, won by 24 year old Isambard Kingdom Brunel in his first major commission, the project was dogged by political and financial difficulties and by 1843 only the Egyptian-inspired towers had been built. Brunel died in 1859 and the bridge was completed as his memorial to be opened, finally, in 1864.

**8th August, 2008**

Much of Lincoln Cathedral dates from the 13th century but its imposing west front has survived from the original Romanesque structure built in 1072.
**15th August, 2008**

Black Rock Cottage with
Buchaille Etive Mòr as
an imposing backdrop, in
Glencoe, the Highlands
of Scotland.
**4th September, 2008**

The illumination of London's Tower Bridge highlights the details of its construction and the results of a four year restoration programme begun in mid-2008, during which the old paintwork would be stripped off and the structure repainted blue and white. Each section of the bridge was systematically enshrouded in polythene-sheeted scaffolding to prevent dust and paint particles polluting the River *Thames*.

**19th September, 2008**

Lindisfarne, also known as Holy Island, lies off the north east coast of Northumberland, connected to the mainland by a causeway flooded twice a day by tides. A monastery was founded there in AD 635 by Irish missionary Saint Aidan. The island was once a centre for the lime burning industry and features well preserved kilns.

**23rd September, 2008**

Facing page: Lindisfarne island is dominated by a 16th century castle, originally in Tudor style, but refurbished in the Arts and Crafts style by Sir Edwin Lutyens for one-time owner Edward Hudson, the founder of *Country Life* magazine, while Gertrude Jekyll laid out a small garden nearby in 1911. Now under the care of the National Trust, the castle, garden and lime kilns are open to the public.
**23rd September, 2008**

A Penfold hexagonal postbox in London, made between 1866 and 1879. From July 1874 postboxes were painted red, replacing the previous green colour scheme.
**3rd October, 2008**

London's Canary Wharf
skyline at sunrise, showing
the United Kingdom's three
tallest buildings (L–R)
8 Canada Square, One
Canada Square and the
Citigroup Centre.
**17th October, 2008**

London's BT Tower, built between 1961 and 1964 to support General Post Office (GPO) microwave aerials that handled the country's telecommunications traffic, has a narrow cylindrical form to prevent excessive movement in high winds that might disrupt the aerial signals. Despite the tower's prominence – it is visible from most parts of city – its existence was, until the mid-1990s, officially a 'secret' and it did not feature on Ordnance Survey maps.

**13th November, 2008**

The Humber suspension Bridge, spanning the River *Humber* Estuary from Barton on the south side, to Kingston Upon Hull on the north. It is the world's third largest single span bridge (after Japan and Denmark) of 1,410m and 71,000km of cable supports. Construction began in 1973 costing £98m pounds and was funded by Government loans, taking eight years to complete.

**18th November, 2008**

The Spinnaker Tower stands like a huge Christmas tree over Portsmouth Harbour in Hampshire, as the lights of the tower have been reset to give it a green trunk and the effect of coloured baubles around the edges.
**17th December, 2008**

A row of classic public telephone boxes in Covent Garden, London. The iconic 'K2' box, designed by Giles Gilbert Scott and deployed in the city and elsewhere in 1926, was made from cast iron and painted red for high visibility, although Scott had specified mild steel, painted silver with a greenish-blue interior. Although more utilitarian designs are now made many of the much loved red boxes still survive.

**15th January, 2009**

A short lived landmark outside the City of Manchester Stadium, *The B of the Bang* sculpture, by designer Thomas Heatherwick, displayed structural problems in its 180 hollow tapered steel spikes, one of which broke off just days before the 184ft sculpture's unveiling in 2005. Subsequently 22 more spikes were removed amid safety concerns. The City Council took legal action against Heatherwick's studio and subcontractors, who paid £1.7m in damages in 2008. Dismantling began in April, 2009.

**22nd January, 2009**

Burns Cottage in Alloway, South Ayrshire, is just one of many locations across Scotland involved with the 250th anniversary celebration of the birth of Scotland's national poet Robert Burns.

**24th January, 2009**

Reopening after an 18-month, £4.5m refurbishment, the Monument to the Great Fire of London – commonly known as 'The Monument' – gleams in the morning sunlight. The 202ft tall Portland stone Roman Doric column topped with a gilded urn of fire, designed by Christopher Wren and Robert Hooke, is located at the junction of Monument Street and Fish Street Hill, 202ft from the origin of the conflagration, which devastated the capital over four days in September, 1666.

**16th February, 2009**

The Boots cosmetics factory in Nottingham is a 1930 Grade
1 listed Art Deco building, which is regarded as one of
Britain's finest industrial buildings. It was designed by the
architect and engineer Owen Williams and pioneered the use
of glass blocks in roof construction and steel framed glazing
to envelope the reinforced concrete structure in glass, which
are now in common use.

**20th February, 2009**

The interior of the Boots cosmetics factory reveals the ground-breaking use of glass blocks in the building's roof canopy.
**20th February, 2009**

The Old Lion Inn or 'Guy Fawkes' House' in Dunchurch, Warwickshire, where Guy Fawkes and other members of the Gunpowder Plot planned and waited for the result of their plan to blow up the Houses of Parliament in 1605.
**21st February, 2009**

Facing page: The ruins of Bishop's Waltham Palace, founded in 1135 by Henry de Blois, a grandson of William the Conqueror, at Bishop's Waltham in Hampshire. The moated residence, now a scheduled ancient monument, was ruined in 1644 after the English Civil War.
**20th February, 2009**

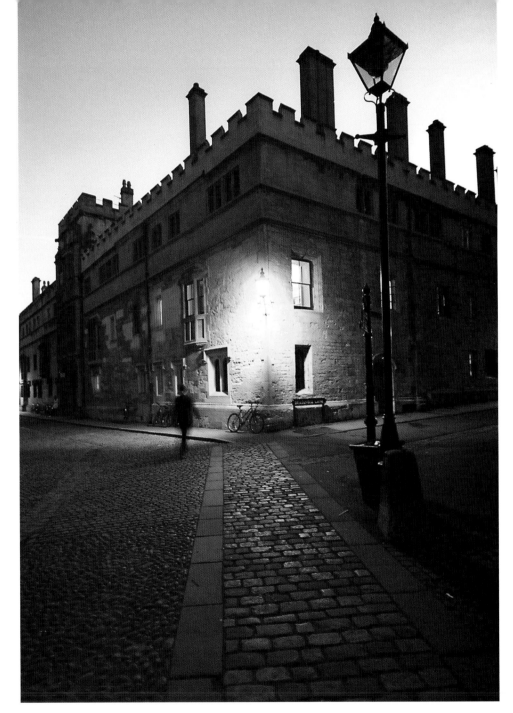

Brasenose College, part of the University of Oxford, is situated on the west side of Radcliffe Square in the centre of the city and comprises three 'quads', the dormitory suites housing four residents. Former students include leader of the Conservative Party, David Cameron, and actor, writer and *Monty Python* star Michael Palin.

**21st February, 2009**

Minster Lovell Hall ruins are all that remains of a manor house built in the 1430s beside the River *Windrush* for William Lovel. In a macabre legend Francis, Viscount Lovel, who supported King Richard III against Henry VII, fled to the manor when Richard was killed at the Battle of Bosworth Field, and hid in a secret chamber. When his trusted servant – the only person to know of the hiding place – died suddenly Francis was left to starve to death.

**21st February, 2009**

Arundel Castle, ancestral seat of successive Dukes of Norfolk for 850 years, overlooking the River *Arun* in West Sussex.
**22nd February, 2009**

The iron clad Rufus Stone in the New Forest marks the spot where William II is believed to have been fatally wounded by an arrow while out hunting. The monarch was known as Rufus due to his ruddy complexion and red hair.
**23rd February, 2009**

A 17th century house in
Chawton near Winchester,
Hampshire where novelist
Jane Austen spent the last
eight years of her life.
**23rd February, 2009**

Visitors relax by former
shipwrights' cottages on the
banks of the River *Beaulieu*
at Buckler's Hard, near
Beaulieu in Hampshire,
where ships for Lord
Nelson's fleet were built.
**23rd February, 2009**

The Science School at
Winchester College, which,
in its entirety, includes nine
Grade I and 84 Grade II
Listed Buildings.
**23rd February, 2009**

A statue of George Loveless, leader of the Tolpuddle Martyrs and also a Methodist preacher, at the Martyrs Museum in Tolpuddle.
**24th February, 2009**

Maiden Castle, near
Dorchester, is the largest
and most complex Iron Age
hill fort in the UK.
**24th February, 2009**

In the heart of Sherwood Forest, Nottinghamshire, according to legend, the Major Oak once served to hide Robin Hood and his men. The huge tree, near the village of Edwinstone, has a girth of 33ft, is estimated to weigh about 23 tons, and could be 1,000 years old.
**24th February, 2009**

Cromford Mill, near Matlock in Derbyshire, was the world's first water-powered cotton spinning mill, developed by the inventor Richard Arkwright, the father of the modern industrial factory system.
**24th February, 2009**

One of two flights of locks,
five in each flight, on the
Grand Canal at Foxton in
Leicestershire.
**26th February, 2009**

The Eleanor Cross at Hardingstone, Northampton, was one of a dozen stone monuments erected in memory of Eleanor of Castile, wife of Edward I, along the route taken when her body was carried to Westminster Cathedral after her death in 1290.
**27th February, 2009**

Town Hall is a Grade I listed neo-Classical building located in Victoria Square, Birmingham. It was originally the venue of the Birmingham Triennial Music Festival, established in 1784 to raise funds for the General Hospital. Between 2002 and 2008 it was the subject of a £35m renovation, and now hosts diverse musical events such as organ recitals, rock, pop and classical concerts, in addition to graduation ceremonies for Aston University.

**27th February, 2009**

George Elkington opened a silver manufacturing business in Newhall Street, Birmingham, in 1840. Elkington's electroplating process revolutionised the manufacture of plated silver and by the late 1850s had superseded most of the trade in Sheffield plate. The building later became the Museum of Science and Industry. Although standing empty, the factory features two blue plaques, one to Elkington, the other to his employee Alexander Parkes, who invented the first plastic.

**27th February, 2009**

Dating from 1530 Llancaiach Fawr Manor in Mid Glamorgan, Wales, is a fine example of a semi-fortified manor house, with walls four feet thick and a single entrance leading to easily defended staircases. A leading 'living history' site, the manor is also claimed to be haunted, and in addition to featuring a 'Ghost Webcam' also hosts guided candlelit Ghost Tours for visitors.

**28th February, 2009**

Caerphilly Castle in South Wales is one of the largest castles in the United Kingdom. The sturdy concentric fortress, built between 1268 and 1272, survived largely unscathed through the ages until the end of the Civil War of 1642-48, when it gradually fell into disrepair and its south-east tower leaned alarmingly 10ft out of perpendicular – although this could be the result not of damage inflicted by Cromwell's Parliamentary Army but subsidence.

**28th February, 2009**

Stokesay Castle, near Ludlow and the Welsh border in Shropshire is a well preserved 13th century fortified manor house – the oldest in England – featuring at its heart a slate-roofed hall 34ft high with four cross gables, a defensive, broadly octagonal South Tower (R), and an unusual timber-framed residence built onto the upper section of the North Tower (L).
**1st March, 2009**

A great arched doorway of Strata Florida Abbey, located just outside Pontrhydfendigaid, near Tregaron in the county of Ceredigion, Wales. Founded in 1164 by a group of monks, the abbey now lies mostly in ruins after the monastery was dissolved in the 1540s by church commissioners under King Henry VIII.
**1st March, 2009**

Facing page: Dolbadarn Castle, Llanberis, Wales, was built by Llewelyn ap Iorwerth some time before 1230 to guard the Llanberis Pass, a major north-south route through Snowdonia in medieval times.
**2nd March, 2009**

Beaumaris Castle, last and largest of the Welsh castles built by Edward I, has four successive lines of fortification and has been described as the most technically perfect concentric castle in Britain, despite the fact that it was never finished due to lack of funds.
**2nd March, 2009**

Gloucester is a port linked to the tidal River *Severn* by the Gloucester and Sharpness Canal. Its wharves and warehouses, and the docks themselves, fell into disrepair until the 1980s, when a major renovation programme was carried out, creating luxury residential apartments, shops, bars, museums and public open spaces.
**2nd March, 2009**

Offa's Dyke is a linear earthwork, which roughly follows
the present border between England and Wales and was
constructed at the end of the 8th century by Offa, King of Mercia.
**4th March, 2009**

Trinity College, Cambridge was founded by Henry VIII and its past students include Francis Bacon, John Dryden, Isaac Newton, Byron, Thackeray, Tennyson, Jawaharlal Nehru and a total of 32 Nobel Prize winners.

**5th March, 2009**

A medieval merchant's
house in Southampton,
Hampshire.
**5th March, 2009**

The county town of Hereford with its Cathedral and late
15th century bridge over the River *Wye*.
**6th March, 2009**

The Angel and Royal Hotel, Grantham, Lincolnshire started life as a hostel for the Knights Templar but eventually became an inn, providing lodgings for several monarchs through the centuries.
**8th March, 2009**

The Workhouse in Southwell, Nottinghamshire, also known as 'Greet House', is considered to be the prototype for the workhouses that were built in the 19th century. Built in 1824, the Grade II listed building is managed by the National Trust, which has restored or reinstated the dormitories, workshops and privies of this early 'welfare' institution as a museum.
**8th March, 2009**

Spring daffodils on the mound of Clifford's Tower, all that remains of York Castle, which is named after Roger de Clifford who was executed by Edward II for treason.
**11th March, 2009**

Rushton Triangular Lodge in Northamptonshire is a folly designed and built between 1593 and 1597 by Sir Thomas Tresham using most features in groups of three (*tres* in French, which was also his nickname for his wife). It has trefoil windows, three floors, three triangular gables on each side, and three Latin texts each of 33 letters.

**12th March, 2009**

Warwick Castle was built by William the Conqueror in 1068
next to the River *Avon* in the medieval town of Warwick.
The Grade I listed building is classified as a Scheduled
Ancient Monument in recognition of its status as a 'nationally
important' archaeological site and historic building. The
British Tourist Authority named the castle one of Britain's top
10 historic houses and monuments.
**15th March, 2009**

Salford Quays is the name
given to a vast docklands
regeneration scheme just
outside the city centre of
Manchester.
**16th March, 2009**

Nine Ladies Stone Circle is located in a large clearing in woodland on Stanton Moor, within the Peak District National Park. Dating back to the Bronze Age, the site is visited by many to celebrate the summer solstice. Owned by English Heritage, the stones have long been the focus of an environmental protest, which aims to protect the site from nearby quarry work. A controversial protest camp has inhabited the site since 1999.

**16th March, 2009**

The Boat House, a wooden shed in which Dylan Thomas worked during the last few years of his life, including creating the classic *Under Milk Wood*, lies 100 yards from his home in the Carmarthenshire town of Laugharne.
**17th March, 2009**

Laugharne Castle stands on
a low cliff beside a stream,
overlooking the estuary of
the river *Taf*.
**17th March, 2009**

Pembroke Castle in South Wales was established in 1093, before the Norman conquest of Wales had been completed, and is surrounded on three sides by water. It is where Henry VII was born and has been used as a set for several films including *The Lion in Winter* and *Jabberwocky*.
**19th March, 2009**

Airport House at what used to be Croydon Aerodrome,
London's first international airport when it opened in 1928.
**19th March, 2009**

Number 8a Victoria Street, the birthplace of English author, artist and poet D H Lawrence, in the coalmining town of Eastwood, Nottinghamshire, is now a museum.
**22nd March, 2009**

The Publishers gratefully acknowledge Press Association Images, from whose extensive archive the photographs in this book have been selected. Personal copies of the photographs in this book, and many others, may be ordered online at www.prints.paphotos.com

PRESS
ASSOCIATION
Images

AMMONITE
PRESS

For more information, please contact:

**Ammonite Press**

AE Publications Ltd. 166 High Street, Lewes, East Sussex, BN7 1XU, United Kingdom

Tel: 01273 488005  Fax: 01273 402866

www.ammonitepress.com

# Reading the Financial Pages

## FOR

# DUMMIES®

### by Michael Wilson

# WILEY

A John Wiley and Sons, Ltd, Publication

**Reading the Financial Pages For Dummies®**

Published by
**John Wiley & Sons, Ltd**
The Atrium
Southern Gate
Chichester
West Sussex
PO19 8SQ
England

E-mail (for orders and customer service enquires): cs-books@wiley.co.uk

Visit our Home Page on www.wiley.com

For general information on our other products and services, please contact our Customer Care Department within the U.S. at 800-762-2974, outside the U.S. at 317-572-3993, or fax 317-572-4002.

For technical support, please visit www.wiley.com/techsupport.

Wiley also publishes its books in a variety of electronic formats. Some content that appears in print may not be available in electronic books.

British Library Cataloguing in Publication Data: A catalogue record for this book is available from the British Library

ISBN-13: 978-0-470-71432-4

Printed and bound in Great Britain by Bell & Bain Ltd., Glasgow

10  9  8  7  6  5  4  3  2  1

WILEY

# *About the Author*

**Michael Wilson** is a widely-known investment journalist and author with more than 25 years of experience in the field of personal finance and professional financial services. He has written around 20 books on business and investment topics for the *Financial Times*, the Longman Group, Dorling Kindersley and Euromonitor. Professional clients have included Nasdaq Europe, the Securities Institute, Goldman Sachs, the United Nations Conference on Trade and Development, and the American Association for Investment Management and Research.

But he generally gets more fun out of writing on tax and investment subjects for private investors, mainly through magazines such as *Personal Finance*, *What Investment*, or the Zurich Club investment newsletter, where he is investment director.

# Dedication

This book is dedicated to my wife Jenny, for her unending support, encouragement, laughter, consolation and occasional telling-off during the months while I was writing it. Not to mention the half a million cups of late-night coffee, and the blind eye she somehow managed to turn to the permanently disreputable state of my office. I'll tidy it up now, honestly.

Also to my beloved daughters Hannah and Georgia, who have made the last thirty-odd years so very special, and who are still getting used to the novel idea that, after a quarter of a century of boring old financial journalism and dense but worthy business books, their dad is finally hitting the bright lights with a volume that people will actually enjoy reading. (We hope.)

# Acknowledgements

I've worked with many, many book editors over the last three decades, but I think I can honestly say that I've never met a team with such patience, thoroughness, consistency and good humour as the editorial people at John Wiley. My particular thanks go to Nicole Hermitage and Simon Bell, who somehow managed to turn my occasionally wayward manuscript into the polished volume you see before you – and who also, remarkably, managed to bring it in on time. Simon's unfailing good humour and sheer unending courtesy are an example to all those of us in the media industry who sometimes take ourselves too seriously.

Thanks also to all the copy and technical editors who worked on the project and whose patience I must certainly have tested at times. Not to mention rescuing my pride from time to time with observations and queries that were sometimes very much to the point!

Finally, to the person who started me on the long and rocky road to financial journalism, more than 25 years ago. Dennis Kiley, the former section head at the *Financial Times,* taught me the most important lesson any journalist can ever hope to learn – namely, that when it comes to a subject as challenging (but also as important) as investing your money, there is simply no such thing as a stupid question. Indeed, the more stupid questions you ask, the better your chances of getting the right answers.

**Publisher's Acknowledgments**

We're proud of this book; please send us your comments through our Dummies online registration form located at www.dummies.com/register/.

Some of the people who helped bring this book to market include the following:

*Acquisitions, Editorial, and Media Development*

**Commissioning Editor:** Nicole Hermitage

**Project Editor:** Simon Bell

**Publishing Assistant:** Jennifer Prytherch

**Development Editor:** Kate O'Leary

**Copy Editor:** Sally Osborn

**Technical Editor:** John Ward

**Publisher:** Jason Dunne

**Executive Editor:** Sam Spickernell

**Executive Project Editor:** Daniel Mersey

**Cover Photos:** ©Tom Grill, GettyImages

**Cartoons:** Ed McLachlan

*Composition Services*

**Project Coordinator:** Lynsey Stanford

**Layout and Graphics:** Christin Swinford

**Indexer:** Ty Koontz

# Contents at a Glance

Introduction ................................................................ 1

## Part I: The Financial Pages ........................................ 9
Chapter 1: Introducing the Financial Pages ............................... 11
Chapter 2: Looking at How the Financial Pages Work ....................... 21
Chapter 3: Relating the Financial Pages to the Stock Market............... 37
Chapter 4: Using the Pages to Your Advantage ............................. 61

## Part II: Using The Financial Pages to Make Basic Investments ........................................................... 77
Chapter 5: Investing in Shares........................................... 79
Chapter 6: Investing in Bonds ........................................... 107
Chapter 7: Investing in Cash Investments ................................ 129

## Part III: Delving Deeper into the Financial Pages ....... 141
Chapter 8: Sharpening Your Understanding ................................ 143
Chapter 9: Watching Out for the Pitfalls................................. 173
Chapter 10: Monitoring the Market's Psychology Using Charts ............. 187

## Part IV: Using the Pages for More Advanced Investments ....................................................... 197
Chapter 11: Going International.......................................... 199
Chapter 12: Delving into Derivatives.................................... 209
Chapter 13: Making Money from Commodities............................... 219
Chapter 14: Investing in Funds and Trusts............................... 243
Chapter 15: Discovering Hedge Funds, Bonds, and ETFs.................... 255

## Part V: Other Places to Go for Financial Information ............................................... 267
Chapter 16: Using the Alternatives ...................................... 269
Chapter 17: Understanding Company Accounts .............................. 291

# Part VI: The Part of Tens ............................................. 307

Chapter 18: Ten Things to Know About a Share......................................309

Chapter 19: Ten Ways to Make Your Asset Allocation Fit.......................315

Chapter 20: Ten Warning Signs that a Company May Be on the Ropes .................323

Chapter 21: Ten Red-Hot Clues to an Opportunity....................................331

# Appendix: Glossary ............................................. 341

# Index ............................................. 355

# Table of Contents

*Introduction* ......................................................................... *1*

About This Book.................................................................2
    More Than Just Numbers ...........................................3
    Finding the Right Strategy for You ............................3
Conventions Used in This Book........................................4
What You're Not to Read...................................................4
Foolish Assumptions..........................................................4
How This Book Is Organised .............................................5
    Part I: The Financial Pages.........................................5
    Part II: Using the Financial Pages to Make Basic Investments .........5
    Part III: Delving Deeper into the Financial Pages .........5
    Part IV: Using the Pages for More Advanced Investments .............6
    Part V: Other Places to Go for Financial Information......................6
    Part VI: The Part of Tens..........................................7
    Glossary ....................................................................7
Icons Used in This Book ...................................................7
Where to Go from Here......................................................8

*Part I: The Financial Pages ....................................... 9*

## Chapter 1: Introducing the Financial Pages ...................11

Getting into the Swim of It..............................................11
Looking at the Key Players..............................................13
    Yesterday's genteel society......................................14
    Today's drones and superheroes .............................14
    Investigating investors ............................................16
    Considering companies............................................16
    Finding out about financial institutions .................18
Seeking Foreign Information ...........................................19

## Chapter 2: Looking at How the Financial Pages Work ...........21

Getting the Most out of the Statistics ............................22
    Share prices in close detail.....................................22
    The daily price movement.......................................24
    Perusing profits.......................................................25
    Puzzling out the price/earnings ratio.....................27
    Considering company size (market capitalisation)......29
    Dividends .................................................................31
Looking Beyond the Numbers .........................................33
    What the Numbers Don't Say ..................................33
    Reading between the lines.......................................35

**Chapter 3: Relating the Financial Pages to the Stock Market.......37**

Revealing What the Stock Market Is and What It Does............................38
    Considering the international angle.................................................40
    Figuring out FTSE................................................................................40
Understanding What Shares Are ..............................................................41
    Grasping the basics on shares .........................................................41
    Getting a share of the profit .............................................................42
    Investigating other types of share...................................................42
Looking at How the Pages Report on the Stock Market ......................43
Understanding Market Sectors .................................................................45
    Recognising the difference between growth
        industries and mature sectors ...................................................46
    Choosing the middle ground.............................................................47
Understanding Stock Market Indices .......................................................48
    Seeing how indices can move shares...............................................49
    Getting into the FTSE-100 index.......................................................49
    Finding indices ...................................................................................50
Looking at Market Realities.......................................................................51
    Understanding how macro factors move markets .........................51
    Avoiding the madness of crowds......................................................54
    Understanding how the standard business cycle works...............56
Interpreting Important Stock Market Buzzwords...................................58
    Sentiment .............................................................................................59
    Momentum............................................................................................59
    Liquidity ...............................................................................................59
    High beta ..............................................................................................60
    Points.....................................................................................................60

**Chapter 4: Using the Pages to Your Advantage ..................61**

Choosing Your Basic Strategy....................................................................61
    Are you a bull or a bear?....................................................................62
    Common investing approaches .........................................................64
Choosing Between Investment Channels .................................................74
    Direct ownership ................................................................................74
    Nominee accounts ..............................................................................75
    Trusts ....................................................................................................76

**Part II: Using The Financial Pages
to Make Basic Investments............................................. 77**

**Chapter 5: Investing in Shares...................................79**

Different Shares for Different People .......................................................80
    Following tortoises and hares...........................................................81
    Focusing on your own risk tolerance...............................................84

Using the Information in the Financial Pages.............................85
    Reading the information correctly ....................................86
    Using the information to make decisions ......................87
    Selling, and why it's harder than buying .....................88
    Taking a closer look at price/earnings ratios................89
    Valuing a company that doesn't have any earnings......94
    Understanding market capitalisation.............................95
    Delving into dividends ...................................................98
    Understanding debt ratios............................................101
    Getting more information about debt ..........................104
Comparing Stocks with Cash ................................................105

**Chapter 6: Investing in Bonds** ............................**107**
Getting Comfortable with Bonds ..........................................108
    Understanding the upside-down logic of bonds...........109
    Knowing what makes a bond price move.....................111
    Browsing benchmarks...................................................113
    Buying bonds...............................................................113
Government Bonds..................................................................114
    Looking at government bonds ......................................114
    Understanding bond rating systems ............................115
    What you find in the papers – and why ......................116
    Getting down to business with some quotations .........117
    Looking at the international scene ...............................119
Corporate Bonds ...................................................................121
Junk Bonds: A High-Risk Alternative....................................124
    Why they call these bonds junk ..................................125
    'Sub-investment grade' paper .....................................126

**Chapter 7: Investing in Cash Investments** .....................**129**
Everybody Needs Some Cash ...............................................129
The Tax Issue ........................................................................130
Talking About Time................................................................132
    Running fast to stay ahead of inflation........................133
Getting Price Information .......................................................135
Knowing Your APRs from your AERs.....................................137
    Working out the APR ....................................................137
    Working out the AER ....................................................138
Dodging Sneaky Bank Tricks.................................................138

## *Part III: Delving Deeper into the Financial Pages ....... 141*

### Chapter 8: Sharpening Your Understanding ...................143

Understanding Statutory Announcements...............................143
   When does a company have to
      make a regulatory announcement?..............................144
   When a company hits the skids ......................................147
   'Responding to press comment': Emergency announcements,
      updates, and what to do about them ..........................149
   Changes to controlling shareholdings ............................152
   The takeover rules...........................................................152
How the Media Is Regulated .....................................................154
Valuing a Company Correctly....................................................156
   Putting a price on a company with no profits................157
   Appraising goodwill, patents, and other intangibles ...160
   Weighing up takeover potential .....................................162
A Closer Look at Fixed Asset Valuations ..................................165
   Considering depreciation ...............................................165
   Valuing property ..............................................................165
   A property sector whose value simply disappears........168
Checking Future Pension Liabilities.........................................169

### Chapter 9: Watching Out for the Pitfalls ......................173

Avoiding Common Mistakes.......................................................173
   Price falls on ex-dividend dates .....................................174
   Scrip issues and consolidations.....................................177
   Collapsing valuations: Falling knives
      and the dead cat bounce.............................................179
   Free float and golden shares: How they affect volatility.............180
   EBITDA ..............................................................................181
Spotting a Company's Hidden Debts.........................................183
Shorting – and Why It So often Ends in Tears...........................184
   'Bear raids': Ganging up on the victim ..........................185
   Getting information about shorting volumes..................185

### Chapter 10: Monitoring the Market's Psychology Using Charts ....187

Understanding What Charts Can Tell You and What They Can't .........187
   Driving on emotions ........................................................188
   Viewing charts realistically ............................................189
Looking for Patterns..................................................................190
   Double tops .....................................................................190
   Head and shoulders.........................................................191
   Rising floors, support levels, and resistance levels .....192
   Triangles ..........................................................................193
   The Elliott Wave theory ..................................................194
Using Charts to Check Your Decisions .....................................194

## Part IV: Using the Pages for More Advanced Investments ............ 197

### Chapter 11: Going International ...................199
Why You Need Foreign Shares in Your Portfolio ....................200
Riding the Macro Waves .......................................201
Investing in Emerging Markets .................................202
Finding Information on International Investments ...............202
    Using comparison charts ...................................203
    Locating information on individual companies .............204
    Overlooking structural differences .......................205
Understanding Currency Risks and
    Using Them to Your Advantage ...........................206

### Chapter 12: Delving into Derivatives ...........209
Finding Out about Futures .....................................210
    The perils of leverage ...................................211
    Hedging with futures contracts ...........................213
    Companies that hedge their own prices! ...................215
    Why you don't find many futures prices in the papers ....215
Weighing Up Warrants .........................................216
Casting an Eye Over Options ..................................217

### Chapter 13: Making Money from Commodities .....219
Introducing Commodities ......................................219
    Understanding the long-term argument for minerals .......221
    Getting started on commodity investing ..................223
    Finding price information ................................224
Investing in Oil .............................................228
    Getting started ..........................................229
    Finding price information ................................230
    Can anyone forecast the oil price? .......................231
    Drillers, explorers, and producers ......................233
Investing in Food Commodities ...............................233
    The DJ-AIG commodity indices .............................234
    Finding price information ................................235
Investing in Gold and Other Precious Metals .................235
    Finding price information ................................236
    Choosing gold certificates and Exchange Traded Funds.....237
    Investing in silver, platinum, palladium, and the rest...238
    Discovering gold collectable coins ......................240
    Finding prices information ...............................241
Investing in Less Glamorous Commodities .....................241
    Uranium ..................................................242
    Finding price information ................................242

**Chapter 14: Investing in Funds and Trusts . . . . . . . . . . . . . . . . . . . . .243**

Employing a Professional Pilot ............................................................... 243
    Utilising expert knowledge ........................................................ 244
    Considering the autopilot advantage ...................................... 244
Sourcing Information ................................................................................ 245
    TIDMs, SEDOLs, and ISINs ........................................................ 245
    Where's your manager gone? .................................................... 246
Unit Trusts ................................................................................................ 248
    Understanding unit trusts ......................................................... 249
    Finding unit prices ..................................................................... 250
    Choosing between a business sector
        and a geographical sector ................................................... 250
    Introducing UCITS and OEICs ................................................... 251
Investment Trusts .................................................................................... 252
    Understanding discounts and premiums ................................ 252
    Finding information on the 'invisible' investment category ........ 253
    Realising why investment trusts are volatile ......................... 254

**Chapter 15: Discovering Hedge Funds, Bonds, and ETFs . . . . . . . . .255**

Assessing Hedge Funds ........................................................................... 256
    Understanding why hedge funds are different ....................... 256
    Considering whether hedge funds are
        becoming respectable at last .............................................. 258
Gauging Guaranteed Income Bonds ....................................................... 259
    Understanding how 'structured products' work ..................... 259
    Locking up your money for a fixed period .............................. 260
    Taking those marketing claims with a pinch of salt .............. 260
    Avoiding precipice bonds .......................................................... 262
Exchange-Traded Funds ........................................................................... 264
    Understanding how ETFs work ................................................. 264
    Finding out what's available in the UK ................................... 266
    Buying foreign-listed ETFs ........................................................ 266

*Part V: Other Places to Go for Financial Information... 267*

**Chapter 16: Using the Alternatives . . . . . . . . . . . . . . . . . . . . . . . . . .269**

Online Resources ...................................................................................... 270
    'Official' websites ........................................................................ 270
    'Unofficial' Websites .................................................................. 272
Discussion Forums, and Why You Need Them ...................................... 279
    Blogs ............................................................................................ 281
Investment Magazines .............................................................................. 282
    Discovering the charm of a monthly read .............................. 283
    Valuing independent reportage ................................................ 284
The Foreign Press ..................................................................................... 284

Reports, Tipsheets, and Newsletters ........................................................286
    Analysing brokers' analyst reports ...................................287
    Assessing tipsheets and newsletters ................................289

### Chapter 17: Understanding Company Accounts ................**291**

Introducing Company Accounts ..............................................................291
    Getting hold of the accounts ............................................292
    Working out how much you really need to know ..........293
Reading a Profit and Loss Account ..........................................................295
Understanding the Balance Sheet ............................................................297
Interpreting the Cash Flow Statement .....................................................300
Understanding What Can Go Wrong .........................................................303
Looking at Five-year Summaries ..............................................................303

## Part VI: The Part of Tens ............................................ 307

### Chapter 18: Ten Things to Know About a Share ................**309**

Knowing What the Share Price Has Done
    During the Last Five Years.............................................309
Knowing the Company's Stock Market Size .............................................310
Knowing the Price/Earnings Ratio............................................................310
Looking at the Dividend, and Deciding Whether
    Current Profits Can Cover It ..........................................311
Finding Out When the Next Dividend Payment Is Due ...........................311
Reading the Profit and Loss Statement....................................................312
Looking at the Balance Sheet...................................................................312
Knowing What Other Debts the Company Has.........................................313
Looking at the Directors' Statements ......................................................314
Checking the Buzz on Online Forums ......................................................314

### Chapter 19: Ten Ways to Make Your Asset Allocation Fit ........**315**

Assessing Your Life Situation...................................................................315
Adjusting the Balance ...............................................................................316
Considering Whose Money You're Managing ...........................................317
Deciding Between Capital Gains and Income for Tax Purposes............317
Deciding How Long You Can Afford to Lock in
    Your Money if Everything Goes Wrong...........................318
Figuring Out Your Attitude to Debt...........................................................318
Asking Whether You Enjoy the Investment Game for Its Own Sake .....320
Figuring Out Whether You're a Herd Follower or a Maverick .............320
Making Sure You Know How Important This Money Is to You............321
Asking Whether You Can Get Over a Mistake...........................................322

**Chapter 20: Ten Warning Signs that a Company
May Be on the Ropes**................................................323

  Profits Are Stagnant or Falling.................................................324
  The Dividend Cover Is Looking Stretched...............................324
  The Share Price Is Below Its 200-day Moving Average...........325
  Directors Are Selling Their Shares.........................................325
  The Sector Is Troubled, with No Obvious Upturn in Sight.....326
  The Company Depends Heavily on a Client Who's in Trouble.............327
  A Merger Approach Looks like Falling Through.....................327
  New Reporting Regulations Have Exposed a Pensions 'Black Hole'.....328
  A Recent Merger Doesn't Seem to Have Produced
    any Useful Synergies.........................................................329
  The Auditors Have Qualified the Company's Accounts.........330

**Chapter 21: Ten Red-Hot Clues to an Opportunity**..............331

  The Price/Earnings Ratio Is Below the Sector Average, but Rising......332
  Like-For-Like Sales Are Up Strongly......................................332
  Brokers' Recommendations Improve......................................333
  The Company Is about to Be Promoted into the FTSE-100.....334
  The Economic Cycle Is Moving to Favour
    Companies like Your Target...............................................335
  The Underlying Macro-environment Is Improving.................336
  The Share Price Has Been Unfairly Devastated......................336
  Predators Are Circling the Company......................................337
  The Company Has Announced a Technical Breakthrough.....338
  The Company Earns Its Money in a Currency
    that's Set to Strengthen....................................................338

*Appendix: Glossary*.........................................*341*

*Index*..................................................................*355*

# Introduction

*I*f you've been feeling the need for a bit more financial savvy in the last few years, you can rest assured that you're not alone. Let's face it, your company's pension fund provisions aren't what they used to be, and so you need to think harder about securing your long-term prosperity. You're also painfully aware that you're probably going to need to have to plan for your own care costs as you get older and live longer. Meanwhile, your kids need to be supported through school and university. And, with every upward lurch in the government's budget deficit, the chances of us ever getting any of those state benefits back recede further into the distance.

Fortunately, investing is getting easier. You can set up a tax-efficient savings plan or a pension plan that will give you 100 per cent tax relief on your payments – and needn't cost you more than £50 a year to run. Your children will get government assistance if you set up Child Trust Funds on their behalf. Everybody is keen to get you investing for your pension.

Best of all, we have the internet, which has revolutionised savings by making it possible to do your own research instead of paying some fool in a blazer to sell you the wrong products and then charge you a fat management fee for the privilege. And you'd really love to do the job yourself, but . . .

The trouble is, you're a busy person, and you really don't relish the thought of having to tangle with all those City people with their obscure language and their convoluted ways of doing things. How do they figure out which companies are on the up-and-up and which are going down? And can you do the same?

Well, you've taken a good first step by buying this book. It'll show you, in reassuringly easy stages, how to get started in the investment game. Whether you're interested in shares or bank deposit accounts or bonds, or whether you're just trying to select a professionally-managed fund that will take all the responsibility off your own shoulders.

I'm not about to make specific share recommendations to you. The heroes and the villains on the stock market are constantly changing places, and I'd be in trouble if I pointed you toward an investment that would only disappoint you – or worse, leave you worse off than before you started.

Instead, I'll make sure that you have the tools and the understanding that you'll need to make your own choices. I'll point you towards information sources that are truthful and reliable, and I'll try to show you how to avoid getting fooled by the ones that aren't.

# *About This Book*

I've been in financial journalism for long enough to have learned – sometimes the hard way – that it's really rather easy to get swept along by other people's blithe assumptions that you always know what they're talking about. When somebody starts spouting city jargon it can be hard to tell him you really haven't got a clue what he's on about.

Well, relax, because you're among friends. One of the really important things they drummed into us at the *Financial Times* was that there's only really one stupid question where money is concerned, and that's the question that you're too scared to ask. Never be afraid to admit your ignorance, is my advice. And if the person who's doing the spouting can't explain things to you in clear, concise language, then either he's a bigger fool than he looks, or else he's talking about something so deep that it really doesn't need to concern you anyway.

I've tried in this book to structure the sections in a sequence that I think you'll find easy to follow. You'll find most of the easier stuff, and all of the really basic stock market fundamentals, in Part One of the book. Parts Two and Three take you a bit further into the more complex areas of the subject matter, including clues as to how you can take better advantage of the information that's already out there. And how you can avoid falling into some of the elephant traps that can await the unwary.

The later Parts of the book look at cash investing, and at bonds, and at managed investment funds. And then we go right off the deep end with a look at some really fancy stuff – futures and options and warrants and so forth.

Toward the end of the book, you'll find a chapter on the subject of understanding company accounts. Now, I don't want to frighten you unnecessarily here. So let me whisper a little secret into your ear. Ready? Okay, here it comes, but don't tell anyone of we'll both be in trouble. You don't really need to understand the finer points of companies' finances to make a success of your investments. Indeed, the majority of investors never even look at their companies' accounts in any detail, and some of them wouldn't know how to interpret what they read even if they tried.

How do they get away with it? Because today's interconnected investment world is constantly buzzing with other peoples' analyses, and if there's anything seriously wrong with a company's books there's always likely to be someone who'll draw it to your attention. That doesn't mean that you don't need to understand anything at all about accounts, mind you. If you don't know a pre-tax profit from a dividend, or a fixed asset from a current debt, then you need to sharpen up your understanding pronto. You've come to the right place. I'll try to make it easy for you.

## More Than Just Numbers

You can't argue with publicly-issued figures because they're facts. (Well, that's generally true of the stock market anyway, because the regulators take a dim view of people who play fast and loose with matters of mathematical accuracy.) But you'll soon find that the real art of investing lies somewhere else. It's the background reading, the company research, the general state of the financial markets, and even the politics that will decide how well you succeed. You'll find that I encourage you in this book to think not just about the companies (or bonds, or whatever) that you're investing in, but also how they fit into the bigger picture.

I'll show you how to look at what's being said in the news broadcasts, in the Sunday papers, and in the many discussion forums on the internet. (They can be a bit scary at first, but don't worry, I'll hold your hand.) The bigger your field of view, the better your chances of not buying the right share at the wrong time. Because that might easily be worse than not buying it at all. But if you can figure out what the Next Big Thing is likely to be, you stand an excellent chance of beating the odds.

## Finding the Right Strategy for You

Now, I'm going to say something rather important. Every reader will get something different out of this book, because every single reader is different from all the others and everyone will have different requirements. Things that will be good for one investor might be an act of reckless abandon for another. One investor might want dividends from his shares, while another might find that they just drive up his tax bill. A younger investor without a family can afford to take risks that I could never recommend to somebody who was approaching retirement. And so on.

So I'm going to encourage you to start by thinking about what kind of an investor you want to be. Are you saving up for something special, or do you just want to have a bit of fun with a few thousand pounds from Auntie Dora's will? Are you going to be depending on the money you'll make through your investments – and, if so, how long will it be before you need to get your hands on it? Can you lock your money up for five years or more?

This is what we mean by deciding on your investor profile. And once you've got your answers we should be ready to go.

# Conventions Used in This Book

A note about internet addresses (or URLs, as they're known). Wherever possible, I've removed the initial *http://* from URLs like http://www.ft.com, because you can get along fine with just www.ft.com But every so often you'll come across an URL that has no *www* but simply goes http://news.bbc.co.uk. There's no obvious reason for the discrepancy, but I expect we can learn to live with it.

When this book was printed, some Web addresses may have needed to break across two lines of text. If that happened, rest assured that we haven't put in any extra characters (such as hyphens) to indicate the break. So, when using one of these Web addresses, just type in exactly what you see in this book, pretending as though the line break doesn't exist.

# What You're Not to Read

I'll be thrilled if you do decide read this book from cover to cover, but I'm going to let you off some of it. Wherever you see any text that's preceded by the Technical Stuff icon, you can safely move on without losing anything significant from the narrative. I use this icon to denote that I'm going off on a momentary tangent to satisfy my insane need for technical detail. If techie details really don't do it for you, just ignore them and move on. Similarly, when you see something set apart as a sidebar (with a grey tint behind the text), you can take it that it's an aside that isn't critical to the text.

# Foolish Assumptions

I'm going to try and assume as little as possible about you, except of course that you've had the very good sense to buy this book. I'm also going to assume that you don't have a PhD in higher maths, and that you're not particularly familiar with the bizarre terminology that the financial markets use. Well, relax, because it's my job to take you through it at a pace which I hope you'll be able to follow.

It'll certainly be helpful if you can find your way around the internet, because you'll find rather a lot of Web links in this book. Investing is getting to be an internet sport these days, mainly for the very good reason that the investing world has speeded up to the point where you ideally need to be on the ball most of the time.But if you don't have an internet connection at home, don't panic. There's still plenty that you can do using just the printed media that land on your doorstep every morning – the newspapers, the magazines and so forth – and also the television and radio news.

# *How This Book Is Organised*

If you've read any of the other *For Dummies* books, you won't need telling that they're laid out in a very regular way that makes them easy to use.

You could, of course, simply start at the beginning and read this book right through to the end. And, if you do decide to do that, you'll find that I've graded the Chapters roughly in order of difficulty and complexity so that the learning process will be reasonably smooth. But it's much more likely that you'll want to use the book as a reference source that you can dip into whenever you've got a query about something.

## *Part 1: The Financial Pages*

In this section of the book I go right back to basics with a look at what the key players in the financial scene actually do and how they interact with each other. I discuss the simplest and most important things that you'll always want to know about a company's shares before you buy them, and I talk about the many different strategies you can use, depending on what sort of investor you are and what your personal 'risk profile' looks like.

## *Part 11: Using the Financial Pages to Make Basic Investments*

This part takes a closer look at the stock market basics that we saw in Part I, and it looks at the relative merits of stocks against cash investments. Then it explores the weird upside-down world of bonds, where everything revolves around the interest rates rather than the bond prices themselves. Finally we return to the cash investing theme with a summary of what's available and what some of the basic terminology means.

## *Part 111: Delving Deeper into the Financial Pages*

This part is probably better suited for readers who've already got a rudimentary grasp of stock market basics. The tricky thing with share investing is that sometimes the devil sits among the details. I'll show you where he's likely to be lurking, and how you can spot him before he sees you coming. We also look at special situations like takeovers, and I show you how to read the official regulatory information sources that are absolutely, positively guaranteed to give you the plain unvarnished truth - on pain of jail!

We end this part with a look at so-called technical analysis, which is the black art of using charting techniques to second-guess what the market's going to do next. Is it a valid analytical technique or just superstition and voodoo? You decide.

# Part IV: Using the Pages for More Advanced Investments

We start to get into slightly racier territory in this section of the book. Chapter 11 explores the many advantages of broadening out your horizons to include foreign shares as well as British ones. Then we discuss the so-called derivatives market - futures, options and so forth – and we take a long look at the fast-growing commodities sector. I show you how to use the new generation of exchange traded funds, which are a cheap and flexible way of backing your hunches on gold, oil and other basic items.

Finally we move on to managed funds - unit trusts, investment trusts, guaranteed income bonds (a kind of stock market tracker), and hedge funds. What do they do? How do they calculate their prices? Why are some riskier than others? And where do you get up-to-date information about them?

# Part V: Other Places to Go for Financial Information

This section takes a long look at the relative advantages of print media and internet-based information sources, and its conclusions might surprise you. Reports of the death of investment magazines are much exaggerated. Even though the sharpest, most up-to-date and most informative sources are online. I show you which sources you can trust and which ones are strictly bargepole territory.

The section concludes with a detailed look at listed company accounts, using a real-live set of figures from a major British company.

## *Part VI: The Part of Tens*

This is where you'll find a set of easy-to-read checklists that will help you focus your attentions where they really matter.

What do you really need to know about a share before you buy it? Does your investment portfolio reflect your personality and your position in life? What are the unmistakeable signs of a company that's on the up and up? And what are the giveaway clues that tell you it's on the way down? You'll find short, pithy answers here.

## *Glossary*

At the end of this book you'll find a handy glossary of the more common kinds of terminology used by the investing fraternity. It won't take you right into the very depths of the City's workings (but then, that isn't what were trying to achieve with this book.) Instead, the aim is to arm you with the basics.

# *Icons Used in This Book*

You'll find a lot of graphical material in this book, which will give you a pretty fair idea of the sort of information that's out there, and what it typically looks like when you find it. But you'll also notice that some of the paragraphs are tagged with the following icons, all of whichhave their own special meanings:

This icon tells you that there's a labour-saving trick you can use to help you get the best use out of your time. Sometimes it'll be a short-cut, and sometimes it might be a link to a resource that will give you a greater in-depth understanding of the subject.

A self-explanatory icon, really. You can save yourself a lot of repetitive work and worry by internalising these little bits of practical advice. And sometimes help yourself make more money....

There's a risk of tears before bedtime if you ignore one of these warning icons. Getting on in the financial world is all about taking risks and managing them properly, but it's important to know where the minefields are. Mostly, the risk is that you'll end up losing money. But sometimes the warning icon will be telling you that you risk breaking the law!

The financial pages are endlessly full of technical verbiage that doesn't need to concern you unless you're really keen on detail. Often you'll find that when you see this icon, it denotes information that you can skip if you want to. Come back later and have another look at it when you know your way around a bit better.

# *Where to Go from Here*

Finally, let me say once again that there are no one-way signs in this book, and therefore there's no compulsion to read it in any particular sequence. Just treat it as a reference book and dip into it as and when the need arises.

Having said that, I've 'graded' the initial Parts of the book so that they cover the most basic concepts that every investor really ought to know before he gets into deeper stuff. If you've glanced through Part I briefly and thought 'yes, I know all that,' then you're all set to take the rest of the book in any sequence.

But if you do find yourself getting a bit tangled up in the vocabulary department, have another look at Part I. Alternatively, you may well find that a quick look-up in the Glossary at the end of the book will get you back up and running. If it's the figures that are doing your head in, you may find enlightenment from Chapter 17 on company accounts

If this really is your first time as an investor, and if you have internet access, do think hard about setting up a dummy portfolio account and running it for a few months before you splash your hard-earned cash on real live stocks and investments. The FT website, the London Stock Exchange website and the Motley Fool website will all let you run portfolios without charge. It's simply got to be the best and the safest way to find out whether you've got the talent, the persistence, and most of all the self-discipline to make a raging success of it.

It only remains for me to thank you again for buying this book, and to wish you a happy, entertaining and above all profitable experience as an investor.

# Part I
# The Financial Pages

## *In this part . . .*

1n this section of the book I go right back to basics with a look at what the key players in the financial scene actually do and how they interact with each other. I discuss the simplest and most important things that you'll always want to know about a company's shares before you buy them, and I talk about the many different strategies you can use, depending on what sort of investor you are and what your personal 'risk profile' looks like.

# Chapter 1

# Introducing the Financial Pages

*In This Chapter*

▶ Getting started

▶ Getting to grips with the major players

▶ Avoiding transatlantic misunderstandings

Strictly speaking, the term 'financial pages' is a bit outdated. Now that we've got the Internet and television business news and all the rest of it, the chances are that not very many people depend solely on what they read in the papers any more. So much detail comes at you from every side, and so many analysts and economists are pushing their own versions of events at you, that the task of understanding this thing I'm calling the financial pages has got quite a lot more challenging.

No longer do you have to make do with whatever little bits of information you can get from magazines and newspapers. Nowadays, the challenge is to know how to sift through all this stuff, sort out the biased dross, and then act on the sources that you've come to trust and respect. That's bound to seem like a tall order at first. But relax; this process isn't as terrible as it sounds. I'm here to guide you through the basics.

## Getting into the Swim of It

If this is your first foray into the strange and maybe frightening world of investing, take heart. Although you can dip in and out, I've structured this book so if you wish you can start at the shallow end of the pool where the water isn't too crowded and the waves aren't too big. Then, once you've got your 10-metre certificate and you're feeling confident enough to get around without your armbands, I introduce you to some of the more ambitious swimmers and the exotic creatures who inhabit the slightly deeper waters. (Only a few of them bite. I make sure you know what they look like and how they behave.)

Throughout the book I introduce you to the lifeguards and referees who are responsible for seeing fair play in the financial markets – and who can order offenders right out of the pool if they don't behave themselves. I show you how to stay in these regulators' good books, and how to read their reports. They're on your side, after all.

The early chapters deal mostly with the stock market. Later chapters describe other ways in which people use the pool, by investing in cash, bonds, and commodities. Not to mention derivatives such as futures, options, and warrants! Yes, we've reached the diving boards, where nobody wears water wings any more, and where you can show off your impressive abilities to the utmost. Providing, of course, that you're happy with the additional risks that you're also taking. Because the lifeguards won't always be able to rescue you if you do get into trouble.

Mention of futures, options, and warrants will probably strike fear into your heart at first. After all, not so long ago bonds cost £100,000 a shot and commodities – raw materials like oil, gold or copper – were strictly for fast-talking experts wearing loud blazers. But these days a small private investor can easily play the commodities game with just as much chance of success as the experts. In Chapter 14 I introduce you to the wonderful new world of exchange-traded funds (ETFs), which work like shares but actually track the prices of oil and copper and gold. They're even tax efficient! You don't pay stamp duty on ETFs. And you can put them in your Individual Savings Account (ISA) if you like.

What do we mean by bonds, incidentally? Well, I don't want to go too deeply into that subject right now – that can wait until Chapter 6 – but let's just say that they're a kind of interest-bearing investment that many people find preferable to shares when they don't want to expose themselves to too much direct risk from the stock market. The general idea is that you're effectively lending money to a borrower – either a government body or a large company – who promises to pay you a (usually) fixed rate of interest for a fixed number of years, plus your money back when that time is over. And what's more, on top of that reliable cash return you've also got the possibility of making a capital gain, depending on how a range of other factors stack up over a period of time.

That sounds really great, doesn't it? But there's the proviso that, if things go badly or if you overpay for your bonds, you could lose some of your capital instead. So it's not quite as simple as it sounds. Even so, a few bonds ought to be in everybody's portfolio because they provide a useful counterbalance to the ups and downs of the stock market.

Slackening off the pace a bit, Chapter 14 takes you through the slightly less unfamiliar world of managed funds, where somebody else does all the work and the only decisions you really need to make are when you buy and when you sell. You've almost certainly got some managed funds already: a few unit trusts, the occasional tracker ISA, and maybe a guaranteed equity bond from your local building society. Furthermore, the chances are that your pension's invested in unit trusts and investment trusts.

Just for interest, I show you how people invest in other countries, and how you can optimise your investments if you're willing to have a little flutter on a few foreign markets instead of only the United Kingdom.

I introduce you to my favourite places for getting hold of the best information. Some of it come from the print media, and a lot of it's from the Internet. These days you can't get away from the web.

I also introduce you, very briefly, to the wild and wacky world of Internet discussion forums and blogs. Now, I'm going to warn you in advance that some of these places aren't suitable for raw beginners, because they can be a little, ahem, robust. If you've ever seen a game of water polo you have some idea of how the discussion board posters sometimes treat each other, and you may decide you want to watch from the poolside for a while before you dive in and get involved. Yes, blogs and discussion forums can get a little brutal – and remember, they're largely unregulated, so you shouldn't always believe everything you read! But then again, you do have the satisfaction of knowing that you're watching world-class sportspeople doing what they do best.

This is the adults' pool, no doubt about it, and it can get rowdy. But I'm not doing my job if I don't at least introduce you to it, because, as I hope to prove, Internet forums can contain masses of good stuff.

Right at the end of the book is a glossary of financial market terminology. I've tried to cover all the basic stuff that's in this book, but you're bound to run into phrases that make you wonder whether you've missed something. You haven't. Instead, I missed it out. But then, I'm writing a book for beginners, not for experts, so the more I can cut the jargon the happier we all are.

# Looking at the Key Players

Back in the grand old days of the 1980s, when stockbrokers still wore bowler hats instead of cycle helmets and Bluetooth headsets, and when share dealing started some time after morning tea and biscuits had ended, nobody had the slightest doubt about who did what, because it was all very neatly ordered.

## Yesterday's genteel society

The investors were the people who telephoned their orders to their stockbrokers, telling them what shares they wanted to buy or sell, or asking for advice. The brokers then telephoned the *market makers* – the people who kept 'buffers' of shares that they bought or sold to the brokers' clients. Assuming the market makers had the stocks on their shelves, they made them available to the brokers, who bought them on behalf of their clients.

The brokers got the paperwork done, and within two or three weeks (often longer) the investors received their share certificates in the post. The transaction typically cost the investor somewhere in the region of £30, which is closer to £80 in today's money. But then, in those days there was no such thing as today's execution-only trading, whereby you simply tell your broker what to do and don't ask for advice. Instead, every customer needed detailed and personal advice about what to buy. Because the stock market was such a complex and confusing place. Wasn't it?

So everybody had his own job to do, and the division of labour was absolute. Everybody would have been horrified at the idea of a broker doubling as a market maker, because that would have put somebody out of a job. And it was illegal anyway. There was also no question of a bank, still less an investment bank, owning a stockbroker, because surely that created a conflict of interest. So that was illegal too. In America a law even existed called the Glass-Steagall Act, which prevented lending banks from getting involved with the securities industry altogether.

And the broker's analyst was the lowest of the low. He spent his days cooped up in the darkest room in the building with an ancient desk, poring over company accounts and trying to think up new ways of making them sound interesting to his bosses, the stockbrokers, and their clients. If anybody told him one day he'd be the superstar and his stockbroker bosses would be the drones who enacted share purchases that came down a wire into their computers, he'd have laughed in their faces.

## Today's drones and superheroes

Today, the investor is still the person who spends the money, but these days he calls all the shots. He generally doesn't need the broker's advice about what to buy, because he can get all the information he needs from the Internet and the financial media; consequently he's more interested in getting his trades done for £8 a time, which is around a tenth of the 1986 cost in real terms. The customer expects to get the important parts of his paperwork done in a few seconds. Indeed, if he's running a *nominee account* (where an intermediary holds the shares on his behalf) he probably doesn't care about getting a share certificate at all. You can go your whole investing career without ever seeing one.

The broker is no longer king of the hill. He does what he's told, and he has to compete hard with his rivals on a cost basis. The fact he doesn't have to pay a market maker any more is good, because he can make markets in his own right if he wants to. (This abolition of the old division of labour was one of the key changes of the 'Big Bang' financial markets deregulation in 1986.) In America the Glass-Steagall Act was repealed in 1999, which was a good thing because the financial markets had widely ignored it for years by that stage.

These days, absolutely no reason exists why a bank shouldn't own a stockbroking firm – and indeed, most of them do. Very few fully independent brokers are still left, and there are no independent market makers at all in London Instead, the whole market-making job is done by brokers and/or the banks that own them.

The same goes for consultancies, accountancy firms, and all sorts of other 'multi-agency' financial firms, which may typically be running broking divisions alongside their lending divisions, their research divisions, and their fund-management divisions. Every single one of these multi-agency outfits is doing practically everything. And the furious heat of progress has melted away every distinction that used to exist between these various roles.

Well, almost. One risk had to be controlled by new legislation. Now that a bank can be advising its own clients what to buy while simultaneously investing its own money in shares to make its funds grow, a potential conflict of interest arises between what its divisions do. Imagine what would happen if an investment bank issued a broker's recommendation instructing its customers to buy a particular company's shares, while simultaneously dumping that company's shares from its own investment portfolios. Wouldn't you be just a little suspicious that it was driving up prices in order to reduce its own losses?

So would I. These days, multi-agency financial outfits are required to maintain so-called *Chinese walls* between their divisions so that their employees can't talk to one another in ways that may be anti-competitive, or that may manipulate the market in any way. Usually the Chinese walls work well. When they don't, the scandal keeps the papers busy for months and can mean a prison term for the company's directors.

And the humble stockbroker's analyst? He's a superhero. Even the ones who don't head their departments get their suits from Armani so they look smooth when they talk to the television cameras. Newspapers hold the front page whenever they speak. The role reversal is complete.

## Investigating investors

Investors have never had it so good. That's the theory, at least. They've got more information, cheaper dealing costs, and access to a share purchase at the press of a computer keyboard. They've got tax-efficient Individual Savings Accounts (ISAs) that put their money into a tax-free shell where it can grow and grow without ever incurring any capital gains tax.

Investors can buy shares listed on pretty well any stock market in the developed world, and put those into their ISAs too. When they can't find a share they like, or when they don't feel capable of running a foreign-share portfolio, they can buy an investment trust that spreads their money over a wide range of suitable shares and still charges them zero in management costs. Or they may prefer to buy an *exchange-traded fund*, which somehow manages to shadow the performance of a big price index (the Nikkei, the German Dax, or even just the price of coal), without ever buying even a single proper share. Weird.

The flipside of all these advantages is that investors need to be much more in touch with the markets than previous generations ever had to be. In the past, people bought old-style heavy manufacturing shares and kept them all their lives. But you don't have it so easy as your grandparents, because you have to live with a fast-changing world. China used to be a mainly agricultural nation, but instead it's becoming the world's number one producer of electronic goods. India and China have overtaken much of the developed world for steel and heavy machinery manufacture, and places like Mexico and Brazil are quickly dominating the international market for low-cost cars in the developing world. Chemicals, energy, mining companies – you name it, the geography of the industry is shifting fast. You have to listen out for the news in ways that nobody else has ever had to do.

You also have to understand information that would've baffled investors from previous generations: new terminology, previously unimagined techniques, fancy accounting systems, and lots and lots of politics. That's where this book comes in. But courage, you'll be fine once you get started.

## Considering companies

Fortunately not much change has occurred over the years in the fundamental concept of a company. A *company* is an independent legal structure (a 'person', legally speaking), which belongs to its shareholders, whoever they may be, and not necessarily to its directors. If a company commits a crime, the directors can be jailed even though they may not own it. That's partly why they get paid so much. They're in charge of an asset that belongs to the shareholders and not to them.

When they make profits, the default assumption is that the board of directors hand out some of it to shareholders as a thank-you for their loyalty and an incentive to stay invested. This incentive is called a *dividend*. In practice, however, the board will generally prefer to hold at least some (or maybe even all) of the money back, in readiness for the day when the company wants to expand, or to buy up a competitor, or simply to go into a new area of business.

As you may expect, companies have debts as well as assets. Some of those debts (usually called the *current liabilities*) are due for repayment within the next year or so, while others (the *non-current liabilities*) can be rolled forward for many years. If you're sensible, you do your homework and get a general picture of how this 'legal person's' debt/asset situation really looks. In Chapter 17 I show you how to read a company's accounts, and especially its balance sheet, and how to read between the lines so that you get a better picture of what's really going on.

One day, the company will probably cease to exist in its present form. It might go out of business altogether, or (more probably) team up with some other company to form a new and bigger entity under a different name. In the second instance, your rights as a shareholder are transferred into the new company in one way or another. Maybe you'll receive shares in the new company, or maybe you'll get bought out with a cash payment that, with luck, will leave you handsomely in profit.

But in the event that the company really does go bust, you need to face the possibility that its investors may lose almost everything they've ever invested in it. That's just how it goes with red-blooded capitalism, unfortunately.

But hold on, surely you'd have some rights if your company went completely insolvent? Couldn't you demand at least some of your money back from the directors and all the other people who've been spending your cash or drawing it down in salary?

You'd better brace yourself. Your company is what's called a limited liability company (or, in Britain's case, more probably a public limited company, or plc) which essentially means that the law sets out very clearly how much it can end up having to shell out if the worst comes to the worst and the company collapses.

Usually, this means that the shareholders will be at the very bottom of the heap. The first people to get paid are the so-called administrators who get called in to sort out the wreckage and extract as much value as possible from the ruins, so that it can be fairly distributed to the right people. Next in line is the taxman. Then come the banks and anyone else who has lent the company money in the form of straightforward loans. Then come the bondholders and the preference shareholders who've invested money in special ways that give them so-called 'seniority' over other people. Somewhere in the line are the trade creditors – the companies who've supplied the failed company with goods and services that haven't been paid for. And right at the bottom are the poor ordinary shareholders who might have to settle for a tiny percentage of what they thought their shares were worth. Or, if they're really unlucky, nothing at all.

But we're in danger of frightening you off before we've even started, and that's really not the idea at all. A portfolio of well-chosen company shares will provide you with income (from dividends), or capital gains (from well-run businesses that will make your company worth more to other people), or ideally both at once. You can't get these sorts of returns on your money from *any other form of investment* – or at least, not without running a lot of risks that we really wouldn't advise you to take without a lot of thought.

But relax, you're among friends, and making good decisions really isn't as hard as I'm probably making it sound. It's just that there are a fair number of things you really do need to know before you start laying your money down on a portfolio of stocks. And a certain number of warning signs that you need to be aware of if you want to come out of it with a big smile on your face. My job is to take you through these things at a pace that won't leave you feeling daunted by a wall of detail. It can be done, and we're going to do it.

## *Finding out about financial institutions*

I can't (and shouldn't) conclude this chapter without mentioning financial institutions. But where and what are they?

Like the proverbial elephant in the room, they're looking right over your shoulder, whether you happen to recognise them or not. They're the banks, the building societies, the pension funds, the insurance companies who make the pension funds work, not to mention the fund providers themselves, who are likely to be subsidiaries of the same banks, building societies, pension funds, insurance companies, and so on.

Plus the hedge funds that try to exploit minute differentials in the markets by slipping in and out, ideally while you're not looking (see Chapter 15 for more on hedge funds). Nobody has the slightest idea how much money the world's financial institutions control, but if you pick a figure somewhere in the £50-100 trillion region you're probably in the right ballpark. (America alone is estimated to have around £30 trillion in wealth assets, including property, of which more than half is managed by financial institutions.) And when it comes to the world's financial assets, you can safely assume that financial institutions control at least 85 per cent.

Now I'm going to say something controversial. I'm absolutely certain that with a bit of help and some study, most people can beat the majority of financial institutions. I can say that with certainty because of an inconvenient fact. *Most financial institutions perform less well than the stock market average.* Look at any ranking of fund manager performance, especially for unit trusts (see Chapter 6 for more on these), and you find that the average year's end performance is woefully short of what the stock market indices themselves have been doing (Chapter 3 covers indices).Which is a curious thing, because it means that somebody else must be doing better, or the averages don't mean anything. And that somebody else can only be private investors.

Institutions under-perform for the following reasons:

- ✔ Because they don't have certain essential freedoms that you do. (They can't hold cash for very long, whereas you can pull your money right of the market during financial droughts.) That cramps their style and gives you the comparative edge.

- ✔ Because they charge you fees that cut into your profits and may indeed chop them in half over the long term. Like a solicitor, they charge you these fees regardless of whether they make you money or lose it instead. Sometimes I think I'm in the wrong line of business.

- ✔ Because the really influential players are so large that their every move is scrutinised. George Soros or Warren Buffett can't turn over in their sleep without the Internet trying to second-guess what they're planning next. And Foreign & Colonial or Citicorp's funds are so vast that when they get rid of even a sliver of their holdings in a company, the news hits the global liquidity pool like a boulder falling from outer space. Everybody knows, instantly! So doing anything secretly is very hard for financial institutions, which also cramps their style.

# Seeking Foreign Information

George Bernard Shaw declared that England and America were 'two great nations divided by a common language'. These two great nations have different laws, different tax systems, and different conventions regarding to talking about the financial markets. Just because the Internet encyclopaedia Wikipedia says something doesn't mean that the same necessarily applies to the UK, because the shading of the terminology might be subtly different – or indeed, completely different! If you act on a recommendation that's only going to be helpful to American investors and not to British ones, that's a real shame.

As a general principle, therefore, try to use online information sources that you know for a fact are written with the UK in mind. That doesn't mean that transatlantic information sources are unreliable, just that you should sometimes seek corroboration from these shores if you read something particularly arresting on a foreign website. That's a counsel of perfection, but one worth aiming for.

To avoid getting caught out by linguistic misunderstandings, include 'UK' when you look something up on a search engine like Google.

# Chapter 2

# Looking at How the Financial Pages Work

*In This Chapter*

▶ Understanding what the numbers mean

▶ Assessing what the numbers can't tell you

▶ Reading news stories

*Y*our intensive search for an investment generally starts with the numbers. No matter how good a company may look from the things you've already read in your newspaper, you're not going to be interested in actually laying down your hard-earned cash unless the underlying figures stack up properly. Okay, you may be prepared to make a few allowances now and then, such as accepting that a struggling company with a bad record may have good prospects if it can only get the better of its debts. Or you may think that a famous-name chief executive can transform your chosen company's fortunes with her incisive management skills. But only a fool ever lays down her money without examining the financial fundamentals first.

In this chapter I talk mostly about the stock market, because that's the main place where you're likely to want to take things into your own hands and begin acting on your own account. If you're experienced enough to be able to use the information in your paper about government bonds, investment trusts, currency exchange rates, and the price of oil and copper, then good luck to you. I discuss those things in more detail in Part III, because they have separate lives of their own that don't mesh too well with the world of the stock market. Here, I keep things simple and focus solely on shares.

# Getting the Most out of the Statistics

You don't need a great head for maths to make the most of the information in the financial pages. Thousands and thousands of expert mathematicians, analysts, and other people do all the hard work for you. They have computers that can spew out detailed and highly accurate computations a million times a day, so you don't need to strain your brain with advanced calculus – unless you really want to, of course.

What you do have to do is apply a little logic to the things you see in the paper, or on your computer screen. And a lot of common sense, and ideally a bit of background study too. Your job as an investor is to fill that gap between the raw numbers and the actual situation with a mixture of experience, curiosity, and downright scepticism. Your big advantage over the geeks in front of their computers is that, unlike them, you haven't got your nose pushed right up against the numbers. You can step back, take a deep breath, and put the things you're reading into their proper context – the business situation, the politics, the state of the competition, and so forth.

Being aware of the overall context means that you soon learn how to spot the pitfalls when you come across them. If a figure in the paper is suddenly twice as high as you're expecting, you don't immediately hit the 'Buy' button. Instead, you stop and check the facts before you make a mistake you may long regret.

If a figure looks too good to be true, it probably is.

## Share prices in close detail

Figures 2-1, 2-2 and 2-3 provide a snapshot of what you can expect to find in typical midweek editions of three of Britain's most popular daily papers: the *Daily Telegraph*, the *Guardian*, and the *Financial Times*.

The first thing you need to know when you look at a share is, of course, its price. That price may be expressed in pounds sterling, or more probably in pence; but it may also come in dollars, euros, or any other currency if its parent company isn't in the UK. If you're getting your share prices from the paper, the chances are that you're told whether or not the denomination is in sterling. If you're using an online source from the UK, the racing certainty is that you're alerted if the share prices are being expressed in anything other than good old pounds or pence.

| PHARMACEUTICALS | | | ▲ 3.19% | | | |
|---|---|---|---|---|---|---|
| 90³₄ | 6¹₂ | Alizyme ............. | 11³₄ | +¹₂ | – | – |
| 33¹₄ | 17¹₂ | Antisoma .......... | 19³₄ | +³₄ | – | 7.0 |
| 117³₄ | 43¹₂ | Ark Therapeutic | 48¹₂ | ... | – | – |
| 2766 | 1748 | **AstraZeneca** ..... | 2301 | +85 | 4.2 | 11.6 |
| 335 | 226¹₂ | Axis–Shield ....... | 284¹₄ | –³₄ | – | 41.7 |
| 462³₄ | 325 | Dechra Pharm .. | 400 | +13 | 2.1 | 18.7 |
| 894¹₂ | 625 | Genus♦ ............. | 676¹₂ | +28¹₂ | 1.4 | 22.1 |
| 1385 | 995 | **Glaxo SmithKline** | 1118 | +32¹₂ | 4.8 | 11.9 |
| 518 | 309 | Hikma♦ ............... | 362¹₄ | +43¹₂ | 1.2. | 15.7 |
| 187¹₂ | 143¹₂ | Neuropharm ..... | 143¹₂ | ... | – | – |
| 37³₄ | 12³₄ | Phytopharm ...... | 13 | –¹₄ | – | – |
| 104³₄ | 46 | ProStrakan ........ | 95¹₂ | +2¹₂ | – | – |
| 60³₄ | 27 | Protherics ......... | 36¹₂ | +3 | – | – |
| 1206 | 734¹₂ | **Shire** ................. | 788 | +14¹₂ | 0.5 | 52.7 |
| 158 | 1¹₄ | SkyePharma ..... | 130 | ... | – | – |
| 70³₄ | 34³₄ | Vectura Group .. | 46¹₄ | –¹₂ | – | – |

**Figure 2-1:** Prices of pharmaceuticals companies from the *Daily Telegraph*

## Top 100 shares

| High | Low | Stock | Price | Change | Yield | P/E |
|---|---|---|---|---|---|---|
| 1128.00 | 500.50 | **3i** | 591.50 | +64.50 | 2.9 | 2.8 |
| 1132.00 | 690.50 | **Admiral** | 909.50 | +24.00 | 4.1 | 17.2 |
| 376.00 | 222.00 | **Alliance Trust** | 252.75 † | +7.00 | 3.2 | 25.8 |
| 961.00 | 459.75 | **AMEC** | 579.00 | +53.50 | 2.4 | 26.1 |
| 3683.00 | 1312.00 | **Anglo American** | 1660.00 | +31.00 | 4.5 | 5.2 |
| 886.00 | 285.75 | **Antofagasta** | 341.50 | -8.00 | 1.9 | 4.1 |
| 940.50 | 590.00 | **Assoc British Food** | 659.00 | +15.00 | 3.0 | 12.4 |
| 2796.00 | 1743.00 | **AstraZeneca** | 2301.00 | +85.00 | 4.7 | 10.3 |
| 1215.00 | 704.00 | **Autonomy Corp** | 818.00 | +38.50 | | 46.3 |
| 785.00 | 379.50 | **Aviva** | 445.00 † | +24.00 | 7.7 | 5.8 |
| 519.00 | 325.00 | **BAE Systems** | 358.50 | | 3.8 | 13.1 |
| 1134.00 | 720.50 | **Banco Santander** | 804.00 | +56.00 | 5.4 | 8.1 |
| 655.00 | 185.00 | **Barclays** | 246.00 | +30.75 | 13.8 | 18.8 |
| 1415.00 | 730.00 | **BG Group** | 836.50 | -11.50 | 1.2 | 15.9 |
| 2205.00 | 880.00 | **BHP Billiton** | 1077.00 | +36.00 | 3.7 | 6.9 |
| 657.25 | 370.00 | **BP** | 446.75 | +28.50 | 5.8 | 7.4 |
| 2060.00 | 1350.00 | **Brit Amer Tobacco** | 1717.00 | +146.00 | 4.1 | 15.0 |
| 450.00 | 105.40 | **British Airways** | 128.90 | +9.10 | 3.9 | 4.0 |
| 785.00 | 453.25 | **British Energy** | 739.00 | +18.00 | 3.8 | 20.9 |
| 1125.00 | 605.00 | **British Land** | 712.00 | +26.00 | 2.5 | 2.3 |
| 698.50 | 360.50 | **BSkyB** | 403.25 | +4.25 | 4.1 | 55.2 |
| 332.25 | 130.00 | **BT Group** | 150.00 | +8.00 | 10.5 | 7.0 |
| 757.00 | 500.00 | **Bunzl** | 612.50 | -3.50 | 3.2 | 14.8 |
| 198.30 | 126.00 | **Cable Wireless** | 148.70 | +11.10 | 5.0 | 21.9 |
| 721.00 | 445.25 | **Cadbury** | 508.00 † | +9.25 | 3.1 | 26.2 |

**Figure 2-2:** A selection of the Top 100 shares from the *Daily Mail*

| Notes | Price | Chng | 52 week High | Low | Yld | P/E | Vol '000s |
|---|---|---|---|---|---|---|---|
| **AEROSPACE & DEFENCE** | | | | | | | |
| BAE SYS .+† 358.00 | | – | 519 | 325 | 3.8 | 12.6 | 22,641 |
| Chemring ....† £18.38 | | +0.10 | £25.86 | £17.80 | 1.5 | 17.2 | 507 |
| **Cobham** ......† 189.50 | | +1.20 | 240.75 | 170 | 2.4 | 16.0 | 8,040 |
| Hampson ..... 112 | | -1.25 | 209 | 104.50 | 2.7 | 15.6 | 165 |
| Meggitt ...♣† 156.50 | | -0.25 | 347.25 | 150.50 | 5.4 | 10.3 | 4,655 |
| QinetiQ ......... 177.25 | | +3 | 235.25 | 156 | 2.4 | 21.5 | 2,129 |
| **Rolls-Ryc** ....† 290.75 | | +8.50 | 554.72 | 242.25 | 4.5 | 9.1 | 11,427 |
| Senior .........† 58.50 | | -3.50 | 135 | **56.50** | 4.4 | 6.5 | 1,790 |
| Thales € ....♣ £26.10 | | +0.36 | £30.99 | £23.68 | 3.0 | 9.6 | 623 |
| UltraElc ...♣† £11.37 | | -0.07 | £14 | £10.18 | 2.0 | 20.0 | 465 |
| **UMECO** ...♣q 370 | | +16.25 | 644.50 | 329.50 | 4.6 | 16.2 | 24 |
| VT ................. 472 | | +13.50 | 724 | 436 | 2.8 | 14.5 | 1,800 |

**Figure 2-3:**
The
Aerospace
and
Defence
section
of the
*Financial
Times*
financial
pages

Every now and then you come across a share price that isn't in decimal format at all. Some mining companies, and a handful of large chemical companies whose shares are worth many pounds each, still insist on quoting their share prices in quarters, eighths, or even sixteenths of a pound. So instead of £14.75, you may find they say £14¾. And if you're really unlucky they may say £14⅝, which has you reaching frantically for your calculator. Fortunately these companies are fast becoming a rarity, but you certainly meet them from time to time.

One of the odd things about the stock market is that you tend to think of a share's price as some sort of take-it-or-leave-it figure that you simply have to accept if you want to buy it. But in practice the stock market is much closer to a street market than it might appear. The people selling the shares set a higher price than they actually expect to get (the 'offer' price), and the brokers (the people who actually buy the shares on your behalf) set a lower price (the 'bid' price) in the hope of getting a discount. In practice, the two usually settle on a mid-price, the 'trade price', and everybody goes home happy.

## The daily price movement

The daily share price is the simplest method for finding out whether a company has become more or less popular during the course of the day, and of course it also tells you what your shares are currently worth or what you have to pay if you decide to buy more.

The prices you see in the morning papers are always the 'closing prices' that show how the last few trades of the previous day were priced.

Be aware that certain strange things happen to online prices after the stock market closes its doors to the public at 4.30 p.m. For about another half an hour, the brokers and the market makers (the people who keep their store-cupboards stocked with shares to sell to the brokers) have free rein to negotiate their own prices as they play catch-up on the day's business with some quite large trades at wholesale prices that aren't available to the likes of you and me. These low-price transactions don't normally affect the prices you find listed in your morning paper, though.

In the share columns in the financial sections of the newspaper, you can also see the highest and lowest prices that share has commanded in the last 52 weeks. Why do you want to know that information? Because it gives you a sense of whether today's share prices are plumbing new depths, or if they're making better prices than at any time in the last year. Rather a lot of things can skew the reality of the lowest and highest prices, however, so don't get carried away with this information.

In the excerpt from the *Financial Times* shown in Figure 2-3, you can hardly fail to notice the clubs, hearts, daggers, and diamonds adorning the second column. These aren't just there to decorate the page – they alert you to all the obscure little things that can affect a share's price, such as an ex-dividend date, a scrip issue, a changed year end, and so forth. Chapter 8 covers these in detail, so don't get too annoyed if I pass over them for the time being. Just register the fact that they're there for anyone who takes the trouble to decode them, and that most successful investors go through their entire lives without ever even bothering to try.

## Perusing profits

Everybody knows what *profits* are, don't they? Well, probably, but I want to make sure your concept agrees with mine.

In the most basic sense of the word, profits are what a company is left with after deducting its operating costs and all its purchasing costs from its *turnover* (the whole amount that it's taken in from all its trading operations – which is sometimes misleadingly called its ~~revenue instead). Profits are what~~ the company exists to achieve, and profits are normally what you're looking for when you're searching for a company to invest in.

So how come people sometimes decide to invest in companies that don't make profits? Indeed, why do they sometimes fall over themselves to buy shares in companies that haven't even started producing any products or services at all yet, or are simply chomping their way through large amounts of investment capital with the aim of making profits in a few years' time? I think everyone knows the answer to those questions. Anyone who's ever invested in high-technology stocks knows the value of owning a piece of a company that may – just may – turn out to be immensely profitable soon; or a company that a competitor may buy out, thus making you immensely rich when it pays you a fortune for your shares. Chapter 19 looks at such speculative investing in more detail.

For a company, profits are an essential goal. For an investor, they can sometimes be strictly optional! (It depends a little bit on the sector, obviously. A retailer which made losses would soon be on the fast track to nowhere, whereas a loss-making engineer could be quite profitable for an investor as long as the price was right.)

I was guilty of a little oversimplification just now when I said that a company's income is the same thing as its turnover, and that its profits are what's left after it deducts its costs. That's not quite correct, because a few things always go into the profit-and-loss calculation that you might not have thought of:

- ✔ **Grants, subsidies, or other financial incentives.** A company commonly includes the value of these in its revenue figures – in addition to its sales, of course. Then again, a big takeover that doubles its sales in mid-year may skew its turnover for the year. (This subject takes us into the difficult waters of like-for-like sales, which I examine in Chapter 21.)

- ✔ **Costs and expenses.** The company might want its costs and expenses to include the cost of paying the interest on its bank loans, or perhaps setting some money aside for a forthcoming legal dispute, or even part of the cost of buying up a competitor. Those sorts of things aren't likely to figure in your personal tax calculations when you declare your earnings to HM Revenue and Customs, but a company has the right to include them in its costs for the purposes of computing its profits. Just to make things more interesting, different rules tend to apply in different countries, so getting your head round the company's accounts isn't always easy. (If you're feeling brave, I tackle the subject in depth in Chapter 17.)

To keep the notion of profit simple, for the moment you can place your faith in the reliability and reputation of the accounting profession. No public company is ever able to get its accounts past HM Revenue and Customs without running them through an external auditor, no matter how much it may like to. And the external auditor makes her calculations according to the law of the land (whichever land it happens to be) and has no professional interest whatever in misrepresenting the true state of the company's affairs. The *pre-tax profits* that you see listed in the financial press are prepared on a level playing field with every other company in the country, and that's good enough for me. The pre-tax profit is the figure that most interests you as an investor.

## Puzzling out the price/earnings ratio

Every investor has a different idea of what she's looking for when she weighs up what a company's really worth. But for many people the most reliable piece of information is something called the *price/earnings ratio*. You don't usually find the p/e ratio listed in tabloid newspapers, but you can be sure that all the serious papers – the *Financial Times*, the *Daily Telegraph*, the *Guardian*, the *Independent*, and the *Times* – carry it every day from Tuesday to Saturday, and often on Mondays as well.

In the simplest terms, a company's price/earnings ratio is the figure you get when you look at the company's last reported set of pre-tax profits and then divide that figure into the market's current stock market valuation. So if the market reckons that your company is worth £6 billion at today's prices but its last set of pre-tax profits came in at £600 million, then its p/e ratio is 10. If it made only £300 million, its p/e ratio is 20.

### Looking at p/e ratios

All things being equal, the higher the p/e ratio, the more confidence the company commands. A p/e of 10 means that when you buy one of your company's shares, the price you're paying is the equivalent of 10 years' profits at the last recorded level, which means that you're reasonably sure of the company carrying on in the same way, or hopefully better. If the p/e is only 5, that implies that investors don't have so much confidence in its ability to keep on producing good profits, or maybe they think that it isn't going to grow much and that, because it doesn't look like such a good risk as the first company, they're only prepared to pay half as much as a multiple of its earnings.

In contrast, if the company's p/e is as high as 20, that implies that investors think its future prospects are so fantastic that going out on a limb with a big risk to buy its shares is worthwhile. In Britain, companies that command p/es of 20 or more are mostly high-tech businesses with brilliant prospects, and a more typical average is in the 12–15 range. Banks, utility companies, and stuck-in-the-mud chemical companies often struggle to make double figures, not because they're risky but because they're 'ex-growth' and have become generally too boring to interest the speculators. Except, as we're about to see, when crisis strikes....

# The 2007/2008 investment crisis, and why banks started it

Okay, you'll probably know all this stuff by now, but it never hurts to run through it again. Banks are not always boring! You'll hardly need reminding that the stock market crisis of 2007/2008 was brought on very largely by banks that overreached themselves and then ran out of luck in a most dramatic fashion. And with frightening consequences for the world . . .

Here's a very simplified account of the disaster. For a couple of decades, a rising property market had encouraged them to lend absurd amounts of money to risky borrowers who didn't really have the means to repay their debts. Which was not a problem as long as property prices kept rising, because the banks' money was safely secured against the properties themselves. But the rot set in when a sharp property price crash in America forced the borrowers to default on their mortgages, while simultaneously undermining the banks' own assets that had been secured against those properties.

At which point a global-scale crisis of banking confidence opened up which eventually created panic right across the financial world. The banks started to mistrust each other so much that they stopped lending to each other. Investors found themselves unable to raise new loans, and they often had to sell off the investments they already had in order to meet their debts. And a worldwide wave of selling started which had knocked around 45 per cent off the value of a typical stock market within a year or so. Dozens of the world's biggest banks collapsed, mainly in America and UK, and many of them ended up being largely or partially nationalised by anxious governments – Northern Rock, Bradford & Bingley, even Lloyds TSB and Royal; Bank of Scotland. As the end of 2008 approached, some of these 'super-safe' and supposedly boring institutions had dropped their price/earnings ratios to pitiful levels. RBS could be had for a p/e of 2.75, and even the once-mighty Lloyds TSB was down to 4.5.

Meanwhile, the investment panic had spread to whole economies in the last quarter of 2008. As soon as it because apparent that some companies were going to suffer because the lending market had dried up, the economists started scaling back their forecasts of everything from export levels to the demand for commodities (minerals, foodstuffs, oil and so forth). And that spread the panic even further, so that all kinds of investments tanked all at once. By November 2008 there were very few world financial markets that hadn't lost 35 per cent-45 per cent of their value – rising to 70 per cent and more in emerging giants like China and India. What had started out as an unpleasant little bank lending crisis had turned the world's financial markets sour.

Banks? Boring? Don't make me laugh.

But I digress. To see what this price/earnings information actually looks like, let's take a look at the *Financial Times* price column in Figure 2-3. BAE Systems, the company at the top of the list, is quoted as having a p/e ratio of 12.6 per cent which, at the time of writing, is pretty close to the average of about 13.

All well and good. But unfortunately, there are several different ways in which the financial pages report their p/e calculations. You'll be glad to know that most of the papers use a *historical* p/e ratio, which means that they compare today's share price valuation with *the last lot* of published profits. That, at least, is nice and simple. But some people insist on using a *prospective* p/e, which tries to guess the current set of profits based on they way they see the business developing next year. And many more go for something in between, by trying to extrapolate this year's profits instead of using the known ones from the last period.

Not all of these people are up to no good. When you've got a company that's growing fast or one that's going through a tough patch that's bound to end soon, fixing your gaze on what next year may bring can sometimes make sense, rather than sticking with the results of the moment that don't really give you the full picture. Of course, you then have to decide what the true picture actually is! But relax, that's what this book's here for. In the following sections in this chapter I show you how to read between the lines and work out what's really going on behind the statistics. For the moment, my purpose is to run through the key figures themselves.

In Chapter 8 I take a look at some of the other weird and wonderful ways in which people value the companies they invest in – price to book values, price to turnover, and so on. Here, I confine myself to p/e ratios.

Newspapers, and most online information sources, stick firmly to the good old historical p/e ratio. If in doubt about a company, looking in two or more places to see whether the sources agree or disagree is never a bad idea. Misunderstandings can happen. And so can misprints!

## Considering company size (market capitalisation)

The stock market's valuation of a company usually refers to something called its *market capitalisation*. The City calculates the market capitalisation of a stock by simply taking the current share price and multiplying it by the number of shares that your company's issued.

Suppose your company's issued 100 million ordinary shares – or common stock, as Americans call them – and that yesterday they were trading at 220 pence each. Your company has a market capitalisation of £220 million:

100 million × 220 pence / 100 = £220 million

Why should you mind whether your company's large or small? After all, if it's turning in a good performance and you own 2 per cent of it, does size really matter? You get 2 per cent of all the cash the company returns to its investors in dividends every year (for more on this turn to the section on 'Dividends', later in this chapter), and if it gets taken over you get 2 per cent of the proceeds. If your company's share price goes up by 5 per cent, your investment grows by 5 per cent.

The size of your company does matter, and here's why. Large companies tend to be more powerful than small ones. They don't get taken over as easily as their smaller rivals, and conversely they're in a better position to launch takeover bids of their own. They can get much cheaper terms from their banks when they go out to borrow money, and launching corporate bonds and other stuff that I cover in Part III is easier.

But the main reason everybody loves a billion-pound company is that it's very stable. Pension funds will nearly always prefer to buy a large company's shares rather than a small company's shares, because they know that all the other so-called institutional investors (organizations that specialize in investing in companies) are doing the same thing, and that makes them all feel more secure. They know that even if one great big fund decides to sell a big batch of a large company's shares without warning, it doesn't cause enough ripples in the great big shareholder pool to start a tsunami – whereas if it does the same thing to a £200 million company all hell breaks loose, and the company may suffer a damaging run on its shares.

Chapters 8 and 9 look at some of the things that can go wrong if you rely too heavily on market capitalisation alone. The company has plenty of other ways of raising money besides issuing ordinary shares – or debts, as some investors choose to call them – and the market capitalisation alone simply doesn't show you what they are. Until you do know what all those other liabilities are, you need to be a little careful about taking the market capitalisation at face value.

But don't let that scare you off, just because you're only a beginner and you still have everything to learn at this stage. For the most part, you'll actually find that the stock market is already wise to these various alternative tricks that companies can play with their debts and their assets – and that these 'side orders' of debt have been calculated into the prices that the market is prepared to pay for them. It's fairly rare for an unnoticed anomaly to be big enough to threaten you. But, just to be on the safe side, let's repeat the mantra again. If something looks too good (or too bad) to be true, it probably is. If you see something that simply seems too tempting, it's very important to spend some time looking for the booby-traps before you commit your money.

## *Dividends*

Most listed companies return some of their profits to their investors in the form of dividends, which – in Britain at least – they pay out either once every twelve months or once every six months. Even, occasionally, every three months. (Different rules sometimes apply outside the UK.) A dividend is your thank-you from the company for being a shareholder, and your incentive for continuing to be a faithful shareholder in the future. It's your financial reward for risking your money on the company in the first place, so don't let anybody convince you that the profits somehow belong to the company. They don't – they belong to you, and to your fellow shareholders.

---

# What dividend yields are

Obviously, a dividend might be worth just a few pence per share, or perhaps a few pounds, depending on the actual share in question. But that cash value doesn't tell us very much unless we already know what sort of price the share commands. You'll follow that a 10p share that's paying a 1p dividend is obviously going to produce more money, proportionally speaking, than a £100 share that pays a 100p dividend, because we'll have far more of the cheaper shares than the more expensive ones. We need a way of relating the dividend payout to the share price if we're to figure out which of the two dividends is going to make our wallets fatter.

That's why we use the so-called dividend yield, which you can see in the right-hand column of Figure 2-3. (It's the last but one column, labelled "Yld"). You calculate it by taking the cash value of *the last dividend* that the company paid out, and then dividing it into *today's share price*, so

as to get a percentage figure. In the example we just considered, our first company (with a dividend of 1p but a share price of only 10p) is paying out a dividend yield of 10 per cent. Whereas The second company (with a dividend of 100p, or £1, but a share price of £100) has a pathetic dividend yield of just 1 per cent. In this case, you'll get a bigger bulge in your wallet by buying large numbers of the very cheap shares than by buying small numbers of the very expensive ones.

In practice, dividend yields aren't usually quite as divergent as this. In Britain, you'll normally get a dividend yield of between 1 per cent and 5 per cent. Anything more, and there's probably some special reason for the company's generosity. As we're about to see . . . And in some cases, of course, you might not get a dividend at all!

---

You normally receive your dividends in the form of a cheque, or perhaps a direct payment into your nominee account, if you have one. (That's a trading account where you hold your investments through a broker, rather than doing all the paperwork yourself. We look at nominee accounts in Chapter 4.) When you get your dividends, the chances are that they'll have had the appropriate UK taxes deducted at source, but you still need to declare it to HM Revenue and Customs, which wants to make sure that you shouldn't pay higher-rate tax on it. The only exceptions here are if you hold your shares through a tax-efficient Individual Savings Account (ISA) or Personal Equity Plan (PEP), in which case the dividend payments are liable for lower rates of tax, so the people who run your ISA/PEP report everything to the Revenue on your behalf.

One thing you soon notice is that some companies make enormous dividend payments to their investors while others make hardly any payments – or indeed, none at all. But don't go thinking that the non-payer companies are all cheapskates: many of them are making very small profits, perhaps because they're very new and vulnerable, or else because they're expanding very fast and they're putting everything they've got into growing the business.

Some companies don't go in for big dividend payouts for other, cultural reasons. American businesses tend to attach less importance to dividends than British businesses; even Microsoft, one of the world's most profitable companies, only started making dividend payments in 2003! And in Japan investors are happy with tiny dividends, often well under 0.5 per cent, that would have the British shouting with rage.

Now, a very general point about dividends. A common feature of dividend payments is that the companies that make big ones fall into one of two very different categories. Either they're in 'mature' or 'ex-growth' industries, such as energy or chemicals, where very few long-term surprises are expected and not much incentive exists for them to sink their spare profits into aggressive takeovers and the like. Or else they're in dead trouble and in danger of going bust! (Which, come to think of it, has not been a bad description of the average UK bank since 2007. But I digress.)

If you ever see that a company's giving you a generous 8 per cent dividend yield – which means that for every £1,000 worth of company shares you own at the present market capitalisation, you get £80 back before tax every year – that means one of two things. Either it's a solid but rather immobile company that's just right for your pension plan. Or else it's a high-risk proposition that's going down the pan so fast that even last year's profits look absurdly handsome when set against today's rather paltry market capitalisation. The chapters in Part II cover how to work out the difference.

## How dividends really work

Company A is a large but rather solid energy utility that made £8 billion profit last year and decided to distribute £4 billion of this profit to its shareholders as dividends. Its market capitalisation last year (that is, its stock market value) was £80 billion, and this year the figure's exactly the same because the company's share price hasn't moved at all. The stock market looks at how the dividend payment for the whole of the current year is likely to work out (probably a little bit of last year's divi and a little bit of the next planned divi), and it divides the resulting dividend figure into *today's* market capitalisation and calculates that Company A has a dividend yield of 5 per cent:

£4 billion/£80 billion = 5 per cent dividend yield

Company B was also worth £80 billion last year and it also made £8 billion profit – but that was before disaster struck! Because it knew trouble was coming, the company only made a rather stingy dividend distribution of £2 billion to its shareholders. The proposition was much worse all round.

The trouble is, in the last few weeks Company B's share price has fallen by three-quarters, so obviously its market capitalisation has come down by a massive 75 per cent to just £20 billion. But look what happens when the stock market calculates its dividend yield in the same way as Company A, by dividing the amalgam of this year/last year's dividend into today's market capitalisation:

£2 billion / £20 billion = 10 per cent dividend yield

Ouch! The company with the biggest problems looks more generous than the one with the healthy business.

# Looking Beyond the Numbers

Numbers are all very well, but this wouldn't be much of a book if I simply told you to look at the figures and make your own decisions. Instead, I show you how to 'get inside' the figures and make your own mind up about what's really going on. You can discover how to read the mysterious runes of statutory publications like the stock market's RNS announcements (see Chapter 8), and, more importantly, how to interpret what you read in the newspapers about the business itself – the politics, the deals, and all the other things that go to making up a company's value. The following sections offer a quick overview of what you can, and can't, find in the financial pages.

## What the Numbers Don't Say

What price information can the newspapers really offer?

- You get a flat, one-dimensional report on how the financial market saw your chosen company yesterday, and on how much people were prepared to pay for the company's shares.

- You find out whether its shares went up or down on that day, and by how much.

- If you happen to be reading one of the more heavyweight papers, you also get to know how much the company was being valued at after yesterday's price movement.

- Maybe you can also find out how the stock market's valuation relates to the profits that your company's been making recently.

All this information's useful, certainly. But it isn't necessarily going to tell you everything you need to know about how the company's doing. These details certainly don't give you enough information on their own to make a investment decision about whether to buy the company's shares, or whether to sell them.

Why not? Partly, of course, because the market may simply have been in a bad mood yesterday – or a good mood. If everyone's bouncing with confidence about the state of the economy – if 'sentiment' is positive – then people are probably prepared to pay a little more for your company's shares than if inflation's soaring, the prime minister's resigned, and the oil price has just gone up for the fourth time in a month. But then again, tomorrow morning's sentiment may be running the opposite way and you may find that all the growth has disappeared. You haven't done anything wrong, that's just the way the cookie crumbles.

A less obvious reason for a fluctuation in sentiment is holidays. If the US had a public holiday yesterday, then you need to allow for the fact that hardly any of the New York traders were at their desks and not so many buyers were about. The whole global market slows down a little – or sometimes a lot! – on days when one of the major national markets is closed. And everything slows down during the summer months when everyone in the northern hemisphere is on their annual holiday.

Even the weather can have a role to play in the stock market's mood. Some of the biggest stock market wobbles in history have followed hurricanes, earthquakes, and other natural disasters.

People run financial markets, not automatons. People have good days and bad days; they make mistakes; they take sides and make enemies. This book looks at ways of reading between the lines and making money out of these little human quirks. They're there to exploit if you can only find the keys that 'unlock' the hidden value in the stock market.

# The fallibility of human beings

Anyone old enough to remember the days of Duran Duran and yuppies waving great wads of cash around will also be old enough to remember the notorious stock market panic of October 1987 – which at that time was the worst that many people had ever experienced, although actually it pales into insignificance beside the financial crisis of 2007-2008.

To this day, nobody is completely certain what caused the global stock markets to crash so badly in 1987. Was it that everybody thought a commitment by the United States to hold up the value of the dollar was about to fail? Was it a whole string of insider-trading scandals had been exposed all at once? Was it that we were finding out just how badly computerised trading programs could get it wrong when they all decided to sell at the same moment (and then persuaded each other that their own wave of sells was itself a sell-off signal?) The truth is, nobody really knows.

One rather obscure factor was that London had a full-blown hurricane the previous night that killed dozens of people, shut off the electricity network, and caused billions of pounds' worth of damage. With one of the world's most important currency centres effectively knocked out, for one day only, the rest of the global financial markets were left to play a guessing game at a time when they were already worried about a whole lot of things. They guessed that things were about to get nasty and they all headed for the door at once. Unsurprisingly, the market did get nasty - and very quickly too. Stock markets plunged all around the world. Hong Kong's market went down so badly that they had to shut it completely for a fortnight while they worked out who owed how much to whom. It was absolute bedlam.

As it happened, there was nothing much wrong with the world's economy in 1987, apart from the fact that it had been growing strongly for rather a long time and some people thought the markets were due for a 'corrective' downturn. No earthquakes, no big wars, not much political uncertainty – this was the middle of Margaret Thatcher's conservative party reign, remember – and not many collapsing banks either. And afterwards the world's stock markets duly recovered, repaired all the damage and returned to normal within a year or so.

We don't have many more clues, actually. 1987 seems to have been a moment of complete madness. But the lesson that's worth learning here is that, when people don't have all the information, they make stupid decisions. Cowardly decisions. Ignorant decisions. And, sometimes, highly profitable decisions. And that's my point.

# *Reading between the lines*

Most importantly of all, however, what the raw figures alone don't tell you is what journalists are saying about your company in the newspapers. They don't tell you whether the company has just announced a soaring set of quarterly financial results, or has just lost an important contract, or has just passed the date on which its shareholders have qualified to get one of its half-yearly dividends. (In Chapter 9, you can see that 'going ex-dividend' can have a really disruptive day-to-day effect on some companies' shares.)

So why exactly should you bother to look at all those figures in the papers if they tell you so little about what's going on with your company? Because they're a quick and digestible way of telling you what's going on without swamping you with detail. If you're the kind of investor who buys a share and holds it for years on end, the figures in the papers give you a snapshot that tells you whether your portfolio's going the right way or not. If something exciting's going on, or something terrible, the daily figures ring an alarm bell and make you go out of your way to find out what all the fuss is about.

So there you are. The share price information in the daily paper is your barometer, and your watchdog too. Most of the time, being a busy person with other priorities in life, you don't want to do anything unless it barks.

# Chapter 3

# Relating the Financial Pages to the Stock Market

. . . . . . . . . . . . . . . . . . . . . . . . . . . . . . . . . . . . . . . . . . . . . . . . . .

*In This Chapter*

▶ Visualising how the stock market is structured

▶ Defining shares

▶ Introducing indices

▶ Considering market sectors and macro factors

▶ Introducing the buzzwords

. . . . . . . . . . . . . . . . . . . . . . . . . . . . . . . . . . . . . . . . . . . . . . . . . .

*K*nowing what you want to achieve from your investing – get rich, work less, and feel more secure probably sums it up for most people – is all very well, but fully grasping the mechanisms you have to use to get there is another matter.

All of a sudden, 'phoning my broker to buy some shares' becomes a lot less simple than it sounds. Today's stock markets don't just link into each other, they compete viciously for your business. The share you think you're buying in London may have crossed three continents and eight time zones to be on your portfolio – silently, electronically, efficiently. And the things that make it move up or down may depend on factors in places you hardly know exist.

The financial press has had to adapt to meet the needs of today's international investment generation. Not only has it had to learn new tricks and acquire new buzzwords along the way, it's also having to widen the scale of the news it brings you to accommodate the new international dimension. A government decision in India, an earthquake in China, or a coup in Latin America are now part and parcel of the essential information the financial pages need to bring you if you're to make the best of your portfolio. Thank goodness, then, for the Internet, which at least gives you the tools you need to make sense of all this.

# Revealing What the Stock Market Is and What It Does

I'm taking a bit of a chance talking about a thing called 'the stock market' at all. The days are long gone when the London stock market was a real, physical place where traders gathered and competed physically for space on the trading floor, all shouting and jabbing each other with their elbows as they jostled for the best bargains and shouted down their telephones to their clients. Ever since 1986, the year when the 'Big Bang' revolutionised the London Stock Exchange, the only people who actually work on Stock Exchange premises are the technicians and the supervisors who exist to see fair play between the participants. Everybody else – the traders, the brokers, and the market makers (Chapter 1 describes what these do) who keep the shelves stocked with shares for people to buy – is probably working at a fair distance from the market itself, maybe hundreds of miles away. What connects them all together is an enormous electronic trading system that allows each and every one to deal with anybody else at the press of a button – and to see the details of every single trade that anybody else is conducting, no matter where they are. That's quite a mind-blowing thought.

But even this isn't really much of an explanation, because you don't have one stock market in every country but several. Some countries may even have as many as a dozen different investment markets, all competing furiously with each other for various niche positions: some specialise in small companies, some are big on mining firms, and a few are turning out to be a natural home for the new breed of mutual funds called exchange-traded funds. (I say more about these in Chapter 15.) New York alone has at least half a dozen electronic exchanges and Chicago has another five. India and Australia are such big countries that their many provincial stock markets have been fused into 'virtual' stock markets that have to cope with many different time zones. Thank goodness for electronic trading is all I can say, or nobody would ever get to bed at all.

What you can say, though, is that each country usually has a single regulatory body that oversees all the shares, no matter which exchange they're listed on. That body makes sure that the rule of law applies and it has the power to fine any offenders. Any company that wants to be traded publicly with the full protection of the law has to apply for a 'listing' of some sort so that the structures can be set up for enforcing the rules. You can, of course, buy shares in 'unlisted' companies, but you don't get nearly so much protection from the authorities if that's what you decide to do.

Just to finish off the illusion of a unified stock market for good, great big international alliances link the stock markets of various countries using real-time electronic platforms. The stock markets of Paris, Brussels,

Amsterdam, and Lisbon are all electronically linked in a huge electronic exchange called EuroNext, which allows any broker in any of these countries to access the shares in any of the member exchanges and to trade on an equal footing with any of the others. The EuroNext system also has special links with the main exchanges in Helsinki (Finland) and in Warsaw (Poland). EuroNext is now effectively the fifth largest stock exchange in the world, broadly comparable to London.

# The Big Bang Revolution

What exactly was this Big Bang in 1986? To today's younger generations, the phrase conjures up theories about the beginning of the world and that enormous particle accelerator thing in Switzerland. But to those of us who are old enough to recall the bowler-hat City generation (and we're talking about less than 25 years ago, remember), it means something that was almost as radical, in its own way. And just as terrifying. Because it all happened literally overnight. . . .

As I explain in Chapter 1, the City of London was a very different place up until Big Bang. Stockbrokers were stockbrokers, banks were banks, and market-makers (the people who kept their shelves full of shares so as to sell them on to stockbrokers) were another breed entirely who stayed completely separate from other financial institutions. What's more, there were laws to stop them encroaching on each other's professional territory. It was a great big closed shop, with a total division of labour, and it was really very inefficient and costly. For the participants, it was a licence to print money. And it was pretty much the same in every other financial centre in the world.

But then, in those days cost-inefficiency didn't matter. Stock market investing was largely a pastime for the elite, and most of the stockbrokers' clients were well-heeled enough not to mind the stiff charges. But that situation had been changing ever since the early 1980s, when Margaret Thatcher's Conservative government had launched a series of privatisations of state-owned industries that had massively broadened the shareholder base. Suddenly, everybody wanted quick and inexpensive access to share dealing.

As it happened, technology was also at a cross-roads. Computers were just getting to the stage where you didn't need a white-coated technician to run everything for you, but you could dio it all yourself. It seems rather quaint to recall a time when the exchange of electronic information was a really difficult thing to achieve and most transactions were done by post, or on the basis of trust between old-style professionals. But yes, it was barely 25 years ago.

Big Bang did away with all that. They called it Big Bang because all the new rules came in on one single day, and all the existing institutions were forced to sink or swim from the moment that trading opened for the morning. (Many of them sank.) By abolishing the restrictive laws that separated all these institutions, Big Bang made it possible for banks to buy brokers, for brokers to set up as market makers, and for everybody to chop their bloated commission charges to the minimum. Which was great for everybody. For a couple of years, London's deregulated stock market was the most efficient in the world. But it didn't take long before New York, Tokyo and (eventually) Frankfurt, Paris and Madrid followed suit and instituted their own 'Big Bangs'. The financial markets had taken on the shape that they possess today.

## Considering the international angle

Since December 2001, the EuroNext network has owned the London International Financial Futures and Options Exchange (LIFFE), which doesn't deal in shares at all but specialises in something called derivatives (I explain what these exotic beasts are in Chapter 12). London is now the beating heart of a whole European complex of these trades. And in recent years the EuroNext system has been a subsidiary of the New York Stock Exchange. Stock markets themselves are all private companies, with their own shares and their own shareholders. And they make bids for each other and buy each other out whenever it suits them.

You can't do all this unifying unless you've already got a pretty good standardised system of regulation in place. If somebody in Amsterdam is buying a stock that's listed in Portugal, he wants to know that his purchase is going to be properly protected against anything going wrong. He wants to be reassured that Portuguese companies prepare their financial accounts in more or less the same way as Dutch ones, and that no peculiar rules give native Portuguese shareholders preferential treatment over foreign share-holders. And so on.

That's why so much pressure exists these days to get all European companies singing from the same hymn sheet. In the next ten years or so, all of Europe's listed corporations will obey the same rules. But for the moment, only the largest ones have to comply with European Union edicts. Still, that's a start. I'm not placing any bets on how long it may take to get American companies aligned with their European counterparts because, as Chapter 11 reveals, the Atlantic ocean marks a pretty major divide in the way the regulators think about stock markets. But one day that alignment will probably happen.

## Figuring out FTSE

In Britain, an independent company called *FTSE*, which is jointly owned by the Financial Times and the London Stock Exchange, draws up all the most prominent stock market indicators. FTSE compiles the mathematical perfor-mance indices that provide an instant snapshot of how the market's moving (the FTSE-100, the FTSE All-Share, the FTSE All-World Index series, and all the rest of them). These indices in turn form the basis for hundreds of stock market trackers, derivatives, and spread bets (see Chapters 4 and 12 for more on these), which go far beyond the stock market itself.

I draw attention to the FTSE because you're bound to notice how often I mention its listings in this book. I do so not because I feel a sense of favouritism towards the *Financial Times* because I used to work on it, but rather, because the FTSE (and, by extension, the *FT* itself) is part of the central mechanism that makes the stock market tick.

There are similar private-sector relationships to be found in pretty well any other major country. In America, the Dow Jones index company and Standard & Poor's rating agency are responsible for the Dow Jones Industrial Average and the S&P 500 Industrial indices, which are the two most talked-about tracking devices on the planet.

# Understanding What Shares Are

Explaining what a share is may seem a little odd, but surprisingly, many people seem to get the wrong idea. When you buy a share, you're not just investing your money. You're actually becoming a part owner of the company, in conjunction with thousands and maybe millions of other people. That means the company has to be nice to you. It has to invite you to its meetings, it has to consult you about any big changes it's making, and it may even have to try to dissuade you if you're tempted to sell your shareholding to a predator who wants to take over the company. Some companies offer perks to their private investors, such as cut-price offers on the goods and services they sell.

Too many people forget that they have this enormous power over the companies they invest in. The board of directors doesn't own the company – the shareholders do! Of course, a bank or a big block of professional shareholders may hold so many of the shares that it can easily outvote somebody like you or me; but on the whole the state imposes limits on just how big these shareholdings can be so that one big shareholder can't bully all the others. (This rule is diluted for unlisted companies and for companies in the lightly regulated Alternative Investment Market. I describe all this in more detail in Chapter 9, where I talk about free float and so-called 'golden shareholders'.)

## Grasping the basics on shares

When you buy a share, what you're getting is a so-called *ordinary share* (known as a common stock in the US). Ordinary shares are the stock market's bread-and-butter investment, and they're simple. A company issues a fixed number of shares and sells them, and after that it can't issue any more ordinary shares without having a very good excuse. This restriction makes sense, because if you've bought 10 per cent of a company's shares you don't want to wake up one morning and find that it's issued another lot with the result that you now own only 5 per cent of the company.

Each ordinary share has a nominal cash value attached to it, which is pretty much for accounting reasons. It may be a pound, or even just a penny, although the value is meaningless to all intents and purposes because what you're interested in is the price at which the share buys and sells on the open market. So a company can float a newly issued ordinary share with a nominal value of 5p but charge £5 for it. And if you buy that share and later sell it to somebody else for £10, nobody's the least bit bothered about the 5p. The only time the value may matter at all is probably if the company goes bust, in which case the 5p value of each share is considered as one of its assets.

## Getting a share of the profit

You are, of course, also interested in getting a share of the profits if at all possible. But then, since the shareholders own the company, why not? So the company usually tries its best to distribute some of the cash in the form of a dividend, probably once or twice a year. It's under no obligation to do this, and some companies don't give any dividends at all. (We tackle this subject in more detail in Chapter 2.) But the important thing to remember is that every ordinary shareholder is treated exactly equally in getting dividends – a bank can't demand a bigger dividend than you for each share it holds. The other time this equality principle applies is if the company goes bust. In that case you get your fair share of whatever's left after the trade creditors, the banks, the liquidators, and the taxman have all had their share of the wreckage.

So does that mean that the company can't come back and tap you for some more money once you (or somebody else) have paid for the first issue of the ordinary shares? In principle, yes, because you can only sell an asset once, and that's what the company does when it first floats the shares. But it might need to twist your arm if it gets into difficulty and requires more cash for developing its business. In Chapter 9 I look at rights issues, which happen when a company needs to increase its cash holdings. Essentially, a rights issue gives every existing shareholder the right to subscribe to a new issue of ordinary shares, probably at a cheap price in relation to the stock market price on the day. The catch is that, if not enough shareholders stump up for the new shares (and who wants to pour money into a company that's in trouble?), the stock market takes the refusal amiss and the share price plummets even further. No wonder everybody hates rights issues.

## Investigating other types of share

Other ways exist of raising extra share capital once the original ordinary shares have been floated, and often nothing sinister's involved. Suppose a company has decided to buy out a competitor and needs to raise some extra cash quickly. One way of achieving this is to issue a set of so-called *'B' shares*, which to all intents and purposes are a separate chunk of market capitalisation and which the stock market treats separately. (You often find the financial press listing 'B' shares separately from 'A' shares.) Sometimes the 'B' shares are amalgamated with the 'A' shares after a few years, so that the two sets of market capitalisation combine to create a bigger stock market entity; sometimes, however, they remain separate for ever.

If the company needs money at very short notice it may decide to issue something called *preference shares*, which are special shares that carry an unusually high rate of interest – a bit like corporate bonds, but without the volatility. One important point with preference shares is that if the company ever goes bust, the preference shareholders get paid before the ordinary shareholders do. Or the company may simply opt to raise the money by issuing a corporate bond (see Chapter 6 for more on these) and have done with all the complications. The advantage here is that by borrowing from the markets instead of selling off its precious equity, the company retains more of its independence.

I introduce these options to make the point that you need to look at more than just the share price and the market capitalisation figure in the papers if you want to know how much your company's worth and how much it owes. But, all things being equal, the stock market generally isn't quite as wet behind the ears as you might suppose, and it doesn't compartmentalise these things as tightly as all that. A company that decides to borrow a lot of money on the side against its assets will almost certainly see the market mark its share price down. Generally, everything comes out in the wash.

In a way, the fact that a company takes any interest at all in what its shareholders think of it is rather strange. After all, once somebody buys the shares for the first time, the company receives its money from them and it isn't going to get any more in the future. If the original buyer later manages to sell his shares to somebody else for a great big profit, the company gains nothing whatsoever from that profit. And conversely, of course, it doesn't suffer directly if the share price later falls so that the shareholders lose some (or even all) of their money.

# Looking at How the Pages Report on the Stock Market

Concentrating on the stock market itself isn't likely to get you very far. Instead, if you want to really understand what's going on, you need to engage with quite a lot of the foreign news coverage in your newspaper, or on many of the excellent Internet sites that exist for this very purpose.

The average British newspaper gives you share price information for most major UK stocks, plus some information about day-to-day movements and perhaps a high and low figure for the last 12 months (Chapter 2 provides a breakdown of this information). The *Financial Times* covers rather more companies, including several thousand foreign companies, and tells you about the price/earnings ratios and dividend yields of the listed companies. Perhaps more to the point, of course, the *FT* also gives you a vast amount of statistical information about world stock markets, commodity prices, bond prices, currency exchange rates, and so on. Don't overlook the digital TV channels or the Prestel/Ceefax services on your television, which give you up-to-the-minute share prices. Ceefax is also available on the Internet, at www.ceefax.tv.

The statistical coverage is rather less ambitious in tabloid newspapers, such as the *Sun* or *Daily Mirror*. The *Daily Mail* and *Daily Telegraph* both do a reasonable job for UK equities, with a decent range of background articles about personal finance that should fill in many of the gaps.

But this is all rather dry stuff and it's unlikely to fill you with the thrill of the international stock market chase unless you get some in-depth company coverage as well, plus a decent grasp of how the UK and international economic scene is moving.

So the real meat of the investment story is likely to lie in the City pages, and also in the newspaper supplements. Better-quality newspapers – those with better business and international coverage – include the *Daily Telegraph*, the *Times*, the *Guardian*, and, of course, the *FT*.

If you're looking for international coverage of stock market events you're generally better off avoiding the US media. Sadly, American newspapers have been scaling back their international reporting staffs for many years, preferring to obtain their non-US copy from news agencies like Reuters, CNN, AFN, and Bloomberg. Probably the best international paper in the US right now is the *International Herald Tribune* (www.iht.com), which is a division of the *New York Times* and has strong roots in Asia and Europe.

The BBC has a first-class reporting staff and also a comprehensive country-by-country summary of the current political and economic situation on its website, at news.bbc.co.uk.

# Understanding Market Sectors

In Chapter 5 I take a deeper look at the thorny question of how the stock market divides its listed companies into sectors that show what sort of industries they operate in, or what sort of companies they are. A company in the clothing industry obviously behaves differently from a mining company in any given set of market conditions. When the economic squeeze is on and consumers are staying away from the high street, people often turn to oil or commodity producers for comfort. Or maybe they decide that food retailing is the safest way to ride out a recession, because people always need food even when they're not buying high fashion.

But you can define sectors in different ways – and not just by their fields of activity, but by their size as well. If you can imagine the companies on the stock market as like a pack of cards, you soon realise that you can sort the cards according to either their suits or their face denominations – you can choose to select either all the clubs or all the queens.

The stock market does this too. Certain industry sectors are more suitable for very conservative investors because they don't jump about much, whereas, by contrast, other sectors are volatile. Some, such as small companies, do very badly when lending conditions are tight because they don't have piles of cash to see them through hard times, while others do well precisely because they pick up business from the losers.

One of the really important things to know about stock market sectors is that they often display a phenomenon that they call *sectoral drag*. If one company's in trouble in a sector, the chances are that the bad news transmits itself through to all the other companies in that sector, both good and bad. If you can only keep your mind sharply focused, you can probably pick up some bargains while the going's good. But why does sectoral drag happen?

Not all press sources allocate a particular share to the same sector. If a company's in the road haulage business, one newspaper may allocate it to the transport sector, another to the support services sector. ('Support services' is the catch-all phrase the stock market uses for any kind of service that companies buy in from an independent source. So it can include anything from railway track maintenance to running government databases or cleaning hospitals. Be careful.)

Just to add to the fun, even the FTSE itself from time to time adjusts and reconfigures the sectors it uses. Whole swathes of companies find themselves plucked out of a stock market sector that's deemed not to exist any more and planted into another sector that didn't exist the day before in its present form. Although the FTSE people studiously re-compute their listing calculations every time they make these changes, quite large anomalies can occur. The moral? Don't set too much store by the long-term statistical aspects of FTSE sectors. Instead, look at them to determine where the sectors and subsectors are going at the moment.

## Recognising the difference between growth industries and mature sectors

The sector a company's in can make an enormous difference, not just to how well it copes with a particular set of market conditions, but also how well it meets the needs of particular sorts of investors. Older investors in search of steady incomes, or people who don't have the time to follow the ups and downs of the stock market, often prefer a 'mature' investment sector that pays them a solid income without robbing them of their beauty sleep.

In Chapter 5 I discuss some of the reasons why certain industry sectors pay better dividends than others. Often they're in mature sectors where nobody expects anything much to change in the foreseeable future. That means, in turn, that the prospects for stellar growth probably aren't all that great, and that the companies need to keep their investors sweet with big and regular payouts.

Of course, a difference exists between 'mature' and 'slowly rotting away'. Many of Britain's high-street stores have all but lost their reason for existing, now that consumers can look up what they want to buy on the Internet and choose from a vast array of goods online at half the price they have to pay locally. Large furniture warehouses in out-of-town business parks have wiped out many small specialist furnishing outfits. And even established household names like music retailer HMV have had to rebuild their entire business models to compete with the onslaught of online music downloads and savage price cutting that characterises the spread of e-commerce.

But perhaps the biggest challenge comes from the Far East. As Britain consolidates its position as a services exporter, cheap competition from low-wage economies badly threatens some of its domestic goods producers. These 'sunset' sectors pay out big dividends because they have no choice if they want to keep their investors. (The chemicals giant ICI was a victim of cheap competition in the years after 2000, although 'sunset industry' is probably a bit strong as a description.) What you have to do as an investor is to decide whether the company understands its damaged performance and has it well under control, in which case you may want to hang on in there. Or is the performance a sign of worse things to come?

At the other end of the scale, of course, are all the high-tech sectors that I talk about in Chapter 5. They start their stock market journeys with fire in their bellies; they burn brightly for a few years on astronomical price/earnings multiples, which reflect the minuscule profits they're probably making; and then half of them disappear down the pan while the other half can make you rich.

## Choosing the middle ground

In the middle ground are other kinds of companies that aren't in either a mature or a growth industry. Either they behave cyclically – they flourish under some economic conditions and nose-dive under others, like oil or house building. Or else they're those very special companies that used to be plodders but have now been elevated to the status of high-fliers. Utility companies are a good example of these unexpected superheroes. Back in the mid-1990s, when Britain's water and electricity boards were first broken up and floated off on the stock market, nobody in the investment community gave them even a chance of becoming giants. Water was just water. People knew how much water they needed, the water companies provided it, and that was that. The industry was completely boring, but safe. As for electricity companies, aren't people going to start using less of the stuff as they get more energy conscious?

Then the takeover boom started. No sooner had Britain split up its dozen or so national monopolies into a couple of dozen competing companies than they started re-amalgamating – not just with each other, but with French, German, American, Australian, and Korean companies. Huge corporations developed like United Utilities, an agglomeration of smaller regional companies that now runs an international operation stretching from Wales to Eastern Europe, Australia, and the Philippines. Everybody wanted a piece of the utilities action and suddenly it was a hot stock sector.

The reason, in retrospect, was that Britain's utility companies were getting an unexpectedly easy ride from the government when it came to letting their prices rise. As the money rolled in from all those higher-than-expected power and water bills, the utility companies were able to pay out not just very generous dividends to their shareholders, but exceptionally safe ones – because their big profits dwarfed even these big dividends. (In other words, their 'dividend cover' was substantial.) I made 100 per cent profit in 15 months on one utility company, and I was hardly even trying.

Keep an open mind about what may lie around the corner for that unassuming little stock market sector you're looking at. Is it going to be tomorrow's utility superstar? Or tomorrow's department store sob story? The numbers alone don't tell you – instead, you can find out by doing some digging of your own. And using a little bit of common sense as well.

# Understanding Stock Market Indices

When you think about just how many thousands of shares are on the London stock market – never mind all the other internationally traded markets as well – you may want to know indices exist that can sweep up this massive tide of information and deliver it back to you in the form of a single number. An *index* figure is a mathematical distillation of what a whole stock market (or a stock market sector, or a currency) is doing at any one moment. And in a fast-moving world, we need the help we can get if we're to make sense of it all.

The mathematical task of performing all those calculations, hundreds of times every day, is simply mind-blowing. And as I explain in Chapter 11, the wonder is that hundreds of indices all around the world are constantly being updated in the same way.

The FTSE wasn't set up until 1984 because only then were computers capable of crunching the numbers and spitting them out fast enough to provide a real-time index. Up to that point, the All-Share index was something that teams of mathematicians calculated every evening after the market had closed for the day.

But indices pay a much more important role than just being useful to investors. Most of the futures contracts that people use to gamble on overall stock market trends (see Chapter 12) are based on the performance of the indices themselves. And most of the index tracker funds that people buy to give them a dead-neutral share of the stock market's fortunes are based on indices like the FTSE too.

What's a *tracker fund*? I explain it in Chapter 14, but for the time being let's just say that it's a very cheap and efficient way of backing a whole stock market index (or a currency, or a commodity) with a single investment. For lots of investors who don't have the time to do their own research, buying a tracker fund from an ordinary fund manager is the best way of keeping up with the market. And although there are hundreds to choose from, they're all guaranteed to achieve a result that's within a very small margin of what the actual index achieves. (Little divergences from the index do happen, but they're rarely serious.)

Of course, you will have to pay a few management charges if you buy an index tracker, but these normally will be in the range of 0.5 per cent to 1.0 per cent a year, so they won't break the bank. Unlike a stock market investment you won't get any dividends from the underlying shares in an index tracker, which is a shame. But it's like floating your money downstream in a canoe. It'll get there at roughly the same speed as the rest of the river.

Sometimes the tracker funds actually buy shares in all of the companies in the FTSE-100 index (or whatever), but increasingly often they simply make carefully hedged bets based on the indices to keep their portfolios exactly in line with whatever the indices are doing. (Don't ask me for the technical details of how they do this, because you need a Nobel Prize in mathematics to understand the answer.)

But either way, the tracker fund managers don't have to make many decisions. Most of them are fully automatic funds that are run by computers, not by human beings at all. And that's where the fun starts.

## Seeing how indices can move shares

You may be tempted to suppose that an index is really just a passive reflection of whatever happens to be going on in the stock market from day to day. You look at the FTSE-100 index – or the FTSE AIM index, which covers the more lightly regulated shares in London's secondary stock market – and you may well conclude that the relationship is one-way: the shares move the index.

If you do, you're wrong. In various subtle ways, the index moves the shares as well. Tracker funds blindly follow the indices they're supposed to be tracking, and many of them buy and sell actual shares in the indices. As a result, whenever (for example) the FTSE's Energy Index rises, the tracker funds rush out and buy all the energy shares in the index, in varying proportions. They don't have any choice. So an upward blip in the index can create new demand for the companies in that index – which in turn drives their shares up still further. Some people seriously doubt whether indices are really such a good thing, because they can actually create volatility.

## Getting into the FTSE-100 index

Much jostling goes on among companies to be in the FTSE-100 index itself. The Footsie, as it's popularly known, consists of the 100 biggest companies in the London market, measured by market capitalisation, whatever they happen to be at the time. So when one company overtakes another one and gets itself into the 100th position on the list, it suddenly becomes much more valuable. All the tracker funds have to go out and buy it! Which is great for the company, but a lot less great for the company that's now demoted to 101st position. That company can expect to see the demand for its share fading noticeably. Volatility rears its ugly head.

The Stock Exchange does its best to reduce this volatility by announcing any changes to its various indices well in advance so that everybody can get into position before the day of the change finally arrives. This helps to keep things running smoothly.

The Stock Exchange also utilises something called *free float*, which skews the weightings of the indices to favour those companies that allow most of their shares to be bought and sold on the free market, where anybody can buy them – while simultaneously penalising the companies that keep most of their shares on a tightly restricted rein where only a handful of shares are actually open to ownership by the general public.

It's pretty common for a company to have a largeish proportion of its shares owned by its bankers, or perhaps by a big co-owner who's unlikely ever to sell them – and there's nothing wrong with this, of course, because it all helps to keep the company's share price stable. But if you're thinking of buying some of its shares for yourself, it might make quite a difference to know that you're one of only a small number of people who are in the 'free' market for those shares. (or, in other words, that the 'free float' was smaller than it looked.) If the company's directors ever decided to do something stupid that would benefit themselves and their backers financially but not you, you'd have very little say in the matter. And indeed, you might have a problem selling those shares to somebody else if things got really difficult.

That's why they call it 'free float'. The bigger, the better! I discuss the issue in Chapter 8, so I won't go into it too deeply here. London's very keen on 'fair' free float weightings, but other countries' stock markets aren't. Indeed, the Dow Jones Industrial Average index in America isn't weighted at all, not even according to market capitalisation (that is, company size), as in Britain or in the rival S&P 500 Industrial index.

There are hundreds of different indices in 60 or 80 different countries. (The *Financial Times* lists daily results from 60 markets, and that's just a small representative sample.) And, in their way, they're all wonderful institutions. Indices can They help you keep your sense of balance when you're confronted by the impossible number of companies you're supposed to track. Because they give you a working average of the bigger picture, they also give you the benchmarks you need to measure your own performance, and perhaps to guess what's coming next.

## *Finding indices*

Where else do you look for index information? According to www.ft.com, the website can provide no less than 100,000 British and international indices, including several hundred that the *FT*'s partnership with the London Stock Exchange (FTSE) has set up. But for an alternative view, try Bloomberg (www.bloomberg.com/markets), Yahoo! (www.finance.yahoo.com/intlindices?e=americas), or the *Wall Street Journal* (www.online.wsj.com/mdc). Or look at one of my old favourites, Bigcharts (www.bigcharts.marketwatch.com), which supplies chart materials to many other publishers.

# Looking at Market Realities

The previous sections in this chapter run through the basics of the stock market – its functioning, rationale, and reasons for existing. Now I open the subject out a little, to explore the ways in which the world in general moves the stock market – and, in turn, how it moves the world.

## Understanding how macro factors move markets

The great investment theorist Benjamin Graham is famous for many things – most notably, the discovery of a system for finding undervalued stocks which he said were likely to come in the long term if you could only hold them for long enough. Graham's ideas were a bit too advanced for a book like this one that's intended for beginners. So, rather than tell you lots of detail about this great man, I'm simply going to say that it was Graham who first set Warren Buffett, now the world's richest man, on his route to riches with his radical ideas about value. But I think one of Graham's best contributions to investing was a simple one-liner that contains more wisdom than whole shelfloads of theory books:

> 'In the short term, the stock market is a voting machine. In the long term, it's a weighing machine.'

And there, in a nutshell, is the truth of it. The financial markets seem to spend so much of their time chasing each other round and round in an endless trivial pursuit of the Next Big Thing – and most of the time, you know that they'll only dump this year's fashionable investment in favour of something equally hot and illogical next year. Surely there's got to be a better way than that?

There is, but you have to work at it to make the best of it. A really successful investor doesn't just look at what his company is doing and how its decisions are changing its prospects. He also tries to 'think ahead of the curve' (to use that rather annoying expression), so as to work out what the wider economic world has in store for us. And some a lot of the time, we're not just thinking about next month, or even next summer. We're trying to weigh up all the possible influences of macro-economic factors that range all the way from the state of the pound to superpower politics and the price of oil.

Quite a lot of what I say in this section is a matter simple of common sense. Having a smattering of economics in your background helps, of course, but on the whole you can make certain assumptions about the ways in which the stock market responds to macro-economic situations.

### Assumption 1: Strong economic growth is a good thing

This is just about the only economic assumption that people don't challenge very often. Everybody likes growth. It creates wealth and spreads it around, generating a snowball effect. The more the merrier. Well, almost.

The main objection is that if economic growth gets too strong for comfort, it can cause big cyclical swings in your economy. I look at the classic business cycle in a moment, but if you need any illustration of this point think about China.

Beijing has experienced a 10 per cent growth rate ever since 2000, and probably for some years before that, except that the statistics at the time weren't clear enough to be completely sure. Anyway, China's opening up to the West has resulted in a massive migration of about 150 million people from the impoverished rural farms to the bright lights of the cities. The Chinese are buying cars, fridges, televisions, and mobile phones at an enormous rate – but the result is that Chinese inflation has become intolerable in recent years. That in turn has encouraged the Beijing government to clamp down hard on foreign shareholdings and foreign property ownership, and the stock market took a steep dive as a result in the first half of 2008. It'll be back one day, but for the time being China looks 'overbought'.

Economists tend to take the view that a 'sustainable' long-term rate of economic growth exists that doesn't pitch a country into cycles of financial boom and bust. For developed countries, economists often cite a growth rate of up to 3 per cent per annum as being the ideal. For developing countries, with hungrier populations and more room to absorb faster expansion, the acceptable rate may be stretched to 6–7 per cent (although opinions vary, obviously.) By that reckoning, India's growth rate of about 8 per cent since 2000 is pretty much on the cusp of safety; China's 10 per cent growth, though, is over the edge.

### Assumption 2: A big trade surplus is desirable

Fine. Except that, in the words of somebody famous, one man's surplus is another man's deficit. America rarely seems to stop berating China, and Japan too, for scoring such enormous surpluses every year in their dealings with the rest of the world.

Up to a point, this is true. If the world's money is flowing in one direction so that it all ends up in one country's bank account, then a real danger exists that it doesn't get spent, ever. And that in turn is a shame, because money oils the wheels of commerce and if it doesn't keep on circulating, the world eventually grows a little less strongly.

Overall, the financial markets always prefer to have a situation where the profits from foreign trade are being spent, and invested in useful things, rather than merely being hoarded in a bank. The freest and most open markets are the ones that generally tend to respond best to positive economic news.

### Assumption 3: A strong currency is desirable

A strong currency is all very well if all you want is a symbol of national pride – but having one means that your exporters find selling their goods in other countries darned hard. American politicians seem to have spent the whole of the last decade getting angry at China for keeping its currency weak, because China is able to export an 'unfair' quantity of goods at cut prices. Continental Europeans have often vented their impatience at the European Central Bank for keeping the euro too strong for their tastes. By keeping bank rates high, they say, their export opportunities are being badly constrained.

To summarise, you can have too much of a good thing. Having a strong currency will help to make foreigners want to invest in your country, because they'll feel confident that every yen or every euro that they change into your currency will give them profits that won't be dulled by a falling exchange rate. But in the end it always cripples your trade balance, because your exporters can't compete.

It won't surprise you to learn that the financial markets are always highly sensitive to currency movements, and that these can affect the stock market in many and complex ways. This is the best reason of all, perhaps, for making sure that you read the commentary pages of the newspapers as well as just the stock market numbers.

### Assumption 4: Inflation is your enemy

Inflation certainly does a lot of damage to the financial markets. For one thing, it undermines the value of your country's currency, because the foreigners who buy its stocks and bonds start getting jumpy about the possibility that their returns can't keep up with rising prices. Also, as Chapter 6 explains, the bond markets tend to go into complete spasm if inflation gets too bad, because the whole mathematics of bond investing revolve around people's expectations of what inflation is likely to be over the next few decades.

Inflation causes labour unrest, because workforces become permanently convinced that everyone else is getting a bigger pay rise than them, and so you get vicious circles of envy and aggression that often get in the way of smooth production. Meanwhile even faithful investors become edgy, because they know that they have to consider this year's dividends in the light of next year's price rises – a logical impossibility!

But you can also have too little of a good thing. Japan has spent most of the last 20 years battling with periodic bouts of actual *deflation*; and for a while, Germany was heading that way too.

If deflation sounds like the kind of problem you want to have, consider this awkward fact. If Mr Watanabe thinks that the car he's got his eye on is going to be cheaper next year than this year, then he's going to hold back and not buy it. That means one less car gets sold. And maybe one less car-manufacturing employee is needed, or maybe somebody even gets sacked. That car-assembly worker isn't going out to buy a new television or a holiday or a new suit any time soon – and he probably can't afford a new car either. The banks also don't need to make him a loan if he doesn't buy a car, so another opportunity to make a profit is lost.

Not surprisingly, then, stock markets really hate deflation. They fear it more than inflation, because it tends to snowball and get out of control.

### Assumption 5: Debt is generally a bad thing

Generally, debt is indeed a bad thing. But with only a little thought you realise that debt can be a thoroughly good thing too. If my company wants to take over your company and it doesn't have the cash in the bank, it's got no choice but to borrow. No merger process, and not much expansion either, can happen without taking on debt. Debt can be a thoroughly good thing – just as long as your (or the company you're investing in) can afford the instalments!

One exception, which I may as well acknowledge, is the thorny question of *pension fund liabilities*. Chapter 8 takes a closer look at these nasties, which can often lurk unseen at the bottom of the balance sheet until their moment finally arrives to burst out of the darkness and frighten everybody silly.

### Assumption 6: Behaving responsibly is good for your bottom line

Ah, if only that were true! Companies that behanve responsibly are trusted more by their market. Trust is generally conducive to doing business. Although it doesn't always work out that way. . . .

## Avoiding the madness of crowds

Unfortunately, understanding macro-economic influences and using them to your advantage isn't always quite as simple as figuring out the sensible thing and then doing it. One of the really awkward things about economic trends is that they tend to follow fashions that can be every bit as silly as those in the colour supplements. But heck, that's all part of the fun. If this shifting kaleidoscope of fashions and opinions didn't exist, you'd learn all you need to know within a year and then you'd stop growing.

### Seeing through the New Paradigm

Back in the late 1990s something called the *New Paradigm* became fashionable in financial circles. It seemed to revolve around a rather dubious claim that wonderful new technologies had pushed the economies of the western world into a new pattern whereby high growth was possible without creating inflation. The idea was rubbish, of course, as everyone found out after the tech-stock crash of 2000. All technology had actually done was give the human race a one-off step-change that lasted for a couple of years and then left people back on the familiar upward grind, just like before.

# Not spending more than you earn

Back in the 1980s, you were considered to be a real economic Neanderthal if your government wasn't borrowing all the money it could to finance its national economic expansion. In America, Ronald Reagan was cranking up the US budget deficit to a peak of 5 per cent of gross domestic product in 1986 – while simultaneously cutting income taxes by 25 per cent – and in the process he and his successor George Bush raised the country's accumulated debt from 30 per cent of GDP to nearly 70 per cent in 1990. But the good bit was that every time President Reagan increased the government's borrowing, the dollar soared a little higher and the American economy grew a little faster. Meanwhile, over in continental Europe, governments competed with each other to see who could borrow the most money through the bond markets, so that they could funnel it into their factories and their transport systems. That was, after all, pretty much what John Maynard Keynes, the inventor of so-called Keynesian economics, had told them to do.

Only Britain, under the newly elected prime minister Margaret Thatcher, seemed to think that what she called 'good housekeeping' made economic sense, and that the country should avoid borrowing, resist the temptation to print money, and generally make the market pay for its own expansion and grow at a rate that the growth of the money supply dictated. (Essentially, this was the 'monetarist' approach.

I've over-simplified the concept here, but you get the general idea.) And so Britain became the only country in Western Europe that tried not to spend more than it earned. Brussels well and truly laughed at the Brits for holding quaint Victorian values, because the country was indeed growing more slowly than either the Americans or the continentals. Britain's stock market suffered a big loss of face for sticking to a principle that you may now regard as pure, simple reason.

The payback for continental Europe didn't come until maybe ten years later, when Germany suddenly found itself pinned down by a huge weight of debt caused by its expensive absorption of the former East Germany. Meanwhile Belgium, Italy, and France were struggling with a colossal backlog of debt that killed their economic growth for a decade. They all had to go on a painful crash diet until the debt situation moderated, while Britain sailed ahead, untrammelled by mountains of debt. The UK stock market boomed magnificently and the Brits tried not to laugh too loudly.

The interesting question is this. Why didn't anybody twig that accumulating massive debts causes such a lot of economic indigestion? The problem seems obvious now, but at the time the financial markets fell for the Keynesian logic hook, line, and sinker.

But at the time you'd have been a complete laughing stock in the City if you tried to point out that the Emperor had no clothes. You'd have missed out on all the tech-stock investing bubble, for one thing, which would have meant that you wouldn't have got your Christmas bonuses, and you may not even have kept your job. And you wouldn't have been invited to many parties if all you were going to do was to wander round declaring that everything was going to end in woe. That's what happened, of course, when the tech meltdown struck.

### Making currency decisions

Sometimes the market gets hold of the idea that having a strong currency is good (Britain in the 1980s). Or alternatively, that a better plan is to have a weak one (China since 2000). Or that issuing lots of bonds makes your currency stronger because doing so creates heavy demand for your country's financial products (America in the 1980s).Or, conversely, that issuing lots of bonds is an absolutely ruinous thing to do because you end up with inflation and a horrible reliance on foreigners to fund your budgets; especially if they all turn fickle and decide to run away at the same moment (Brazil in the 1990s).

### Keeping your head

The point I'm making is simply that the financial markets are not the sane, rational places people often assume they are. Instead, at times the whole market goes crazy for some insane idea, maybe for years on end. And all you can do is go along with everyone else if you don't want them to think you're a bit strange.

Not that you necessarily need to sit and suffer in silence, of course. If you'd managed to ride the technology boom of the 1990s to the max and then sell out your shares as the millennium approached, you'd have multiplied your money many times and still had cash in your wallet when the dream turned sour on everybody else.

Can you achieve that clever trick? Yes, but only if you're very, very careful and if you do a lot of background reading to develop your own sense of when the fools' dance may be coming to an end. And you won't be alone, by the way, because a few sane people always warn everyone about the folly of the markets.

People like Warren Buffett, for instance. The world's richest investor has always refused to invest in any business he says he can't understand. Which is why he sat out the 1990s tech boom and lost the initiative for a while. But does he look like a man in need of a bit of small change now? That's the best argument for treating fashions with the disdain they sometimes deserve.

## Understanding how the standard business cycle works

It hardly matters how smart (or otherwise) we investors might think we are. At the bottom of every economic situation is a reality that we all dismiss at our peril. Yes, the plain fact is that everything we do, and every decision we take, is undertaken against the background of something we call the *business cycle*. And you just can't argue with it, worst luck. Although you can try to work around it.

Most countries' economies don't grow in long sustainable straight lines. Instead, they go through phases of strong growth, consolidation and then contraction, before they eventually bottom out and start back on the road to growth again. And if we're clever investors, we can learn to read the economic cycle so that we're always on top of the situation.

Well, that's the theory anyway. In practice, reading the economic cycle is a lot harder than it looks, and not very many investors have the self-discipline to act in accordance with a changing situation even if they know what's going on. How many people in Britain carried on buying property stocks long after the boom of the mid-noughties was clearly over?

But I digress. In its purest form, the business cycle can be summed up in a very few sentences. When economic growth is going well, consumers want to buy more and more things. And this creates inflation, because retailers will always try to push their prices as high as the prevailing sentiment in the market will allow. As long as interest rates are reasonably low, this isn't really too much of a problem. Big companies, small companies, technology companies and boring old engineering companies will all tend to prosper. Unemployment figures drop to very low levels because so many jobs are being created, and eventually it'll become so hard for businesses to recruit new staff that even rather poor employees can start to command large wage packets.

Eventually we'll reach a point where all this gets too much for the Bank of England. If inflation rises too fast, the falling purchasing value of the pound will start to undermine the strength of the national currency, and people in other countries will start to wonder just how safe their money is going to be if they invest it in Britain. At the same time, the prices of government bonds will start to fall, because (as we'll see in Chapter 6), the value of bonds is very sensitive to the inflation figures. Suddenly that great consumer splurge doesn't look like such a good idea at all.

So, eventually, the Bank of England will decide that it's got to take action to slow the inflationary boom. It has several ways of doing this, but the usual way is that it increases the bank rates, so as to make people think twice about buying that new sofa. And, with luck, the public will take notice – it often takes 6-12 months before people really respond, but it'll happen eventually – and then the inflation rate will start to moderate because they're less keen to buy stuff and the retailers have to compete harder for their business.

This is bad news for business, of course, because nobody likes to see sales dropping. But the worst is yet to come. The cost of borrowing starts to rise, because those higher bank rates soon start to make it harder for businesses to pay their way, and eventually it becomes harder to keep some businesses going. As the weaker businesses are forced to lay off their staff, unemployment goes up at *exactly the moment when demand is already falling.* And so company profits fall and the economy goes into the downward stage of the economic cycle.

It's likely to stay that way until the day when the Bank of England (or its foreign counterpart) decides that enough is enough. As long as inflation is low enough to be acceptable, the central bank will try to bring down the cost of borrowing so that customers start to venture back into the shops and businesses are able to start growing again. Profits go up, borrowing costs go down, unemployment starts to fall, and eventually we get back into the upswing part of the economic cycle. The chances are that it'll stay that way until the evil day when inflation rears its ugly head again and the central bank feels the need to put the brakes on again.

Now, I ought to point out that not all countries experience the business cycle in exactly this way. In developing countries like China or India, where the underlying push for growth is enormously strong, consumer demand can withstand even quite steep rates of inflation. And sometimes the governments of those countries are very happy for their currencies to be pushed down by high inflation, because that makes it easier to sell stuff to other countries. But, in developed and industrialised, on the whole, the business cycle works pretty much the way I've described it.

How can we use the business cycle to our advantage? Well, firstly we can try to figure out what sort of companies do badly when the business cycle turns downwards, and then take it from there. We could probably argue the toss all day, but my vote would go to smaller companies that aren't producing profits yet, but which have lots of expensive debt to finance. (Or rather, that's where my money *wouldn't* go.) If the cost of borrowing is rising, at precisely the same moment when customers are keeping their wallets firmly shut, then you can bet that times are going to get hard for these very indebted companies.

So which companies should you choose instead when the cycle goes downward? Generally, it'll be the bigger companies that sell things people always need – food retailers, electricity suppliers and so forth. You'll notice that these sorts of so-called '*defensive*' shares suddenly become popular with pension fund managers who simply can't afford to take too many risks with their clients' money.

And when the economic cycle turns upward again? That's when people will start to spend on 'discretionary' items which they only buy when they're not having to save hard just to pay the bills. Sofas, cars, house-building programmes, and endless quantities of consumer electronics get sold when times are good. Understanding this simple principle can help you to change the shape of your investments so that you're not just a helpless bystander when things turn ugly in the business cycle.

# Interpreting Important Stock Market Buzzwords

You find yourself bombarded with some pretty obscure terminology once you start getting seriously into investing. No matter whether you're into stocks or commodities or currencies or even futures, the way's strewn with phrases that you have to go and look up.

Fortunately the Internet makes locating terms easy. A website like Investorwords (`www.investorwords.com`) puts you straight pretty quickly. The glossary at the end of this book is helpful as well.

The following sections cover some of the basic terms.

## Sentiment

You're probably not used to thinking of the stock market as a sentimental place. Unless you count the barely suppressed anger of the wounded, or the genuine joys of victorious investors, not much scope exists for expressing your feelings.

And yet 'sentiment' is one of those words that you keep on running into in the media. In its most general sense, the term describes how the stock market's feeling about itself on a given day: its optimism, its dark moods, its perception of how the overall economic climate is moving, and so on. Sentiment may also be low because not very many people are buying shares at the moment. (Perhaps they're only on holiday?)

## Momentum

Momentum is another of those expressive words that tend to defy definition as soon as you look at it closely. But in practice, a comparison with the much more physical idea of momentum in the real world is a fair guide. If thousands of investors are trampling a path in one particular direction, you can say that the momentum for the shares in question is positive, and that the trend's likely to continue.

Some investors swear by something called *momentum investing*. According to them, if you can pick up on a trend and buy shares that are already in strong demand, you should be able to turn a modest profit as long as you remember to sell the shares in time before the herd starts running in the opposite direction. Statistical studies have shown that, in the long term, momentum investing works well. But you need to have great timing and nerves of steel. Oh, and you need to take almost no interest in the companies you're buying. You're buying into the momentum, not the company.

## Liquidity

Liquidity is easy to define but almost impossible to measure. If I've got a batch of shares in some small company that I'm trying to sell but nobody else is interested in buying that company, then liquidity in that stock is very low. Even if I can persuade somebody to take the shares off my hands, the chances are that I get a lousy price for them. I may do better to sit tight and wait until the market picks up a bit before I try to sell.

This is why if you want to cash in your shares in a hurry, people usually advise you to buy big, 'liquid' shares where you can always bank on finding somebody who wants to buy them from you when the time comes to sell.

## High beta

*High beta* simply means that the shares it refers to are likely to behave in an exaggerated way in relation to whatever else the stock market (or the relevant sector) is doing at the time. High beta shares are fine for adventurous investors, especially those who have lots of time to spend on researching their shares. But many investors with longer-term outlooks are better off looking at 'low beta' stocks, which smooth out the bumps by underperforming any severe downward blips in the market, even if it means sacrificing a little of the topside growth.

How can you find out which shares are reckoned to be high beta? Well, that's a tricky one. The City pages won't normally tell you, because often the term 'high beta' isn't being used as a technical term – instead, it's just a rather subjective description that some analysts have decided to use. There are mathematical formulas that will get you some of the way toward understanding high beta – but, since we're trying to keep things simple, let's stay away from them. 'High beta' means (among other things) that you're significantly cranking up the risk in the hope of getting a significantly bigger profit. And that, I suspect, is a more ambitious undertaking than most beginners will want to attempt.

## Points

The phrase 'the base rate was up 50 points (or 'basis points') today' simply means that the base lending rate rose by 50 hundredths of one percentage point (that is, from 2.5 to 3.0 per cent).

This is not the same as saying that the base rate rose by 0.5 per cent, because that means it rose from 2.5 to 2.5125 per cent. When people are talking in billions, knowing exactly what they're on about is crucial. Errors cost money – and decimal points cost jobs!

# Chapter 4

# Using the Pages to Your Advantage

- - - - - - - - - - - - - - - - - - - - - - - - - - - - - - - - - - - - - - - - - - - - - - - - - - - - - -

### In This Chapter

▶ Identifying your investment style

▶ Choosing between direct ownership or a nominee account

- - - - - - - - - - - - - - - - - - - - - - - - - - - - - - - - - - - - - - - - - - - - - - - - - - - - - -

*B*efore you can make the most of the financial information available to you, you have to establish a few simple points about the sort of person you are, and how much time and energy you're prepared to expend on the pursuit of financial nirvana. This chapter aims to help you achieve a perfect balance between making money and having a life.

## Choosing Your Basic Strategy

I start this section by asking a few simple questions about your basic outlook on life, and on the investment world in particular. Your responses are important because they shape not just the way you use the information you get from the financial pages, but also the kind of information you go looking for in the first place.

Some people seem to be born with sunny dispositions, and some are the broody type. Some make friends easily and spend a lot of their time communicating busily with everyone around. Others are more private and self-sufficient, and achieve their best work when they're working alone on something too deep and complicated to be easily explained to other people.

That's fine. Life would be pretty tedious if everyone was the same. And, if you think about it, the financial markets would become pretty volatile if everyone was trying to achieve the same thing all the time. As soon as an opportunity opened up at the gates of Company A, people would all rush towards it at once so that it quickly became so crowded no point would exist in being there any more, and everyone would head to Company B or Company C, or wherever the action happened to be on that day. So thank goodness that whenever some of the investment herd starts driving up the prices of Company A, other people are taking advantage of the fact that Company B and Company C have suddenly got cheaper.

What you've got, then, is mutual synergy between the bulls and the bears, the old 'uns and the young 'uns, the steady hands and the over-excited. A kind of biodiversity keeps things on an even course. And that can't be bad, can it?

## *Are you a bull or a bear?*

A *bull* is someone who reckons that stocks are likely to rise in the nearish future, and therefore that this looks like a good time to buy before prices go up. Bulls are, as they say, 'long' on equities.

That doesn't necessarily mean that bulls are optimistic about all shares. They might very well be talking about only one sector. You can be bullish on oil but bearish on banking stocks, for instance (or the other way round). You can be a FTSE bull (that is, you're planning to buy a tracker investment that shadows the performance of the FTSE-100 index, because you think the whole market will rise), or a dollar bull, or even a gold bull. But you're unlikely to be bullish on one particular stock – normally you're talking about a general mood that's lifted your spirits and made you want to splash your cash.

What sorts of things make people bullish? Mostly the usual macro-economic suspects:

- ✔ Improving economic growth
- ✔ Falling bank rates or lower inflation
- ✔ Weakening energy prices
- ✔ Strong employment statistics
- ✔ Positive consumer/producer surveys
- ✔ Fast-growing demand from some major export market

Certain positive factors don't normally elicit the term bull in the papers. For instance, if a takeover boom is going on within a stock market sector that's certainly excellent news for its investors, but calling it a bull market isn't quite right. Instead, the term tends to imply that something deep down in the economic bowels of the stock market is giving cause for optimism.

# Shorting

Some bears reckon that you can turn a decent profit out of a falling market using a tactic called shorting. Chapter 9 describes shorting in detail, but the basic idea is that you borrow shares from a broker and then sell them at today's price in the confident expectation that you're able to buy them back in the future at a lower price.

Suppose you borrow 1,000 shares that you think are going to plunge and sell them at 800p apiece. That gives you £800 in hard cash (minus trading costs) in your trading account. But suppose the price then drops to 600p. You're able to buy the 1,000 shares back for only £600, which leaves you with £200 profit, minus your costs. Congratulations, you've just made some money on a falling market.

But hey, what happens if you're wrong and the shares rise rather than fall? You're going to have to move pretty fast if you want to buy back the shares at an affordable price before they clean out your trading account. Because make no mistake, you're going to have to repay the loan of those shares somehow, no matter what happens. Panicky traders who have to sell quickly like this are said to be 'closing out their short positions', and it isn't a pretty sight.

If a short position goes really, really wrong, you may need to shell out many times what you've invested when you re-buy those shares so you can give them back to the lender. That's especially true if you're the type who likes to buy 'falling knives' – companies that have fallen precipitously from grace but then bounced back a bit. Examples of these shares have included the bank Northern Rock, the services provider Jarvis, and the electronics giant Marconi, all of which were driven so close to bankruptcy that several of them had to be sold off or nationalised.

People who reckon they're good enough to compete with the best by shorting stocks when the markets look gloomy have lost (and won) fortunes. But the unspoken terror for all of them is if the company being shorted goes completely bust, because if that happens then you're not able to buy the shares back at any price. In which case you're going to have some explaining to do to the person who lent them to you on the understanding that you'd give them back.

Shorting really isn't recommended for beginners. However, you do need to know a bit about it because shorters really do have an important impact on the behaviour of ordinary stocks. If you've bought some shares 'long' (that is, to keep) in a particular company but its shares are falling much faster than the circumstances seem to warrant, then a good chance exists that the share price is being 'driven down by shorters' who are trying to create a self-fulfilling expectation that the price is going to drop. This situation is also known as a 'bear raid'. And if you really know your stuff, this can be one of the very best moments to go in as a buyer while prices are being driven unnaturally low.

Can you get information in which stocks are being shorted at any one time? That's not particularly easy, because this sort of information isn't usually released to the general public. The authorities worry that, if everyone starts to get the idea that a share is being driven down, it might start a stampede which will just create a lot of counter-productive volatility. But if you're serious about it, there's a company called Data Explorers which publishes a newsletter. Not for beginners!

Equally, saying you're a bull just because you think some technical thing's about to happen isn't appropriate. For instance, if you expect a big share-purchasing spree at the end of the year as the City types scramble for their Christmas bonuses, that hardly makes you a bull, just a sharp observer with an eye for market timing. A *bear*, on the other hand, thinks that things are soon going to the dogs. Like bulls, bears are viewing the macro factors. And again, bears aren't usually talking about just one investment. Rather, they're looking at the whole blackening sky and reckoning that the thunderstorm is due to start any time soon, for example:

- ✔ Declining economic growth
- ✔ Rising bank rates or higher inflation
- ✔ Energy prices going up
- ✔ Disappointing employment figures
- ✔ Gloomy high-street surveys
- ✔ A sinking currency that may make foreigners avoid UK investments

A bear's first instinct is to sell whatever she thinks is about to go steeply downhill as a result of the impending storm. That may even include selling her house. (Yes, some property bears spend years living in rented accommodation in the hope of being able to buy back into the property market at a cheaper price.) But on the whole, one of the major differences between bulls and bears is that bulls go out looking for investment opportunities while bears are inclined towards damage limitation. After all, once you've sold your shares you can't do much else, can you? Well, bears can consider shorting, as described in the nearby sidebar.

## Common investing approaches

People tend to stick to their own approaches to they invest their money. And for good reason. No two investors are every the same. People are in different life-situations: some of them are young and able to take risks, while others are nearing retirement and need to keep their risks under control. Some people are investing 'fun money' that they won't miss if they lose it, while others know that their lives will change for the worse if they get it wrong. Some people get a buzz out of picking their shares, while for others it's just a bore and a worry. In which case they'll be better off backing a range of investments and letting somebody else do all the work, even if it means having to pay them a commission. We're all different, and that's the way it ought to be.

You don't have to sign up for anything when you become a contrarian investor, a day trader, or a long-term buy-and-hold devotee (see the following sections), and you don't have to learn any Masonic handshakes or funny walks to be accepted in any of these circles. But reading a few books is a good idea before you start laying down your money, because each of these groups has its own little vocabulary of specialist language, its own preferred techniques, and its own ways of reacting to any bits of news – good or bad. Spoiling a solid, tried-and-tested investment approach because you jumped to the left when the rest of the gang were jumping to the right is a shame.

Read the following examples and see whether you recognise your own approach in any of the outrageously extreme stereotypical investing behaviours.

### Income investing

Income investing makes some people yawn. The press use the term to describe buying an investment mainly for the sake of the dividends or the interest cheques, rather than for the capital gains that you make if you've bought and sold your shares wisely. Most cash investments, such as bank or building society deposits, are income products. But the same can apply to any kind of share that happens to pay high dividends to its shareholders. Or, of course, to the tax-free National Savings investments (bonds, equity funds and cash accounts) that brighten so many retired people's lives.

In Chapter 5 I talk about the sort of people who favour income investments. They tend to be long-term investors who don't like surprises and who try to avoid risks whenever possible. Often their tax situation means that they're better off with income than with capital gains. Thus, for example, a person setting up a trust to save for a child's school and university fees probably opts for income investments: partly because they can effectively use up her income tax allowances, and partly because their low level of risk makes them attractive.

A third type of people go looking for income, and they're the people who use tax-effective instruments such as Individual Savings Accounts (ISAs) or self-invested pension policies (SIPPs) to 'roll up' surprisingly large sums of money over several decades.

According to Albert Einstein, the most powerful force in the universe is *compound interest*. If you invest a £10,000 lump sum in a share that gives you a reliable 4 per cent dividend (after tax) just once every year, come rain or shine, and if you carefully reinvest it every year, you quadruple your money in 36 years even if the share price doesn't budge at all – see Figure 4-1. But if that yield goes up by just a measly 1 per cent to reach 5 per cent a year, you very nearly sextuple it – see Figure 4-2.

The growth rate's even faster if the dividend payments are half the size but come in twice a year instead of just once. Impressed? Aye, perhaps those old pipe-smoking bores are wiser than they look.

The issue, of course, is that you do have to be really very sure that your income investments really are as reliable as they seem. In Chapters 2 and 3 I show you a few supposedly safe and predictable bets that turned out to be anything but. So take care, and don't get misled by mere numbers.

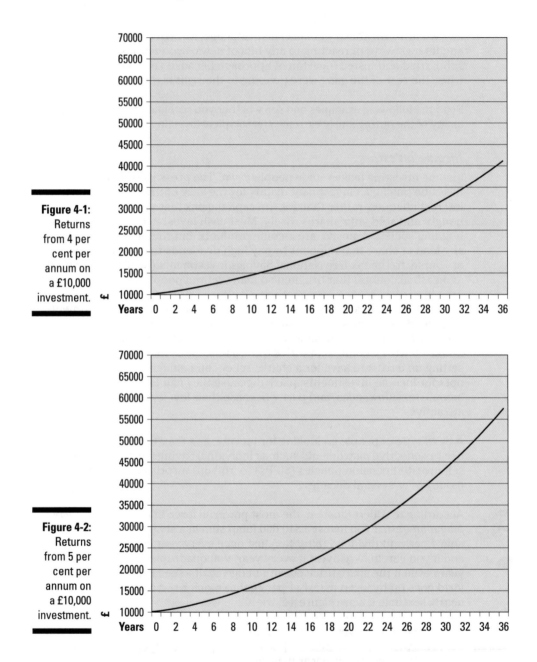

**Figure 4-1:**
Returns
from 4 per
cent per
annum on
a £10,000
investment.

**Figure 4-2:**
Returns
from 5 per
cent per
annum on
a £10,000
investment.

You also need to spend a little time deciding whether an Individual Savings
Account (ISA) or some other form of investment may give you the best protection from HM Revenue and Customs. At one time an ISA was the ideal way
to get your dividends tax free; but now that the special dividend tax breaks

through ISAs have more or less vanished, a self-invested pension policy (SIPP) or even a trust of some sort may be a more tax-effective way of going about the task. But that's getting outside the scope of this book, which is about the financial pages. For more details on these thorny issues, read the excellent guides to *Investing For Dummies* and *Investing in Shares For Dummies*.

### Long-term buy-and-hold investing

Long-term buy-and-hold (LTBH) strategies are still the most popular techniques among investors. Basically, you buy a share that you think's going to be a good 'un for the long term, and you don't worry too much about whether it happens to be up or down by 5 per cent or so on this particular week because you've got your eye fixed firmly on the far horizon.

An averagely active investor probably spends a lot of her time worrying about nothing. If the price of Acme Screws goes down 5p when the market opens in the morning, she's going to watch the price all day to see whether or not some bad news is unloaded on the market, or if Washington is about to launch an embargo on European screw imports, or whatever. And nine times out of ten, she hasn't done anything about it by the time the market closes at the end of the day. No buying, no selling, just watching. Active investors spend a lot of time watching. And drinking coffee, and chewing their fingernails.

In contrast, LTBH investors spend a lot of time sitting in their armchairs, or getting on with their work, or playing with their families and thinking about what they're going to have for supper. LTBH investors have more fun!

They also have the pretty considerable advantage of being able to sleep much better at night, because they don't clog up their brains with stressful stuff. Staying fixed on the long-term horizon is an excellent way to stay sane.

Back in the good old days before the Big Bang revolutionised the London market in 1986 (see Chapter 3), LTBH was the only kind of investing that really made sense for an ordinary citizen. High broking commissions and heavy taxes meant that making a share purchase cost you around £30 in mid-1980s money – probably closer to £70 in today's money. So you weren't exactly going to be nipping in and out of the market every few days in search of a hairline profit. Instead, you relied on your financial adviser (usually your broker) to set you up with a portfolio that didn't need too much trimming and adjusting. You probably feel the same way about your pension plans right now: you just want to set something up and let it run for years on end with very little attention from you.

That said, of course, you do have a choice. The Web is full of cheap broking deals that let you trade as often as you like, and at the instantaneous push of a button, for as little as £6 per trade. And since you only pay stamp duty on purchases, not on sales, you may find just going ahead and trading very tempting.

---

# The true LTBH investor

This investor:

- Checks her portfolio maybe once a month.
- Relies on the Sunday papers, TV and magazines for investment information
- Is probably over 35 years old
- Likes getting dividends, but doesn't worship them
- Has plenty of other interests outside investing
- Is quite annoyingly hard to frighten

---

## Value investing

Value investing is for people who are in a hurry to get places and don't intend to wait around. If you hold that the market is inefficient and prices are often 'wrong' in relation to the underlying value of the companies involved, all you really have to do is buy the shares while they're cheap and sit tight until their real value's revealed. And then you cash in. Dividend yields mean next to nothing, except that they can be a useful flag to show that something's out of kilter in the share valuation; and, according to some value investors, even debts don't count for much – you're after capital growth, and a share price ignores both of those things when things are going well.

But you can't be a value investor without taking bigger than average risks, and you have to be a bit of a whiz with the calculator (not to say an expert in company accounts) to work out which shares the market's outrageously ignoring and which ones are just putting on a brave face to disguise the fact that they're genuinely rotten to the core. If the idea of taking on this task doesn't frighten you, then you may qualify to join the gallant band of value investors.

Where value investors really differ from most people is that they don't mind digging around among the fallen ruins of once-mighty companies for their trophies. And nor are they afraid to tread in those two warrens of booby-traps that pass by the innocent names of the Alternative Investment Market (AIM) and the over-the-counter (OTC) market.

AIM shares are more lightly regulated than normal listed shares, meaning first that the financial reporting requirements are relaxed for these companies, and secondly that most of the normal protective restrictions on how much of a company one person can own go right out of the window, so you can sometimes find yourself well and truly snookered by a management that plays fast and loose with its own power. Buyer beware, unless you have deep pockets and an unerring instinct for a bargain.

A value investor's response is normally to say: 'Yes, AIM companies are also ineligible to go into a tax-efficient ISA or a PEP, a fact that may be of some concern to you if you consider that probably half of all AIM-listed companies go bust. And rather more in the case of OTC shares.

I understand all that. Now please stand aside and let me invest my money. I'll buy 20 companies, and if 10 of them go completely under at a 100 per cent loss I'll still have made a good profit because the other 10 will have cleaned up.'

The remarkable thing is that they're generally right in the long term. Over the two and a half decades since the first lightly regulated companies were allowed into their own corner of the stock market, AIM-type investments have soundly beaten the overall long-term stock market averages.

Overall. Long-term. Note those words carefully. One of the biggest problems that value investors have to face is that value opportunities tend to come and go in cycles. During some periods, maybe years on end, AIM companies absolutely bomb – mostly when interest rates are high (because troubled companies tend to be in a lot of debt), or because the market is just wobbly and all the main-stream investors have pulled back their money into lower-risk investments.

Where do you look for enlightenment if value investing's your chosen path? To the company accounts, of course, and also to Internet-based forums like ADVFN (www.advfn.com) and the Motley Fool (www.fool.co.uk). You spend a lot of time scouring blogs for clues, but you're suitably careful because an awful lot of rampers exist. (Rampers are people who buy cheap but rotten shares, then tell everybody how good they are and sell as soon as the price goes up, leaving their victims to choke in the dust.)

Apply a share-filtering system. They're available for free on the Internet from the likes of ADVFN, iii (www.iii.com.uk), and Hargreaves Lansdown (www.h-l.co.uk/shares). At the press of a button you can apply a filter to the whole stock market that lets you find the highest yields, the lowest price/earnings ratios, the best debt ratios, and all sorts of other useful stuff that helps you find candidates for the bargain share of the year.

---

# The true value investor

This investor:

✔ Checks her portfolio most days.

✔ Relies on the Internet, discussion forums, and her own research for information

✔ Is hoping to retire by the time she's 45

✔ Doesn't think dividends matter at all – in fact, she says they just get in the way

✔ Accepts failure readily – failure's part of the cost of success, she says

✔ Looks pretty grim most of the time, but that's because she's concentrating

### Day trading

Back in the mid-1990s, when the Internet was just starting to make home share trading seem like a viable option for the average punter, day trading briefly became *the* dinner party subject. I must have met dozens of clever young people with big black circles under their eyes who told me they were making fortunes by buying and selling shares at the push of a button, maybe a dozen times a day, in the comfort of their own home. The trick, they said, was to find a share that you thought was looking a little bit peaky on a particular day, and then buy it in the hope of offloading it later the same day at a modest profit. If you did this often enough, they said, all you had to do was make enough to pay your rock-bottom dealing costs (£6–10 per trade, typically) and you'd be laughing. Every night you 'closed down all your positions' (that is, sold all your holdings) and went to bed on your profits or your losses. Keeping your positions open for two days or more was strictly for wimps.

Ten years on, I doubt whether many of these people are still using the comfort of their own homes in the same way. Their partners have left them, their children hardly recognise the square-eyed creatures they've become, and in some cases their homes are no longer their own. You struggle very hard to find anybody who's making money in any consistent way through day trading.

And yet the lure of the quick day-trading buck endures. Intelligent people are still gambling with both their money and their sanity in a practice that's only half a step higher than going down to the local betting shop, and twice as addictive.

Day trading's twice as addictive as gambling because, unlike a horse race, you really feel completely sure – instead of only fairly sure – that your skills can help you turn a small profit. You're not being greedy either – just a 3 per cent profit on the day suits you fine. And when things go wrong you always have a convenient reason to hand.

If you can't resist the allure of day trading (against my best advice), you need a specialised online account that lets you see every deal, everywhere in the country, listed in real time. (But it'll cost you extra. Normal mortals only get access to so-called 'Level 1' share prices, which are usually released only after a 15–20 minute delay.) You also need a battery of statistical tools, including those for charting (see Chapter 10), to help you make your snap decisions.

I think I've made my point. But if you really, really insist on this ridiculous practice, you can day trade more effectively by using one of the many spread-betting services that companies like CMC (www.cmcmarkets.co.uk) or Paddypower (www.paddypower.com) can offer you. With these services you're backing whole stock market indices, rather than single companies, and your profits are tax free.

## The true day trader

This investor:

- ✔ Checks her portfolio 20 times an hour.

- ✔ Relies on online forums, blogs, charts, intravenous caffeine, her corns, and a lucky penny for investment cues

- ✔ Is unlikely to be over 35 – day trading's just too hard on the nerves

- ✔ Doesn't really know what a dividend is

- ✔ Had a social life once, but didn't like it

- ✔ Has an impressive collection of facial tics

Of course you want up-to-the-moment charts, and the ones you can get for nothing from LiveCharts (www.livecharts.co.uk) are better than most.

Be under no illusion, though, that day trading has anything to do with proper investing. You take no interest in actual companies or their fundamentals – you only second-guess which way the market is likely to move in the next six or eight hours. That's not much better than tossing a coin, except that you're paying commissions for each toss. The dealer always wins.

### Contrarian investing

Despite some superficial similarities, know-it-all tactics such as conventional value investing and day trading are about as far as you can get from the stunning investment habits that have made Warren Buffett the world's richest man. With a net personal worth of $62 billion, the 'Sage of Omaha' shot past Bill Gates in *Forbes* magazine's March 2008 survey, having earned another $10 billion during a year when the American stock market had fallen by 4 per cent. Yes, the S&P 500 index had got 4 per cent poorer and Buffett had got 19 per cent richer – in the same year.

Many things make Mr Buffett such a successful investor, and if I knew even a tenth of them I'd be writing this book on the deck of my very own yacht. Nobody else seems to know, that's for sure. I can start by saying that Buffett's essentially a value investor with that essential extra streak of genius that lifts him well above the crowd. But then, I can also say that Buffett does a prodigious amount of research work that hardly anybody else is bothered to do. That he can dissect a company's accounts with more precision than almost anyone. And that his intelligence, his rigorous approach, and his cheerful resilience have stood him in good stead. But ultimately, Buffett's success is down to one very simple strategy. He believes that the market is wrong so much of the time that you can actually build a successful investment strategy out of always doing the exact opposite of what everybody else is doing.

Well, not exactly *always*. That's a popular misconception. Quite a lot of the time the markets have the situation sized up pretty well and although opportunities exist, they really aren't big enough to be worth exploiting. But every so often – maybe only once or twice a year – the chance is available to make a big profit out of the market's error. And so you spend your life looking out for these so-called *contrarian opportunities*. When you're not doing that, you sit on your wallet and resist the urge to buy anything at all.

According to Buffett:

> 'Investors should remember that excitement and expenses are their enemies. And if they insist on trying to time their participation in equities, they should try to be fearful when others are greedy and greedy when others are fearful.'

Like I say, contrarianism takes discipline, and more than most people ever possess. Indeed, Buffett takes discipline to an extreme that few think worthwhile. Whereas you or I buy a cheap share, let it ride upwards, and then hope to sell it at its peak, Buffett says that once he's bought a share he tries his very hardest never to sell it. That's because he likes the big dividends that large 'mature' mainstream industries can afford to pay. Buffett's a secret long-term buy-and-hold fan as well.

So, assuming that you don't have Buffett's towering intellect or his humungous wallet, can you gain anything useful from the financial media to help you spot the occasions when the Emperor's tailors have sold him a see-through suit?

Indeed you can. You can, and should, do your very best to read as much as possible of the great man's thinking on life, money, and the follies of the financial world. They call Buffett the Sage of Omaha because his annual shareholder addresses at his company Berkshire Hathaway's shareholder meetings attract hundreds of thousands of people who enjoy his unfussy, down-to-earth, and often witty style.

---

# The true contrarian investor

This investor:

- ✔ Checks her portfolio every few days, but deals only rarely

- ✔ Devours huge amounts of investment information from every available source, and disagrees with most of it

- ✔ Is probably under 50, but looks older

- ✔ Regards dividends as a piece of information, not a benefit

- ✔ Rarely switches completely off, but has other interests too

- ✔ Has played the long game for so long that she's seen everything before

Read Buffett's best gems online at www.berkshirehathaway.com under Shareholders' Letters. Or make a start by looking him up on Wikipedia (www.wikipedia.com), which may keep you supplied with enough anecdotes to keep you laughing while you learn about the secrets of the contrarian/value approach he's made his own.

That's not much of a starting point for a beginner to follow, is it? Better, perhaps, to try to establish a mindset that simply isn't afraid to ask even the stupidest-sounding questions. Because every so often they turn out to be the sensible questions that nobody else thought to ask. That's what they taught me at the *Financial Times*, and the advice hasn't failed me yet.

### And finally, a bit of everything

I may not shock you too much by saying that most successful investors don't restrict themselves to just one of these approaches. I've got a sprinkling of LTBH investments in my portfolio, together with a couple of industrial stocks that were just too much of a bargain to miss when I saw them going cheap a couple of years ago. I have some utility shares that bring in fat dividends come rain or shine, which is a great comfort to me when the investment skies are darkening. And I've dabbled in small company shares, although without much success, I must admit.

I've been known to buy shares on the contrarian principle that a stock that everybody hates must have something going for it. That was how I bought the transport operator Stagecoach's shares back in 2002 for 27p and sold them a year later for 70p when the market had come to its senses. The one thing I've never tried my hand at is day trading. But then, I do need my beauty sleep.

---

# The true bit-of-everything investor

This investor:

✔ Checks her portfolio every couple of days, but doesn't actually like admitting to it

✔ Picks up quite a lot of her information from the papers, but gets a special kick out of using the online media to chase up her hunches

✔ May be any age at all

✔ Finds something fascinating and new in everything she reads

✔ Feels pangs of guilt at the amount of time she spends on the Internet

✔ Has long since realised that you've got to be pretty terrible at investing not to make more money every year than your pension fund

# Choosing Between Investment Channels

The two most common ways in which you can own shares – or bonds, or unit trusts, or practically anything else, really – are in your own name, or through an expert who holds them in a so-called nominee account, which means that although the expert's the holder, the law recognises you as the beneficial owner.

I also make a passing reference to the use of trusts in which to hold your investments. I don't go into much detail here, because trusts are more of a taxation issue than an investment issue – and besides, they're quite fiendishly complicated, and are subject to tough laws that change all the time.

## Direct ownership

For most people, owning your investments directly and having them in the drawer is simply the most logical thing to do. You're spending your money, after all, so why shouldn't you have all the paperwork and all the ownership documents made out in your personal name?

The advantage, obviously, is that you know exactly where everything is, and that you don't need to worry about the honesty and good behaviour of people far away whom you've never met. Also, if you should pop your clogs unexpectedly, your inheritors can find all the necessary bits of paper right there in your desk drawer – or, more probably, in your bank's vault – rather than having to go online and track down your holdings the hard way via some faceless office in the Channel Islands where you're known as a user-name and a password.

More importantly, perhaps, you know that your name and address appear on the company's shareholder register, instead of the name and address of the Channel Islands office. This means that you, and not somebody else, get the invitations to attend the annual shareholders' meeting and munch the company's Jaffa cakes with your fellow investors. If the company decides to do anything controversial, such as accepting a takeover offer, you're invited to have your personal say in the matter, instead of the Channel Islands person you've nominated to exercise your rights for you.

You also get the benefit of any shareholder perks: the little favours, discounts, and sometimes quite big handouts that some companies make available to their shareholders (see Chapter 3 for more on these).

The downside, however, is that you may need to do a little more of the tax paperwork yourself if you're the one with all the documents. And a slightly bigger chance exists of you getting nuisance calls from people who've looked you up on the register in the hope of selling you other investments.

## *Nominee accounts*

Sorting out your own investments nearly always costs you more than doing them through a nominee account. You're hard pressed to find a private stockbroker's dealing costs that can compete with the £6–8 that now passes for normal among the cut-price, 'execution-only' brokers on the Web. ('Execution-only' brokers don't offer you any advice about what to do – instead, they simply obey your instructions.)

Of course, you don't get the personal service and advice – or indeed, any advice at all! – from the nominee accounts these people provide. Nor are they quite so flexible as a private broker if you decide to leave a limit order. (That's a standing instruction that the broker buys or sells something if a particular price ever moves above – or below – a specified level.)

So you face a trade-off between cost and flexibility, inconvenience and possible nuisance, with the added disadvantage that a nominee account doesn't normally get you your shareholder perks. (Of course, you may decide that you rather like the anonymity of not being on the shareholders' register.)

One time you're definitely going to find a nominee arrangement an advantage is if you decide to buy gold certificates or some other kind of proxy gold. Gold certificates like the Perth Mint Gold Certificates run by the government of Western Australia allow you to hold the legal equivalent of a bar of gold without ever needing to have the physical object shipped to your house – where it makes a useless doorstop that just keeps you awake at night and pushes your insurance bills up.

Then again, you're already using the services of half a dozen nominees, whether you know it or not. Your pension funds, your endowment mortgage, and your five-year stock market-linked bond from the building society are just three examples of nominee arrangements. Your child trust funds are very probably being administered by a nominee account set up by the fund arranger. And if your life assurance policy is designed so as to build up a nest-egg alongside the normal cover it gives you against death, that's another one.

The all-important question is, are any risks involved in letting a stranger get between you and your financial holdings in this way? What happens if your intermediary turns out to be a crook who disappears off to Bolivia with your cash? What if an unforeseen emergency forces her company into bankruptcy?

Relax, you're fine as long as the nominee company is registered with the Financial Services Authority, which includes any company that's legally allowed to solicit your business on the UK mainland. Any nominee accounts with these companies are rigidly policed and controlled, and the FSA 100 per cent protects and guarantees your money in the event of any cataclysm. Even if a financial disaster wrecks the bank that's handling your private banking account (that's another nominee arrangement for you), you're okay because your holdings are in another pot entirely. The bank's shareholders might whine, but you don't need to because your money is safe.

## *Trusts*

Trusts are a complex and fast-changing environment in which to hold your shares, and one that's neither fish nor fowl as far as the law's concerned. I'm not going to discuss them too deeply here, partly because trusts are *so* complicated, but partly also because you can't set one up without engaging a solicitor, who's much better placed to advise you than I am.

Some unscrupulous people use complex 'blind' trusts to try to make sure that HM Revenue and Customs can't find out who the beneficial owners of an asset happen to be. (But watch out, because the Revenue's bloodhounds are getting better at their job these days.) Others use trusts in a less obviously underhand way to ensure that their children's tax allowances are used to the best effect in an offshore location.

Still others use trusts to manage foreign property portfolios or to reduce their inheritance tax liability– activities that may involve moving large quantities of cash, bonds, or other securities to some location that's temporarily beyond the Revenue's reach (this is perfectly legal as long as you declare the eventual profits).

Special trust rules apply to people who aren't British nationals. Certain Islamic investment instruments must be handled through a trust in order to comply with Shari'a law. And so on. You get the idea.

What all these devices, both legal and otherwise, have in common is that an apparent stranger – who may indeed be a genuine stranger, but often isn't – becomes the agent the authorities have to deal with, instead of the beneficial owner herself. The general effect is that a kind of legal fog is allowed to develop between the beneficial owner, who's theoretically powerless to control the actual assets, and the Inland Revenue, which generally prefers to treat her as the owner and administrator.

Trusts work well for some investors and not for others, so if you think you may benefit from one seek out professional advice from a solicitor.

# Part II
# Using The Financial Pages to Make Basic Investments

## In this part . . .

*T*his section takes a closer look at the stock market basics that we saw in Part I, and it looks at the relative merits of stocks against cash investments. Then it explores the weird upside-down world of bonds, where everything revolves around the interest rates rather than the bond prices themselves. Finally we return to the cash investing theme with a summary of what's available and what some of the basic terminology means.

# Chapter 5

# Investing in Shares

. . . . . . . . . . . . . . . . . . . . . . . . . . . . . . . . . . . . . . . . . .

## In This Chapter

▶ Working out what sort of shares suit you best

▶ Making the most of the financial pages

▶ Understanding debt

▶ Considering how stocks shape up against cash

. . . . . . . . . . . . . . . . . . . . . . . . . . . . . . . . . . . . . . . . . .

*Y*ou don't need me to tell you that stocks and shares aren't the only way of running your investment portfolio. But they're always a good place to start, because the performance of the stock market pretty well determines what happens in a lot of other parts of the investing universe. And besides, a company's share price is one of the most reliable ways of telling what the business world thinks about that company – or, indeed, about the state of the business economy in general.

I'm going to tell you now that there are quite a lot of things you need to be aware of when you go out looking at stocks. But this chapter sets out some of the basic principles that underlie the stock market, and it shows you how the financial pages cover them. Chapter 6 will give you a bit more chapter-and-verse detail about the mote technical aspects.

First, I just want to say – don't panic! Much of the information in this chapter may sound very strange if you're new to the investing game, and unfortunately an awful lot of terminology's involved. But I explain the process of investing in shares in an easy-to-follow manner and you're going to be fine.

If you find yourself itching to discover more about any of the subjects I covered in this chapter, or indeed in any chapter, you can gain a wealth of detailed information in *Investing For Dummies* and *Investing in Shares For Dummies*. My purpose is to run you though some of the fundamental concepts and to show you exactly how you can interpret the information in the financial pages to your best advantage.

You can't find everything you need to know in the statistical pages of the financial press, though. The figures can only give you quite a small (although important) part of the overall picture when you look at a share. What makes the difference is how you use that information as a springboard for further research – on the Internet, in the papers, on discussion forums, and simply by keeping your ears open for the little scraps of news that give you a competitive edge.

# Different Shares for Different People

Not every share appeals to every kind of investor. What you want out of a share is very likely to be affected by your risk profile – that is, by what sort of person you are and how much risk you can sensibly afford to take, bearing in mind your age and how much you depend on your shares. If investing's just a hobby, and if you can genuinely afford to be relaxed about possible losses, then your attitude to risk will probably be quite different from how it would be if your investments were crucial to your future well-being. And if you're genuinely interested in chasing down bargains and generally keeping on top of the daily hurly-burly, then you're going to take a different approach from someone who would really rather buy solid stocks and keep them for longish periods. If you think the whole subject is just a bore, but you still want to be invested, you'll probably be better off leaving the whole process to a professional agent, or perhaps buying a tracker fund that will automatically shadow the stock market's overall performance, rather than doing all the buying and selling yourself.

But your risk tolerance doesn't really get to the heart of the issue of how to choose shares, because even the most risk-tolerant investors know that sometimes stepping back and thinking about putting their money somewhere a little safer for a while makes sense. That might mean selling a lot of your shares (see 'Selling, and why it's harder than buying', later in this chapter, for more on this) and sitting tight on cash, or perhaps switching into bonds (take a look at Chapter 6) for a while.

Certain circumstances, such as an impending economic downturn, can also mean that you should think about dumping your more racy investments in new technology and the like, and opting for slow-and-steady plodders that won't set the world alight but which ought to keep you protected from the worst of whatever the market's getting ready to throw at you until it's finally finished throwing it. Then again, a family event such as a birth or a death or an illness – or, especially, a looming redundancy! – might mean that it's sensible to step back from the brink of risk until you're back on an even keel. That's what we mean by tailoring your risk to your circumstances.

# *Following tortoises and hares*

How do you find out which companies belong in the safer categories and which ones are risky? As you may expect, you're not going to get many direct answers to this question. Nobody wants to say straight out that XYZ Technologies is a high-risk company that's suitable only for the very solvent or the totally scatty, because that sort of finger-pointing may frighten off a lot of potential investors and cause a panic that does XYZ Technologies no good at all.

But several ways do exist of finding out whether or not your company belongs to a very high-risk category or a very low-risk one. You can start by asking what industry sector of the stock market your share belongs in, and then home in on other companies in that sector to see how they're doing.

Figure 5-1 shows a page from the FT Actuaries Share indices, which are produced by the Faculty and Institute of Actuaries in conjunction with the *Financial Times* and form the basis for pretty well every stock market tracker in the UK. For the time being, I want to look at the price/earnings ratio (covered in detail in Chapter 2), because the p/e can give a rough-and-ready idea of how much confidence the stock market has in a particular company, or a particular sector. The p/e is the *risk ratio* that divides a company's share price by its last set of pre-tax profits. Or, in other words, it tells you how many years' worth of profits you're paying for your shares if you go out and buy them today.

## FTSE UK Index Series Values

Data as at: 22/10/2008 (download)

| Index name | Index value (GBP) | TRI (LOC) | PE Ratio | % Change on day | % Change on quarter |
|---|---|---|---|---|---|
| FTSE 100 Index | 4040.89 | 2428.52 | 8.45 | -4.46 | -24.67 |
| FTSE 250 Index | 6232.62 | 3560.47 | 10.60 | -3.27 | -30.61 |
| FTSE 350 Index | 2083.61 | 2547.49 | 8.65 | -4.33 | -25.41 |
| FTSE All-Share Index | 2038.43 | 2524.97 | 8.76 | -4.27 | -25.41 |
| FTSE Fledgling Index | 2550.91 | 3792.77 | 31.07 | -1.14 | -20.49 |
| FTSE AIM All-Share Index | 468.15 | 468.05 | 27.62 | -1.71 | -43.84 |
| FTSE SmallCap Index | 2041.67 | 2299.52 | 16.89 | -2.34 | -25.34 |
| Flemings Index | 1253.59 | 1712.56 | 10.00 | -2.98 | -30.28 |
| FTSE TMT Index | | | | | |
| FTSE All-Small Index | 1374.58 | 1988.31 | 17.92 | -2.19 | -24.76 |
| FTSE AIM 100 Index | 2109.80 | 2193.00 | 11.44 | -1.98 | -50.61 |
| FTSE AIM UK 50 Index | 2088.49 | 2158.16 | 8.22 | -0.98 | -51.74 |

**Figure 5-1:**
FTSE UK
index series
values

What's the first thing you notice when you look at the fourth column, the one with the p/e ratio? Right, it tells you that the FTSE-100 index, which comprises the 100 largest companies in the UK, carries a very much lower p/e ratio than the FTSE-250 index, which consists of the next 250 largest companies. This means that the FTSE-250 is significantly more expensive than the FTSE-100. And if you buy a typical selection of companies in the FTSE AIM (that's the Alternative Investment Market, which is only lightly regulated) All-Share index, you're paying a sky-high p/e of 76.04!

That figure represents a lot of risk. You can conclude from this information that, generally speaking, the larger the company, the smaller the risk you take when you buy a share. Of course, exceptions to this occur from time to time. (Northern Rock was a pretty big bank until it went almost bust in the last quarter of 2007.) But as a general rule, the assumption holds up fairly well. *The lower the p/e, the lower the risk.* In some sectors, such as the FTSE Fledgling company section, the risks and returns from these tiny companies, some of them virtually start-ups, are so high that you're not safe to pin a p/e figure on them at all.

Should that detail worry you? Later in this chapter, I take you through some of the main arguments that make people want to invest in ultra-risky stocks, and I also explain how the market arrives at valuations for these smaller companies that aren't producing any profits at all (take a look at 'Valuing a company that doesn't have any earnings', later in this chapter).

But you can also choose your risk ratios so that they reflect the industries themselves. Table 5-1 shows a sample of the main sectors that make up the FTSE Actuaries in April 2008.

| Table 5-1 | FTSE Actuary indices, 29 April 2008 | | | |
|---|---|---|---|---|
| | Actual yield | Dividend cover | P/e ratio | % Annual |
| **FTSE main indices** | | | | |
| FTSE-100 | 3.71 | 2.35 | 11.49 | −5.58 |
| FTSE-250 | 3.07 | 2.31 | 14.13 | − 16.11 |
| FTSE-350 | 3.63 | 2.34 | 11.77 | − 7.19 |
| FTSE SmallCap | 2.74 | 1.77 | 20.57 | − 23.72 |
| FTSE Fledgling companies | 3.08 | | n.a. | − 20.95 |
| FTSE –Aim | 0.66 | 2.01 | 76.04 | − 17.36 |
| FTSE All-Share | 3.60 | 2.33 | 11.91 | − 7.75 |

|  | Actual yield | Dividend cover | P/e ratio | % Annual |
|---|---|---|---|---|
| **FTSE sector indices** | | | | |
| Oil & Gas | 3.02 | 3.04 | 10.89 | 21.43 |
| Basic materials | 1.29 | 6.18 | 12.50 | 49.45 |
| Industrials | 2.97 | 2.24 | 15.00 | − 15.52 |
| Consumer goods | 3.17 | 2.01 | 15.68 | − 4.89 |
| Healthcare | 4.16 | 1.82 | 13.21 | − 22.26 |
| Consumer services | 3.43 | 2.46 | 11.87 | − 27.25 |
| Telecommunications | 4.67 | 1.69 | 12.64 | − 1.01 |
| Utilities | 4.02 | 2.10 | 13.37 | − 5.97 |
| Financials | 5.14 | 1.89 | 10.31 | − 23.91 |
| Non-financials | 3.08 | 2.58 | 12.57 | − 0.82 |
| Technology | 2.12 | 1.97 | 23.94 | − 21.54 |

What do you notice first about the fourth column in Table 5-1, the one that contains the p/e ratios? Certain industrial sectors command higher p/es than others. Technology stocks are running price/earnings ratios of nearly 24, while old staples like oil and gas are almost down into single figures. And if you think banks have a licence to print money, you're probably surprised to see they're the cheapest stocks in the market in terms of their p/e ratios. (Admittedly, this table was compiled in the aftermath of the 2007 credit crisis when several large international banks were looking shaky, but it isn't actually all that untypical of what the market normally gives you.)

Now look at the second column, which tells you what dividend yields you can get from these various sectors. Yields are especially important to some investors, particularly to people who are looking for security for the long term and aren't particularly bothered about making a lot of capital growth from their shares (Chapter 2 covers yields in detail).

Surprise, surprise, the slow and steady sectors turn out to be delivering the biggest dividends. Financial stocks were turning in an enormous 5.14 per cent return on the day this table was compiled – which goes a long way to explain why so many retired people hold bank stocks. And steady, 'mature' sectors like telecommunications and utilities (that is, gas, water, and electricity) are all producing relatively good returns of 4–5 per cent; whereas technology stocks only give 2.12 per cent, maybe less. Indeed, a large proportion of them were paying nothing at all, because they were focusing all their money on developing their businesses, not handing it back to their investors.

But the final column of Table 5-1 probably widens your eyes. In a year when the UK stock market had fallen by an average of 7.75 per cent (that's measuring by the FTSE All-Share index, which contains every share on the market), the basic industries – mining companies, utilities, and consumer goods industries – performed much better than all the industrial and technological shares. And this is entirely typical for a period of downturn. When the going gets tough, so-called mature industries show their worth.

If I showed you the really detailed breakdown, which lists the individual sub-sectors one by one, you'd see that some big variations existed between them as well. For instance, that steep 22.26 per cent decline in healthcare stocks was almost completely due to a 23.21 per cent collapse of pharmaceutical companies' share prices. The companies that supply actual healthcare services had seen their prices falling by a more modest 8.87 per cent. Mobile telephone companies like Vodafone had seen their share prices actually rising by 10.46 per cent, whereas fixed-line providers like British Telecom had fallen by an appalling 29 per cent. And within the consumer services sector, which fell by 27.25 per cent, the general retailers (department stores, furniture retailers, and so on) took a 43.51 per cent dive, while the food stores and chemists got away with a rather less alarming 12.74 per cent fall during the year.

You can find this full breakdown in the print edition of the *Financial Times* every morning. Oddly, it doesn't appear in any other paper, or anywhere online, even though it provides the central benchmarks for the London stock market.

## Focusing on your own risk tolerance

You can control your risks more easily than you probably think. I can't stop you from buying a bad company, or from having a bout of sheer bad luck. And I don't want to stop you from taking a bigger risk on a company that may bring you enormous success if everything goes right.

Some sectors, however, fit your own risk profile better than others and a good place to start looking is on the *FT* website (media.ft.com). This site provides a definitive breakdown of which companies belong to which stock market sectors. It contains a pretty exhaustive list, including well over 2,000 different companies, and it ought to give you a decent start.

# Using the Information in the Financial Pages

How often do you look at investment opportunities? Are you the kind of investor who checks up on his investments every day – or even several times a day? Or do you simply look out for a share you like and then stick with it for months, maybe years?

I'm a five-times-a-day man. Although I normally hold a share for an average of 18 months – which makes me quite a lot more faithful than the average UK investor, apparently – I'm possessed with a continuous urge to know the very latest about how my investments are doing. Sometimes I rely on the information I find in my daily newspapers, especially the news and reviews sections, which can encapsulate the spirit of a day's trading more effectively than any amount of detailed stuff on my computer screen. And sometimes I prefer to use the huge resources on the Internet, including intra-day price data, flexible charting, and up-to-the minute news coverage. Both have their strengths.

But in one area the traditional financial press always scores over the Internet. Unlike me, the average financial journalist doesn't spend his whole time watching share price movements. Instead, he's on the phone, talking to fund managers, analysts, bankers, and brokers – not to mention the secretive hedge fund managers who rarely raise their heads above the parapet for long enough to attract attention (see Chapter 15 for more on hedge funds).

In short, a well-informed financial journalist has a better grasp of what's going on, and who's doing what, than almost anybody else you're likely to meet. For instance, currently the leader writers in the papers are talking about how the hedge funds are distorting the patterns of commodity markets – gold, copper, wheat, and so on – by buying and selling commodity futures at short notice. And since hedge fund managers don't ever report publicly on what they're doing, you're never going to find out about these things unless you read them from somebody who's got the inside track.

Of course, you can pick up these same rumours in the Internet chat rooms if you're enthusiastic enough to want to give them a try. But you need to remember that chat rooms, blogs, and discussion forums are all very well, but they're populated by people who have their own agendas and don't always know what they're talking about. In contrast, a newspaper has a sub-editor whose job is to look for inconsistencies, and an editor who fires any journalist who isn't careful enough with his fact checking.

That's why the statistics alone are only a small part of what you get when you look stuff up in the papers. You get wisdom as well, and years and years of experience, and a fact-checking regime that's properly worthwhile. In an age when the Internet's laying everything before you in unending detail, I encourage you to take the good old financial press seriously.

## *Reading the information correctly*

They say you can lead a horse to water but you can't make it drink. Certainly you can lead some investors to the facts but you can't make them think. Personally, I don't have any problem with investors who don't think. I wait until they make mistakes, and then I make money out of those mistakes.

Not many absolute truths exist in the financial markets. If you think that big dividends are always a good thing, or that low price/earnings ratios are always a sign of a bargain, you need to remember that one man's meat is another man's poison.

Some investors need to sprint for fast capital growth and aren't interested in getting dividends from their companies. And others don't care about capital growth as long as their dividend income's secure. Some cross the road to avoid anything that appears remotely risky, and others look at a risk and say: 'Bring it on. The bigger the risk, the bigger the payout.'

Tax considerations have quite a lot to do with people's different approaches to investment decisions. Some investors prefer to take their investment winnings in the form of earnings – perhaps because they've already used up most of their capital gains tax exemptions and they don't want to have to pay a flat-rate CGT on their winnings. Others, however, are set on maximising their capital gains at the expense of income – perhaps because they've got their investments stashed into Individual Savings Accounts (ISAs) or pension plans that roll up their capital gains or even disregard them completely for tax purposes. Either way, ne'er the twain shall meet.

My task in this chapter is to bring all these conflicting needs together in one place, and to talk in quite general terms about how to evaluate the information in the financial pages. What you do with that information once you've got it is coloured very largely by your own investment objectives, and by where you are in life and where you want to be in ten years' time.

# *Using the information to make decisions*

I'm going to assume, for the moment, that you've found the information you're looking for in the financial press, and that it's opened your eyes to some big opportunity. So what do you actually do with the info? Do you get straight on to your stockbroker and tell him to buy (or sell) the shares right away? Or do you sit on your hands and wait a while, to be as sure as possible that you're doing the right thing?

Everyone has their own personality and their own ways of doing things, of course, but I've got to admit that I don't like acting quickly, no matter how pressing the need seems to be. If a share starts to look promising to me, that's my signal to go out and do some urgent research. I want to know how well the company's performing in relation to other companies in its sector. I'm looking for clues about how the whole sector's getting on, especially with regard to things like borrowing costs, foreign trade opportunities, and simple economic growth – the macro factors.

I probably take a good look at the company's last set of trading accounts, and I check out its website for news – or, at the very least, write to its registrar for details of its financial statements and any new press releases. I want to know all about its price/earnings ratios, and I'm interested in its dividend payments. When was the last dividend paid and how much was it? Is another dividend due to be paid soon?

And then, last but by no means least, I look at the company's share price performance chart, just to double-check whether my hunches are correct or if I've made some ghastly mistake. I want to know about every blip and twitch in the share price over the last five years. And I want to see whether there's a seasonal pattern to the share price. One of my favourite power utility companies always rises in the late autumn and falls in the summer. You don't need to be a genius to figure out why, but you don't know for sure until you've seen the trend with your very own peepers. You can find more about the idea of charts (known as 'technical analysis') in Chapter 10.

One of the very useful things you can do with an Internet connection these days is to set up a dummy portfolio that lets you shadow your potential investments over a period of weeks or months at a time, without ever laying down a penny of your hard cash for the privilege. If you're new to investing, or just unfamiliar with a particular neck of the investment woods, then shadowing a portfolio like this is one of the very best ways of finding out whether or not you've got a feel for what you're doing. You can set up these investments for free through the London Stock Exchange website (www.lse.co.uk), the *FT* (www.ft.com), or Yahoo! (www.yahoo.co.uk). If you want to get really serious, you can even play an online game called Virtual Trader (www.virtualtrader.co.uk) and pit your wits against all-comers.

But the really great thing about these online portfolios – apart from the fact that you're not making a fool of yourself if you turn out not to have the Buffett genes – is that you can also instruct the websites to send you an email if any of the shares in your portfolio starts moving into your 'target zone'. With an automatic bloodhound like that on the case, you can be sure of never missing an opportunity to buy your shares at a real price that you've pre-selected.

You can also pre-set your buying price by simply giving your stockbroker what's called a limit order, which means that you give him permission to buy the shares for you if they ever fall below a certain price that you've specified in advance. Most stockbrokers can do this for you, and so can a few of the cut-price execution-only online brokers. But you have to have put enough liquid cash into your trading account before you give the instruction in the first place, and that isn't necessarily the way you want to operate. By using an online price-gathering site instead, you can keep your cash in your bank account where it belongs until almost the last moment.

## *Selling, and why it's harder than buying*

What about selling your shares? Should you hold out until the very last minute, in the hope of squeezing the final drop of profit out of a winning position? Or are you better selling while the going's good, in the hope that you've called the top of the market correctly.

A saying in the investment world strikes a chord with me: 'Always leave something for the next guy.' That doesn't mean holding out till the last minute has no merit. Instead, it means that you have a life to lead, and that spending it hunched over your morning paper is such a shame when all you're trying to do is extract a few last pounds of profit that probably aren't going to change your life anyway.

Besides, if you can keep on telling yourself always to leave a little for the next guy, you have the perfect excuse in the event that your guess goes wrong and the price carries on rising after you've sold.

I'm going to admit something that hardly anybody else knows. I'm reasonably good at picking a winning share, but I'm absolutely terrible at knowing when to sell it. Sometimes I hold on to shares for far too long, in the vain hope of making just a little more profit against a falling market, so that the share price goes down while I'm actually watching my shares. (Drat!)

Or else I simply don't accept that I've bought a bad share in the first place and that I should take my losses and admit my mistake. So I carry on for months on end, holding that dud share and hoping against hope that something good eventually comes along to let me off the hook and keep my self-respect intact.

What a lot of investors do is impose a *trailing stop-loss* on themselves. Basically, they say:

'I've paid 400p for this share, and I'm not ever going to hold on to it if it falls to 20 per cent below its best price. (You decide the level.) So if the share falls to 320p next week (that is, 80 per cent of 400p), I sell it without a twinge of conscience. But if it rises to 500p, then I increase my stop-loss price to 400p (80 per cent of 500p), so that I sell it as soon as it drops back to 400p. Result: I've got an automatic trading program that continually ratchets up my minimum holding price, while at the same protecting me from excessive downside. How can I lose?'

How indeed? But the real beauty of a stop-loss is psychological. It takes all the responsibility off your shoulders if you ever have to sell because of a falling share price. You can safely tell yourself that the stop-loss has made the painful decision to sell, and not you. So you can safely curse the stop-loss and walk away from your loss with your pride intact.

This is a particular comfort if you have an emotional connection with a company's shares. Maybe they're your employer's shares and you feel a special affinity with them. Maybe you were the person who spotted the company when nobody else thought it was worth looking at, and so maybe you've been rooting for it and cheering it on as it finally broke through and gained recognition from the whole stock market. A fat lot of good that does you if the tide turns and the time's come to sell the shares again. But are you prepared to sever that old emotional link, that sense of being personally vindicated?

Never fall in love with a share; it doesn't love you back.

## Taking a closer look at price/earnings ratios

Many different definitions of a price/earnings ratio exist (Chapter 2 covers p/e ratios in detail). Some analysts think that an investor should be looking forwards, not backwards, whenever he weighs up a share. What use is comparing last year's profits with today's share price, they ask. Doesn't looking at the company's current trading projections and then calculating a p/e ratio based on the way things seem to be going at the moment make more sense? And if the company's growing fast, aren't you even better off taking a stab at next year's profits and working out the maths from there?

### Interpreting historical price/earnings ratios

For most people the best method is still the historical p/e ratio (often called the *trailing p/e*), which is what you get if you divide the company's current share price by its last reported set of pre-tax profits, diluted to take account of the number of shares currently in circulation. In other words, you're calculating what's known as the earnings per share figure and using that as the basis of your calculations.

The historical p/e is a useful bedrock for your calculations, because you're using real numbers instead of just something some analyst's dreamed up after a long lunch with a client. If somebody's using a different measure of a company's profitability to calculate a p/e ratio you'd normally expect them to tell you.

Unfortunately, p/e ratios aren't always that simple. You find big discrepancies arising even between the print and online editions of some British newspapers, perhaps because somebody somewhere has read a broker's report that gets his imagination working overtime, and the good news somehow hasn't filtered through to the print room yet.

The stock market itself sometimes makes mistakes. Wrong prices turn up on the London Stock Exchange's own automated listing screens, usually because somebody's made a keyboard error and a price may be ten times too big or ten times too small. Or maybe it's even a price for the wrong stock altogether. These errors generally get sorted out in a matter of minutes, but goofs can occasionally stay on the record overnight. That does your blood pressure no good at all if you stumble on them inadvertently!

These things shouldn't happen, but unfortunately they often do. If something you see on the screen or in the paper looks startling or unusually attractive, go away and double-check it before you commit your hard-earned cash to a figure that may just be due to a misprint or a keyboard operator with a fat thumb.

Even the good old historical (or trailing) p/e ratio can cause some serious problems if the company happens to be going through a period of rapid change. If it's just bought a massive new division from one of its competitors, or closing down one of its manufacturing plants and taking the costs straight on the chin instead of spreading them out over a number of years, some very strange distortions can happen.

Figure 5-2 presents an example of a distorted p/e ratio. In 2007, the company in the illustration closed down a couple of its European factories and moved some of its operations to China. That was expensive, of course. And during the same year its operating profits rose by about 10 per cent, to £40 million or thereabouts. Things were looking good. But by the time it offset the cost of the move against its annual earnings, it only had about £6 million of pre-tax profits left! So this thriving, fast-expanding business was left carrying what on paper appeared to be a price/earnings ratio of – wait for it – 266.

Why did this company choose to write down all of its relocation costs at once, rather than diluting them by taking on some borrowing and then paying it back over several years? Because it wanted the tax break, presumably.

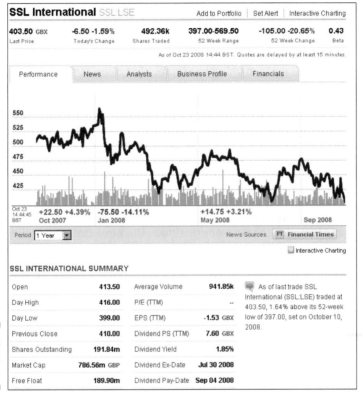

| SSL International | SSL:LSE | Add to Portfolio | Set Alert | Interactive Charting |
|---|---|---|---|---|

| 403.50 GBX | -6.50 -1.59% | 492.36k | 397.00-569.50 | -105.00 -20.65% | 0.43 |
|---|---|---|---|---|---|
| Last Price | Today's Change | Shares Traded | 52 Week Range | 52 Week Change | Beta |

As of Oct 23 2008 14:44 BST. Quotes are delayed by at least 15 minutes.

Performance | News | Analysts | Business Profile | Financials

Oct 23 14:44:45 BST  +22.50 +4.39%  -75.50 -14.11%  +14.75 +3.21%
Oct 2007   Jan 2008   May 2008   Sep 2008

Period 1 Year

News Sources FT Financial Times

☐ Interactive Charting

**SSL INTERNATIONAL SUMMARY**

| | | | |
|---|---|---|---|
| Open | 413.50 | Average Volume | 941.85k |
| Day High | 416.00 | P/E (TTM) | -- |
| Day Low | 399.00 | EPS (TTM) | -1.53 GBX |
| Previous Close | 410.00 | Dividend PS (TTM) | 7.60 GBX |
| Shares Outstanding | 191.84m | Dividend Yield | 1.85% |
| Market Cap | 786.56m GBP | Dividend Ex-Date | Jul 30 2008 |
| Free Float | 189.90m | Dividend Pay-Date | Sep 04 2008 |

As of last trade SSL International (SSL:LSE) traded at 403.50, 1.64% above its 52-week low of 397.00, set on October 10, 2008.

**Figure 5-2:**
A distorted
p/e ratio.

## Avoiding p/e traps

How can you protect yourself from falling into price/earnings traps? The general rule is: If something seems too good to be true, it probably is. But then again, if something seems too bad to be credible, doing some investigation to find out exactly what's been going on is worthwhile. If you've been fooled into thinking something's worse than it is, you can bet a lot of other people have as well. That's when you can move in quickly and bag a bargain. All you have to do then is wait until the world comes to its senses.

Do your own research. In the case shown in Figure 5-2, you'd have looked up the company's market capitalisation figure (see 'Understanding market capitalisation', later in this chapter), which is listed on any financial website or in Monday's copy of the *FT*. In this case it's nearly £900 million.

Then you'd have checked up on the latest trading reports – either on the Internet, or perhaps by writing to the company's head office if you couldn't find them in the newspapers. In this case you'd have discovered that the company had turned over a record £530 million in the previous trading year, and that it was expecting its profits before tax to hit £65 million. And straight away you'd have worked out that its true p/e was really somewhere in the 14–18 range.

But for the moment I'm going to assume that none of these confounded special circumstances is in play, and that what you see's really what you're going to get. Under these circumstances you can say quite clearly that the higher the p/e you're paying for a share, the better the stock market thinks the company's prospects are. And the lower the p/e, the more you should start sniffing round for the reason. It may be something as innocent as the company being in a slow-moving stock market sector, or its products being overtaken in the marketplace by something new.

Or possibly another company in the sector has recently had some bad luck that's dragged down the market's expectations for the whole sector, your company included. Never underestimate the power of 'sectoral drag', which happens when all the tracker funds in a particular sector are driven into forced selling. (Chapter 3 covers this in detail.) Sectoral drag can often create marvellous buying opportunities!

But the real puzzle happens when you find two similar-looking companies in the same stock market sector with widely-varying p/e ratios. If one company's sporting 25 and the other's on 11, you can safely assume that something's up. The market may not be quite as efficient as some people may have you believe, but it isn't *that* inefficient!

---

# Which transport company should you buy?

Consider four large British transport companies. All of them divide their activities between bus routes and train services. All of them are worth between £1.3 billion and £2.6 billion, so none of them looks like a particularly unacceptable risk. The business they're in is fairly unexciting and not very much new technology exists that can sweep them all away. In any case, they mostly lease their buses and trains rather than owning them outright, so they haven't got a lot of their capital tied up in depreciating assets.

Also, these companies aren't in a discretionary spending sector – if you need a train you need a train, and that's the end of the matter, so you shouldn't regard them as particularly recession prone. All the companies have higher p/e ratios than the UK average, which was about 12 at the time the table was compiled. And that means, obviously, that they're more expensive to buy than an average UK listed stock. The stock market appears to like them.

In the table below one of these companies stands out from the others. Can you see which?

| | Price | 52-week high | 52-week low | Yield | P/e | Market cap (£m) |
|---|---|---|---|---|---|---|
| Company A | 689 | 853 | 607 | 3.3 | 15.8 | 1370 |
| Company B | 932 | 1337 | 819 | 4.1 | 15.5 | 1420 |
| Company C | 575 | 825 | 493 | 2.8 | 18.0 | 2520 |
| Company D | 258 | 295 | 165 | 1.7 | 14.1 | 1840 |

Yes, Company C. It's the largest of the four companies, by quite a long way, and it's also carrying the highest p/e ratio (18), which means that you pay the equivalent of 18 times its pre-tax profits per share if you go out and buy its shares today. It's also paying a historical dividend yield of 2.8 per cent – a good 30 per cent less than Company B. And that higher dividend yield in turn suggests that the stock market thinks so highly of this company that it's willing to accept a lower earnings return from it.

Clearly, Company C is the one to buy. It's big, it's confident, and it's got everything going for it. And who in their right mind would buy Company D? It may be on an affordable p/e ratio of 14.1, but its dividend yield of only 1.7 indicates that it must surely be struggling to make ends meet.

Alas, I'm afraid things aren't quite that simple. As soon as you do some basic statistical work on this company, you run into a few surprises. And when you delve a little deeper, you discover some home truths that Company A really might not want you to know about.

Look at today's share prices in the first column, and then look at the second and third columns to see how those prices compare with the highest and lowest levels the prices have reached in the last 52 weeks. What you get is a table that looks like this:

| | Current price as % of 52- week high | Current price as % of 52 week low |
|---|---|---|
| Company A | 81 | 114 |
| Company B | 70 | 114 |
| Company C | 70 | 117 |
| Company D | 87 | 156 |

Lo and behold, Company C is trading at only 70 per cent of its best over the last 52 weeks, and only 17 per cent above its worst. Company D is at 87 per cent of its 52-week best and an impressive 56 per cent better than its worst. Clearly, the company that's on the move here isn't Company C but Company D. And in terms of its price/earnings ratio, it's the cheapest of the four!

The real fun starts when you look beyond the numbers and begin doing some proper background digging in the newspapers. This is what the latest press report about Company D says:

*(continued)*

*(continued)*

"[Company D] yesterday became the second transport operator in less than a week to say trading had exceeded expectations in recent months. The operator of XXX Trains and part owner of XXX Trains said that its annual profits, excluding exceptionals, would almost double this year to 20p a share, compared with 11.7p last year."

So what about Company C? Well, this is what the last major news story said:

"[Company C], the UK's largest train operator, was warned on Tuesday that it could lose its most important franchise unless it implemented an unprecedented set of performance-improvement measures imposed by the government. The Department for Transport said it was serving a formal notice on [Company C], requiring it to reduce the number of cancellations on its XXX franchise and to make other improvements costing a total of £29m."

No wonder Company C's feeling unloved. With the government threatening to take away one of its businesses, its investors will be lucky if it manages to keep up even its present feeble dividend performance next year. The share price seems very likely to fall. In contrast, Company D's pretty awful dividend performance from last year looks set to improve its payouts massively in the future – always assuming it doesn't decide to blow the additional profits on an expansion or acquisition instead.

Just for the record, the four companies featured here were Arriva (Company A), National Express (Company B), FirstGroup (Company C), and Stagecoach (Company D). The snapshot situation I've portrayed was correct when I wrote it. I stress that things will certainly have changed by the time you read this book, so don't go thinking that FirstGroup is a perpetual clunker and that Stagecoach is on the fast track to riches.

Choosing a company to invest in is a bit more involved than simply looking at the p/e figures and taking things from there. A price/earnings ratio is a very useful piece of shorthand information, and you should never ignore a figure that looks surprisingly high or surprisingly low. But if you think of the ratio as a spur to some deeper research, rather than treating it as if it inevitably represents good news or bad news in its own right, then you can't go far wrong.

## *Valuing a company that doesn't have any earnings*

What are you supposed to do when a company isn't producing any profits at all? Or not yet, anyway. Maybe it's a technology company that's working hard on something earth-shatteringly important that isn't yet in production. Maybe it's a new Internet service like Skype or Facebook or one of those price-comparison websites that depend on advertising revenues, and looks like it may rule the world in a few years' time if you can only summon up the courage to back it now. Surely these companies are still worth investing in, but how exactly are you supposed to put a value on them if they don't even have a price/earnings ratio? (No profits, no p/e. Simple really, isn't it?)

This is one of the best questions an investor ever has to ask himself. And the answer is that you weigh up the company concerned, and the prospects for its products, and then the general macro-economic environment, and then you take a flying guess, open your wallet, and hope for the best.

If that thought doesn't exactly fill you with pleasurable anticipation, you're not alone. Warren Buffett, the wealthiest man in the world, has repeatedly said that he won't have anything to do with a company that doesn't make money. And that he'll never, ever invest in a company if he can't understand what it does.

Fortunately not everybody's that hidebound, but you can see Buffett's point. History's littered with brilliant technological inventions that got trampled in the dust. The combined weight of competition and regulation has flattened any number of web-based marvels. Guessing which companies may conquer the planet and which may founder quickly really isn't easy.

When you have barely any information on which to base a decision, pretty well the only thing you can do is ignore the p/e ratio question altogether and try to gauge how much other investors want to buy a certain company's stocks. Like you, they're all looking at the size of the potential market. They're all focusing on the value of the company's patents, which might be pretty much all it's got. They've all spent a lot of time analysing the company's debts and assets, and they know who the major shareholders are.

Sometimes the pundits try to extrapolate a p/e ratio out of a loss-making situation by projecting the company's sales forward and talking about a *forward p/e ratio* (or a prospective p/e ratio). These guesses always incorporate a bit of flannel, but on the whole they mean well. But you can bet that, even if the company makes a profit, the p/e ratio would be into the 50-plus range, which means that the shares are at least four times as expensive as normal shares in real terms. American Internet stocks like Yahoo! have been traded as high as 100 during the peaks of market euphoria.

That brings me to the next stage in my considerations, the question of market capitalisation – see the next section.

## Understanding market capitalisation

Market capitalisation is a fancy term to describe the whole value that the stock market places on your company's shares. And it's the basis on which the p/e ratio and a whole lot of other things are calculated. You can find a quotation for any listed company's market capitalisation in Monday's *Financial Times*, or on most Internet share price sites, or from the London Stock Exchange's own website (www.londonstockexchange.com).

A hefty market capitalisation is generally considered to be a good thing. Bigger companies are less liable to get thrown about by the slings and arrows of outrageous fortune than their smaller counterparts. They've got more money than their less gigantic rivals, so they can afford to ride out a temporary downturn in the economy. If they need to borrow money, they can get it at better rates than the minnows. And if they decide to issue corporate bonds (see Chapter 6 for more on these), they can get those on better terms as well because their credit ratings are more favourable than those of their competitors.

No wonder the pension funds are so keen on investing in large companies. You get far fewer nasty surprises. And you have the additional benefit of knowing that if a bruising takeover battle ever occurs, nobody's going to be able to bully your champion gladiator.

By comparison, a company with a small market capitalisation is more vulnerable but probably much more flexible. If you want to launch a £10 billion multinational company into a new field of activity, you've got to endure months and maybe years of feasibility studies, focus groups, in-depth audits, competition studies, and unending shareholder battles. Whereas if you're running a £100 million company where the board members already own 25 per cent of the shares, you can call a meeting with your main backers and get started. I'm making a huge generalisation, of course, but small companies are generally sparkier, more fun, and (from an investor's point of view) rather more likely to make you a fortune even if you allow for the large proportion that undoubtedly go bust along the way.

So what does market capitalisation mean? Does it mean that this amount of money is what the entire company's worth? Or just the bit that operates in the UK? Does it include all the company's activities and all its obligations? Or may it not cover things like private debts, assets, and liabilities that aren't obvious to the naked eye? In short, does the market capitalisation give a complete picture of what the company's really worth?

I'm afraid that the answer may disappoint you. Indeed, you may even think that somebody's trying to dodge the awkward questions. Because the plain truth is that that tidy little figure you see listed in the financial pages isn't rooted in reality at all. Instead, the market capitalisation figure tells you what the stock market thinks your company's worth, at this precise moment, and without any detailed knowledge of how much the company owns, or what it owes, or anything else. The market capitalisation's a guess, and a half-informed one at that.

Market capitalisation is the figure you get if you take today's share price and multiply it by the number of shares currently in issue. So if the share price is 200 pence and you know that 100 million shares have been issued, the market capitalisation is £200 million.

What's wrong with that? Well, you may think I'm nit-picking, but the calculation doesn't reveal anything much about what the company's actually worth on paper – only what the stock market thinks it's worth, as of today. If you're looking for a valuation that correlates with what the company's last balance sheet says, you're out of luck. The balance sheet contains no in-depth consideration of the company's assets, and no analysis of its debts. No examination of how many shares it's giving away to its employees at cut-price rates in form of stock options. No formal attempt to value its brands or its patents, or anything at all of that kind.

You can, however, get a rough approximation of the company's true valuation by looking out for a *price to book value* (PTBV), which quite literally compares the market capitalisation with what the company's own figures actually say.

So, having shattered all your illusions about the solidity of the information you read in your morning newspaper, where will you find information about this flawed thing we call the market capitalisation? Well, to tell you the truth it can be tougher than you might think. But the better British newspapers will usually give you a figure at least once a week, and pretty well all the online service providers include this sort of information all the time.

Make very sure that you're clear about what currency a market capitalisation is quoted in. Even the *Financial Times* isn't immune from quoting a dollar figure as if it were expressed in sterling from time to time – a failing that can seriously distort your understanding of the situation. And if a company lists various batches of shares on different stock markets around the world, the local stock exchanges may treat those issues as if they give the size of the whole global company instead of just the little bit that happens to be parked on their soil.

One more cautionary note: being the biggest fish in your particular pool is all very well, but that situation does impose certain constraints on you. If the authorities think a company's dominating things too heavily, you're quite likely to find that it isn't as free as its rivals when it comes to developing its business. Indeed, in an extreme case the authorities can even force a large company to split itself into two or more entities, or to hive off some of its more profitable arms to the competition. That can be bad news if you're an investor! See the nearby sidebar on measures to limit the power of huge companies.

## Controlling the giants

Tesco provides a good example of how bias against super-large companies tends to work. Britain's biggest supermarket chain now accounts for £1 in every £5 that the UK consumer spends on food. And that gives it enormous clout in driving the sharpest deals with its suppliers, who have no option but to cut their prices if they want to have access to its shelves for their products. That situation's good for the customers, of course, and good for the shareholders, but it doesn't do much to help the poor old food producers. And conversely, if a large supermarket wants to drive out a rival store that's just opened up in town, it can afford to chop some of its prices so sacrificially low that it may even force the newcomers out of business.

Being so very large and affluent, Tesco and its main rivals Sainsbury's and Morrisons have spent a lot of money over the years on buying up any plots of vacant building land that may provide a foothold in town for one of their competitors. And then turning them into car parks! Planning committees all over Britain are getting cross about the way they say big supermarkets are stifling competition by sitting on all the land. And in the last few years both the British government and the European competition authorities have been weighing up ways of forcing them to sell some of their land banks.

In the meantime, Tesco and its main rivals are finding permission for building new stores increasingly hard to get. So much so, in fact, that the stock market now regards Tesco as an 'ex-growth' company in the UK. That doesn't stop it from expanding abroad, of course – indeed, Tesco's planning to quadruple its income from Asia within half a decade or so. But the chances of Tesco being allowed to merge with another supermarket chain in Europe are close to zero.

That's a point worth bearing in mind, perhaps. When you're looking for a large company to invest in, don't just assume that the biggest can continue to grow. Often you do better by backing the second or third largest, which doesn't operate under so many legal and regulatory constraints.

## *Delving into dividends*

Dividends can give you an income from your investments that may (or may not) prove to be steady and reliable over the years – in addition, of course, to the prospect of making capital gains from your shares (Chapter 2 gives you the complete lowdown on dividends, while Chapters 3 and 4 cover capital gains).

In a very general sense, the best dividends come from companies with low p/e ratios. That's not a cast-iron rule, but it makes more sense if you remember that, in the long run, dividends are ultimately paid for out of profits. And that the bigger the pre-tax profits a company makes in relation to the level of its share price, the lower the p/e ratio. Therefore a company with a sky-high p/e ratio (that is, one that isn't making much profit in relation to its market capitalisation) isn't going to be in a very good position to line your pocket with large dividend payouts.

Not every company issues dividends, however. Some industry sectors are more prone to these outbreaks of generosity than others. Let me try to explain why.

Certain industries are, to be frank, a bit over the hill as far as thrills and surprises are concerned. Not much excitement's to be had from making chemicals, for instance, and the growth potential of running a water company's also rather limited because you can make a pretty fair guess at how much water people are going to need over the next 20 years, and that probably isn't much more than today. So, if these companies want to hold on to their shareholders' loyalty during a period when the prospects of exciting share price growth are (to be gentle) rather limited, then they need to compensate them with big dividend payouts that keep them on side.

This sort of arrangement works out just fine for retired people who don't really care much for the thrill of the chase and prefer a sizeable payment coming into their bank accounts at regular intervals. Tax considerations are also important. People on incomes that aren't large enough to attract higher-rate tax (or indeed, any tax at all) are more likely to want an income from their shares than others who worry about having to pay capital gains tax on the proceeds from their investments.

All clear so far? Good, because I have to tell you the market's been suffering from a bit of an anomaly during the last few years, one that's made rather a mockery of some traditional assumptions about high-dividend stocks.

Until maybe 2005, the highest yielders on the Stock Exchange included two sectors that were so 'mature' as to be virtually comatose. On the one hand were the high-street banks, which had long since ceased to be dynamic and were paying sky-high dividends. Lloyds TSB, the most generous of the bunch, delivered a fantastic yield of around 8 per cent for the best part of two decades, and as you may expect, it gained a loyal following among so-called long-term buy-and-hold investors – the sort who like to buy a share and never sell it at all.

The other high-dividend payers were the mining companies who extract boring stuff like coal and copper ore and uranium, and who hardly saw any growth in their overall businesses for a decade or more. Like the banks, the mining sector had fallen into the habit of paying out big yields because they seemed to have little chance of giving investors very much in the way of capital growth.

By the end of 2007, the fact was already clear that both of these models were under strain, and for two very different reasons. Banks were plunged into a global credit crisis by a series of major scandals involving high-risk housing loans, which effectively left them unable to lend new money while simultaneously holding unknown quantities of bad loans. Lloyds TSB's dividend yield had suddenly become a millstone, because although its profits were down, it didn't dare cut the expensive yield for fear of causing panic among its investors.

As for those mining companies, their historical yields were slashed by a sharp rise in their share prices, caused by the explosion of demand from China. The Australian company BHP Billiton, the world's largest miner, is still dishing out pretty much the same healthy cash sums it used to, but a sevenfold increase in its share price within five years has left its handouts looking pitiful in relation to its market capitalisation. Like most other miners, Billiton's now spending every last Australian cent on new capacity, which leaves very little for handing out to shareholders. Overall, the FTSE Basic Materials index companies dropped to just a 1.29 per cent dividend yield by mid-2008, which made then the stingiest and most ungrateful companies in the UK market.

How can I say that the miners and the other basic materials suppliers are stingy? Just take a look at the right-hand column in Table 5-2, labelled Dividend cover, and notice that figure of 6.18.

What that figure means, in very simple terms, is that companies in this sector are making profits equivalent to more than six times what they're paying out to their investors in the form of dividends. And that's rather a big surprise, considering that traditionally, British-listed companies have tried particularly hard to distribute their earnings to their investors. (The investors do, after all, own the companies, so that doesn't seem an unreasonable expectation.)

But you gain more enlightenment if you compare this situation with what other companies are doing. The average FTSE company currently runs a dividend cover of 2.35; that is, for every £100 it distributes to investors, it makes a pre-tax profit of £235.

Where does the rest of the money go? Partly it goes towards paying interest on any bank loans. A lot of it typically gets ploughed back into the business, perhaps for building up a new division or for making an acquisition. And some of it may end up written off to absorb some unusual cost, such as a plant closure or a big backdated tax bill.

Either way, the dividend cover ratio's a pretty reliable way of figuring out whether a company can really afford the dividends it's paying out to its loyal shareholders.

| Table 5-3 | FTSE Actuary indices, 29 April 2008 | |
| --- | --- | --- |
| | *Actual yield* | *Dividend cover* |
| **FTSE main indices** | | |
| FTSE-100 | 3.71 | 2.35 |
| FTSE-250 | 3.07 | 2.31 |
| FTSE-350 | 3.63 | 2.34 |
| FTSE SmallCap | 2.74 | 1.77 |

| | *Actual yield* | *Dividend cover* |
|---|---|---|
| FTSE Fledgling | 3.08 | |
| FTSE –Aim | 0.66 | 2.01 |
| FTSE –All-Share | 3.60 | 2.33 |
| **FTSE sector indices** | | |
| Oil & Gas | 3.02 | 3.04 |
| Basic materials | 1.29 | 6.18 |
| Industrials | 2.97 | 2.24 |
| Consumer goods | 3.17 | 2.01 |
| Healthcare | 4.16 | 1.82 |
| Consumer services | 3.43 | 2.46 |
| Telecommunications | 4.67 | 1.69 |
| Utilities | 4.02 | 2.10 |
| Financials | 5.14 | 1.89 |
| Non-financials | 3.08 | 2.58 |
| Technology | 2.12 | 1.97 |
| Oil & Gas | 3.02 | **3.04** |

# Understanding debt ratios

People generally want to know how much debt a company's carrying. And you can't blame them.

If a company goes into insolvency, the cash creditors are the first people who get paid after HM Revenue and Customs and the administrators have both had their share. The shareholders are a long way down the queue!

But the level of debts can tell you many more important things about how a company's doing. For one thing, once you know how much your company owes, you're in a better position to figure out how a big change in lending conditions is likely to affect it. If bank rates go up, can your company honestly say that it won't be affected? Of course it can't.

But don't take too gloomy a view. Practically every company you can name has debts of some sort. Realistically, you can't start a business properly without either borrowing money or getting somebody to invest in you – and you can't expand it later on unless you can persuade the banks or the stock market to give you still more money, all of which you owe until you eventually pay it off. Indeed, a company that doesn't have any debts at all is a company that isn't really trying hard enough.

### Allowing for assets

How does the market measure this situation? Normally it likes to talk about a *debt ratio*; that is, the entire debt burden the company's carrying, from all sorts of sources, divided by the total asset value. The result is a ratio that probably looks like 1:1, or 1:1.25, or 1:1.5. And generally speaking, the higher the debt ratio, the further out on the plank the company's standing at the moment, and the bigger the risk of failure if everything goes wrong. But conversely, if the company hasn't got a very high debt ratio at all, then that may signify it hasn't got much imagination and really isn't the right place for you to invest your money.

For the moment, I can keep this simple and say they comprise two separate parts, current assets and long-term assets. Current assets include the value of any stock that happens to be in hand, plus the value of any liquid cash the company happens to have in its bank account at the time. And long-term assets include plant, property, equipment, land, manufacturing inputs, and so forth. Everything, in fact, except for so-called intangibles such as the value of any patents the company holds, or the goodwill from its business relationships, or the market value of any brands that it owns.

How does a company fix a value on its tangible assets? That's a good question, because accountants are allowed to play all kinds of games with depreciation, historic cost analyses, and all that sort of jiggery-pokery. What they view as assets can be pretty subjective. I'm not criticising here, merely trying to make sense of the situation. Not for the first time, you have little option but to trust accountants to know what they're talking about when they list a company's assets. And they do.

### Accepting that debt is good

A debt ratio of some sort is clearly a necessary and desirable thing. You probably have a debt ratio of your own, which sets things like your mortgage, credit card debts, and overdraft against your *assets*, which include your home, car, savings, and the money in your bank account. But the difference in your case is that, unlike a company, you're not trying to conquer the world, and therefore you have nothing much to gain from leveraging yourself up to the hilt with more debt than you really need in order to attain a comfortable standard of living.

Investors often talk about an overall debt ratio, which provides the big-picture view of how exposed a company is to the debt markets. This figure's usually expressed as a percentage. Thus, a company that has a 111 per cent debt ratio is borrowing slightly more than the sum total of its assets, which is getting moderately risky. But for a listed company in the UK, a more commonly used definition is the *debt/equity ratio*, also known as the *gearing ratio*. Essentially, that's the figure you get when you divide the company's total debt, from all sources, by its shareholders' equity (broadly speaking, its market capitalisation – see the section of that name earlier in this chapter).

Occasionally, a debt/equity ratio can be in minus numbers if the company's holding more assets than debts. But that's a pretty rare eventuality. For a company, debt is good!

Does that statement surprise you? Remember that your shares are also a kind of debt. After all, the company floated them on the stock market, probably by issuing new shares in a so-called *initial public offering* (IPO), in which it sold them to you (or, more likely, to your predecessors) for a flat, once-only sum of money. And after that first influx of cash it had nothing further to gain financially from having sold the shares in the first place – unless you count the various peripheral blessings that come from having a thriving share price and a big stock market capitalisation.

That was when the company's growth pains really started to bite. I mean, what's a company to do once it's sold its shares to the market and spent all the proceeds on developing the business? If it now gets the chance to buy up a competitor or build a new factory, or maybe even develop an entirely new line of products, the easiest place to go for the cash it needs is to the money markets. It starts by weighing up the pros and cons of a good old-fashioned bank loan of some sort. And then it asks its advisers to look into issuing a corporate bond (Chapter 6 covers these). Only if neither of those things looks workable does it decide on the third course of action, to undertake a rights issue.

### Using a rights issue

A *rights issue* is when a company opts to twist its investors' arms so violently that they agree (usually reluctantly) to buy a whole new set of shares in the company. And this action usually signifies that the company's in some sort of trouble. Investors really hate being ordered to shell out more cash for a company that probably isn't performing well anyway, because it upsets their asset allocations and makes their portfolios look top heavy – by which I mean that the extra shares that they're being 'forced' to buy leaves an excessive proportion of their overall shareholdings in vested in just the one company.

Okay, the company generally makes sure that the rights issue shares are attractively priced in relation to the current share price, so that investors are effectively getting the shares on the cheap. And it doesn't usually dilute their shareholdings in any particularly damaging way, because even if they exercise their perfect right not to buy the rights issue shares, that merely leaves them owning a smaller piece of what is now a larger company, so they come out roughly quits.

The company's market capitalisation goes up once the rights issue shares are floated and sold because the market capitalisation is the figure you get when you multiply the share price by the number of shares in issue. So when you increase the pool of shares, by any means at all, you inevitably increase the market capitalisation – unless, of course, the share price has fallen for some other reason.

Chapter 17 looks at a company's accounts and you can see there that a rights issue goes on the balance sheet alongside all the other debts and liabilities the company acquires along the way.

### Disguising debts

A company can draw a discreet veil over its borrowings in lots of ways, and not all of these debt types show up in the debt ratios unless you actively go looking for them (Chapter 6 has more on this).

A company may, for instance, choose to issue preference shares – a kind of private loan arrangement whereby 'preferred' people receive a cast-iron guarantee of getting a certain rate of interest in perpetuity in return for lending their money at a critical time in the company's history. It may dish out massive quantities of options or warrants or other less obvious devices, all of which are really just more or less invisible ways of giving selected people the opportunity to buy the shares at a heavily discounted price in the future.

The nearby sidebar, 'How options and similar devices short-change investors', describes an extreme example of how options, warrants, and so on can bring the good name of equity investing into disrepute.

In the great heyday of technology stocks during the late 1990s, up-and-coming young hopefuls often paid not just their staff but their directors, advisers, and financial backers in the form of options. All these options eventually returned to torment the shareholders, assuming of course that they hadn't already been wiped out by a complete share price collapse during the dot-com crash of spring 2000. Chapter 6 tells you more about options.

For the time being, the markets are taking a saner view of options releases, and fewer of the ultra-generous types are generally being issued.

## Getting more information about debt

At least eight different definitions of debt exist, and precise definitions tend to vary from country to country. Accountants also have an awful lot of leeway when deciding what to categorise as debt, and in what form. Defining debt's a minefield.

Does debt actually matter, though? Well, a surprising number of people reckon that the whole subject doesn't add up to a hill of beans. *Value investors* (those are people who like to buy up cheap stocks and watch them run) often like to say that they're not really interested in a company's debts, only in its profit potential. They're not really concerned with what a company does, only with how it performs. The stock market itself automatically 'prices in' a factor for the perceived levels of debt, they say, and that's all that you need to make money out of your stocks.

## How options and similar devices short-change investors

Suppose you've a £200,000 legacy burning a hole in your pocket, and you spend it on buying 10 per cent of a company that you think has issued 2 million shares, currently trading at 100p.

But now suppose you discover – alas, too late! – that your company's already pledged to hand out another million shares to its staff at a fixed price of 50p. You're pretty annoyed.

And quite rightly so. Because instead of a company worth £2 million:

2 million x 100p = £2 million/100

you've actually got a company worth £2.5 million:

2 million x 100p = £2 million/100 *plus* 1 million x 50p = £500,000/100

The problem is that effectively you don't own 10 per cent of the company at all, but only 6.666 per cent.

So the real market value of your shares isn't £200,000 (10 per cent of £2 million), but only £1.66 million (6.66 per cent of £2.5 million). You've been had.

I'd say that's a little like crossing your fingers and hoping that number 13 doesn't come up twice in a row. Being at least vaguely aware of the debt issues, and keeping a sharp eye on the news columns for anything suggesting a company's debt levels may be rising or falling sharply, makes sense for most people. Any company's half-yearly or year-end financial statements can keep you informed of the current debt situation.

You need to read the accounts of a company you've invested in – and, more specifically, its balance sheet statement, which ought to tell you everything you need to know.

Where can you find out more about your company's debt ratio? Not in the newspapers, that's for sure. Not one of the main UK dailies tells you about a company's debts in any regular format. For that, you need to go online.

ADVFN (www.advfn.com) provides as many debt breakdowns as you may ever find a use for. The funeral director Dignity, for example, gets 11 different leverage measures, and it isn't even in a growth industry. Reuters (www.reuters.com/business/quotes), however, settles for just two.

# Comparing Stocks with Cash

Looking at the benefits of stocks and cash offers a fascinating comparison about the long-term benefits of stock market investing.

If you want to persuade your friends that shares really do outpoint cash investments in the long term, you really can't do better than to take the annual edition of the good old *Barclays Capital Equity Gilt Study* down the pub. It compares the UK stock market against the cash and government bond market all the way back to 1899 – or to 1925 if you want information for the US markets too.

Broadly speaking, the Barclays survey shows that equities have returned an average of around 7.2 per cent a year during the last half-century or so, after allowing for inflation. (That's using data for the period from 1957 to 2007.) But if you'd put your money into UK government bonds (gilts, about which more in Chapter 6), you'd have been crying into your beer – if indeed you'd been able to afford your pint at all. Your bonds would have made you just 2.4 per cent a year over the same period! (Again, in inflation-adjusted terms.)

But only if you reinvested your dividends. If you'd bought £100 worth of shares in 1945 and had simply taken the dividends as income, you'd be sitting on an investment of only £296 by the end of 2007. But reinvesting the dividends would have given you an extraordinary £4,577 – almost a 46-fold increase.

There's no denying, though, that times aren't quite as easy for shares these days. During the ten years to 2007 the average real return on equities was down to barely 3.1 per cent, which means they were only a whisker ahead of gilts, which would have given you 3% per cent. Even cash in the building society would have got fairly close to that if you'd been clever enough with your investments.

You won't be able to get your hands on a full copy of the Barclays Capital annual report unless you're a customer of the investment bank, or unless you're prepared to pay for the privilege. But do look out for press reviews and summaries of the report, which is usually released some time around mid-February.

# Chapter 6

# Investing in Bonds

●　●　●　●　●　●　●　●　●　●　●　●　●　●　●　●　●　●　●　●　●　●　●　●　●　●　●　●　●　●　●　●　●　●　●　●　●

## In This Chapter

▶ Introducing bonds

▶ Taking the safest entry route with government bonds

▶ Moving out a little with corporate bonds

▶ Considering the high-risk alternative of junk bonds

●　●　●　●　●　●　●　●　●　●　●　●　●　●　●　●　●　●　●　●　●　●　●　●　●　●　●　●　●　●　●　●　●　●　●　●　●

*W*hen it comes to making money, nothing will keep you glued to your seat more firmly than the stock market. The thrill of taking risks, the satisfaction of getting it right – and even, sometimes, the learning experience of getting it wrong – is all very absorbing stuff, no doubt about it. And in the long term, as every available study on the subject will confirm, a policy of backing shares over cash or other investments will bring better results every time.

But there's another way to run a portfolio. The credit crunch of 2007 and 2008 did much more than just concentrate peoples' minds on the fallibility and the vanity of the equity markets, which crashed by 45 per cent and some-times more during the ensuing panic. It also focused our minds on the impor-tance of making room for safe, steady earners that have the ability to keep us provided for, no matter what might happen in the future.

That's when *bonds* come into their own. When you buy a bond, you're putting your money into something that you know won't ever go bust, no matter how bad things might get. Providing you can buy your bonds at the right price, they should normally provide you with a decent income for life – with the added possibility of being able to make a capital gain when you eventually sell them. Bonds are great for people who don't like extreme risk – people like pensioners, children, and people who simply haven't got the time or the energy to chase the stock markets day in and day out.

Well, that's the theory. And it contains a good-sized grain of truth, too. Unless you really insist on going all-out with a high-risk bond, you always know that the chances of anybody actually defaulting on your investment are pretty slim, so your baseline investment is pretty safe. But that's not quite the same as saying that your money's 100 per cent secure when you buy a bond. Only a part of the money you invest is literally guaranteed against loss: the value of the rest is likely to rise and fall in line with its own peculiar rhythms, and your timing's going to be just as important as when you're buying shares.

If that doesn't sound too reassuring, perhaps I can say straight away that if I were lost in a desert and I had to choose between two guides, one of whom was a shares analyst and the other was a bond analyst, I'd go with the bond analyst every time. Bond people know their stuff and they do their calculations properly. They don't allow the madness of the moment to sway them like so many shares people do. That's because they're dealing with a type of investment that's fundamentally rather boring. Bonds go up and down in line with the market's economic expectations – and, rather peculiarly, they often tend to do best when the outlook for shares is at its worst.

So, boring's good. But I'm going to warn you now that some of the following is going to stretch your brain a little. Bond investing is an upside-down world in which the things you may think are important (like prices, for instance) are hardly ever mentioned in the press, while the stuff you may think is less important (like yields) is right up there in the centre of things. The tail wags the dog!

Worse, the prices go down when the bank rate goes up, and up when the bank rate goes down. That's not at all what you may expect from an investment that focuses on yields. But bonds have their own peculiar logic, which I hope becomes clearer in this chapter. They're not driven by their own strengths but by the weaknesses of other competing investments. So when other investments do badly, bonds tend to prosper.

# Getting Comfortable with Bonds

Some investors need more safety than others. Some people are simply cautious and don't like being ambushed by big surprises. Others are too busy to be able to follow the markets on a daily basis, and prefer to keep their money in places where they know it's fundamentally safe, and where it also earns them an income that doesn't vary from one month to another. (Although some of these people may still be in for a surprise if they buy the wrong sorts of bonds.)

The most persuasive reason for having bonds in your portfolio is if you're getting toward one of those turning points in your life where absolute reliability's likely to become really crucial. Usually that means you're nearing retirement, and so you're about to depend heavily on your future income from your investments. Many financial advisers tell you that, once you get within five or ten years of retirement, you should start looking out for the right moment to sell some of your riskier stock market investments to 'lock in' your well-earned gains, and then stash the cash safely into income-bearing investments instead.

Another good reason for choosing bonds may be that you're managing some money for somebody who can't do it themselves – your elderly mother's savings, for instance, or the money your uncle Ted left you to see your kids safely through university. You simply can't take risks with a nest egg like that, because you couldn't live with yourself if it all went wrong.

So what is a bond anyway? Well, in its simplest form, it's just an IOU (I owe you). It's a piece of paper that says you've lent an organisation some of your money, and the organisation agrees to pay you a certain rate of interest (usually fixed) for a certain number of years, after which you get all your money back. The organisation that gets the money might be the British government, which uses the funds to cover its annual budget overspend. Or it may be the government of some other country. Or then again, it might be a large company that needs to raise some cash quickly and decides that issuing a bond is easier than floating some new shares or taking on a loan from its bank.

An incredible number of different bonds exist. What most of them have in common, though, is that they have a redemption date, when you're due to get the basic sum of your investment back in full. Just a few don't, such as Britain's War Loan bonds, still paying out something like 5 per cent a year after more than 60 years – and of course Premium Bonds, which don't pay out anything at all unless your numbers come up. But those aren't what this chapter's discussing. No, we're talking about bonds that might make you some cash in addition to the guaranteed annual interest rate payouts – or losses, if you manage to get it wrong. Whatever else you might have heard about how bonds are a safe option, the brutal truth is that you can lose money on a bond too if you buy the wrong one, at the wrong time, at the wrong price. My job is to try and give you some pointers as to how you can avoid these mistakes.

How many bonds should you have in your portfolio? Well, everyone has their own idea, but one way of working out a suitable ratio is to look at your age in years, deduct 20, and then reckon on having that percentage invested in bonds of one sort or another. Plus another 20 per cent in cash, perhaps. So if you're 60 years old you might be looking at 40 per cent bonds, 20 per cent cash, and 40 per cent shares. But if you're only 40 you may want to have 20 per cent in bonds, 20 per cent in cash (or maybe a bit less), and the rest in shares.

## Understanding the upside-down logic of bonds

As I hope I've intimated, buying a bond isn't just a simple matter of laying down your money and collecting a lifelong interest yield from it. So you won't need me to tell you a second time that it isn't quite that straightforward. Oh no.

First, most bonds don't last for ever. Unlike shares, which are yours for keeps once you've bought them, bonds usually have a fixed term, rather like your mortgage, and they don't pay back you the capital until a final 'redemption date'. But you do have the advantage of always knowing that whatever happens (within reason), you get the original value of your money back on redemption day. That nearly cast-iron certainty is precious, and it's the main reason people turn to bonds when everything else in life is looking dicey.

Okay, let's at least start this section off with a nice simple example. Suppose you buy a brand new £100 bond from the government, with a ten-year term, and suppose it carries a 10 per cent interest rate. You can be completely certain to get £100 of interest on your bond, in the form of ten annual payments of £10 each, assuming that you keep it right up until its redemption date. You're getting a *yield* of 10 per cent from your bond. Remember that word, please, because we come back to it in a moment or two. Then eventually you get your original £100 back from the government, meaning that you've made a £100 profit on your original £100 investment. All clear so far?

Good, because this is where it starts to get more complicated. Most people who buy bonds don't buy them when they're first issued – and they don't keep them until their redemption date either. Instead, they buy and sell bonds in the second-hand market, where they might very well fetch less, or more, than the £100 they originally cost. The actual price of a bond is constantly going up and down in line with things like inflation, economic worries, and the state of other investment markets like the stock market. Generally, the more worried people are about shares, the more they're tempted by the security of bonds.

So, suppose I buy one of these £100 bonds at a time when the stock market's feeling nervy. That means I'll probably have to pay over the odds for it – £120, say. But am I going to get a 10 per cent interest rate return on my £120? Nope, that wasn't the deal when the government originally issued the bond at £100. It was only offering £10 a year, remember? And that £10 a year is what I'll still get, even though I paid £120. So the first thing to say is that my yield on my bond is only 8.5 per cent, instead of the 10 per cent the original buyer was getting.

In addition, the higher the bond price goes, the lower the yield gets. It's literally a fixed ratio. If I'd been foolish enough to pay £200 for my £100 bond with the 10 per cent 'coupon', my yield would have been only 5 per cent. But if I snap it up for the bargain price of £50, my 10 per cent coupon gives me a tasty yield of 20 per cent.

# *Knowing what makes a bond price move*

But hang on. Does that mean the interest yield on your bonds is the only thing on your mind when you go out to buy a bond? Absolutely not. Yields are only important to those people who buy a bond with the intention of keeping it for ever – or rather, until it matures. For everybody else, a capital gain is very much in the picture. When times are hard in the stock markets, people come looking for cash gains from the bond markets as well as just security.

Little changes in the bond yield can be very important. Because bond yields and bond prices are so tightly locked together by the sheer convoluted logic of the financial pages, a small upward twitch of the yield puts a disproportionately large amount of value on the bond price.

Suppose last month my bonds were worth £100 and the newspaper said they were carrying a yield of 5 per cent. That's another way of saying I can expect to get an interest payment of £5 a year from them. But this morning the paper says that the yield on my bonds has suddenly fallen to 4 per cent bear in mind that lower yields are good and higher yields are bad).

That little 1 percentage change in the yield, from 5 to 4 per cent, doesn't look like much. But it's actually a 20 per cent reduction in the quoted yield. That means, in turn, that instead of needing to spend £100 to get that £5 a year return, the buyer now has to shell out £125. In effect, my bonds have gone up in value by 25 per cent!

So a tiny shift in the bond yield inevitably translates into a large shift in the capital value of a bond. But what makes people want to pay more for a bond this week than last week?

Bonds are attractive at times of stock market stress because they have the bottom-end reassurance that can only come from knowing that the issuer (in this case the government) promises to pay back their initial loan value (the 'redemption value') come hell or high water. Of course, that might be less than I actually paid for my bond – but then again, it might be more. Either way, this promise is substantially better than no guarantee at all, which is what I get from a share.

But the financial markets play a deeper game than this. At all times, they're comparing the yields from the bond markets with the yields they can expect to get from the cash markets – bank deposit rates and so forth. If the markets think UK bank rates are soon coming down, they may very well decide that a fixed 'coupon' rate of 5 per cent on your bond's a pretty good deal, and so they all pile in – your lucky day!

# The dreaded yield curve

Explaining the yield curve of a bond in a simple way is challenging, but I'll do my best. Investment professionals often talk about the yield curve when they refer to a bond, and unfortunately they're not just trying to blind you with unnecessary science.

You don't need to understand the specifics, but it helps if you can at least understand the principle of yield curves, because newspapers' economics columns are always talking about them and why they're important.

A bond has two different kinds of interest rates operating at the same time – and they can be quite different from each other. First is the interest that the issuer offers to pay you when the bond's first issued: the 'coupon'. That represents a flat, fixed rate of interest that the issuer intends to pay to anyone who buys that bond, either new or secondhand. £10 a year interest on a £100 bond, and that's the issuer's final offer, take it or leave it.

Second, and more important, is the yield you actually get when you buy the bond – the one listed in the newspapers. The bond yield is the figure you get when you divide that £10 a year into however much you actually paid for the bond. So, for instance, if you paid a hefty £120 for your £100 bond, your £10 coupon gives you a yield of only 8.33 per cent, whereas if you paid only £80 for it, you're looking at a tasty yield of 12.5 per cent.

So the yield and the coupon are generally quite different from each other. The coupon's fixed from day one, but the yield effectively depends on how badly the markets want to buy those bonds. But here's the interesting bit: the closer your bond gets to its redemption date, the closer together those two rates will become. If the yield's higher than the coupon, it comes down. If it's lower, it'll rise.. Why? Because only

a complete idiot would buys something for £120 if she knows she's only going to get £100 back when redemption day comes along next year. The bond price and the bond yield always revert to the original face value and coupon yield as redemption day approaches.

The longer a bond still has to run before its redemption, the higher the offered yield (and hence, the lower the actual bond price). That's because buyers expect inflation to eat away at their gains over the next 25 years, or whatever, so no way do they pay the full asking price for the bond while all those uncertainties still exist. But as the years roll by and the possibility of losses to inflation diminish, they're more tempted by the bond and its yields fall as its prices rise.

Well, at least that's the way the yield ought to work. But sometimes instead we get what the markets call an inverted yield curve. This happens when the long-term yield's lower than the short-term yield! What does that mean? It means that the markets think hard times are coming, and soon. There won't be much inflation, they think, because there won't be much growth going on. Wiser heads than mine tell me that an inverted curve has accurately predicted five out of the six last economic slowdowns in the United States since 1970, and that the Federal Reserve (the American central bank) uses it to actively predict recessions as much as a year and a half in advance.

You're more than welcome to dismiss this as a load of mumbo-jumbo, but bond analysts are pretty clever people who don't jump to conclusions easily. What this discussion does reveal, anyway, is that the yield you get on your bonds is in constant motion, according to how long the bond has left to go.

But all the news isn't good. The bond markets also keep a keen eye on the state of inflation, which might easily drive down the real returns they can expect to get from those fixed coupon rates on the bond in the future. If the markets ever think inflation might hit 10 per cent in the next five years, your permanently fixed coupon yield of 5 per cent won't impress them, because it'll soon be worth less than zero to them. And the consequence is they all run away, and your bond price comes crashing down until the bond yield effectively stabilises somewhere very much higher than 5 per cent. That's very bad news indeed.

These, of course, are exaggerated examples. Under normal circumstances it would be rare for a bond yield to shift by more than 3 per cent or so. Rare, but not impossible – bond yields moved by 6 per cent and more during the heavy inflation of the late 1970s, and fortunes were made – and often lost – by speculators playing the bond markets.

Bond investing isn't the safe, reliable ride it used to be. Owning a portfolio of bonds can still be a great way to secure a long-term income, which is why people nearing retirement still do it. But you do need to make sure you buy the bonds at the right price, and the right moment. Few areas of investing are quite so time sensitive.

## Browsing benchmarks

How does the market deal with the problem of continually changing maturities and ever-shifting yields? Simple. It doesn't even try. Instead of attempting to cope with the endless permutations of the marketplace, your typical financial page carries only a carefully selected handful of sample bonds, called benchmark bonds, and then leaves you to fill in the gaps yourself.

The paper probably gives you the yields for bonds with one-year, three-year, five-year, and most importantly ten-year maturities, plus a sprinkling of twenty-year and twenty-five year dates. Your own bonds are incredibly unlikely actually to be listed on the page – but hey, that doesn't matter much, because the market treats all bonds of a particular maturity as much of a muchness in terms of their value and price. The benchmarks give you a good idea which way bonds are moving.

## Buying bonds

So, assuming that we haven't put you off completely, how do you buy bonds?

Most people are best leaving the task to a professional such as a stockbroker or an investment adviser at your bank. You're unlikely to be able to buy bonds directly in your own right, unless you're willing to deal in very large denominations. But generally the principle is much the same as with shares, except that you don't pay stamp duty on bond purchases.

The big exception, which you forget at your peril, is National Savings and Investments, which you can buy in tiny quantities at your local post office. NS&I's products are government bonds issued to help fund the Treasury's deficits.

You buy them when they're fresh and new and hold them until maturity, when you redeem them. (A second-hand market in them does exit, but it isn't readily accessible to amateurs.) NS&I products nearly always pay better rates than high-street banks, and they're tax free.

A more practical way to feel the benefit from buying bonds for many people is simply to buy a collective fund such as a unit trust or an investment trust that will do all the hard work for you. You can now put bond funds into your Individual Savings Account (ISA) or your Self-Invested Pension Policy (SIPP), by the way.

# Government Bonds

Most of what I've been saying up till now has referred to government bonds, which are still the only sort that I'd really recommend an amateur investor to get into. Sure, there are corporate bonds, which might take a very varied range of forms – some of them very scary indeed, as I'll show you shortly. And then there are junk bonds, which are another way of frightening yourself silly in the pursuit of high returns on your investments.

But with government bonds you're unlikely to run into anything toomuch more complicated, than what I've talked about already, which makes them an excellent place to start.

## Looking at government bonds

One of the really great things about investing in government bonds is that you know the government that issued them isn't ever going to go bust and leave you in the lurch. Well, that's almost true. If you really insist on lending your money to the government of Russia or Colombia – and you can do that, by the way – you might not be quite so easily able to dismiss the risk of something going horribly, terribly wrong.

Russia, Argentina, and Mexico are just three of the countries that have given their bondholders sleepless nights in the last 10–15 years. But countries like Britain, America, or the continental European states aren't going to fold up any time soon.

In Britain, government bonds (*gilts*) are free of all taxes on capital gains, although you nearly always have to pay tax on the yield interest (see the nearby sidebar on how to work out a bond's yield interest). Another good reason for sticking with them! You can certainly buy bonds from other countries, but you might not be able to get your hands on the tax concessions if you don't have the right passport. For a beginner, you're best off sticking to gilts until you know your way around.

## Understanding bond rating systems

We said just now that a bond is merely a loan you make to somebody else in return for a fixed interest rate, plus a firm promise to pay you back when the term's up and the redemption date comes around. But you don't need telling that a world of difference exists between lending your money to a reliable borrower and lending it to some spendthrift who's going to blow it all on fast living and then renege on his debt.

That, of course, is putting things rather colourfully. But investors have come badly unstuck even with supposedly stable governments in various parts of the developing world. And frankly, the situation isn't any better with large companies that also issue bonds of their own (corporate bonds). Some of the world's best-known companies – Ford, General Motors, General Electric – have found themselves downgraded by the credit rating agencies whose word is practically holy writ in the financial world. A company that's been downgraded will find it harder to raise new money, and it'll have to pay more interest on its bonds. Worse, it's likely to find it hard to attract investors to its shares, which are likely to plummet in value.

So who decides what kind of a debt rating a bond issuer ought to get? Well, you might be surprised to learn that this incredibly important task isn't handled by an intergovernmental agency, even if a national government's being put under the microscope. Instead, the task of rating bonds falls to a handful of commercial credit ratings agencies, with names like Standard & Poor's, Moodys, and Fitch IBCA, which advise the banking community about the soundness of these various agencies and their likelihood of defaulting.

Just to make it more interesting, each of these agencies has a different way of setting out its grades, with most of the major agencies opting for three digits and a few other signifiers: the nearer a bond gets to three As ('Triple A'), the better the risk. Most developed countries, including Britain and Ireland, get a Triple-A status, with a larger number of less developed markets getting a lower grade of A rating and some getting down into the B ranges.

In general, whether you're talking about a government or a company, a bond is reckoned to be 'investment grade' if it gets at least a BBB– (that's BBB minus) from Standard & Poor's, or a BAA3 rating from Moody's, or a BBB from Fitch IBCA.

# What you find in the papers – and why

So let's ask the $64,000 dollar question. Can I look in my newspaper and check up on the price of my bond? No, I can't. Tens of thousands of bonds are in existence, and the financial pages simply don't have enough room to list them all, even if you had the patience to track yours down.

You face another problem, too. Your bond may have originally started out as a ten-year bond, but by the time you buy it might have only five years left to run.

(Or, as you might say, it has a *maturity* of three years.) Then again, it might have three years to run, or maybe even one. If I now say that the market price of a bond changes according to how much longer it's got to run before redemption, you soon realise that the range of variables is truly mind-boggling. Tens of thousands of bonds, all priced differently at the time they were issued, and every single one of them on a sliding scale between being brand new and nearly ready to expire. How on earth do the financial pages cope with such unending variety?

The answer is that they do it by treating all bonds as if they were the same! Just one great big generic product. If I tell my broker to buy me some British government bonds with ten years left to run before their redemption date, he won't bother to ask me which ones I want. Instead, he dips into the great big lucky-dip bag and buys me whatever bonds he can get on the day. And – this is the good bit – everybody else does the same thing. Because the British government backs all these bonds, the financial markets take the view that they're all as risky as each other (which, in Britain's case, means they're not very risky at all).

If I had two bonds and they both shared the same redemption date – and if they were issued at the same coupon yields, which is quite likely – I'd find that the market treated them as a homogenous whole, and that it was constantly forcing their prices precisely into line with each other. If somebody ever tried to sell one of these 'generic' bonds at a higher price than other bonds of its type, the power of market forces quickly knock him back into line and his price would drop until it matched what the market was paying for other bonds of that type on that day.

So, when I go looking for my bonds in the paper, all I need to do is specify how much longer they've got to run – which in my case is five years – and it tells me what the yield is on all bonds of that type and maturity.

Well, almost. You can probably understand that the market for information about six-and-three-quarter-year-old bonds is rather scarce, and seventeen-and-a-quarter-year bonds aren't a whole lot more fascinating. So what the papers do is select a handful of so-called benchmark bonds that provide a snapshot of which way the markets are moving. For instance, currently the *Financial Times* is listing prices for British government bonds that are due to mature in each of the years up to 2016, then for intermittent years up to 2038, and finally for a long shot that runs all the way until 2055. Does the morning paper tell you the actual price of your bonds? No. Instead, it tells you what the yield is on all bonds of this type and maturity. Because that's the one thing they all have in common. Big ones and little ones, £100 ones and £10 ones, all share the same yields, thanks to market forces continually whipping them into line.

Bond prices are one of the toughest areas of all to understand. To recap:

- ✔ When the financial markets say that bond *yields* have *fallen*, that means that bond *prices* have *risen*. And that's good if you own those bonds! It means that your bond investment's worth more than it was yesterday.

- ✔ Conversely, when the financial markets say that bond yields have *risen*, watch out because that means that bond prices have *fallen*.

Yes, that situation's crazy, and it seems counter-intuitive too. The bond yield tail's wagging the bond price dog. But this arrangement is the only way the market can cope with the unending multiplicity of all tens of thousands of bonds with constantly changing redemption dates. The approach makes a kind of sense, honestly.

## Getting down to business with some quotations

Figure 6-1 provides a sample listing of bond prices from one of Britain's better sources for international bonds, the *Financial Times*. The prices quoted here are from Reuters, and as you can see they carry the most important data very clearly set out. You can find these tables either on the *FT*'s website at www.ft.com, or in the daily print edition of the paper.

## UK GILTS – cash market
www.ft.com/gilts

| Oct 15 | Price £ | Day's Chng | W'ks Chng | Int Yield | Red Yield | 52 Week High | 52 Week Low | Amnt £m | Last xd date | Interest due |
|---|---|---|---|---|---|---|---|---|---|---|
| **Shorts (Lives up to Five Years)** | | | | | | | | | | |
| Tr 9pc '08 . . . . . . .z | 100.00 | -0.13 | – | 9.00 | – | 103.48 | 100.00 | 687 | 3/10 | Ap13 Oc13 |
| **Tr 4pc '09** . . . . . . . . | 100.41 | -0.02 | +0.29 | 3.98 | 2.94 | 100.66 | 98.27 | 16,974 | 27/02 | Se7 Mr7 |
| Tr 8pc '09 . . . . . . .z | 104.13 | -0.26 | +0.34 | 7.68 | 3.50 | 106.22 | 102.93 | 393 | 17/09 | Mr25 Se25 |
| Tr 5.75pc '09 . . . . . | 102.44 | +0.03 | +0.36 | 5.61 | 3.55 | 103.48 | 100.39 | 12,124 | 27/11 | Je7 De7 |
| **Tr 4.75pc '10** . . . . . | 101.46 | +0.10 | +0.30 | 4.68 | 3.82 | 102.33 | 98.54 | 17,137 | 28/05 | De7 Je7 |
| Tr 6.25pc '10 . . . . . | 105.00 | +0.13 | +0.30 | 5.95 | 3.76 | 106.67 | 101.75 | 5,256 | 17/11 | My25 Nv25 |
| **Tr 4.25pc '11** . . . . . | 100.30 | +0.10 | -0.28 | 4.24 | 4.12 | 101.48 | 96.79 | 13,750 | 25/02 | Se7 Mr7 |
| Cn 9pc Ln '11 . . . . . | 112.43 | +0.09 | -0.45 | 8.00 | 4.15 | 116.22 | 109.49 | 5,664 | 4/07 | Ja12 Jy12 |
| Tr 7.75pc '12-15 . .z | 109.91 | +0.14 | -0.82 | 7.05 | 4.46 | 113.34 | 106.76 | 804 | 18/01 | Ja16 Ja26 |
| **Tr 5pc '12** . . . . . . . | 102.15 | +0.15 | -0.83 | 4.89 | 4.31 | 104.32 | 98.51 | 17,897 | 28/02 | Se7 Mr7 |
| Tr 5.25pc '12 . . . . . | 103.03 | +0.21 | -0.87 | 5.10 | 4.34 | 105.34 | 99.09 | 10,250 | 30/05 | De7 Je7 |
| Tr 9pc '12 . . . . . .z | 115.62 | +0.17 | -1.13 | 7.78 | 4.34 | 120.09 | 112.50 | 403 | 27/07 | Fe6 Au6 |
| **Tr 8pc '13** . . . . . . . | 115.25 | +0.22 | -1.57 | 6.94 | 4.52 | 119.75 | 111.41 | 6,553 | 19/09 | Mr27 Se27 |
| Tr 4.5pc '13 . . . . . . | 100.13 | – | -1.29 | 4.49 | 4.47 | 102.57 | 95.97 | 9,500 | – | – |
| **Five to Ten Years** | | | | | | | | | | |
| **Tr 5pc '14** . . . . . . . | 102.82 | +0.17 | -1.48 | 4.86 | 4.45 | 105.80 | 98.20 | 13,699 | 29/08 | Mr7 Se7 |
| **Tr 4.75pc '15** . . . . . | 101.26 | +0.09 | -1.72 | 4.69 | 4.53 | 104.23 | 96.70 | 13,782 | 28/08 | Mr7 Se7 |
| Tr 8pc '15 . . . . . . . | 119.76 | +0.19 | -2.18 | 6.68 | 4.71 | 124.87 | 115.47 | 7,744 | 27/11 | Je7 De7 |
| **Tr 4pc '16** . . . . . . . | 96.63 | +0.08 | -1.76 | 4.14 | 4.51 | 99.67 | 91.61 | 13,500 | 30/08 | Mr7 Se7 |
| **Tr 8.75pc '17** . . . . . | 128.39 | +0.27 | -2.80 | 6.82 | 4.78 | 134.11 | 123.62 | 8,136 | 17/08 | Fe25 Au25 |
| Ex 12pc '13-17 . . .z | 133.60 | +0.23 | -1.86 | 8.98 | 4.60 | 140.39 | 130.22 | 57 | 4/12 | Je12 De12 |
| **Ten to Fifteen Years** | | | | | | | | | | |
| Tr 5pc '18 . . . . . . . | 102.18 | +0.27 | -2.42 | 4.89 | 4.71 | 106.07 | 98.04 | 15,000 | – | – |
| Tr 4.75pc '20 . . . . . | 98.95 | +0.29 | -2.57 | 4.80 | 4.87 | 103.61 | 95.09 | 10,743 | 28/02 | Se7 Mr7 |
| **Tr 8pc '21** . . . . . . . | 129.39 | +0.44 | -3.08 | 6.18 | 4.86 | 135.38 | 124.41 | 17,573 | 28/05 | De7 Je7 |
| **Over Fifteen Years** | | | | | | | | | | |
| Tr 5pc '25 . . . . . . . | 99.21 | +0.56 | -5.25 | 5.04 | 5.07 | 107.52 | 97.84 | 16,348 | 27/02 | Se7 Mr7 |
| **Tr 4.25pc '27** . . . . . | 90.58 | +0.54 | -5.33 | 4.69 | 5.02 | 98.44 | 89.16 | 13,500 | – | – |
| Tr 6pc '28 . . . . . . . | 112.50 | +0.63 | -6.25 | 5.33 | 5.01 | 121.86 | 110.89 | 12,462 | 29/11 | Je7 De7 |
| Tr 4.75pc '30 . . . . . | 96.21 | – | -6.03 | 4.94 | 5.04 | 105.44 | 95.75 | 11,000 | – | – |
| Tr 4.25pc '32 . . . . . | 90.29 | +0.58 | -5.83 | 4.71 | 4.95 | 99.01 | 89.71 | 17,497 | 28/05 | De7 Je7 |
| **Tr 4.25pc '36** . . . . . | 91.99 | +0.77 | -5.52 | 4.62 | 4.78 | 99.62 | 91.22 | 16,285 | 28/02 | Se7 Mr7 |
| Tr 4.75pc '38 . . . . . | 101.44 | +1.00 | -5.24 | 4.68 | 4.66 | 108.94 | 99.83 | 14,958 | 29/11 | Je7 De7 |
| Tr 4.5pc '42 . . . . . . | 96.81 | +1.08 | -5.43 | 4.65 | 4.69 | 104.56 | 95.73 | 15,000 | 28/11 | Je7 De7 |
| **Tr 4.25pc '46** . . . . . | 92.77 | +1.20 | -4.96 | 4.58 | 4.66 | 100.32 | 91.57 | 13,750 | 29/11 | Je7 De7 |
| Tr 4.25pc '49 . . . . . | 92.80 | – | -4.82 | 4.58 | 4.64 | 99.79 | 91.62 | 4,500 | – | – |
| **Tr 4.25pc '55** . . . . . | 94.90 | +1.40 | -5.32 | 4.48 | 4.51 | 102.70 | 93.50 | 13,852 | 29/11 | Je7 De7 |
| **Undated** | | | | | | | | | | |
| Cons 4pc . . . . . . .z | 77.20 | +0.81 | -5.86 | 5.18 | – | 85.36 | 76.39 | 358 | – | – |
| War Ln 3.5pc . . . . . | 72.90 | +0.83 | -6.00 | 4.80 | – | 81.28 | 72.07 | 1,939 | 23/05 | Je1 De1 |
| Cn 3.5pc '61 Aft. . .z | 71.27 | +0.79 | -5.72 | 4.91 | – | 79.26 | 70.48 | 89 | – | – |
| Tr 3pc '66 Aft. . . .z | 59.99 | +0.66 | -4.72 | 5.00 | – | 66.58 | 59.33 | 53 | – | – |
| Cons 2.5pc . . . . . .z | 51.22 | +0.57 | -4.14 | 4.88 | – | 57 | 50.65 | 272 | – | – |
| Tr 2.5pc . . . . . . .z | 52.07 | +0.59 | -4.29 | 4.80 | – | 58.06 | 51.48 | – | – | – |
| **Index-Linked** | | | | (1) | (2) | | | | | |
| 2.5pc '09 . . . .(78.8) | 275.80 | -0.21 | +0.41 | 3.30 | 3.30 | 276.86 | 261.23 | 3,304 | 12/05 | Nv20 My20 |
| 2.5pc '11 . . . .(74.6) | 284.58 | +0.26 | -8.78 | 2.51 | 2.94 | 296.97 | 277.29 | 4,631 | 15/08 | Fe23 Au23 |
| 2.5pc '13 . . . .(89.2) | 235.40 | +0.29 | -12.93 | 2.76 | 3.01 | 253.68 | 232.87 | 7,347 | 8/08 | Fe16 Au16 |
| 2.5pc '16 . . . .(81.6) | 259.59 | +0.01 | -21.26 | 2.50 | 2.67 | 287.95 | 259.58 | 7,696 | 18/07 | Ja26 Jy26 |
| 1.25pc '17† . .(193.725) | 90.10 | +0.19 | -8.85 | 2.49 | 2.49 | 103.20 | 89.91 | 9,300 | 14/11 | My22 Nv22 |
| 2.5pc '20 . . . .(83.0) | 263.82 | +0.60 | -24.02 | 2.21 | 2.32 | 300.10 | 263.22 | 6,409 | 8/04 | Oc16 Ap16 |
| 1.875pc '22† (205.65806) | 95.04 | – | -11.45 | – | – | 113.42 | 94.34 | 6,750 | – | My22 Nv22 |
| 2.5pc '24 . . . .(97.7) | 231.66 | +1.63 | -26.86 | 2.06 | 2.15 | 273.84 | 230.03 | 6,827 | 9/07 | Ja17 Jy17 |
| 1.25pc '27† .(194.06667) | 91.30 | +0.82 | -11.26 | 1.84 | 1.84 | 110.32 | 90.48 | 7,975 | 12/11 | My22 Nv22 |
| 4(1/8)pc '30 . .(135.1) | 228.56 | +2.15 | -27.03 | 1.68 | 1.76 | 270.54 | 226.41 | 5,021 | 12/07 | Ja22 Jy22 |
| 2pc '35 . . . .(173.6) | 140.81 | +1.74 | -17.98 | 1.36 | 1.42 | 171.06 | 139.07 | 9,389 | 18/01 | Jy26 Ja26 |
| 1.125pc '37†(202.24286) | 98.86 | +1.91 | -11.21 | – | – | 119.13 | 96.95 | 8,325 | – | – |
| 0.75pc '47† .(207.76667) | 96.35 | – | -9.58 | – | – | 116.17 | 93.47 | 2,800 | – | My22 Nv22 |
| 1.25pc'55† .(192.20000) | 122.82 | +3.90 | -8.27 | 0.77 | 0.77 | 144.32 | 113.93 | 5,738 | 12/11 | My22 Nv22 |

**Figure 6-1:**
The UK gilts market listing.

All UK Gilts are Tax free to non-residents on application. xd Ex dividend. Closing mid-prices are shown in pounds per £100 nominal of stock. Weekly percentage changes are calculated on a Friday to Friday basis. Gilt benchmarks and most liquid stocks, are shown in bold type. A full list of Gilts can be found daily on ft.com/bond&rates.
Prospective real redemption rate on projected inflation of (1) 5% and (2) 3% (b) Figures in parentheses show RPI base for indexing (ie 8 months prior to issue and, for gilts issued since September 2005, 3 months prior to issue) and have been adjusted to reflect rebasing of RPI to 100 in January 1987. Conversion factor 3.945. RPI for Jan 2009: 209.8 and for Jun 2008 216.8. † For those bonds indicated, with a 3m lag, the 'clean' price shown has no inflation adjustment. The yield is calculated using no inflation assumption. Source: REUTERS Ltd.

What a lot of them exist!

## *Looking at the international scene*

Once you've found your feet in the UK bond scene, you may well want to build up a holding in the international market. The countries listed in Figure 6-2 are very definitely low risk: all of them get Triple-A ratings, or something very close, from Moody's, Standard and Poor's, and all the rest.

(See 'Understanding the bond rating systems', earlier in this chapter.)

So, for instance, Figure 6-2 lists two types of bonds for Australia: one with a year or so to go to redemption ('Red Date' 08/10) and the other with ten years to go (03/19). The coupon, which tells you the issuer's original interest rate, is listed in the second column, and the bid price (the price you have to pay if you buy the bond today) is in the third column. But the fourth column tells you the most important element of all, the yield (assuming you're paying the bid price). Notice that the yield's definitely not the same as the coupon! In the case of the 2017 bond, the yield's more than the coupon, which tells you that the markets aren't too happy at all about the prospects for inflation and economic growth in the next nine years. When they're feeling more san-guine about the future for bonds, they offer less than the coupon rate.

The next few columns tell you how the yield on these bonds has changed in the last day, the last week, the last month, and then the last year. The yield's risen by around 0.45 per cent (45 basis points, in the jargon) since a year ago. Can you figure out whether that's good or bad?

The fact that the bond has risen is bad. If the yield goes up, the price of the bond must have gone down – in this case, actually, by quite a lot. If today's yield on the nine-year bond is 6.29 per cent and it was 0.45 per cent lower last year, that suggests the yield was 5.84 per cent a year ago. That in turn means the bond price has fallen by around 7 per cent in the last 12 months.

Take a look at those minuscule yields in Japan, by the way. 1.25 per cent doesn't seem like much of a yield in Britain, where people expect at least 4.5 per cent and often more from bonds. But the yield is enough to keep Japanese investors happy, because they hardly have any inflation to worry about. Of course, if Japan's inflation rises in the future it may be a different story, because everybody may look at those microscopic coupons and say, 'You've got to be joking.' Whereupon Japanese bond prices may crash horribly.

## BENCHMARK GOVERNMENT BONDS

| Oct 15 | Red Date | Coupon | Bid Price | Bid Yield | Day chg yield | Wk chg yield | Month chg yld | Year chg yld |
|---|---|---|---|---|---|---|---|---|
| **Australia** | 08/10 | 5.25 | 101.5880 | 4.33 | -0.12 | +0.25 | -1.17 | -2.30 |
| | 03/19 | 5.25 | 99.1460 | 5.36 | -0.08 | +0.42 | -0.23 | -0.91 |
| **Austria** | 01/10 | 5.50 | 103.0040 | 2.98 | -0.16 | +0.01 | -1.17 | -1.27 |
| | 03/19 | 4.35 | 99.1300 | 4.45 | -0.04 | +0.19 | +0.09 | -0.02 |
| **Belgium** | 03/10 | 3.00 | 99.4230 | 3.41 | +0.06 | +0.16 | -0.61 | -0.83 |
| | 03/18 | 4.00 | 95.6900 | 4.57 | -0.07 | +0.18 | +0.09 | +0.04 |
| **Canada** | 12/10 | 2.75 | 100.9200 | 2.30 | -0.03 | +0.12 | -0.24 | -2.06 |
| | 06/18 | 4.25 | 103.6300 | 3.80 | -0.01 | +0.22 | +0.37 | -0.68 |
| **Denmark** | 11/10 | 4.00 | 100.1690 | 3.91 | -0.19 | -0.12 | -0.20 | -0.48 |
| | 11/17 | 4.00 | 95.5530 | 4.61 | -0.04 | +0.09 | +0.24 | +0.11 |
| **Finland** | 09/10 | 2.75 | 99.1600 | 3.21 | -0.15 | +0.05 | -0.57 | -1.05 |
| | 07/19 | 4.38 | 100.1150 | 4.36 | -0.14 | +0.02 | +0.05 | -0.13 |
| **France** | 09/10 | 3.75 | 100.9400 | 3.23 | -0.16 | +0.06 | -0.60 | -1.05 |
| | 07/13 | 4.50 | 102.3600 | 3.94 | -0.10 | +0.17 | -0.05 | -0.43 |
| | 04/18 | 4.00 | 97.5600 | 4.32 | -0.03 | +0.18 | +0.03 | -0.19 |
| | 10/38 | 4.00 | 88.2950 | 4.74 | +0.04 | +0.45 | -0.01 | +0.03 |
| **Germany** | 09/10 | 4.00 | 101.5500 | 3.14 | -0.11 | +0.03 | -0.43 | -1.09 |
| | 10/13 | 4.00 | 101.3130 | 3.70 | -0.07 | +0.21 | +0.03 | -0.61 |
| | 07/18 | 4.25 | 101.0200 | 4.12 | +0.02 | +0.27 | +0.14 | -0.30 |
| | 07/39 | 4.25 | 93.9200 | 4.62 | +0.05 | +0.44 | +0.03 | -0.03 |
| **Greece** | 03/11 | 3.80 | 99.3800 | 4.06 | -0.01 | +0.07 | -0.16 | -0.31 |
| | 07/18 | 4.60 | 97.2000 | 4.96 | -0.01 | +0.18 | +0.17 | +0.27 |
| **Ireland** | / | – | 99.4850 | 4.16 | – | – | -0.32 | +0.07 |
| | 06/19 | 4.40 | 96.5200 | 4.82 | – | +0.29 | +0.29 | +0.34 |
| **Italy** | 08/10 | 4.50 | 101.5300 | 3.63 | -0.09 | +0.05 | -0.43 | -0.67 |
| | 04/13 | 4.25 | 99.9200 | 4.32 | -0.15 | +0.15 | -0.04 | -0.14 |
| | 08/18 | 4.50 | 98.0100 | 4.81 | -0.03 | +0.12 | +0.06 | +0.17 |
| | 02/37 | 4.00 | 82.9950 | 5.21 | +0.01 | +0.27 | +0.01 | +0.20 |
| **Japan** | 12/10 | 1.90 | 102.4410 | 0.76 | -0.08 | +0.02 | – | -0.15 |
| | 12/13 | 1.40 | 101.1450 | 1.17 | -0.03 | +0.19 | +0.09 | -0.13 |
| | 09/18 | 1.50 | 99.3560 | 1.58 | -0.01 | +0.19 | +0.09 | -0.16 |
| | 09/28 | 2.10 | 100.2810 | 2.08 | -0.08 | +0.09 | -0.04 | -0.18 |
| **Netherlands** | 01/10 | 3.00 | 100.0800 | 2.93 | -0.06 | +0.08 | -1.12 | -1.31 |
| | 07/18 | 4.00 | 97.0800 | 4.37 | -0.02 | +0.20 | +0.11 | -0.12 |
| **New Zealand** | 11/11 | 6.00 | 100.5200 | 5.81 | -0.09 | +0.45 | +0.10 | -1.13 |
| | 12/17 | 6.00 | 99.5700 | 6.06 | -0.10 | +0.36 | +0.27 | -0.43 |
| **Norway** | 05/13 | 6.50 | 108.5000 | 4.40 | -0.09 | +0.63 | -0.14 | -0.60 |
| | 05/17 | 4.25 | 98.0000 | 4.53 | – | +0.68 | +0.07 | -0.51 |
| **Portugal** | 05/10 | 5.85 | 103.5540 | 3.48 | -0.08 | +0.07 | -0.55 | -0.79 |
| | 06/18 | 4.45 | 98.7000 | 4.62 | -0.07 | +0.10 | +0.05 | -0.01 |
| **Spain** | 07/10 | 3.25 | 99.8460 | 3.34 | -0.11 | -0.01 | -0.57 | -0.89 |
| | 07/18 | 4.10 | 96.3900 | 4.56 | -0.10 | +0.13 | +0.04 | +0.07 |
| **Sweden** | 03/11 | 5.25 | 104.2850 | 3.36 | -0.04 | +0.17 | -0.52 | -0.96 |
| | 03/19 | 4.25 | 104.3780 | 3.73 | +0.03 | +0.47 | -0.04 | -0.72 |
| **Switzerland** | 08/10 | 3.50 | 103.4200 | 1.55 | +0.01 | +0.24 | -0.26 | -1.11 |
| | 01/18 | 3.00 | 99.8200 | 3.02 | -0.01 | +0.46 | +0.20 | -0.12 |
| **UK** | 12/09 | 5.75 | 102.3800 | 3.60 | -0.08 | +0.35 | -0.42 | -2.11 |
| | 03/13 | 4.50 | 100.1100 | 4.47 | -0.07 | +0.51 | +0.11 | -0.70 |
| | 03/18 | 5.00 | 102.1400 | 4.72 | -0.03 | +0.43 | +0.31 | -0.43 |
| | 12/38 | 4.75 | 101.3690 | 4.67 | -0.05 | +0.37 | +0.32 | +0.02 |
| **US** | 09/10 | 2.00 | 100.7109 | 1.63 | -0.17 | +0.01 | +0.01 | -2.58 |
| | 09/13 | 3.13 | 101.0938 | 2.89 | -0.10 | +0.19 | +0.40 | -1.50 |
| | 08/18 | 4.00 | 100.0156 | 4.00 | -0.04 | +0.29 | +0.59 | -0.68 |
| | 05/38 | 4.50 | 104.3125 | 4.24 | -0.03 | +0.17 | +0.16 | -0.67 |

**Figure 6-2:** Benchmark bonds.

London close. New York close. Source: Reuters.
Yields: Local market standard Annualised yield basis. Yields shown for Italy exclude withholding tax at 12.5 per cent payable by non residents.

## Eurobonds

Surprisingly, not every government always issues bonds in its national currency. Some countries denominate some of their bonds in US dollars, in euros, or even in yen – or even a mixture of all three. These so-called eurobonds started in the 1970s and early 1980s, as a way of attracting investors from the bigger industrialised countries and getting them to lend their money to parts of the world where the money was needed. And by denominating them in a currency that the lender regarded as relatively safe, the governments were reassuring those investors that they wouldn't lose their shirts if the national currency tumbled. If you lent £1,000 in sterling to Mexico, you got £1,000 in sterling back, even if Mexico ended up with hyperinflation and a worthless currency (which it duly did).

Other countries didn't take long to cotton on to this brilliant idea. If an American bond issuer thought the yen may be about to tumble, issuing a eurobond denominated in Japan's currency instead of the dollar made good sense. That made the costs of repaying the bond much cheaper if everything went well.

Over the last five years or so, the dollar has lost a lot of popularity as a denomination for eurobonds. These days, more countries (and more corporations too) issue their bonds in euros than in good old greenbacks. That fact has come as something of a shock to the United States during the mid-noughties, when the dollar has struggled for supremacy against the euro. Although obviously we can't know what the future will bring: as the start of 2009 approached, it looked increasingly as though the euro might be heading for a period of uncertainty that would send bond hunters back toward the dollar again.

# Corporate Bonds

Big companies issue corporate bonds, which immediately raises the unmentionable subject of *defaults*. No matter how big or powerful a company is, it can always find itself in trouble in five or ten years' time. Think about industrial giants like Ford or General Motors, which have been getting very close to junk bond status (see the section on junk bonds later in this chapter) in the last few years because of their looming pension fund overhangs. Or the big airlines, which are feeling the pinch, or even British banks like Northern Rock, which was lucky to escape a complete collapse in 2007. You soon see that no guarantee exists that a successful company is going to be in good shape forever.

Companies that issue corporate bonds have to work harder than governments to sell their debt obligations to the markets. If you look at the yields from a typical high-rated corporate bond, the chances are that it's several percentage points higher than you get from a government bond.

Suddenly the whole upside-down logic applied to bond markets falls into place (see 'Understanding the upside-down logic of bonds', earlier in this chapter). The reason you're getting a higher yield from a corporate bond is that the risk of default from the borrower is higher. And this factor in turn means that the cash value of the bonds you're buying is lower than it if you buy a similar bond with a similar coupon (the original interest rate) from a well-respected government. Corporate bonds are cheaper because the markets demand to be reimbursed for the extra risk they take on when they buy these things. A *risk premium* is thus attached to a corporate bond.

This risk premium will vary from time to time, in line with how the financial markets are feeling about this particular company's prospects. But you often find that the general level of certain benchmark corporate bonds, and their divergence from traditional government bonds, are the subject of much hot gossip in the financial pages.

If ten-year government bonds are giving a 5 per cent yield and benchmark corporate bonds a 6 per cent yield – not an improbable gap, actually – then that tells you the market thinks the extra default risk is equivalent to about another 20 per cent on the bond price. But if the gap between the two widens to 2 per cent or even 4 per cent, you know the financial markets are in a seriously blue funk about the immediate outlook for the corporate sector.

But do benchmark corporate bonds exist? No, because you can confidently say that no two companies are alike. And that no two companies offer their bonds over the same two periods, with the same coupon yields, and in the same currencies. That's why the financial pages always pick just a handful of really top-quality corporate bonds and leave you to fill in the gaps the best way you can.

Figure 6-3 provides an example of the kind of bonds that make it into the *FT*'s daily listings. They're all rated by the big three ratings agencies, Standard & Poor's, Moody's, and Fitch IBCA. And they're all top-quality bonds – in other words, they all score high enough ratings from these agencies to merit a mention.

Consider: do you see Ford listed there? And why does General Motors merit only a B– rating from Standard & Poor's? How many banks get into the top rankings? And isn't the number of utility companies that make the top grades rather high? And the number of airlines quite low?

This is all useful information. You're not just getting information about corporate bonds, you're also getting a ratings-agency view of how financially secure these very large companies are thought to be. This is all going to be grist to your mill when the time comes to invest in their shares.

## GLOBAL INVESTMENT GRADE

| Oct 15 | Red date | Coupon | S* | Ratings M* | F* | Bid price | Bid yield | Day's chge yield | Mth's chge yield | Spread vs Govts |
|---|---|---|---|---|---|---|---|---|---|---|
| **■ US $** | | | | | | | | | | |
| Canada | 11/08 | 5.25 | AAA | Aaa | – | 100.02 | 4.66 | +0.43 | +1.83 | +4.42 |
| DaimlerChrysler | 09/09 | 7.20 | A- | – | A- | 94.63 | 13.98 | -0.60 | +8.56 | +12.83 |
| Wal Mart | 08/09 | 6.88 | AA | Aa2 | AA | 101.33 | 5.17 | -0.20 | +1.00 | +3.97 |
| Du Pont | 10/09 | 6.88 | – | A2 | A | 99.38 | 7.53 | -0.67 | +4.41 | +6.35 |
| Philipps Petr | 05/10 | 8.75 | A | A1 | A | 110.65 | 1.98 | -0.01 | -0.12 | +0.20 |
| Unilever | 11/10 | 7.13 | A+ | A1 | A+ | 105.59 | 4.23 | +0.52 | +0.92 | +2.59 |
| Bank America | 01/11 | 7.40 | A+ | Aa3 | A | 104.10 | 5.49 | – | – | +3.27 |
| JP Morgan | 02/11 | 6.75 | A+ | Aa3 | A+ | 101.23 | 6.16 | -1.04 | +0.48 | +4.56 |
| France Telecom | 03/11 | 7.75 | A- | A3 | A- | 106.87 | 4.65 | +0.10 | +0.60 | +2.87 |
| Petronas | 05/12 | 7.00 | A- | A1 | A | 105.00 | 5.46 | +1.22 | +1.48 | +2.98 |
| Bk of Scotland | 02/17 | 5.25 | AAA | Aaa | AAA | 91.22 | 6.64 | +0.11 | +1.30 | +2.56 |
| Goldman Sachs | 11/14 | 5.50 | AA- | Aa3 | AA- | 97.94 | 5.90 | – | – | +3.32 |
| Italy | 09/23 | 6.88 | A+ | Aa2 | AA- | 116.07 | 5.30 | -0.09 | +0.59 | +1.24 |
| Pacific Bell | 03/26 | 7.13 | A | A2 | A | 100.25 | 7.10 | -0.15 | +0.22 | +3.00 |
| Deutsche Tel | 07/13 | 5.25 | BBB+ | Baa1 | A- | 95.87 | 6.26 | +0.21 | +0.21 | +3.79 |
| Temasek | 09/15 | 4.50 | AAA | Aaa | – | 94.94 | 5.38 | +0.20 | +0.76 | +2.41 |
| DaimlerChrysler | 01/31 | 8.50 | A- | A3 | A- | 101.45 | 8.35 | – | +0.26 | +4.04 |
| FHLMC | 03/31 | 6.75 | AAA | Aaa | AAA | 125.44 | 4.87 | +0.08 | +0.34 | +0.63 |
| GE Capital | 03/32 | 6.75 | AAA | Aaa | AAA | 96.85 | 7.03 | – | – | +2.95 |
| Gen Motors | 11/31 | 8.00 | B- | B3 | B+ | 54.00 | 7.46 | – | – | +2.23 |
| Deutsche Tel Int | 06/32 | 9.25 | BBB+ | Baa1 | A- | 131.40 | 6.64 | – | – | +2.03 |
| Abu Dhabi Ntl | 10/36 | 6.50 | AA- | Aa2 | – | 80.50 | 8.30 | – | +0.28 | +3.90 |
| **■ Euro** | | | | | | | | | | |
| TPSA Eurofin | 12/08 | 7.75 | BBB+ | A3 | BBB+ | 100.83 | 2.04 | +0.09 | -0.21 | +1.78 |
| BAT Int Fin | 02/09 | 4.88 | BBB+ | Baa1 | BBB+ | 99.61 | 5.83 | -1.93 | +0.34 | +2.59 |
| VW Int Fin | 05/09 | 4.13 | A- | A3 | A- | 99.79 | 4.42 | -2.65 | -0.99 | +1.12 |
| SMBC Int Fin | 06/09 | 8.50 | A | Aa3 | BBB+ | 103.70 | 3.02 | -0.08 | -0.01 | +1.80 |
| Depfa Pfandrbnk | 01/09 | 3.75 | AAA | Aaa | AAA | 97.12 | 15.87 | +0.19 | +10.77 | +13.34 |
| Vodafone Fin | 05/09 | 4.75 | A- | Baa1 | A- | 97.21 | 9.48 | +0.01 | +3.81 | +6.12 |
| Deutsche Fin | 07/09 | 4.25 | AA- | Aa1 | AA- | 97.35 | 7.82 | +0.87 | +2.29 | +4.48 |
| Repsol Int Fin | 05/10 | 6.00 | BBB | Baa1 | BBB+ | 100.80 | 5.42 | -0.08 | +0.13 | +2.28 |
| Elec de France | 10/10 | 5.75 | AA- | Aa1 | AA | 102.80 | 4.27 | -0.16 | -0.23 | +1.13 |
| HVB | 09/11 | 5.00 | – | Aa1 | AAA | 101.28 | 4.52 | -0.07 | -0.30 | +1.12 |
| CDC Fin | 06/12 | 9.00 | AAA | Aaa | AAA | 114.86 | 4.45 | -0.19 | -0.32 | – |
| Citibank Cred | 04/11 | 5.38 | AAA | Aaa | AAA | 96.45 | 6.97 | -0.02 | +2.90 | +3.43 |
| Banco Bradesco | 04/14 | 8.00 | – | A2 | – | 98.00 | 8.64 | – | +1.73 | +5.11 |
| Teliasonera | 05/15 | 4.13 | A- | A3 | A- | 86.07 | 6.82 | +0.22 | +1.06 | +2.90 |
| **■ YEN** | | | | | | | | | | |
| Toyota Motor | / | – | MATD | MATD | – | 100.00 | 0.62 | – | – | – |
| KFW Int Fin | 03/10 | 1.75 | AAA | Aaa | – | 101.04 | 1.02 | – | +0.18 | +0.22 |
| Chubu Elec | 07/15 | 3.40 | NR | Aa2 | AA | 111.49 | 1.53 | +0.03 | +0.22 | – |
| Hutch Fin | 08/17 | 7.45 | A- | A3 | A- | 95.34 | 8.20 | +0.16 | +1.65 | +4.54 |
| Takefuji 8 | 06/22 | 4.00 | BBB- | Baa1 | – | 77.64 | 7.27 | +0.15 | +0.15 | +5.29 |
| **■ £** | | | | | | | | | | |
| Network Rail | 03/09 | 4.88 | AAA | Aaa | AAA | 100.26 | 4.06 | +0.12 | -0.73 | +0.38 |
| Boots | 05/09 | 5.50 | NR | WR | BBB | 93.00 | 18.03 | +1.11 | +6.56 | +14.57 |
| France Telecom | 03/11 | 7.50 | A- | A3 | – | 101.61 | 6.79 | – | – | +2.46 |
| Goldman Sachs | 02/17 | 6.13 | AA- | Aa3 | AA- | 13482.12 | 7.03 | -0.02 | -0.07 | -53.98 |
| Vodafone | 11/32 | 5.90 | A- | – | – | 86.71 | 6.94 | +0.06 | +0.12 | +2.40 |

US $ denominated bonds NY close; all other London close. *S - Standard & Poor's, M - Moody's, F - Fitch.

Source: Reuters

**Figure 6-3:** Global investment bonds.

In the next couple of sections I take a closer look at some of the riskier government bond investment markets, and at some of the less well-known ones from Europe and South America. It gives you another opportunity to see those debt ratings from Moody's and Standard & Poor's and Fitch IBCA in action. But perhaps I can say for the time being that the list in Figure 6-3 reinforces my point about just how important the ratings agencies are when weighing up a bond from an issuer who may not be 100 per cent reliable.

What do you do if your corporate bond isn't listed in the *FT*? You need to do some serious digging on the Internet for details of the daily prices on these bonds, because you certainly don't find most of them in the papers.

But at times like these you may very well consider the advantages of getting somebody else to do all the worrying on your behalf. Any number of specialised bond funds can take your money and invest it in a suitably diversified range of corporate bonds from any part of the globe you happen to specify. Some bond funds are even allowed into your Individual Savings Account (ISA), where you can stash them safely away from the grasping reach of HM Revenue and Customs.

You can find any number of these corporate bond funds listed on Trustnet (www.trustnet.com), or Yahoo! (uk.biz.yahoo.com/mutualfunds/ specialist/corporate_bonds.html). Most of them take an annual management charge, but you may well think that's worth the trouble they take off your shoulders.

Once you start getting deeply into the bond markets you're going to be hit by a tidal wave of variants on the bond theme. You can get split-capital bonds, convertible bonds, eurobonds, zero-coupon bonds, and extendable and retractable bonds – bonds that pay fixed rates, floating rates, Libor-related rates, and bonds in every conceivable currency.

# *Junk Bonds: A High-Risk Alternative*

Do you buy junk? I certainly don't. Or not knowingly, anyway. 'Junk' is surely the ultimate insult for a serious investor. So how can anybody even consider compromising her principles to stoop to such depths? Let alone devising an entire investment strategy that revolves around such an unlikely concept?

Well, perhaps surprisingly, an awful lot of people are interested in buying exactly this sort of 'garbage'. A *junk bond* (or high-yield bond) is any kind of bond that doesn't make what the ratings agencies call 'investment grade' – which means it doesn't meet certain threshold standards from the likes of Moody's or Standard & Poor's (see 'Understanding the bond rating systems', earlier in this chapter). But as you may expect, these bonds offer you a very much bigger yield than a normal 'investment grade' bond from a government. That's just what the market expects to get from an investment that carries a sizeable risk of default.

So cast out from your mind any idea that junk bonds bear any relation to the ultra-safe government bonds that you might want to buy for your maiden aunt's retirement fund. Junk is red in tooth and claw. It's lightly regulated, so all sorts of sins and omissions may pass under your nose before you find out what's been going on. But on a good day, junk can make you very rich.

You can't always get reliable prices for junk bonds, and only the very best of them are ever likely to make the pages of your daily newspaper. You can get quotes from the Internet, but you do need to remember that this is an obscure market where deals are done in the half-shadow, and where you may not get exactly what you were expecting. Liquidity, in other words, is poor, and the more of a hurry you're in, the less likely you are to get a fair price.

## *Why they call these bonds junk*

Two main kinds of junk bond exist, and the meaning of each has shifted slightly over the years. What both these bond types offer, however, is the chance to do much, much better than you can ever do if you limit yourself to top-grade investments.

The original junk bonds appeared during the takeover boom of the late great 1980s, when the likes of Jimmy Goldsmith and Lord Hanson were romping through the stock markets like there was no tomorrow.

They would buy a big stake in a victim company, just below the threshold that sparked an automatic takeover manoeuvre, and they then tried to intimidate the company's owners into accepting a takeover offer that probably undervalued it by a mile. Then, if they succeeded with their takeover, they moved in, stripped the company's assets bare, and sold off the remaining shell, having made an enormous profit.

To do this, they needed very large amounts of speculative cash that the banks wouldn't even consider lending them because it was far, far too risky. So they started issuing so-called 'junk' bonds that carried stupendously large 'coupons' – 25 per cent and more – in return for the fairly good chance of a handsome payback if the takeover attempts were successful and the victims' assets were duly stripped. And the punters absolutely loved them.

Everybody knew where they stood with a junk bond. The bond had a chance of being worth zero, but the likelihood of success made the manageable risk of failure handsomely worthwhile.

Over the years, the junk bond concept came to be extended to any company that offered an unusually high yield in return for quick funding. Often, no speculative takeover activity was involved – instead, we were being asked to invest in the companies that reckoned they could raise money more effectively in the bond markets than by going to their usual banks for a loan. And quite reasonably, these companies were reluctant to start selling off their equity through share issues, because that would be a commitment for life and they only wanted the money for five or ten years.

Among the biggest junk bond issuers have been giant industrial companies that have gone down the bond route in order to finance some enormous expansion or other. Car companies sometimes issue junk to cover their outlays on the car-finance groups that help to keep their own wheels turning. Energy groups use junk to buy up their rivals, or to build new facilities. And so forth. All very laudable.

But the question you always need to ask yourself is whether a junk bond can buck the general stock market trend and leave you laughing when the bottom falls out of the economy and the equity scene goes into crisis. The answer, perhaps unsurprisingly, is that it can't. At the end of the day, when you buy a junk bond (or any corporate bond, for that matter), you're backing the company's corporate performance just as much as if you're buying its shares.

If you have any illusions left about how this particular corner of the bond field might be suitable for widows and orphans, prepare to abandon them now. Before you, or somebody you love, gets hurt.

## *'Sub-investment grade' paper*

Figure 6-4 provides a nice example of how you can't necessarily take the Triple-A credit ratings from Moody's, Standard & Poor's, and Fitch IBCA for granted. First look at the lower part of the figure, where the 'Emerging US$' and 'Emerging Euro' markets are listed. Mexico, South Africa, and Russia get a BBB+ from Standard & Poor's, which means it regards them as 'investable' markets: Solid enough to be reasonably safe, and definitely not sub-investment grade. And Poland even rates an A–, which means it's not far out of the top league. But Turkey's right down there with the Philippines and Venezuela among the high-risk countries, getting only a BB– from Standard & Poor's. The worries are not so much that these countries aren't growing well, but reflect a fear that they may get their economies into such a state that inflation wipes out the gains from the yield, and that they may even default on their debts.

## HIGH YIELD & EMERGING MARKET BONDS

| Oct 15 | Red date | Coupon | S* | Ratings M* | F* | Bid price | Bid yield | Day's chge yield | Mth's chge yield | Spread vs US |
|---|---|---|---|---|---|---|---|---|---|---|
| ■ **HIGH YIELD US$** | | | | | | | | | | |
| Gazprombk | 10/08 | 7.25 | BBB- | – | – | 98.73 | 41.55 | +29.53 | +35.43 | +37.55 |
| Gazprom | 03/13 | 9.63 | BBB | – | BBB | 89.00 | 13.00 | +0.38 | +4.61 | +9.00 |
| Kazkommertsbk | 04/13 | 8.50 | BB | – | BB+ | 46.62 | 31.46 | +0.02 | +16.46 | +27.46 |
| TNK-BP | 07/16 | 7.50 | – | Baa2 | BBB- | 51.37 | 20.15 | +0.83 | +7.79 | +16.15 |
| ■ **HIGH YIELD EURO** | | | | | | | | | | |
| Astana Fin | 06/10 | 7.88 | – | Ba1 | BB+ | 65.00 | 41.00 | +0.17 | +22.17 | +37.00 |
| Gaz Capital | 09/10 | 7.80 | BBB | A3 | BBB | 90.47 | 13.71 | +0.06 | +6.63 | +9.71 |
| ■ **EMERGING US$** | | | | | | | | | | |
| Fiat Fin | 05/11 | 6.75 | BBB- | Baa3 | BBB- | 91.01 | 10.87 | +0.85 | +4.66 | +6.87 |
| Ukraine | 06/13 | 7.65 | B+ | B1 | BB- | 55.00 | 24.34 | +4.94 | +15.10 | +20.34 |
| Mexico | 03/15 | 6.63 | BBB+ | Baa1 | BBB+ | 96.25 | 7.37 | -0.21 | +1.57 | +3.37 |
| Brazil | 03/15 | 7.88 | BBB- | Ba1 | BBB- | 96.00 | 8.70 | +0.47 | +2.03 | +4.70 |
| Turkey | 03/15 | 7.25 | BB- | Ba3 | BB- | 87.31 | 9.98 | +0.85 | +3.24 | +5.98 |
| Peru | 05/16 | 8.38 | BBB- | Ba1 | BBB- | 97.00 | 8.93 | -0.38 | +2.55 | +4.93 |
| South Africa | 06/17 | 8.50 | BBB+ | Baa1 | BBB+ | 95.00 | 9.35 | -0.29 | +2.59 | +5.35 |
| Philippines | 01/19 | 9.88 | BB- | B1 | BB | 103.00 | 9.41 | -0.80 | +2.65 | +5.41 |
| Colombia | 02/20 | 11.75 | BBB- | Ba1 | – | 121.50 | 8.72 | +0.14 | +2.06 | +4.72 |
| Venezuela | 09/27 | 9.25 | BB- | – | – | 60.00 | 16.02 | +0.84 | +2.59 | +12.02 |
| Russia | 03/30 | 7.50 | BBB+ | Baa1 | – | 87.50 | 9.82 | -0.32 | +3.09 | +5.82 |
| Ecuador | 08/30 | 10.00 | B- | B3 | CCC | 53.69 | 19.98 | +0.48 | +4.35 | +15.98 |
| Argentina | 12/33 | 8.28 | B | – | – | 41.00 | 20.38 | -1.01 | +5.87 | +16.38 |
| ■ **EMERGING EURO** | | | | | | | | | | |
| Brazil | 02/10 | 11.00 | BBB- | Ba1 | BBB- | 102.85 | 8.50 | +0.05 | +2.45 | +4.50 |
| Poland | 02/11 | 5.50 | A- | A2 | A- | 100.63 | 5.19 | -0.08 | +0.48 | +1.19 |
| Turkey | 02/17 | 5.50 | BB- | Ba3 | BB- | 82.25 | 8.56 | +0.06 | +1.66 | +4.56 |
| Argentina | 11/26 | 11.75 | DEF | DEF | CC | 26.00 | 45.08 | +0.01 | -2.14 | +41.08 |

US $ denominated bonds NY close; all other London close. *S - Standard & Poor's, M - Moody's, F - Fitch.

Source : Reuters

**Figure 6-4:** High yield bonds.

Worse, Ecuador and Argentina get B– and B, respectively, from Standard & Poor's: both countries have actually defaulted on their foreign loans in the past, and both have historically had high inflation rates too. So don't get too sidetracked by the fact that they're both offering high bid yields.

These bonds are, in effect, junk. And don't forget it.

# Chapter 7

# Investing in Cash Investments

. . . . . . . . . . . . . . . . . . . . . . . . . . . . . . . . . . . . . . . . . .

## *In This Chapter*

▶ Understanding why you need cash in your portfolio

▶ Staying protected

▶ Facing the evil truth about interest rates

. . . . . . . . . . . . . . . . . . . . . . . . . . . . . . . . . . . . . . . . . .

*Y*ou can easily think that stocks and shares are the only really challenging area of the investment business, and the only area that needs a lot of explaining in this book. But tens of millions of investors actually prefer to place their faith in cash investments of one sort of another.

And a good thing, too. As the saying goes, you never miss your water till the well runs dry, and lots of investors were left feeling very illiquid indeed when the stock markets failed to perform in the credit crunch of 2007-2008. The problem wasn't just that their equity investments weren't doing the business for them: people who hadn't set aside enough cash provisions to tide them through a difficult period found themselves suddenly running into quite serious problems with their banks, which were starting to take a tougher line on everybody's finances and had developed a distinct tendency to downgrade the credit ratings of those who hadn't got much in the way of liquid assets.

Meanwhile, people who put their money into safe but boring cash investments were enjoying investment returns that dwarfed what the stocks and shares investors were getting. Cash doesn't often beat equities over a prolonged period, but this has been one of those times.

## *Everybody Needs Some Cash*

Even the biggest stock market bull needs to invest in cash as well – no matter whether you're doing this to diversify your risks and protect yourself from stock market downturns, or whether you simply need a place to keep some of your cash between selling a stock and buying something else.

Being able to park your money in cash from time to time is one of the things that make you different from a professional fund manager. A fund manager doesn't have the option of keeping large sums of money in cash, the way you do – or not for long periods, anyway. If he does, he's in breach of his fund's rules that basically require him to stay invested all the time, with only short breaks in cash. (Things are a bit different for hedge fund managers, who can do anything at all; see Chapter 15.) But for a more conventional manager, the minimum-cash rule applies.

The reason this requirement is a problem for a fund manager, but good news for you, is that being able to take your money out of stocks and into cash from time to time is probably your best hope of beating the market! Doing so allows you to 'time the market' (if you're lucky and/or very skilful) by picking your entry and exit points carefully. During the bear market (see Chapter 4 for what these are) of early 2008, I shifted most of my investments out into cash, which allowed me to wait until the market had dropped quite a lot before I bought back into my shares. Timing the market precisely isn't easy, though. I'd have been in trouble if I'd been wrong about my suspicion that the market was about to fall steeply, because if shares had risen instead of falling then I wouldn't have gained anything at all – instead, I'd have been forced to buy the shares back for more than I paid for them.

For most people, the main point about having some cash investments is that they bring in interest instead of capital gains. The question is, what sort of interest do you need, and how do you intend to go about arranging it?

That probably sounds like a stupid question. But you need to be clear about two major issues: tax and time.

# The Tax Issue

Most people don't spend much effort thinking about the tax on cash investments. Unless you've got a fairly sophisticated portfolio and a very astute financial adviser, the money probably comes to you with the tax already deducted at source. You've probably seen the annual statements that the bank (or the building society, or whatever) sends you in the spring for the end of the tax year on 5 April. The statement tells you the gross amount your savings have earned during the outgoing financial year, and the amount of tax that's been deducted and paid straight to HM Revenue and Customs. All you ever see is the *net amount*.

The chances are that you stick your statements in a drawer and forget about them because nobody ever asks you for them. But steady on. The tax that's deducted at source is calculated at the standard rate of income tax, currently 20 per cent. That's all very well as long as you're not paying higher-rate tax on either your earnings or your savings. But if the combined weight of your salary and your interest income takes you over the threshold and into the higher band, then HM Revenue and Customs makes an additional deduction – either through your PAYE (Pay As You Earn) or through your twice-yearly tax bill if you're not a full-time employee. HMRC knows who you are because you provided the bank with your National Insurance details when you first opened the account.

The main exception to all this is if you don't pay any tax at all – for instance, if you're a child or a very low earner. Your bank or building society supplies you with Form R85 on request, which is a declaration that you're ineligible for tax and want your interest paid to you gross instead of net.

Some investors, especially wealthier individuals, find that being asked to pay income tax at the higher rate (currently 40 per cent) spoils the game. For these people, the attractions of having an income from cash investments are somewhat diminished – especially when you remember that if they invest in stocks and shares instead they could get an annual exemption of around £10,000 on all their capital gains. And that even if they had to pay capital gains tax (Chapter 5 has the lowdown on this tax) on what they made above that limit, it would still betaxed at only 18 per cent, which has been the standard capital gains tax level since spring 2008.

And, further, that if they choose to invest their money through tax-efficient ISAs, they don't have to pay any capital gains tax at all under any circumstances, although some income tax is payable on any dividends their shares pay out.

 Cash investments aren't for everyone. Before you automatically assume that cash is the right way forward for you, make sure that it really suits your lifestyle.

---

# Religious considerations

Devout Muslims don't want to earn interest on their cash balances because Shari'a law prohibits profiting from money lending.

A range of alternative arrangements is available to British Muslims, some of which involve accepting what amount to gifts in return for lending their cash. Other methods may mean effectively placing the money in trust.

This is a rather specialised area of investing, and requires more information than I really have room to include here. If you want to find out more, try contacting the European Islamic Investment Bank plc (www.eiib.co.uk). The EEIB was the first independent, Shari'a-compliant Islamic investment bank to be authorised and regulated by the UK Financial Services Authority, and it's still the best place to go for advice.

# Talking About Time

How long can you really afford to lock up your money for? Consider four basic questions:

✓ Are you just keeping a few thousand pounds in a current bank account so that you can feel secure in the knowledge that it's there if the car's gearbox goes bang tomorrow? People tend not to worry so much these days about having ready cash for such purchases, because credit cards and convenient bank loans have given us easy ways of plugging a gap of a couple of months in our finances. (Although we might like to add that these avenues haven't been quite so easy or so convenient since the credit crunch of 2007 forced the banks to rethink their easy lending policies.)

✓ Are you trying to build a nest egg over the long term, by making regular payments into a savings account to fund a big event later in your life? Paying for your children's university education, a holiday home, or a world cruise? A 'notice' or 'term' account is obviously the way to go.

With a notice account, you know that you aren't able to withdraw money at less than (say) a month's notice – or, if you can make a withdrawal, you either pay a charge or lose a chunk of the higher interest that these accounts normally pay.

✓ Can you positively guarantee that you don't want to access your money at short notice? And are you willing to lock up your money for a long period? If so, two obvious options are open to you.

One option is to take advantage of the National Savings & Investments bonds available from your post office, which often beat anything you can get from banks or building societies. Best of all, NS&I interest is paid tax free.

Another option is a cash ISA, which builds your nest-egg in a tax-free environment for as long as you like. You can pay in a limited sum every year (£3,600 per annum at the time of writing) and you can get at your money at any time.

✓ Are you saving to build a nest egg for a child? If so, consider child trust funds, which allow parents or grandparents to make regular payments into a tax-efficient growth fund, and either to claim the tax relief for themselves or to allow it to be paid back into the fund. The fund can be self-administered, or the management can be left to a professional; either way, the fund attracts two cash payments of £250 from the government at two separate stages of the child's life. (Additional government payments are available for children from deprived backgrounds) Then, when the child reaches the qualifying age (currently 18), the money in the child trust fund can be 'rolled over' into a tax-efficient ISA, even though it's probably much larger than the normal annual contribution limit for an ISA. More details are available at www.childtrustfund.gov.uk.

You have a lot of choices available, and most of them involve looking closely at your own lifestyle and figuring out what's right for you. If you're like most people, you decide you need a little of everything. You may, for instance, want to have £5,000 on instant access, another £20,000 or more in notice accounts, and the rest invested in cash ISAs and bonds for the longer term.

I probably ought to say that 'bond' is one of the most over-used words in the financial market's vocabulary. It can mean anything from the premium bonds you buy in the hope of a million-pound win, through to the 'guaranteed income bonds' that your building society offers (see Chapter 19), and of course the 'proper' kinds of bonds, which Chapter 6 covers and which are in a different league entirely because they carry risks and rewards that are hard to predict. That's not what you want for your cash investments at all!

# Running fast to stay ahead of inflation

An interest rate return is only worth having if it beats the inflation rate. I can well remember my father, back in the inflationary 1970s, discovering to his surprise that borrowing the money for his new car was cheaper than saving up his money for two years and then paying cash. That's because the interest rate he had to pay was below the inflation rate (what's called a *negative real interest rate*).

Negative real interest is a rare thing, of course, and its occurrence doesn't do anybody any good because it destabilises the whole of the financial system. If inflation is running at 10 per cent, you aren't going to lend £1,000 to your bank if that amount's only going to bring you a 5 per cent interest rate return, because this time next year you'll need £1,100 to buy what your £1,000 buys you today, whereas your 'increased' cash pile's only worth £1,050!

But then, you aren't so stupid as to sign up for a deal that delivers less than inflation, are you? Well, perhaps. If you buy a fixed-interest government bond that gives you a fixed 5 per cent for the next five years, you may be a bit perturbed if inflation suddenly picks up to 10 per cent. And if you lock up your money in a deposit account that pays you a variable rate, you may be a bit annoyed if the bank lowers the rate while still locking you in – or worse, if it moves your high-yielding account onto the back burner while you aren't looking, so that the interest rate quietly fades away. These things shouldn't happen, but they do.

The bottom line is that you really do need to stick a finger into the wind when you look at an interest rate, to try to measure how fast the inflation rate is moving. You may be surprised at how rare a *real interest rate* of more than about 2.5 per cent actually is.

# How safe is your money? Lessons from the credit crunch

Your money is safe in any bank or building society that's been authorised by the Financial Services Authority – and you're most unlikely ever to encounter one that isn't, because for anyone to offer you a deposit scheme in the UK without being registered is illegal. Even if the bank goes belly up, the Financial Services Compensation Scheme means that at least the first £50,000 of the money you hold in any one bank is secure, so you'll get your money back.

Okay, that's not strictly true. That's what a lot of people *think* happens if your bank goes bust. But in practice the arrangements are a bit more complicated, and there are a few pitfalls you ought to be aware of.

Firstly, let's stress again that the government guarantees your deposits up to the value of £50,000 in any one bank. (It used to be only £35,000, by the way, and even that protection was only partial.) Many investors who had more than £35,000/£50,000 have very sensibly tried over the years to sidestep their risk by making sure that they spread their money around between various banks, so that none of their accounts holds more than the guaranteed minimum. Thuis, somebody with a million pounds would need to open 20 accounts with 20 banks in order to be completely safe!

Unfortunately, even that probably wouldn't be enough. The current rules of the Financial Services Compensation Scheme say that, if you have two banks owned by the same financial group, then you only get one set of protection, worth just £50,000. You might not be aware that Royal Bank of Scotland and NatWest are simply two divisions of the same company, and that even if you had two separate accounts, one with each bank, your total protection would still only be £50,000 and not £100,000. The same thing applies with the Halifax and the Bank of Scotland, which are another pair of twins. Or

with Lloyds TSB and Cheltenham & Gloucester, which are another. Or with Abbey and Alliance & Leicester, both of which have been part of the Spanish banking group Santander for some time now. (Santander also owns the banking operations at Bradford & Bingley, which also collapsed completely during late 2008.)

And that brings us to the point. Because the credit crunch has now forced so many banks into shotgun marriages, it has effectively reduced the number of places where you can go if you want to keep your money safely spread around. The government is aware of this problem, and it might eventually agree to give you 'multiple cover' for several accounts within the same banking group. But at the time of writing it was still an issue that savers needed to be aware of.

Ironically, not all banks have this problem. Some banks have been nationalised since the credit crunch began, including the failed Northern Rock and, briefly, Bradford & Bingley. In these cases the government has extended an unlimited 100 per cent guarantee to savers' deposits, on the reasoning that these banks are now owned by the state, and that the state won't go bust. Some other European countries, including Germany, have also guaranteed 100 per cent of their countrymens' savings.

Finally, there's another group of savers who have been perspiring mightily in recent times. Investors who've stashed their money in offshore tax havens, such as the Isle of Man, are still very unsure of where they stand on the deposit guarantees. And those who have invested their money directly into certain exotic bank products issued by foreign banks - especially in Iceland, where the banking system collapsed in 2008 - may not get all of it back. Frankly, we don't know what will happen to these people.

That's not to say you're necessarily better to put your money into stocks and shares, of course. As investors found out in the first half of 2008, when the stock market dropped by nearly 20 per cent, many things are worse than a 2.5 per cent real interest rate!

If you have a conventional account with an old-fashioned broker who handles your affairs for you, the chances are that you're able to use these interludes to make a bit of interest on the side while your money's out of the game. But the situation isn't so good if you're running a tax-efficient self-select Maxi ISA (Individual Savings Account; see Chapter 1 for more on these) instead.

Sad to say, you probably aren't able to get much interest on your money while it's sitting in a share ISA provider's trustee account waiting to be redeployed. They don't offer much interest, if any, because they know full well that the ISA rules don't exactly encourage you to swap your money out of the ISA and into a bank at will. The thing is, every in-payment to an ISA counts as part of your annual ISA contribution quota, even if you've only parked it somewhere else temporarily. So if you move, say, £1,000 into the building society and then back into your ISA, and then repeat the action seven or eight times in a year, you use up all your annual ISA entitlement and eventually the ISA provider refuses your money because you've exceeded your quota.

# Getting Price Information

Where can you find price information on the returns you can expect to get from your cash investments?

Almost anywhere, is the answer. The Sunday papers are full of listings that tell you which are the top-performing deposit accounts this week. They don't tell you about accounts that have been closed, or about deals that are now off the table – unless they're talking about National Savings bonds, where they often give you figures that relate to closed issues.

Just for once, the *Financial Times* is probably not the best place to go looking for a listing of interest-bearing accounts. Because its emphasis is on business-related matters for professionals, it tends to pass over the small private investor. The main exceptions are the *FT*'s Weekend section, and the occasional supplements it publishes for wealthier investors.

The *Daily Mail* and *Mail on Sunday*, the *Times* and *Sunday Times*, and the *Daily Telegraph* and *Sunday Telegraph* get the mix about right. You'll find comparison tables that set out the best buys, the lowest rates, and details of where to get more information.

You can also get excellent advice and information from price comparison web sites such as www.comparethemarket.com, or from so-called fund supermarkets and portals like Interactive Investor (www.iii.com) that will present you with a huge range of options, together with details of the special conditions that often apply to these products. (You'd be surprised at how often an attractive 'headline rate' is only available for the first twelve months, after which the interest rate heads straight back down to something much less attractive.)

But for many investors, the best and most comprehensive resource for making price comparisons is still the good old Motley Fool. The UK incarnation of the Fool, at www.fool.co.uk, is set up especially to meet the needs of British investors (as distinct from the parent site www.fool.com, which is aimed primarily at Americans).

## The Fool School

The Motley Fool UK website runs online tutorials called Your Money (the original Fool School operates in the United States for investing beginners of all ages). The tutorial articles are backed up by specialist articles that appear in your inbox almost every day, and they contain a variety of sharp and often witty observations.

The Motley Fool is very keen on a practice called *stoozing*. This involves borrowing money from a credit card at a zero rate for balance transfers and then investing the money in some sort of cash deposit account at maybe 6 per cent. Net result: you're in profit even if you have to pay a fee for the 'free' transfer. Just as long as you remember to draw the money out again and pay off your credit card balance before the free period ends. If you forget to do so, you're likely to find that your interest rate reverts to the standard cash withdrawal rate, which will probably be eye-watering - rates of 25 per cent and more are not uncommon. You've been warned!

The Motley Fool is also hot on the heels of the bank and credit card practice of charging ridiculously high fees for overstepping your overdraft limit, or for missing a payment instalment. The Office of Fair Trading has repeatedly stated that a bank should only make a charge that relates to its actual costs in these circumstances – which means that the banks are underhand when they hit you for fees of up to £35 a time, because their true costs are probably closer to £5 when you overstep your limits. This is an issue that will probably run and run, because the banks are contesting it through the courts. They insist that, if it weren't for these charges, they'd have to charge all their customers for routine banking services that they're currently getting for free.

But in the meantime, The Motley Fool runs an entire discussion forum devoted solely to the practice of getting your unfair bank charges refunded. Some people have had refunds of several thousand pounds.

The Motley Fool's articles are presented in blog format so readers can add their own comments about them. Although not everybody talks sense, on the basis that you can hardly go wrong by listening to all points of view, you can only benefit from the discussions.

If you're not sure which sort of deposit rate is right for you, or if you don't know how much you can put into your cash ISA, or if you want to know your APRs from your AERs, then the Fool School's the place to be.

# Knowing Your APRs from Your AERs

In theory, you shouldn't any longer have a problem understanding the interest rates banks charge when they lend to you – or offer when you're doing the lending and they're the borrowers. The regulators thought they'd done the job years ago when they required all lending institutions to print their offered rates as Annual Percentage Rates (APRs). But they were wrong, because the banks and lending institutions soon discovered a hundred different ways to tweak the figures, for better or (usually) for worse.

## Working out the APR

In theory, the APR wasn't a bad idea. It was supposed to tell you how much your loan would really cost you over the course of a year, by adding in the cost of any up-front fees to the nominal cost of the loan. That sounds simple, doesn't it? And to be honest, the APR's still the best way of comparing the rates from two lenders.

So what was life like before APR? Well, back in the bad old days, if a lender intended to charge you 10 per cent a year, he could tell you he was going to do that in any one of three ways:

- 0.7974 per cent effective monthly interest rate.
- 9.569 per cent annual interest rate compounded monthly.
- 9.091 per cent annual rate in advance.

And all of them produced exactly the same result. So guess which way he chose to sell you the loan? The first way, of course, if he thought he could get away with it, because you'd think you were only paying seven-point something instead of ten-point nothing.

The old 'effective monthly interest rate' is still common among loan sharks, pawn shops, and other people who don't do everything in writing and who don't think their customers are very bright. So the introduction of APR did at least force all the mainstream lenders to standardise and come clean, so that you're in with half a chance of making an informed choice.

Why is APR still too complex for most people to calculate for themselves? Because your brain simply isn't wired to deal with what accountants call *amortisation*. If I tell you that you're going to pay 10 per cent APR on a £1,000 one-year loan, with 12 equal capital repayments and no up-front fees, you probably figure out that you'll end up paying £100 in interest. You're wrong.

The reason you're wrong is that, although you certainly pay £8.50 in interest (£1,000 x 10/12) in the first month, your second month's interest payment's less than that. Remember, you've paid off one-twelfth of the capital as well as the interest, so now you only owe maybe £917 instead of £1,000. In the second month you're paying £7.63 in interest (£919 x 10/12), and in the third month £6.94 in interest (£833 x 10 / 12). Over the year as a whole, your average capital debt at any one time is exactly £500, or half of your original loan, because you're paying the loan off in equal instalments.

Even that model's too simple, though. Mostly people don't pay back loans and mortgages in equal capital instalments at all. Instead, the lender smooths out the taper to keep the monthly payments equal. In practice, that means that in the first months the lender only deducts a small capital repayment from the loan balance, so that a large part of the monthly payment is interest. By the end of the term, conversely, most of the payment is capital and only a tiny part is interest.

This *amortisation effect* makes working out exactly how much you're paying, for what, and at what point of the loan pretty well impossible for anyone without a degree in advanced maths. That's why investors depend so much on the benevolent rule of the Financial Services Authority to maintain order on their behalf and stop them from getting fleeced.

## Working out the AER

When it comes to investing your money in a savings account (or whatever), you want to know the Annual Equivalent Rate (AER). The AER is the real, absolutely genuine amount that you get from your savings account after a year, after making allowance for the effects of compounding. That's why it's also known as the *effective interest rate*.

But please note that the AER doesn't normally include the effects of any front-end charges, which may increase the bill. And AER gets into a right tangle if the loan is a multi-year arrangement that pays a different rate in the first and second years. That's quite common, by the way, in cash ISAs and savings builder accounts that try to lure you in with big first-year rates followed by not-so-big rates in the following years. Tread warily.

# Dodging Sneaky Bank Tricks

You may need the banks, but that doesn't mean that you have to put up with *everything* they decide to do to you.

As much as 85 per cent of a normal bank's revenues is estimated to come from the fines and fees it earns from people who don't manage their accounts well. I've talked about the very large fees of £35 or more that some banks charge on unauthorised overdrafts. But they're after your money in other ways too.

One is by holding your money for up to a week between the time you pay it in and the time it appears on your account. If you pay in a cheque today, the money may not be available for withdrawal until four or five working days have passed – and it probably won't be earning interest for you. This is nonsense, because banks can flash money across to each other in a couple of hours, and they have access to your cash a long time before you do. In effect, they're borrowing three or four days' worth of your interest.

How much interest are you getting on your current bank account? 75 per cent of people have no idea, and the rate's often just 0.1 per cent. You can make a difference by shopping around. At the time of writing Barclays were offering 2.5 per cent a year on a standard account, while Halifax were going as high as 5.12 per cent providing that you paid in at least £1,000 a month. But clearly, you'll need to do your own research if you want to know what's current right now.

Another favourite bank tactic, and one that annoys the regulators considerably, is the habit of persuading you to include *Payment Protection Insurance* (PPI) when you take out a bank loan. The general idea is that if you lose your job or fall ill, the PPI scheme carries on making the minimum payment instalments on your loans until you're fixed up again.

That may sound like a good idea, but it can add as much as 11 per cent to the annual interest rate on a typical loan. And all too often the PPI providers forget to mention that PPIs are mostly unsuitable for self-employed people, because you have to go through about a year's grief with HM Revenue and Customs before you get the paperwork that you need to be 'officially' out of work.

Worse, some banks have been caught slipping these PPI policies into their loan packages as part of the deal, so that their customers have no real choice about whether to take them up. A few online loan provider sites have sneaked them in by including an opt-out button for the PPI, which they hide so well that punters never even see it. All of this is illegal, and with luck it ought to stop soon.

PPIs are to the banks what extended warranties are to the electrical goods retailers in your high street – that is, they're three or four times too expensive in relation to what you get. The telephone salesperson trying to get you to sign up tells you that the PPI is only going to cost you 80p a month for every £100 you borrow. But when you realise that this is equivalent to £9.60 a year, or 9.6 per cent extra on top of your interest costs, it looks a little different.

Also consider routine service charges and premium accounts. Some high-street banks charge you a fee every time you cash a cheque or make a credit card transfer, and some credit cards make an annual charge, plus a withdrawal fee for cash. Some give you cash back, while others charge you a flat monthly fee for an account including a bundle of goodies that you probably don't need – such as travel insurance or Airmiles – but don't charge you for transactions.

 Some let you open foreign currency accounts at attractive prices, while others struggle with a euro cheque. They give a lousy exchange rate and charge up to £30 for even looking at the cheque. Choose wisely.

You do have a choice.

# Part III
# Delving Deeper into the Financial Pages

'He was a lousy economist but his charts caught the eye of a famous art critic & dealer.'

Part III

Delving Deeper

Into the Financial

Pages

## In this part . . .

This section is probably better suited for readers who've already got a rudimentary grasp of stock market basics. The tricky thing with share investing is that sometimes the devil sits among the details. I'll show you where he's likely to be lurking, and how you can spot him before he sees you coming. We also look at special situations like takeovers, and I show you how to read the official regulatory information sources that are absolutely, positively guaranteed to give you the plain unvarnished truth – on pain of jail!

We end this section with a look at so-called technical analysis, which is the black art of using charting techniques to second-guess what the market's going to do next. Is it a valid analytical technique or just superstition and voodoo? You decide.

# Chapter 8

# Sharpening Your Understanding

## In This Chapter

▶ Reading the statutory announcements for fun and profit

▶ Understanding how the market values a company

▶ Considering why asset valuations can throw everything off balance

▶ Facing the dreaded pensions liability issue

*I* don't think I'm going to shock you too badly if I say that the financial media is really only one of the places to look for clues when you set out to choose a new investment. Or for news about how the investments you've already got are faring. In this chapter I explore some of the less obvious routes that help you fine-tune your strategy and hopefully pick up more profitable signals. Sometimes – just sometimes – the market isn't wrong at all when it decides to avoid a stock, or maybe even mark it down quite savagely. The market's often illogical but it isn't stupid. Ever been struck by how every fish in a shoal simultaneously changes direction in a split second, apparently without reason? And then, as often as not, the real cause becomes clear – a larger fish comes into view ,or they've encountered a cold current. This chapter helps you understand the pack behaviour of investors: why they suddenly veer off in one direction or dodge out of the way without warning. You, too, can spot the subtle signs and know how to respond. But only if you know where to look. . . .

# Understanding Statutory Announcements

Trading updates, profit warnings, and interim statements – as you can imagine, a comprehensive regulatory system exists, which you can utilise to keep tabs on what listed companies are doing. What you may not expect is that looking up these company announcements is not the least bit complicated. And on many occasions, as a journalist and an investor, I've been able to get the scoop on the market by reading such statements before the rest of the press and the media have woken up.

These statements are called regulatory announcements, and they're ferociously policed and enforced. I once worked for an agency that wrote the announcements and then passed them up to the relevant official scrutineers to approve them for release to the public through one of the officially approved channels. Often we had only hours to get the announcements ready, because companies are required to give *immediate* notice to the regulators if any one of a hundred different things happens. So we were up all night talking to the regulators, and we knew we could only publish once they'd picked over every last little dot and comma. Any mistakes, and we were in court. You don't mess with the regulator.

## When does a company have to make a regulatory announcement?

A company must make an announcement when:

- ✔ It knows the final date on which its financial results are being published. Those might be its full-year trading results, or perhaps the figures for the first six months of its financial year, or even just a trading update to let the shareholders know whether it's on course to meet its forecasts.

- ✔ Those results are finally published and available to view.

- ✔ A new director's been appointed, or one's about to leave.

- ✔ It receives a takeover offer, or it thinks one may be coming soon.

- ✔ Takeover talks end, or the offer is rejected, accepted, or updated.

- ✔ It changes its accountant.

- ✔ It issues a dividend.

- ✔ It changes its accounting date.

- ✔ Its shares are suspended, cancelled, or delisted.

- ✔ Its Annual General Meeting is due, or its AGM results are published.

- ✔ Any director buys or sells even a tiny quantity of the company's own shares.

- ✔ A big shareholder has tripped a regulatory tripwire by buying or selling a quantity of shares that takes that shareholder into a new category (more than 3 per cent, more than 20 per cent, less than 10 per cent, and so forth).

- ✔ The company's planning a rights issue (extra shares to shore up the balance sheet with new money) – or at any significant time thereafter in the rights process.

And that list's only a sample. But you've got to admit that, as an investor, that's just the kind of stuff you want the company to tell you about. Nobody's ever going to call these official announcements a riveting read, but you need to know where they are when you want to lay your hands on them. Nothing's better than having the raw facts.

The Regulatory News Service section at the London Stock Exchange should be one of your Favourites in your web browser. You can find it at www.london stockexchange.com, hidden away in the section labelled Information Products and Services. (Or simply select a company through the Investor Centre section, and that company's recent RNS reports will come up alongside all the charts and other information.)You can also get reprints of the same information from Citywire (www.citywire.co.uk), the *Financial Times*, the Motley Fool's UK-Wire service (fool.uk-wire.com), supplied by Prestel, Investegate (www.investegate.co.uk), or many cable television channels. The announcements also turn up on financial news agencies like AFP, Reuters, or Bloomberg, although you may have to pay for those.

Why are the regulations about announcements so strict? Simply because the authorities are absolutely paranoid about wrong information being passed to investors. And they're just as paranoid about the chance that one investor may get better access to the latest red-hot news than all the rest. So once an announcement's finally been published on one of the approved channels, it goes out at the same split second to every financial institution, every news agency, every broadcasting channel, and everyone who can be bothered to look it up on the stock market's own website.

The RNS, which belongs to the London Stock Exchange itself, is the best-known channel for releasing official information in Britain. AFX UK Focus is another regulations publisher, but I'm trying to keep things simple.

I don't want to raise your expectations – 90 per cent of these statements are as fascinating as boiled mud, and they mean about that much too. And most of the big stories make it into the papers fairly fast. But when you really want to know what the company actually said, rather what somebody's trying to kid you it said, you find no substitute to getting it from the horse's mouth.

Besides, most RNS announcements don't happen all that often – ten times a year, maybe less – and so seeing what's going on when a new RNS announcement gets flagged up is always worthwhile.

Okay, I want to look at a couple of typical RNS announcements that you're very likely to see from time to time. As you can quickly gather, they usually have pretty self-explanatory titles. A simple example follows, which says that Capital Group International now holds more than 3 per cent of Future. The market needs to be told this because it may want to keep an eye on Capital in case it decides to sell or maybe engage in a takeover at some future date.

**Holdings in Company**

**TR-1: NOTIFICATION OF MAJOR INTERESTS IN SHARES**

1. Identity of the issuer or the underlying issuer of existing shares to which voting rights are attached: Future Plc – GB0007239980

2. Reason for the notification (please indicate with an X):

An acquisition or disposal of voting rights: X

An acquisition or disposal of financial instruments which may result in the acquisition of shares already issued to which voting rights are attached:

An event changing the breakdown of voting rights:

Other (please specify):

3. Full name of person(s) subject to the notification obligation: Capital Group International Inc.

(Sections 4–6 left out: they're not that interesting)

7. Threshold(s) crossed or reached: 3 per cent

8. Resulting situation after the triggering transaction:

| Class/type of shares | Number of shares | Number of voting rights | Percentage of voting rights |
|---|---|---|---|
| Ordinary | 10,112,875 | 10,112,875 | 3.0945 |

The announcement in the following paragraph reveals that the company has taken on extra debt by issuing some corporate bonds. (It's calling these debts 'Notes', which is usual.) The bonds are nothing to get excited about, because they're just a routine instalment of a very large pre-planned programme of debt releases that was announced a long time ago. But if they're a new and unexpected issue you may be within your rights to wonder whether your equity's being diluted!

**Issue of Debt**

**SEVERN TRENT UTILITIES FINANCE PLC**

Issue of debt

Severn Trent Utilities Finance plc announces that it has today issued £700,000,000 5.25 per cent Notes due 11 March 2016 unconditionally and irrevocably guaranteed by Severn Trent Water Limited under its £3,500,000,000 Euro Medium Term Note Programme

The bond issue shouldn't affect the value of your shares, because the stock market was expecting it and presumably 'priced it in' to its calculations a long time ago. But £3.5 billion is a lot of money all the same. You can see why the regulators are so keen on your knowing about it.

## *When a company hits the skids*

Subsea Resources was a wreck-diving company that went under for the last time in 2008, having failed to get its vessels into the right wrecks at the right time because of bad weather, equipment failures, and some awkward tangles with its suppliers. Figure 8-3 shows the RNS that carried the first indication that the game was probably up.

### Suspension of Shares

SubSea Resources PLC 04 March 2008

Suspension of shares and decision to seek to secure sale of the assets and business of the Company

SubSea is an AIM-traded company which specialises in the research, survey and salvage of high value non-ferrous metals and other valuable cargoes from deep-water ship-wrecks

### Suspension of shares

The Board announces that it has requested the suspension of its ordinary shares and warrants from trading on AIM pending clarification of its financial position.

### Decision to seek to secure sale of the assets and business of the Company

As noted below under 'Discussions – Update', since the announcement of 27 December 2007, the Board has been in discussions with a number of parties, including with the Company's Bondholder. Most regrettably, these discussions have not been successful.

Suspending the shares simply means that the stock market's saying, 'Whoa, hold everything while we clarify this situation.' Until the shares are reinstated, if ever, the shares can (in theory) be traded privately, but not on the Stock Exchange platform. In practice, they're almost worthless when they're in this state.

The death knell was sounded before long, as this announcement demonstrates.

### Appointment of Administrator

SUBSEA RESOURCES PLC ('SubSea' or the 'Company')

### Notice of Intention to Appoint an Administrator

On 4 March 2008 the Board announced that, 'it has requested the suspension of its ordinary shares and warrants from trading on AIM pending clarification of its financial position'. The Board further announced inter alia its 'decision to seek to secure the sale of the assets and business of the Company and the appointment of Kroll as sale agent'.

The Board also noted that '... there can be no assurance that such a sale will actually complete or that, if it does, after repayment of all monies due to the Bondholder, the Company will be able to continue to trade.'

Having reviewed the current status of the sale process, the Board has considered the options available to it and has concluded that no viable option is available to meet the Company's cash needs in the short term. Consequently, the Company has today instructed its lawyers to file a notice of intention to appoint administrators over the Company.

The shareholders in this situation know that their chances of getting anything at all back on their investment are very limited. And the final *coup de grace* came a week later when FTSE, the company that runs the London stock market listings, announced that Subsea Resources had been struck off the FTSE register.

From here on, a couple of months were required to tidy up and then everyone went home. As Figure 8-1 shows, the shares plummeted from 14p in January 2007 to practically zero 14 months later.

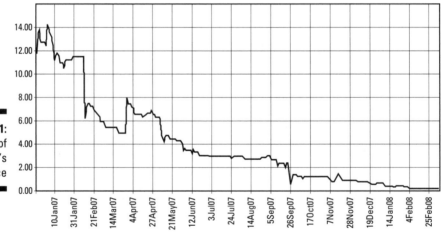

**Figure 8-1:**
Graph of
SubSea's
share price

What can you learn from the RNS that you can't get from the company's directors themselves? Guessing's disrespectful, because this particular board went to a lot of effort to keep its investors very well informed of the various crises, hopes, chances, and disappointments that preceded its eventual disappearance between the waves. But if the thought ever crosses anyone's mind that they may get away with a less open approach, the regulatory announcements system keeps them on a very short leash indeed – which is reassuring news for all of us.

## 'Responding to press comment': Emergency announcements, updates, and what to do about them

Situations often arise in which a company decides to use the RNS system to make a statement that the law doesn't strictly require. It's perfectly free to make these statements, and they're just as rigorously checked and policed as any other kind of RNS statement, so you can rely on them just as much. Except, that is, that you're hearing the words of the board of directors, which may not be wholly disinterested.

Mostly, these statements are completely benign. Nearly all of them are just interim trading statements, which are really just routine buzzings intended to reassure the shareholders that the company's on target to achieve its projected goals. A typical interim trading statement from a major British engineering company might look something like this.

> XXX p.l.c., the industrial switchgear importer, provides an Interim Management Statement for the three month period to 31 June 2008.
>
> Order intake has continued the strong trend which was referred to at the time of the preliminary results, being 25 per cent higher in the second quarter than the same period of 2007. On a like-for-like basis, excluding the YYY acquisition, order intake was up 19 per cent. Increased demand for XXX's products was spread across our geographic regions, end user industries and business divisions. Cost pressures continue to be mitigated by sourcing and engineering cost reduction initiatives. The order book at the end of March reached GBP185m, which is 28 per cent up on the position as at 31 December 2007 or, adjusting for the YYY order book on acquisition it increased by 24 per cent.

Boring, isn't it? And what's more, this announcement doesn't offer you any audited figures, but only a sort of keep-it-up-lads encouragement that tells the investors everything's going okay. The company isn't releasing the final audited figures for quite some time yet, but the announcement ought to give you the flavour of the way things are going if you're an anxious investor. That's good for you and good for the company, because you're more likely to hold onto the shares while you wait for the final announcement.

In this particular instance, you notice that the company's been keen to make allowance for the fact that it bought company YYY during the year, and that this acquisition boosted the overall speed and performance by strapping an extra engine on the back. So if you're impressed by its 25 per cent sales growth, you're being reminded that the like-for-like growth (without that extra engine) was only 19 per cent.

This is good, honest reporting that doesn't try to pull the wool over your eyes. The next paragraph offers another official release, from a North American company that extracts a type of petroleum through a special industrial process:

> During the first quarter, industrial operations were negatively impacted by a weather-related outage, and by lower than anticipated production following the outage. There were also some technical problems with the upgrader, which have now been resolved. Reflecting the loss of production volumes in the first quarter and moderated expectations for the remainder of the year, the Board has reduced its forecast for annual petroleum production to 7 million barrels.

Also, why do you query using the name of the company for Rotork but not Canadian Royal Sands? Is the above verbatim and do you need perm to reproduce it? See my comments on Rotork above, thanks.

The report in Figure 8-7 is honest, straightforward, and gives shareholders the information they need. In fact, they didn't take much persuading to forgive the company for its acknowledged failings: the share price rose by 16 per cent in the next four weeks, and the company was soon able to raise its dividend to the shareholders significantly. Official announcements can be a great way of confessing problems to shareholders in a way that won't make them think you're trying to dodge the dicculties.

But I'm missing the point if I don't say that many such announcements are issued mainly to fend off speculation during a crisis, and to give the board of directors a bit of a break while they think about what to do next. The next few paragraphs are a couple of RNS extracts from a specialist retail operation that was struggling pretty badly:

> During Q1 the sales from our seasonal product areas were poor. This held back sales at our out-of-town retail centres, which have predominantly a seasonal bias. The broader product range now being introduced is having a positive effect, but because the weather adversely affected footfall in Q1 this has not increased sales as much as expected. Like for like sales (including pre-acquisition sales from our recent acquisitions) decreased by 28 per cent.

> Whilst sales currently remain strong it is increasingly unlikely that we will recover all of the shortfall. Sales and profits are therefore expected to be somewhat below current market expectations for both H1 and the full year.

# Mind-boggling minutes

Not every RNS announcement takes its duties so seriously. Because the announcement normally carries the full text of the chairperson's speech, some quite outrageously cynical, funny, and downright scurrilous things find their way into the stock market regulator's official records.

There was, for instance, the company which held a special shareholders' meeting at which one director demanded the immediate removal of all directors except himself. The other directors responded by alleging that the complainant was an incompetent troublemaker who'd been having an affair with his secretary. And all of this was soberly recorded in the official records – as any good meeting's minutes are.

Meanwhile, old RNS hands always keep a lookout for the RNS statements from one South American mining company registered in London, whose Chairman's statements never fail to amuse. Here's a recent extract from one of his offerings, published at the height of the 2008 credit crunch:

" . . . The gruesome truth has now emerged that Bankers and their hired-hand Magicians, intoxicated by greed and dancing with the devilry of Derivatives, far from fostering a Golden Goose, have succeeded in nearly extinguished the Western financial system . . . Those of us who retain that deluded belief in Gold, that Barbarous Relic, fortified by its mystique and durability over thousands of years, can only wonder at the swift acceptance of the ultimately insane trust in Swaps and Derivatives, incomprehensible to all but their progenitors, and very likely including them . . .

'The warnings of the wise against "Financial Weapons of Mass Destruction" went unheeded, and the downward spiral of the United States into a humiliated entity led by a former Master of the Universe, and teetering on the edge of Bankruptcy, threatens to bring down the Banking system as it has evolved over centuries. The Emperor has been discovered to have no clothes, and his cohorts have been found to be swimming naked . . . '

Etcetera, etcetera:

What happened next was:

> On 10 August 2005 Gemstar Acquisitions Limited , a company formed at the direction of funds managed and advised by Camdec Finance Limited [a venture capital company] announced that it was considering making a offer for the issued share capital of XXX, and that Loseley Partners Limited [a team of 'activist shareholders' that held 27 per cent of the company] had undertaken to accept such an offer if it was announced by 2 December 2005 at a price of at least 580 pence per share.

> The Board does not believe the continuing uncertainty as to a possible takeover is in the best interests of the Company or its shareholders and, accordingly, the Board has terminated discussions with Camdec Finance.

The chairman blustered on for a while about how the whole takeover approach had been a 'massive distraction' that prevented his staff from getting on with the winter season and damaged the company's prospects still further. But the chief executive resigned, and six months later the company fell to another raid by a private equity group, and that was the end of that. If you'd been reading the RNS reports, blow by blow, you'd soon have found what you needed to make a thumping profit out of this takeover. I did – I made a quick 30 per cent in a few months.

## Changes to controlling shareholdings

The stock market keeps a very sharp eye on who owns how much of each company, because it's determined that everybody should know in advance if one shareholder has a controlling stake. If a lot of smaller shareholders each hold a few percent of the company, then matters may get difficult if they all gang up together and try to remove the board by force, or if they launch a hostile takeover bid for the company.

The previous section describes that kind of bluster occurring in the retailing takeover story. When the going gets tough, which investors are aligned with which other ones can really start to matter. And in only a single day someone can launch a coup that upsets everybody's plans. That's another reason the RNS people are so hot on your being told of any changes in the shareholding patterns – immediately, and on pain of prosecution!

## The takeover rules

Britain's takeover rules can be pretty complex, because things like competition rules are always getting in the way of deals that may otherwise seem straightforward. And different criteria apply to companies of different sizes. But to keep things simple, under normal conditions the following rules apply to a listed company:

- ✔ If any one shareholder (or any group of shareholders acting together as a so-called concert party) accumulates 30 per cent of the equity in the company, the law requires that shareholder to make a formal offer for all of the remaining shares in the company.

- ✔ The law says that the price the shareholder offers mustn't be less than any price she's paid for her shares during the last three months. In other words, if the shares are worth 30p, I can't go round buying up other people's shares for a generous 50p each, but then drop my bid back to 35p as soon as I've got the required 30 per cent of the equity. That's just playing dirty. In this case I have to price my bid at a minimum of 50p.

✔ I now have to make a formal announcement through the official channels – which effectively means that I'm doing it through RNS. I have to state my honourable intentions and name my opening price; although in practice I may very well raise that price as the negotiations go on. I can't breathe a word about the takeover approach to a living soul until I've issued that first formal statement.

✔ If, by any chance, word does leak out to the press that a bid's on the cards before I lodge my actual bid (and yes, that does happen), I have to make a public statement straight away, confirming or denying that I'm considering a bid. But I'm not asked to name a price until I'm ready, or until I've got 30 per cent of the shares.

✔ Conversely, if the object of my desire notices that its share price is being affected by takeover speculation, it usually makes a statement to say that talks with (normally) unnamed suitors are in progress. The company may also decide to open itself up to other offers and start a bidding war for itself!

Since I'm a gentleman, I try for an 'agreed offer', in which the target company appears on a balcony with me and implores its shareholders to accept my kind offer of marriage. But if I'm in Dick Dastardly mode I may simply try to win the shareholders over without their board's approval. To do this I have to persuade enough shareholders to part with their investments to leave me with 90 per cent of the equity. Then I can steamroller the remaining 10 per cent, no matter how much they may not like it.

Something called the Rules Governing the Substantial Acquisition of Shares used to force a large shareholder to start making declarations as soon as her equity holdings reached 15 per cent. But that has become rather cumbersome now that big financial institutions own such large chunks of listed companies, and so the rules have been dropped.

You can always find out who owns large parts of a company by checking the company's own website, or by using online resources such as Hoovers, a well-known financial firm offering company information (www.hoovers.co.uk), or Hemmington Scott (www.hemscott.com). Alternatively, the company's latest annual report will have details of the big shareholders.

Don't be surprised if company reports turn out to include the company's own pension scheme, by the way – this is normal and doesn't suggest the company's slipping down the same route as Enron, the US energy giant that dragged its pension funds down with it when it went bust. Modern legislation is much more robust than that.

Check the state of a company's 'free float'. This is the percentage figure that tells you how many of the company's shares are genuinely in the free market for the world in general to purchase, as distinct from the proportions that so-called captive shareholders (banks, subsidiary owners, and other big guns closely connected to the company) hold. In a small company that doesn't have a full stock exchange listing you may easily find that the board itself holds 51 per cent. This can seriously cramp an aspiring acquirer's style. (Chapter 9 covers free float in detail.)

# *How the Media Is Regulated*

In Britain, the financial markets (not just the stock market) are regulated by the Financial Services Authority, a pretty fearsome beast that takes a very direct interest in how the press handles itself. As a financial journalist, I'm always talking to people who can give me information about a company that the general public aren't aware of, so no surprise that the regulator's hand is never very far from the back of my collar. Which is fair enough. The editors responsible for the newsletters on which I work are required to be specially registered, qualified, and accredited by the FSA, so that they don't accidentally fall foul of the publishing rules about financial products. The course of qualifications is gruelling, often takes six months, and involves an awful lot of exams.

Sometimes I even have to warn my friends and family not to talk to me about things going on in the companies where they work. For all I know, those companies may be entering the annual 'closed period' – that's the month or so before the date its audited accounts are published, when the company's under orders to remain absolutely silent to the press about anything financial (also the period during which the directors and other insiders aren't allowed to buy or sell any shares in their own companies). Oh yes, the freedom of the press doesn't come without a few limitations on my civil liberties.

One thing that really worries the FSA is that I may get involved in a so-called 'insider trading' scandal, using my privileged knowledge about the company to buy shares that only I know are about to make it big. (I might, for instance, get wind of an impending takeover offer that hasn't been released to the media. While I was working on the RNS releases, this sort of privy information was everywhere I looked.)

Of course, if I'd been a director of the company the situation would have been just the same. I'd have been immediately under the FSA's lens if I, as a director, had bought or sold any shares just before the price jumped sharply. Or, indeed, if any of my friends had done the same. Both they and I would have been in terrible trouble if anything of the kind was suspected.

In practice, nobody really doubts that insider trading goes on all the time in the London market – and far more often than that in some other countries. People talk in the bars, they cadge favours from friends in the big financial institutions, and last but not least, as we saw in the 1990s, situations occur in which the big multi-agency accounting firms allow gaps to appear in the 'Chinese walls' that are supposed to stop the investing sides of their operations from knowing what their colleagues in the consultancy divisions are saying to the very same companies in which they're investing (Chapter 1 has more on Chinese walls).

In some parts of the world insider trading is still regarded as a natural perk of the job. It used to be universal in Italy until the rules were tightened up. In Germany insider trading wasn't a crime at all until the 1990s! And in various emerging markets the liberal use of what people euphemistically call palm oil is still pretty widespread. The regulator's task is to combat insider trading, but realistically the chances of stopping it are pretty limited.

But I want to return for a moment to my responsibilities as a journalist. If I were anything less than the towering paragon of virtue I am, I might try to use my inside knowledge to perform a different trick. I might decide to short-sell shares that I know are about to land in trouble. If I were to find out that some merger talks have collapsed but that the news hasn't made the paper yet, I might make a killing – and get 12 months in jail for breaking the insider trading rules. Hmmm.

But the worst sin of all occurs if I engage in some sort of 'pump-and-dump' scam. In theory I could pick any company's shares, good or bad, buy a load of them, and then write an article telling you how great they were. Once you've all rushed out and bought a barrowload of the things, I sell up and pocket the profit, with a big thank-you to my readers for driving up the share price so nicely.

That one would probably land me in the Old Bailey, followed by a long stretch at Her Majesty's pleasure. So to protect people like you from people like me, special rules govern my behaviour that don't apply to you.

I can't, for instance, buy or sell shares in any of the companies I mention in my articles, within a certain period before or after the date when the articles are written and published. (The same goes for the editors, the designers, even the print room staff and the newspaper despatch van drivers, all of whom could make a lot of money in a few hours if they didn't have any morals.)

You won't find me in Ladbrokes putting any bets on who's going to be in the Queen's New Year's Honours List, because half of Fleet Street knows the full list of recipients a week in advance. And if I do have any long-standing investment interests in any of the shares I mention – which does happen – I'm expected to declare them to my editor and then make sure I don't trade them for at least a month after the publication date.

As a final defence, many of my most sensitive publications (newsletters and tipsheets, for instance) employ teams of beady-eyed compliance checkers, whose entire function consists in doubting everything I say and then forcing me to prove it. If I can't prove it, the information doesn't go in the publication. Finally, a lawyer looks everything over to make sure that I haven't done anything even obscurely illegal. And all that system is in place at the FSA's insistence.

Why am I telling you all this?

Partly to remind you that the press's honesty is not something people simply take for granted. The system has teeth, pretty big ones, and everything falls apart if the safeguards don't work properly. And partly to remind you that when you go onto Internet chat rooms to seek out the wisdom of total strangers, you're entering a world that the regulatory system hardly reaches. And a world where the ground is ripe for ploughing by rampers and pump-and-dumpers, all hiding behind pseudonyms, who would simply love you to see things their way.

Never take anything you read on a blog seriously until you've double-checked it against a reliable, reputable source where the writers and journalists are properly trained – and punished if they goof. Laws do govern bloggers, but they're utterly unenforceable because so many of the posters are untraceable.

# Valuing a Company Correctly

Prepare to shed any illusions you may have about just how solid the numbers are that underlie the way the stock market values a company. I'm about to reveal the stock market's dirtiest secret to you: nobody – but nobody! – has any real idea how much any company is worth.

Yes, folks, the valuation's all down to guesswork, smoke and mirrors, and lots and lots of statistical manipulation. A determined accountant can use so many little weasel holes, an analyst can tell so many great big fibs, and so many different opinions exist about how much a bit of vapourware is worth that you can't ever put a finger on the truth. Trying to is like attempting to nail jelly to a wall – the harder you try, the more baffled and frustrated you're going to get.

Here's my advice. Accept what the stock market says, go with the flow, and then do some solid research of your own to figure out whether or not you agree with it. If you don't think the stock market's figures stack up against harsh reality, then quietly take your coat and leave. But conversely, if you feel sure that the stock market's underestimating the value of your chosen company, then get in there and good luck to you.

The earlier chapters in this book talk repeatedly about market capitalisation. That's the figure you get when you multiply today's share price by the number of shares the company happens to have issued up to now. If a company has issued 100 million shares and they're currently worth 200p each, then the market cap is £200 million. Easy, eh?

Sadly, no it isn't. I say in Chapters 5 and 6 that there are loads of other ways in which companies can raise money, or acquire assets, that simply don't appear in the market capitalisation. Or not in any way you can measure, anyway. I'm talking about corporate bonds, pension fund balances, options, employee share schemes that dilute the equity in the shares – all kinds of stuff. And that's before I've even talked about property, which probably widens your eyes more than anything.

The following sub-sections cover some of the hundreds of things that happen off-balance sheet, and off the profit and loss account as well. If your head's starting to swim a bit with the impossibility of ever understanding the true worth of a company, remember this simple truth:

A company is worth what the market is prepared to pay for it. No more, no less. That's because when you buy a share you're buying a piece of its future, and nobody knows for sure how that may work out. Your chosen company may produce nothing visible at all, but if it invents the next great wave in creating energy for the planet, it can rule the world. Great ideas are just as powerful as good products, and they're just as valuable as decades of proven trading success in the past.

## *Putting a price on a company with no profits*

If you think it looks as if I'm trying to dodge the crucial issue here, you might very well be right. You won't ever get two experts to agree on the best way of attaching a value to a company that's never made any profits at all – and that's a problem that the entire stock market has to cope with, because if the market can't agree on a basis for a valuation it'll never be happy trading the shares at all.

Obviously, as you'd expect, some analysts think they've got better ideas on this subject than others. Some of them apply complicated mathematical fomulae based on the things they can actually measure – such as turnover, growth rates and the rate at which losses are diminishing. Others simply stick their fingers into the wind and take a flying guess, based on instinct, or perhaps because they know and trust the people who are running the company. Others again will look at how the company's competitors are doing and will pitch their guesses on the assumption that the company itself should be able to achieve an equal level of success.

You can also, of course, look at the company's turnover, and then look at its costs. And then, as long as the turnover's accelerating faster than the costs, you can project a date in the future when the two cross over so that the company enters the profit zone.

In many cases that's exactly what the market tries to do. Figure 8-2 demonstrates this concept.

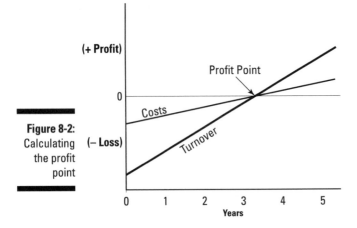

**Figure 8-2:**
Calculating the profit point

The problem, however, is that the future's rarely quite as simple as our example company suggests. If the idea behind the company is any good, and especially if it's in some buzzy area of new technology, either it explodes into prominence or else it bombs in some other, much less desirable way.

Besides, the straight lines you see in Figure 8-2 aren't straight at all in real life. If sales are growing exponentially, you'll get a parabolic curve that keeps on rising at an ever-steeper rate, not a straight-line trend like this. And if costs are rising at the same time, that's two non-straight lines you're looking at instead of just one. The intersection of the two might end up almost anywhere.

Two other big problems may bend the line about quite a lot. The first is that the competition's likely to make some inroads into the exponentially growing sales, which could dent the prospects in unforeseeable ways. The second is that the product itself might run into a problem. What if somebody invents something better, so that everybody goes off and buys that product instead? Or what if the innovation reaches market saturation – the point where it's sold the product to everyone who's likely to want it – and sales go off a cliff?

You simply can't know the answers to these questions. So when faced with a bright new product that isn't making money, the stock market sucks its teeth, looks at the numbers, inspects the competition's products, listens to the directors to decide whether they sound credible, and checks which way the economic wind's blowing. And then it considers what all the rest of the market's doing about this company, and jumps right in. But it wants a big return on its investment because of the increased risk it's taking. And if the market ever thinks it's going to get anything less than a big return, it's out of the company like a cork out of a bottle. Shares with no profits are always more volatile than other types of shares. After all, they've got no bottom line – no safe, reliable, well-known underpinning – if things should go wrong.

Can you, as a mere privateer, get any help from the financial pages when dealing with this situation? Well, you don't find much in the way of numbers, that's for sure. But you can access newspaper reports, RNS statements, the company's website, and discussion forums like ADVFN (www.advfn.com ) and The Motley Fool (www.fool.co.uk) to give yourself the best possible chance of assessing all the available information.

# The view from inside

Many years ago, when the Internet was still in its infancy, a colleague and I dreamed up a truly innovative online information product that was really good. We had a fantastic international team of experts ready to work on it, we had the prototypes up and running, and we only needed £100,000 to develop it. But could we find anybody prepared to invest such a trifling sum? No, we couldn't. Nobody was willing to risk less than a million, because they said it would cost them £100,000 just to check us out properly (the so-called due diligence tests) and it simply wouldn't be worth their while to invest so little in us.

But that really wasn't going to be a problem, according to the private equity backers. 'Hey, this idea's going to make a fortune,' they said to us. 'We really want to invest in you. But we need to know how big the market's going to be in the next five years, and how big you're going to be.'

'Impossible,' we said. 'It's the Internet. It's growing exponentially and changing all the time. We honestly haven't got the foggiest idea.'

'That's no good,' they said, 'we need projections. Just take a good guess at the likely trends, and then make the figures work together realistically so that we can see the way your company's potential will unfold.'

So we did, and they looked fantastic. 'Great,' said the investors, 'but we've just changed our business model. £3 million is now our minimum investment. So make your projections bigger please. And convince us that you really *want* to be a billion-pound company.'

We did. We imagined ourselves running a global empire. We imagined the hotels and the travel and the corporate jets. And the awful thing was, the backers loved it. And the even more awful thing was, we still only wanted £100,000 to get our idea off the ground. But we were being forced to bid for £3 million!

Just as everything was getting really crazy, the dot-com bust of 2000 happened and the whole ridiculous edifice collapsed like the illusion it really was. The backers snatched back their cash and went home, because they were getting scared at the increasing rate at which their other investments were turning into dust. We never did get our £100,000, we had to abandon our amazing idea, and we folded the company.

You have to put yourself inside the minds of high-tech entrepreneurs to see the pressures they're under. If they sometimes seem a bit hyped up, that's because they haven't got a very good grasp yet of a still-unknown world that's taking shape under their very feet. Fantasies are about as good as these projections can ever get at times like these. Most such products fail, but the really good ones clean up in explosive style. And all the time, the owners of these companies are under relentless pressure from the backers to make the projections better, faster, more exciting, more risky.

But then, why not? Just look at Yahoo!, Facebook, Google, eBay, and even the granddaddy of them all, Microsoft, if you want to see where a genius idea can take you. Think about James Dyson, the vacuum cleaner inventor who was struggling to keep going 20 years ago in the face of a bitter patent infringement dispute with Hoover, but who now has a third of global market share. Or consider the chap who invented the ring-pull tab that you find on an ordinary drinks can – and who swiftly became the world's wealthiest inventor on a royalty of about 1 US cent for every can that people bought.

Set up a free dummy portfolio service with iii, Hemmington Scott, the FT, Yahoo!, Motley Fool, or even the London Stock Exchange. You can then use this online service to alert you automatically by message to your inbox or mobile phone every time a company you're watching makes the news for any reason whatsoever. That's a remarkably good way of keeping tabs on higher-risk companies. (Chapter 5 covers dummy portfolio services in more detail.)

## Appraising goodwill, patents, and other intangibles

The *Price to Book Value* (PTBV) is the figure you get when you look at the market capitalisation of a company and compare it with its rock-solid tangible assets – its cash, property, shareholder funds, and so forth. (The market capitalisation is the stock market's own valuation of a company – the value you get when you multiply the price per share by the number of shares in circulation.) Many investors reckon that the PTBV comparison gives you a useful reality check, because it shows how much of the company's share price is being held aloft by nothing more than hope, froth, and hot air. The bigger the discrepancy between the market capitalisation and the book value, the more you know that things you can't regard as 100 per cent reliable are driving the company.

And yet before long you recognise that without all those intangible things you don't have much of a company. Apart from mining companies – almost the only companies that don't really do anything but trade in raw, rock-solid commodities that you can weigh by the tonne – the intangibles make a business what it is, and make you want to invest in it.

One of the toughest jobs a stock market analyst has to face is that she needs to put a value on all of these things that you can sense but you can't touch. Often these intangibles are a company's biggest possessions – its product patents, its goodwill, and, of course, its brand names.

## Patents

If I'm going to invest in a drug company, I want to know three things:

- ✔ What patents or copyrights has it already got?
- ✔ How long have the patents still got to run before they expire and the market opens up to imitators from all quarters of the globe?
- ✔ Is a steady 'pipeline' of new products being developed to replace the existing patents as they expire?

How does the stock market price up the value of these patents? Well, it can generally get precise breakdowns from a company's annual reports that show exactly which patented products are producing exactly how much turnover at the moment. And you can get the same information yourself if you study the accounts and the annual reports yourself. But then you have to decide whether you agree with the market's assessments – and that's the hard part.

## Goodwill

When the woman who runs your local all-night convenience store finally sells her business to take a well-earned back seat after a busy working life, the most important thing she wants to sell to the new owner is the goodwill in her business. Not the stock. Not the premises. Not even the name of the business. But the simple fact that a thousand people in the neighbourhood have been buying their stuff from her for 20 years, and they've generally found her a pleasant person to deal with. So, with luck, they're going to keep on coming back to the new owner when he takes over. He may have their addresses and their phone numbers, and he may know exactly what kinds of things they like, because his predecessor's written all this down in the trading records.

More importantly than that, the whole town knows that if they need a bottle of milk at 2 a.m., this shop is the place to go for emergency supplies. You can't put a value on this sort of asset – but a company's accountant has at least to try. That's why you nearly always find an item on the company's balance sheet for goodwill. The figure's a wild guess, frankly, and you shouldn't ever make the mistake of thinking it's solid just because it's there in black and white. But nor can you ever afford to ignore it completely.

Can you make a better guess than the company's accountant; who is, after all, a kind of interested party? Probably not, but you may like to take a good look at the figure and decide for yourself. For instance, far too many software companies overrate their importance to their clients while simultaneously underestimating the value of their competitor's products.

And great seismic shifts are going on all the time. Record store chains like HMV have seen their neighbourhood-store goodwill bashed to pieces in recent years by the arrival of cut-price Internet shopping at Amazon and eBay. And car manufacturers are finding that their customer loyalty levels have plummeted, as cars have become more reliable and more identical to each other in every way. These days, many people switch their make of car just because they fancy a change. Goodwill can be awfully fickle.

### Brand names

Brand names are reliable, aren't they? I certainly hope so, considering how much money advertisers spend on trying to convince us they are. For businesses, brands are often inextricably linked with both patent and copyright law, and with goodwill (that is, customer loyalty). The spread of counterfeiting in China is a backhanded compliment to the advertisers' achievements. But as an investor, can you put a value on them?

Most of the time, you aren't able to take a properly informed view of the value of branding, and you're better off going with what the City thinks. But if you're thinking about consumer services, many experienced investors reckon you should walk around town with your eyes wide open and just watch. The high street can give you all kinds of clues as to which brands are on the up, and conversely which fashion chains or electrical retailers or even banks are looking a bit dog-eared. This is all useful information – and all too often, it's information that the City forgets to notice for itself.

## Weighing up takeover potential

The stock market's always looking out for a company that seems as though it may come under offer from a rival. Or perhaps a company that wants to transfer some of its assets to another company, to improve its corporate focus.

Six major kinds of takeovers spring to mind, and all of them are different.

- ✔ Because the company is struggling and the market thinks it may do better under new ownership.

- ✔ Because the company's original founders want to turn it over to a management buy-out (MBO), so they can sell up and retire on the proceeds. (With an MBO, the employees will either borrow money from a bank and then buy the shares for themselves, or else they'll persuade a big investor such as a private equity group to take a stake in the company and then eventually float the shares on the stock market so that a true market value can be established.)

✔ Because the company's equity backers (for instance a private equity company) have achieved the improvements they were hoping to make, and now want to make a scheduled exit so that they can cash in.

✔ Because the company has a product that one of its rivals desperately wants to own.

✔ Because there are simply too many companies in the sector, and some consolidation is regarded as essential.

✔ Because a rival wants to buy the company up and close it down, just to get rid of it!

The risks involved in these five scenarios are also quite different. The second and third scenarios are unlikely to produce very much of a shareholder bonus, because no significant disagreement exists about the merits of the company. To be frank, no greed or fear is involved in these types of buy-outs! So you probably just get a handshake, a 'recommended offer' announcement from the board, and an agreed buy-out figure. You'll be lucky to come out of this situation 10 per cent ahead. And don't forget, once the 90 per cent approval threshold is reached (i.e. when 90 per cent of the shareholders' votes have been cast in favour of the deal) you can't hold out on your own against a merger that you don't like.

The fourth and sixth scenarios can be quite a lot more profitable, but saying farewell to a share that you think may have carried on bringing in profits if only you were allowed to keep it for a bit longer, instead of being forced to sell, is always a shame.

The fifth scenario is probably the most reliable route to riches if you can get your timing right. Some stock market sectors always desperately need to consolidate for one reason or another – perhaps because the optimal shape of the industry has changed, or perhaps because consumers have changed the way they buy its products – and with only a little background reading you can identify them and home in on the companies that look like the best targets.

For example, the media has generally agreed in recent years that the world airline industry contains too much competition, and that some very major players need to combine forces to avoid a global glut of excessively duplicated air services that does nobody any good. Or that the international market for utilities, especially water and electricity, can benefit from the constructive synergies that bigger corporations can achieve. Or that the hundreds of struggling biotechnology companies make tasty morsels for the giant drug corporations whose top-earning patents are running out. Or that the fast pace of mining industry mergers since 2005 is likely to go on and on. And so forth.

But the first of the five scenarios is the real peach if you can only spot its takeover potential early enough. How many times have you seen a company being grotesquely mismanaged by a poor board of directors, only to watch its shares going into hyper-drive as soon as the prospect of a new owner heaves into view?

Where do you start looking for information about possible takeover candidates? Well, you don't have much luck with the mainstream news sources, because early-stage takeover talk in the press is both scurrilous and also liable to upset the stock market regulators; see 'How the Media Is Regulated', earlier in this chapter. A potential takeover's also deeply destabilising, so companies don't want to talk about it either.

You may have more luck scouring the Internet forums at The Motley Fool (www.fool.co.uk) or ADVFN (www.advfn.com), many of whose members make a permanent habit of looking for these situations. But investment magazines seem to make a better job of identifying the bigger top-down opportunities, such as the sector-wide mergers I talk about earlier. *The Economist* is often a good place to start searching for these things.

Timing is obviously going to be critical in these situations. Suppose you've got a solid takeover offer on the table, which has been announced in the RNS listings. Are you too late to buy in, or is the share likely to have hit its ceiling by the time you open your paper?

Hard to say, but on balance the chances are that by this stage the cat's well and truly out of the bag and heading off down the street, with the world chasing after it. You may make another 10 per cent, but unless a very angry bidding war takes place, that's probably all.

Better by far if you can pick up on a situation where a company's forced to confirm, in an RNS, that 'approaches have been received', and that more news is to follow. In this situation, the company is said to be 'in play'. My experience suggests that, although one bid may fail, a fair chance exists that another succeeds once the hounds have got the company's scent on their noses.

How much profit can a takeover bring you if you get in soon enough? Hard to generalise, but a quick look through my own records over the years suggests that I've scored an average of around 30 per cent from successful mergers. And that's good enough for me.

When to sell? Should you wait for the final offer to be accepted, or should you get out and take a smaller profit while it's still on the table? My personal preference is always for the second course of action. I may be missing out on 10 per cent of the action, but I'm also eliminating the chance of a 100 per cent failure of the discussions. That's just my own investing style, but if your nerves are stronger than mine, good luck to you.

As the old stock market adage has it: Buy on the rumour, sell on the fact.

# A Closer Look at Fixed Asset Valuations

I'm afraid this is going to come as a bit of a shock to you. No firm agreement exists on what intangible assets are worth, except for what the stock market happens to think at the time. Unfortunately, pretty much the same kind of uncertainty applies to fixed assets, too – plant, equipment, vehicles, and property.

## Considering depreciation

First, depreciation. Just how fast does a truck depreciate? Strangely enough, the amount depends on which country the truck's in, and how big or small the company that owns it happens to be. That's rather odd, because a truck is a truck is a truck, isn't it?

Yes, you guessed it. Tax considerations have a massive impact on how fast or how slow your company's accountants choose to let the assets depreciate on the balance sheets. I can't give you exact figures for depreciation rates even in the UK – not only because they vary enormously across the business range, but because the allowable depreciation rates seem to change with every new Budget from the Chancellor of the Exchequer, so the subject's too much of a moving target to be a suitable subject for this book. Instead, I'm just alerting you that the situation may not be quite as clear-cut as you expect.

Should you mind? Perhaps not, because you can't really do anything about the shifting patterns of asset depreciation. At least, not as far as plant and equipment are concerned. You just have to go with the company's own presentations.

## Valuing property

You enter a whole different world when you start looking at property valuations. For many British companies, property's a bigger deal than you may suppose. Not only big industrial corporations have thousands of acres of land sitting on their balance sheets, so have transport and distribution companies, which may be sitting on vast amounts of disused railway land. But the biggest holders of prime urban land are probably the big supermarket chains – Sainsbury, Tesco, Morrisons, and Asda – all of which keep great swathes of land aside, either using it for car parking or perhaps sitting on it with the intention of stopping rivals from getting their hands on it. I talk about this in a little more detail in Chapter 5.

The point is, however, that these land banks can create quite a nasty little booby-trap for the unwary in the company's balance sheets. For reasons that only an accountant understands, companies are not required to value these property portfolios at their current market value. Instead, they can (and generally do) enter them at 'historical cost' – which effectively means, a lot of the time, that these vast real estate assets are valued at the price at which they were acquired, maybe 20, 30, or 40 years ago! So a piece of land that today's worth £10 million may be in the accounts at £1 million, or even less. The only time a property normally gets revalued is when the company needs to mortgage it, or do anything else that involves being forced to acknowledge its true value.

Does that matter? Well, yes. In effect, the company has assets that the accounts aren't reflecting properly. In 2007, for instance, Tesco's assets were listed at £16.6 billion, of which you can be sure that land represented a very substantial part. According to the Office of Fair Trading, in 2006 the supermarket chain had 4.5 million square feet, enough to add another 20 per cent to its existing acreage, spread across 185 different sites. And, at the time, the property was all listed at historical cost.

What's the fuss about? Well, if Tesco ever comes under offer from another company, which admittedly seems unlikely considering its size, the company presumably needs to think pretty fast about how it values its property portfolio if it wants to get the right price. Its assets, quite simply, are vastly bigger than they appear.

But the situation at Sainsbury's is yet more peculiar. Many of its valuations go back to the early 1970s, which means that they're reckoned to be even more dramatically understated. However, in 2006 the company finally re-valued about half of its land assets while re-mortgaging itself (all part of a complicated scheme to plug a gap in its pension funds, actually), and this half-share of the land suddenly appeared to be valued at £4 billion – quite a lot of money, since the whole company was supposedly carrying a market capitalisation of only £5.5 billion at the time!

If you think the supermarket situation's a bit of an eye-opener, take a look at the share chart in Figure 8-3. It's from a company called UK Coal, which operates a somewhat worked-out portfolio of coal mines, mostly in the north of England. In addition to its mines it has about 14,000 acres of mostly scrubby land, much of it too far out of town to be of any great value to developers.

Nothing very interesting happened to this company for years. And then suddenly, in mid-2007, the share price almost quadrupled. That was a bit odd, considering that its turnover by the end of the calendar year had actually fallen slightly to £328 million, barely half the levels of 2003 – and that its deep mining output had practically halved.

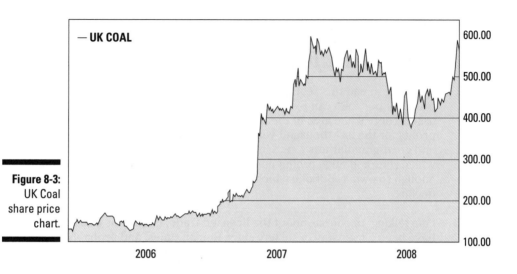

**Figure 8-3:**
UK Coal
share price
chart.

Had the company struck oil? Gold? No, just drains and concrete and mechanical diggers. By getting planning permission to build a couple of industrial estates and a housing development on a small part of its hopelessly scruffy land bank, the company had transformed its fortunes without even sticking a shovel in the ground.

That's not completely accurate, because UK Coal did have a couple of very small developments already on the go at the time. But until the house price collapse of 2008 came back to remind us all of the vanity of all things to do with property, UK Coal was sitting pretty for a while. As you'd probably expect, the share price subsequently took a bit of a beating in the summer of 2008. But as an example of what an apparently useless land bank can do for one of the most clapped-out industries, this story still has plenty to teach us.

You don't find companies like this everywhere you look, but if you think a land bank's attached to any of your companies, do a little digging in the statistics, check the news stories, and see what you can come up with. You don't even need a fork. Just a set of company accounts, a decent subscription to an Internet-based news retrieval service (for which you might have to pay, say, £100 a year), and a bit of common sense.

## *A property sector whose value simply disappears*

I'm going to end this section with a cautionary note about how having a big property portfolio can play havoc with what seems to be a solid investment asset. There's one area of the property market that's been producing big profits for the last thousand years. One which our fathers and grandfathers and great-grandfathers found indispensable in their daily lives, and one which returned huge profits per square foot to those who were fortunate enough to own it. But one which now seems to be pitched into terminal decline.

I am talking, of course, about the licensed trade. Pubs, inns and road houses have been a mainstay of society since Roman times, and probably even further back than that. Over the centuries pubs have been meeting places, rallying points, places of ill repute, places to do business, place bets and pass the time – and, of course, places in which to settle arguments, sometimes violently.

But in the last 20 years television and stricter drink-driving laws have been driving increasing numbers of pubs out of business. Hefty alcohol taxes and tough price competition from supermarkets have combined to send the licensed trade into steep decline, at just the moment when a nationwide ban on smoking in pubs was driving away the working-class males who had typically fed the fruit machines. In late 2008 it was estimated that 40 pubs went out of business in Britain every week. There are simply too many pubs to support the market.

So what becomes of the companies that own the pubs? Companies such as Punch Taverns or Enterprise Inns, both of which have long since stopped brewing beer and which now largely operate as landlords to their own (self-employed) landlords? Both of them have been forced to watch their vast property portfolios being downgraded by the market: Enterprise's market capitalisation dropped from about £4 billion in the spring of 2007 to less than £500 million in the space of 18 months. Ouch!

It's clear, obviously, that the value of the pub properties themselves didn't fall by 90 per cent during those 18 months: it was probably more like 40 per cent. Falling trading profits had at least as much to with the share price disaster. But the City was letting the company know, in no uncertain terms, that its property portfolio was no longer a meal ticket.

How can the people who own the pub properties respond to the challenge? They can try to rebuild the pub industry's profits by encouraging it to turn itself into a restaurant business instead – although that's unlikely to work in all parts of the country. They can sell off their tied properties for redevelopment as housing, assuming that they can keep the planners onside. Or they can try to curry favour with their investors by using tax-efficient vehicles such as Real

Estate Investment Trusts (REITs), which give both the the investors and the company useful tax breaks. In the end, however, many analysts reckon that the game is up for pub properties. You'd have to be aware of the why this seismic shift in the property market has happened before you could be in a position to decide whether this 'undervalued' sector was a gamble.

But you'd certainly be in trouble if you fell into the trap of supposing that last year's desirable property investment could automatically become next year's property meal ticket. For all any of us knows, it may never happen.

# *Checking Future Pension Liabilities*

As we get through the aftermath of the 2007/2008 stock market crisis, I suspect that we're going to be hearing a lot more about pension liabilities. Some of the biggest companies in the Western world are now starting to be marked down by the markets because of the large deficits that they (allegedly) run on the pension funds that they maintain for their staffs. Or, to put it simply, people are saying that these companies haven't got enough cash in their funds to guarantee that they'll be able to pay their future retirees as well as they've undertaken to do.

I think we can all agree that that's bad news. But the reasons for the change in the market's mood go a bit further than the mere fact that all pension funds' portfolios have taken a knock in recent years, along with practically everybody else who got caught up in the stock market crisis of 2007/2008. Instead, the company accounting rules themselves have been amended in such a way that the goalposts have moved. And, as investors we ought to at least take an interest in the matter, even if we don't really need to understand every single detail of the issue.

I'll try and take you gently through the main points of these changes. Remember, you don't need to know absolutely everything about this rather obscure subject. But if the explanation that follows helps you to at least ask some intelligent questions about a company you're interested in, then I'll have done my job. Ready? Here we go, then.

 Back in 2000, the rules governing British companies' pension arrangements were turned upside down by a rather substantial new set of requirements known as FRS-17. (Later on, in 2007 the rules were amended again, to bring them into line with something called IAS-19. But we'll get hopelessly lost if I take you too far down that road.)

In layman's language, FRS-17 said that it wasn't enough for companies simply to carry on logging the amounts of the pension contributions that they were getting (and making) on behalf of their staff, year by year. Instead, they had to calculate the total cash value of their future commitments to their retired employees, *as if they had already retired now* – and then set down in their balance sheets exactly how well or how badly their pension funds were getting on in relation to those future commitments. Yes, the companies were being asked for an annual progress report on how their pension funds were getting on.

That doesn't sound so bad, does it? In fact it sounds like a good idea. But the problem was that this FRS-17 figure that the companies were being asked to produce for their annual pension fund was going to form an integral part of their balance sheets in future, just as if it was a loan or a debt on the company!

What's wrong with that? Well, companies' pension funds are always run as a separate legal operation from their day-to-day trading operations – indeed, in most cases the pension funds are a completely separate company, so that the parent company's board can't simply dip into the pension funds whenever they need a little extra cash. But for the purposes of the annual accounts, they were going to be run together as if they were one company. For many large companies, especially old ones, the pension fund was (and is) bigger than the trading company that set it up. So there's a lot of potential for something bad in the pension fund to throw a whole company's accounts right off balance.

Even that wouldn't be a problem, if it weren't for one thing. Pension funds invest most of their money in stocks and shares and other investments, just the way you expect. And the value of that fund goes up and down quite a lot over the years, in line with the financial markets. But under FRS-17, whatever state the pension fund is in on the last day of the accounting year – for better or worse – gets frozen in time and hangs like a lead weight on the company's balance sheet for the next 12 months. That's the one you look at when you check out the company's finances, remember, so the figure's going to give you a bad impression.

So if the stock market has a bad year, every single company in the stock market's likely to take a hit on its annual balance sheet – even the successful ones! The hit may be quite big if the economic wind's blowing the wrong way at the time the company makes up its accounts. It might even be enough to tip the company into technical problems, or for it to breach the conditions of its bank loans. (*Breaching its covenants*, as it's known.) And a perfectly good company's accounts can look absolutely stupid just because the stock market's having a bad year. Conversely, if the market's having a good year, even a lousy company can look good. FRS-17 and its successor, IAS 19, are mad.

Table 8-1 presents an example from a UK corporation's accounts for 2008. Thanks to FRS-17, this company's balance sheet wobbled by nearly £600 million between 2007 and 2008, for no reason that had anything to do with its business performance.

| Table 8-1 | Sample balance sheet showing effects of FRS-17 | |
|---|---|---|
| | **2008** | **2007** |
| | £m | £m |
| Present value of funded obligations | (3,668) | (4,395) |
| Fair value of plan assets | 4,171 | 4,298 |
| *[Balance]* | *503* | *(97)* |

In 2007 this company reckoned that its obligations to its pensioners were £4.395 billion, but that its pension plan assets were only £4.298 billion. That left it with a shortfall of £97 million. But by 2008 the company had turned the situation back into surplus. Its pension fund was still only worth £4.171 billion, but its projected obligations had shrunk, rather amazingly, to just £3.668 billion. So the FRS-17 element of the statement changed back from a deficit into a surplus.

How did the company do that? Had some of its staff suddenly walked off an inconvenient cliff, so that they no longer needed those pension handouts when they retired? That seems doubtful.

More probably, the company reduced the workforce's entitlements under its final-salary pension scheme – perhaps by shunting some of them into 'cash-purchase' schemes where they had no final-salary rights but were forced to rely on whatever the stock market had made of their pension funds FRS-17 has been accused in some quarters of sounding the death knell for final-salary pension schemes in Britain. I wouldn't be surprised if that's true.

So the next time you see a company whose balance sheet seems to have been snaking about for no obvious reason, give the figures a second look to see whether the poison's coming from its pension liabilities. If so, the chance is good that you're looking at an undervalued stock.

On a more positive note, for the first time in history investors have proper information on how much companies owe their employees, instead of having to guess. And although the information you get may be flaky, perhaps that's better than having no information at all.

# Chapter 9

# Watching Out for the Pitfalls

· · · · · · · · · · · · · · · · · · · · · · · · · · · · · · · · · · · · · · · · · · · · · · · · · ·

*In This Chapter*

▶ Avoiding heart-stopping frights

▶ Locating those pesky debts

▶ Understanding the shorting trap, and where it leads

· · · · · · · · · · · · · · · · · · · · · · · · · · · · · · · · · · · · · · · · · · · · · · · · · ·

*N*othing gets the heart racing like a good fright, and the stock market can deliver one in spades if you're a beginner. Not everything this chapter describes is necessarily bad news, though – just some peculiar bits of behaviour that may make you stir a bit now and then.

This chapter helps you get wise to some of the market's wiles. I can't send you out into the investment jungle without alerting you to at least a few of the beasties that lurk in the undergrowth.

# Avoiding Common Mistakes

Don't get me wrong, I'm not trying to say that everyone's out to get you when you venture out, as a mere privateer, into the world inhabited by hoary old professional hands. Indeed, all the evidence seems to show that if you're any good, you can beat the professionals at their own game without too much difficulty.

Look at things this way. When a big investor controlling lots of money makes a move, the whole jungle crashes with the reverberations of what he's done, and everybody knows he's done it. But when *you* make a move nobody's any the wiser. That's because you're likely to be dealing in a thousand pounds or two, not a million or two.

Obviously, an error involving a thousand or two hurts you just as much as the man with a billion in his portfolio – proportionally speaking, of course. But a little time spent looking at some of those mistakes can help you work out why making them can be so easy.

# Price falls on ex-dividend dates

One of the things they never seem to tell you in investing school is that the ex-dividend date is one of the most important times in a company's year (or half-year, if the company makes six-monthly dividend distributions). That essential date can cause absolute chaos if you don't know it's coming, because it hits the share price. Absolutely, definitely, every single time.

I look at the question of dividends in Chapter 5. A dividend is the company's way of thanking you for your fidelity as a shareholder. In making the dividend payment, it's handing out some part of the profits that it's been making recently. And quite right too, because they're your profits – you do own the company, after all.

The dividend process normally occurs in four stages:

✔ The announcement date itself, which is (guess what?) nothing more than the date on which the company informs the stock market of the impending dividend.

✔ The record date, which is the date on which you need to be a fully registered and stamped-up shareholder if you're going to receive the dividend. But since getting the paperwork sorted when you buy a share generally takes a couple of days, practically all companies use another date, about two days before the record date, as the final shut-off for deciding who qualifies for a dividend and who doesn't.

✔ The ex-dividend date is the watershed that most companies use. That's the date on which whether you hold the shares or not no longer matters, because you're too late to buy them and get the dividend.

✔ The payment date. This may be many weeks after the ex-dividend date, and indeed it usually is. Even if you've sold your shares by then, you still get the payment.

You may not be very surprised to hear that the share price generally tends to rise in the weeks leading up to the day before the ex-dividend date. Everybody wants a piece of the payout! Indeed, the rise in the share price will roughly mirror the value of the dividend – so if the dividend's going to be worth 5 per cent to shareholders, that's roughly the amount by which the share price will rise.

But on ex-dividend day, guess what happens? Yes, the share price takes a hit, because anyone who was waiting for the dividend now has no incentive to hang on any longer.

That the share price should fall on ex-dividend day is perfectly logical. But what isn't so logical is that some people seem to think they can make some free money by buying a share in the run-up to the qualifying date and then selling once the dividend's been stripped out. Any stock market that's even remotely 'efficient' knocks that idea on the head by dropping the price on ex-dividend day. Doesn't it?

Well, almost. If a strong underlying upward current is still supporting the shares, you can sometimes find that the price fall will be muted, or even completely cancelled out, by the other supporting factors on ex-dividend day. Suppose that your shares have just delivered a 3 per cent dividend but they've risen by 2 per cent on ex-dividend day instead of falling as you expected. What that's telling you is that the shares have effectively risen by 5 per cent during the day! (That is, they've 'fallen' by 3 per cent and 'risen' by 5 per cent to leave them 2 per cent ahead.)

If you've set some sort of limit on a share price, whereby something particular will happen if the share crosses a certain threshold, ex-dividend movements might catch you out. For example:

- ✔ If you've set a 'limit order' on an instruction to your broker: 'Sell my Glaxo shares immediately if they drop below 1.200p' or 'Buy 3,000 British Airways shares if you can get them for less than 300p', and he does so without checking the factors affecting the share price.

- ✔ If you've set up an automatic price alert from FT.com or the Stock Exchange website, whereby you get an urgent email as soon as that threshold is reached and you respond to an inevitably lower price by selling without checking the dividend date information.

- ✔ If you've been running your own unofficial stop-loss programme on the side (an ideal way to keep a firm grip on your investing nerves and stop yourself from getting sucked into the destructive patterns of self-denial; see Chapter 5). A typical stop-loss resolution says: 'I'm going to sell my Lloyds TSB if its price ever drops more than 12 per cent below my all-time high for this share'. But if you haven't actually *noticed* that Lloyds TSB went ex-dividend on an 8 per cent dividend yesterday, then you're going to be somewhat flummoxed by the 8 per cent drop in its share price this morning. And if you're not paying attention, you might hit the panic button on a share that's well worth holding.

What can you do to protect yourself against making a goof over ex-dividend dates? First, make sure that you know in advance when the dividends are due to become payable, and keep a written list somewhere that you can look up in a hurry if the wobbles ever seem to have struckstrike the share price. Even if you don't know the precise date of the next one, you're pretty likely to find that it's within a few days of last year's date.

Where can you find about about ex-div dates? The company's last dividend statement, which is always available on the Stock Exchange Regulatory News Service, will generally give you a good idea as to when the next one's due. Or if the next date has been finalised, you can find out in an instant either from RNS or by by checking the *FT*'s website (www.ft.com).

Figure 9-1 shows a summary of the trading position of Arriva shares.

**Figure 9-1:**
Summary of
Arriva trad-
ing position.

| ARRIVA SUMMARY | | | |
|---|---|---|---|
| Open | 614.00 | Average Volume | 1.03m |
| Day High | 636.50 | P/E (TTM) | 12.38 |
| Day Low | 595.50 | EPS (TTM) | 49.16 GBX |
| Previous Close | 608.50 | Dividend PS (TTM) | 23.21 GBX |
| Shares Outstanding | 198.66m | Dividend Yield | 3.81% |
| Market Cap | 1.21bn GBP | Dividend Ex-Date | Sep 10 2008 |
| Free Float | 196.70m | Dividend Pay-Date | Oct 01 2008 |

You occasionally find that the *FT* and London Stock Exchange listings can't give you enough information about foreign-registered companies, even if they happen to be listed in London. If this happens to you, don't take no for an answer: Try Yahoo! instead. It provides an impressive spread of information about the company's financial fundamentals, and its announcements too, though its finance site (http://uk.finance.yahoo.com).

Unfortunately, the printed media aren't quite so good at giving you ex-dividend information at the time. But if you're reading the *Financial Times* share price pages, or some other listing with a similar amount of detail, you're likely to find the initials 'xd' for 'ex-dividend' buried among the hearts and clubs and other miscellaneous footnotes in the left-hand column. That's a sure sign that your company has passed its ex-dividend date, although usually you'll need to do some more research to find out exactly when.

Try also to make sure that you know about any special dividends the company may be making to its shareholders. A special dividend is a one-off cash distribution to shareholders – something that often happens after the company's sold one of its divisions, so that it's sitting on a cash pile that it would rather 'return to the shareholders' than keep in its war chest for a future acquisition. If the market has been expecting one of these special dividends for a while (and it may be quite big), it'll definitely dent the share price on ex-dividend day.

The same thing might apply if any other kinds of distribution are taking place. When Britain's big privatisations were going on in the 1980s and 1990s, it was common to find that investors were offered *bonus shares* if they held onto their shares until a given date. These distributions sometimes hit the share price in exactly the same way as a dividend.

Not every country organises its dividends in the same way as Britain. Some Canadian companies make cash distributions every single month! And an Australian company like BHP Billiton may structure its dividends, share buybacks, or bonus shares in ways that favour Australian taxpayers over non-nationals.

## *Scrip issues and consolidations*

It would be interesting, although also rather depressing, to wonder just how many investors have gone face first into their porridge from the near-terminal shock of discovering that their shareholdings have halved in value overnight thanks to the unexpected arrival of a scrip issue. And how many other people have gone out on an insane spending spree, believing themselves to be suddenly rich because a share price consolidation has sent the price of their shares rising tenfold?

Thousands, probably. Tens of thousands, possibly. And in both cases, the survivors won't have been much consoled by the morning-after realisation that one of the strangest tricks in the stock market's repertoire has temporarily misguided them. A trick that doesn't make anyone richer or poorer. A trick that's really quite expensive to perform, and leaves everyone exactly where they were before. So why on earth do companies do it?

A *scrip issue* (also known as a 'capitalisation issue' or a 'stock split') is what happens when a company decides to multiply the number of shares on the stock market by the simple device of issuing a lot more shares, free of charge, to all of its existing shareholders. Whereupon, inevitably, the stock market promptly adjusts the price of all the shares downward (the new shares and the old shares too), so that the market capitalisation of the company ends up exactly the same as it was before the change.

Suppose that you've got 200 shares in XYZ Co. and that they're worth 1,000 pence each. That's a £2,000 investment. Now suppose that the company decides on a one-for-one scrip issue, which means that you get one free share for every share you already own.

You now have 400 shares instead of 200. But you're not getting free money. The stock market will look at the shares, and it'll look at the company – and, not unreasonably, it'll figure that since the company has now got twice the number of shares it had yesterday, but becasueit's still the same company, the correct price for those shares will be 500p instead of 1,000p. Result: you now have ($400 \times 500p = £2,000$) worth of shares. Just the same as before. Plus a possible cardiac arrest if you haven't been paying attention.

Why would any company do anything so stupid? I'm sorely tempted to say because a whole lot of daft people don't like paying £10 or more for a share, no matter how much of the company that gives them. In the same way that some people are addicted to 'penny shares', which cost small numbers of pennies, other investors are simply allergic to big numbers and would rather pay 500p for a share that only gives them half as much as a 1,000p share.

Of course, the company might not have gone for a nice and tidy one-for-one split. A nine-for-one scrip would have reduced the share price by 90 per cent from 1,000p to just 100p, in this particular instance. A two-for-three split would have left the company worth 600p per share, because there'd now be five shares doing the job that three used to do. And so on.

But the weird thing is that scrips seem to work. If a nine-for-one scrip chops the share price back to 100p, you can be pretty sure that within days it creeps back to 110p. Why? Smoke and mirrors, or human psychology. Maybe the reason is the rules of certain investment trusts, which don't allow their managers to buy a share for over 500p without consulting the boss, but give them the freedom to buy something cheaper on the nod. Who knows? Scrips do work, that's all I can say.

*Consolidation issues* are the same as scrip issues but in reverse. If a big company has seen a corporate disaster devastate its share price – candidates have included the jeweller Ratners or the rail contractor Jarvis – an issue of pride may be involved in 'relaunching' the shares at ten times their deflated valuation. It ought to make no difference that your 100 shares are now worth exactly the same as your old 1,000 shares were. An image question is at stake here.

How can you find out about scrip issues? Well, the official Regulatory News Service announcements always flag them up clearly in advance, for a start. But very occasionally, the information sources you find in the papers, and in the press too, haven't been adjusted as they should have. They're only run by machines, after all, and common sense isn't built into many computers. So from time to time you get an uncorrected figure that sends you running for the Alka-Seltzer. I've seen some pretty weird online charts produced after scrip and consolidation issues.

Remember, if a figure looks too good (or too bad) to be true, it probably is. So don't do anything until you've checked the market capitalisation figures in at least two places, because they jolly well ought to be the same as they were yesterday and the day before, give or take a bit. Only if the market capitalisation is out of kilter should you have to face the terrible possibility that your worst nightmare may actually have happened.

# Collapsing valuations: Falling knives and the dead cat bounce

An old stock market adage states that you should never catch a falling knife. It's a gruesome image, certainly, but it's weirdly descriptive of the truth. If a share's in free-fall, twirling and twisting, your chances of grabbing it safely by the handle and avoiding injury from a dozen unforeseeable jagged edges are pretty minimal.

Yet at the same time, you're told that the best time to bag a bargain share is when panicky markets have driven it right down. A very good friend of mine, who was a pretty good investor considering his job was essentially manual farm labouring, made an absolute packet out of the electronics giant Marconi after it collapsed back in. And by getting out again a week later, he managed to lock it all in.

Other friends have not been so lucky, however. If you've been persuaded that a deeply stricken share is your best bet for a strong bounce-back, the advice is probably right. If you backed six companies in this situation and only one of them recovered as planned, you're probably still ahead.

To grab a bargain, then, what should you be looking for in the financial pages? Forget about the historical price/earnings ratio and the dividend yield), because a recent plunge may have skewed both out of all recognition. Focus instead on the debt situation, including the profile of the debt; that is, how much money the company owes in the next twelve months, and how much can wait till later. You find this information in the company's last set of accounts, and with luck it's also among the Regulatory News Service announcements.

How much competition exists in the sector? And what are the chances of a takeover? Again, background textual research is most likely to tell you what you need to know.

Beware the dreaded dead cat bounce. This theory says that even the most extinct feline, when dropped out of a high window, will bounce a few feet when it hits the pavement. Another gruesome image, to be sure, but it contains a kernel of wisdom. Don't mistake the laws of stock market physics for any sign of corporate life, and still less for any realistic chance of a full return to health.

That said, an investor with the right sense of timing could trade a dead cat bounce and make money nearly every time. If you're good enough to be able to do that consistently, you don't need to be reading this book.

## Free float and golden shares: How they affect volatility

Free float is one of the most important of the many subjects that the trade prefers not to talk about .When you talk about a listed company and the way its shares behave, you may assume too easily that all the shares in the company are up for grabs all the time, and that the market's behaviour is a fair and free reflection of the changing values of those shares.

Not so. Every company has a proportion of shares that are simply not for negotiation, no matter what. They may include the directors' personal shareholdings; the shares the company's original backers hold; those of any venture capitalists; any larger companies that may control the target company, either partially or completely; and even in some cases, national governments themselves.

How do governments come to be such big shareholders? Mostly, as you can imagine, though partial privatisations that leave them still controlling large chunks of equity in the industries they used to own 100 per cent. Germany, Italy and France all have particularly large 'golden shares' that can obscure the view for private investors. But one thing you can definitely say is that whatever happens, the eventualities of the moment are unlikely to sway the holders of these shares when buying and selling. To all intents and purposes, you can regard their loyalty as a permanent fixture of the company.

That creates an interesting situation when a rush is on to buy these shares. When everyone wants to buy, an invisible bottleneck suddenly appears that stops them from getting the shares they want in the free market. And so the bottleneck can quickly create a horrific short-term imbalance between supply and demand. Companies with only a small free float are almost bound to be more volatile than companies with bigger free floats, because the supply's so tight.

The situation gets worse. One of the characteristics of automatic index trackers, a type of managed fund that will typically follow a whole stock market sector (see Chapter 14) is that often their managers have no autonomy whatsoever when deciding whether to buy the shares or not. Their statutes quite literally *force* them to buy shares at any price that becomes necessary. This means, in effect, that the issue of tight liquidity resulting from free float problems becomes so important that entire national governments occasionally come to blows about it.

In Britain, for instance, a company listed on the main market rarely has a free float of less than 50 per cent; in continental Europe or Japan, however, the ratio's often much lower than that because banks hold enormous proportions of their client companies' stocks. In 2007 only about 40 per cent of Volkswagen's shares were in free float, and Porsche, the company trying to take it over, had only about 10 per cent of its own shares available to the open market.

But before you run away with the impression that Britain's a temple of virtue where the free float's concerned, remember that different rules apply in the more lightly regulated Alternative Investment Market (AIM). Indeed, only a tiny proportion of an AIM-listed company needs to be in free float at all. So if the board owns 60 per cent of the equity and another 35 per cent is parcelled up among the institutions, your chances of getting a free and open-market price when you sell your shares are small indeed. Conversely, of course, if the AIM company ever becomes flavour of the month, you're the one who's laughing.

If this fact's any consolation, all of the FTSE indices these days are fully 'weighted' to take account of free float; that is, a company with a small free float gets a much smaller emphasis in the index's calculations than a company with a 75 per cent-plus free float (the level at which they get a 100 per cent weighting). But in America this doesn't apply so frequently. That's one of the reasons US stock market trackers tend to be so much more volatile than British ones.

You find information about free float? Unfortunately it's not that easy, mainly because different analysts have different ideas about how many shares are genuinely free and how many are effectively captive. But one popular source is the Financial Times website at `markets.ft.com`, where you can get a quote for the number of free-float shares for almost any UK-listed company. You then divide that number of free-float shares into the total number of shares in issue, which will give you a percentage figure.

So, for instance, the FT said in late 2008 that Tesco had a free float of 7.78 billion shares, against a total 7.86 billion shares outstanding. The free float ratio was therefore an impressive 99 per cent. But British-American Tobacco, which has several large 'strategic' investors, had 1.38 billion free float shares against 2.00 billion shares in issue - a ratio of only 69 per cent.

# EBITDA

Ah, EBITDA. The Enron meltdown in 2001 possibly first drew Britain's attention to the transatlantic fashion for *Earnings Before Interest, Taxes, Depreciation, and Amortisation*. Or, as it soon became popularly known, 'Earnings Before I Tricked the Dumb Auditors'. Here's why.

Enron was one of the world's mightiest electricity, gas, paper and communications companies, with a reach that extended all the way from its native Texas to India, China and beyond. Fortune magazine named it as 'America's Most Innovative Company' for six consecutive years But all that glory ended in 2001, when it was revealed that its innovative instincts had been turned to setting up the biggest case of creative accountancy the world had ever seen. Lax supervision by the US financial authorities had allowed Enron to bypass some of the normal checks and balances on its reporting standards, and it had been playing fast and loose with the facts in a number of ways – not least, by inventing fictitious trades between its various divisions so as to boost its apparent earnings way beyond their actual level. And by mis-stating the cost of its borrowings and expenditures through a range of dubious activities too dubious to mention.

Normally, this massive fraud would have been picked up by a routine examination of the company's accounts. But it had been able to falsify its figures, among other things, by diverting investors' attention toward its EBITDA figures, which really weren't the real deal at all. I'll spare you the gory details of what followed: suffice it to say that the company went bust, several of the directors went to jail, and the workforce lost most of its accumulated pension funds.

Anyway, Enron spelt the end of Arthur Andersen, the accounting firm that had made such ultimately disastrous use of EBITDA's simplistic appeal. And the world became a safer, wiser place. But many great ideas haven't been properly tested until they've been through the furnace, and now that Enron's demise is firmly in the past, the time may have come to conquer the scepticism and take a closer look at this friendly little beast.

Friendly is certainly a good word to start off with. You don't have any trouble finding mentions of EBITDA in the financial media. If you look up any set of company accounts, or (more particularly) any investment analyst's survey of a listed company, you're likely to find the EBITDA figures right there in front of you, in black and white. Any PR company worth its salt makes sure that the media get told about the EBITDA results, because they're often easier on the eye than the more complex results the authorities are interested in.

EBITDA is great. Unlike the cashflow statements on any normal company's accounts, EBITDA does away with all the boring bits. It abolishes the complexities of figuring out the cost of servicing debts, the depreciation and write-down rates for capital assets like factories and equipment, and a whole lot of other boring things besides. Instead, EBITDA focuses attention purely on important stuff like sales, operating profit margins and so forth. It behaves almost as if the whole question of buying and affording assets was a bit of an irrelevance to the way you should be looking at companies.

Are any alarm bells ringing in your head yet? Good. Warren Buffett, the world's most successful investor, once accused the people who use EBITDA of believing in the tooth fairy. Who else, he asked, did they think was magically bringing in the essential plant, equipment, and expansion funding for all these companies? Aren't people kidding themselves if they think they can safely ignore the cost of these things?

Bearing in mind how badly some companies are already in debt, he had a point. But for me, what makes EBITDA even less reliable is that it has absolutely no firm rules for the calculation, only a sort of general agreement on the principles. The accountants who cook up these figures have enormous scope for 'creativity'. Don't take everything the EBITDA figures say as the absolute truth. Instead, remind yourself that the main American accounting protocol, the US GAAP rules, doesn't acknowledge the validity of EBITDA. And nor do I, for that matter. . The next time you see it, reach for the salt and take a large pinch.

# Spotting a Company's Hidden Debts

A company's market capitalisation doesn't always tell you everything you need to know about how much the company's worth. Looking at the share price and working out a market capitalisation is all very well, but a company can raise money in lots of other ways too:

- ✔ Bank borrowing
- ✔ Bond issuance
- ✔ Preference shares

Options (see Chapter 12) are another method of raising cash while simultaneously rewarding the loyalty of a company's employees and backers. But options can undermine the company's share price because they're practically equivalent to a set of shares that haven't even been issued yet. The market may think it's got the measure of the number of shares in issue - but unless it knows how many more potential shares are out there, in the form of options deals, it won't be able to anticipate successfully how far the company's value ought to be diluted. That means, in effect, that the shares are likely to be priced higher than they really serve to be.

Does that matter? In the case of a large company with options worth perhaps 5 per cent of its issued share base, maybe not. But for a small high-tech company with maybe 25 or 30 per cent's worth of potential shares written as options rather than shares, it could knock a sizeable amount off the actual value of the shares when the options are eventually 'exercised' (i.e. commuted into shares).

Company pension fund liabilities are another kind of debt – and one that the markets are taking more and more notice of, especially now the FRS-17 declaration rules have forced companies to confess to their funding gaps. Chapter 8 describes how FRS is a badly flawed piece of legislation because it takes a once-a-year snapshot of the state of the pension funds and then dumps that figure right into the middle of the company's balance sheet – where it really doesn't belong!

A company's pension funds have no relationship at all to the day-to-day operations of the company itself. Great companies can have defective pension plans, and terrible companies can have magnificently performing ones. So if the balance sheet looks terrible this year but wasn't so bad last year, do stop and examine the accounts to check whether a temporary hole in the investment market's performance is causing a great big blip. Doing so helps you see the true reality.

Don't run away with the idea that pension deficits don't matter at all, though. America has some giant companies, including Ford, General Motors, and General Electric, that the stock markets have savaged at various times because of the huge long-term burdens they have to carry. German companies, too, are much more likely than their British counterparts to be weighed down by pension responsibilities.

As for the more conventional liabilities, you can learn everything you need to know from the accounts, and more specifically from the balance sheets. In Chapter 17 I show you how to navigate your way through these minefields.

# Shorting – and Why It So often Ends in Tears

Shorting is the only halfway sensible way to make money out of a falling stock market. And, according to some people, it isn't particularly sensible either! Why would anyone want to cast aspersions on a company's prospects in such a brutal way – not just by selling shares that they own, but shares that they *don't* own? And how, exactly, does this help to make the world a better place?

Short-sellers have a ready response. By selling shares that they think are about to go down, they draw attention to companies' weaknesses and help to deflate any overblown expectations about those companies' prospects. That, in turn, helps to keep the market a safer place. Oh, and incidentally, shorting can be a jolly good way to make a lot of money, providing that you're ruthless enough and also completely well-informed.

A short seller sets up a special account with a service provider that will enable him to borrow shares from somebody else, for a borrowing fee, and then to sell them in the open market in the hope that before long he'll be able to buy them back for less than he sold them for – thus allowing him to pocket the difference.

Obviously, shorting only makes sense if you're pretty sure that the shares (or indices) you're shorting really are going to fall. If you're wrong and they rise instead of fall, not only do you have to buy them back for more than you sold them for, but all the additional fees and trading costs may make you wish you'd stayed in bed with a nice mug of cocoa instead. By the time you realise that you really do have to buy back the shares at a higher price, the chances are that ten thousand other people who've been shorting the same stocks have also gone into reverse mode, so the price is likely to go even higher than it may otherwise do because of the sheer pressure of competition between the repenting short sellers. (The shorting specialists of this world have a tendency to choose the same candidates for their special attention, so when the tide turns they all reverse their steps together.)

As a beginner, stay well away from shorting until you really know what you're doing. Many of the best investors I know have lost large sums of money on shorting over the years, and only a relatively small number have consistently been able to turn the technique to their advantage.

## 'Bear raids': Ganging up on the victim

Can you measure the effect short sellers have on the overall market? And can old-fashioned 'long' investors (i.e. people who buy shares for long -term capital growth) discover any useful information ?

Short sellers can do a lot of damage to a company's share price performance. If a large group of people identify a troubled company as a candidate for shorting, they often push its share price down well below the level which the majority of people might call a 'sensible level'. That situation's called a 'bear raid', and it can be pretty horrible for the company on the receiving end.

A *bear raid* works like this. Word tends to get round the City rather fast once a group of investors has identified a share for shorting. Other traders then look at the share with fear and trepidation, because they figure that its price may dive under the bear pressure before long – and some of them sell. That action, in turn, sets up a downward spiral that continues until somebody wakes up to the fact that the share's now absurdly under-priced. At this point, I want to be in there looking hard at the risks and thinking about buying into the share.

## Getting information about shorting volumes

Where do you find out who's shorting what? Up to a point you're on your own, because stockbrokers don't usually hand out this sort of information willingly. If they ever did let the world know how much stock they were lending out to short sellers, they'd quickly start new waves of shorting even bigger than the ones they were reporting.

The awkward fact is that a very large proportion of the shorting going on in Britain is the work of hedge funds (Chapter 14 covers these). Hedge funds are unique for two reasons. First, they can deal in literally anything they like – gold, currencies, commodities, futures, emerging markets, anything – and they can shift their strategy in the time they take to press a button on a keyboard. And second, hedge funds are notoriously secretive about their activities. You can't easily establish just what a particular hedge fund has been doing on any one day. (Your best bet is probably to read the gossip columns of the key financial newspapers, because I doubt that anybody else can give you any more solid information.)

But don't despair, because some private research agencies give you an informed online guess of how many shares have been lent out for shorting. The most prominent one is called Data Explorers (www.dataexplorers.co.uk), which provides a series of feeds to the newspapers. You might like to try Googling the company's name to see which papers have been reporting its findings recently. An alternative approach is to look up one of the many websites run by professional shorting specialists, for example Simon Cawkwell A particularly famous example in Britain is Mr Simon Cawkwell, who styles himself Evil Knievel and who has built up a dedicated following among professional bears. But of course, by the time you read this the chances are that somebody else will have stolen his limelight.

Data Explorers runs a shorting blog at shortstories.typepad.com, which is probably going to be a bit more detailed than a beginner would really feel comfortable with. But then, I wouldn't recommend that you try your hand at shorting until you've been sitting on the sidelines and watching for a while. It can be a steep learning curve – but then, when you consider the downside risks, you'll probably agree that it's worth finding out everything you can before you give it a try.

# Chapter 10

# Monitoring the Market's Psychology Using Charts

*In This Chapter*

▶ Working out if charts are just a load of mumbo-jumbo or an essential investing tool

▶ Understanding patterns and the psychology behind them

▶ Introducing charts for even the biggest sceptics

*I*f you're the sceptical type, you may prefer to skip this chapter and spare your blood pressure. At the risk of annoying a lot of very experienced and successful investors who insist that using charts is a load of superstitious nonsense, this chapter talks about the theory suggesting you can learn useful things from the shapes that price trends make when you draw them on a piece of paper – or, more probably, on your computer screen.

Fans of the charting approach have a special name for their hobby that helps to ward off the cynics. They call it *technical analysis* – a term suggesting some sort of scientific basis for what they do. Personally, I prefer to call this approach market psychology. I don't claim to know much about the workings of the human brain, but I can tell you that when a group of people are all in the same situation, they have a definite tendency to think in the same way. And that's where charting can help to figure out what's coming next. Sometimes, anyway.

## Understanding What Charts Can Tell You and What They Can't

The last time I cricked a bone in my back, I went to my doctor for advice. She said I could fix it the official or unofficial way. The official way, she said, was to rest my back for a couple of weeks, take a lot of painkillers, and let nature take its own time to heal me. The unofficial way was to get myself down to a chiropractor, for her to massage my poor aching bones, apply a bit of electroconvulsive therapy, feel the muscles around my spine, and manipulate the affected joints until they realigned.

He wasn't officially recommending the chiropractor, he said, because he wasn't allowed to do that under the medical profession's rules. Chiropractic is an alternative medicine. Practitioners train for a much shorter time than the seven-plus years required to be a doctor, and often have only a working knowledge of the body they're treating. But the discipline also has a habit of getting the treatment right, thanks to years of physical observation of patients. And that's exactly how things worked out with my chiropractor. She had me back up and about after forty minutes of pummelling, and within a week I was completely fixed.

I want you to view technical analysts (TAs) in the same way as chiropractors. They don't always know why the things they do work out as well as they do. And yes, they do come unstuck every so often and get their analysis completely wrong. But they're right often enough to acquire a lot of followers in the investing world. That's why chartists/technical analysts really do have a place in this book. Charts of one sort or another belong in every investor's armoury.

## *Driving on emotions*

How does mass psychology work in the financial markets? Two basic emotions drive the markets: greed and fear. The balance between those two is what keeps the markets on a stable course, because people usually veer about somewhere in the middle. (You can exclude the other great emotion, love, as most people don't have an emotional attachment to their shares. At least, they shouldn't, because that really does get in the way of rational decision making.)

Looking at the way markets invariably over-react to almost any stimulus best proves this greed/fear dichotomy. Once somebody's spotted a bargain and started running in one direction, you can bet your life the greedy herd isn't far behind. Closely followed, of course, by all the fearful ones who follow the greedy people simply because they don't dare to be left out. That situation's all fine and dandy until the day somebody realises that the herd has now run too far in one direction, and prices are getting much too high to be sensible. So a 'correction' occurs, in which the herd retreats and prices swing back towards a sort of equilibrium.

At this point, some of the latecomers probably start to realise that they've lost money on the correction, and they may very well attempt to persuade other investors to launch a renewed push for the 'summit' price so that they can recover their positions. A price recovery may then happen. And the rally may even succeed, if enough genuine reasons exist for the market to think it can squeeze a bit more growth out of this investment. Sometimes you can transform even the most exhausted marathon runners by shouting encouragement at them.

Nevertheless, as often as not, the rally quickly falters and fades. Maybe it goes into a sulk while everybody waits to see what happens next. But more probably, it pitches steeply back downwards. People start saying things like: 'Well, I've had a good run out of this share, and yes, it was very nice when that last-minute rally came along to save it from a decline. But if even the late rally didn't hold the share up for long, that tells me this share really hasn't got enough support from other investors. I'm out of here before it falls any further.'

At that point fear comes surging back into the equation and everybody else joins the rush for the exit door.

Does that story have a ring of truth? And surely a behaviour pattern like that does create certain unmistakable patterns on a share price chart? If so, perhaps people shouldn't be quite so dismissive of technical analysts' belief that they can identify these trends from looking at a chart.

## Viewing charts realistically

Observing behaviour patterns isn't necessarily proof that you can use charts in a predictive way. Knowing what's happened in the past (and why) doesn't give you a cast-iron guarantee that you can figure out what may happen next. But if a chart can teach you something about the mass psychology of the mob, that's useful information.

Lots of extraneous reasons also account for why a rally, for example, fails to stick. Maybe the whole economy's gone into shock and everybody's selling shares, full stop. Or maybe something really exciting's going on somewhere else, and people are pulling their money out of one stock to buy another. A chart can't tell you that. So, on the clear understanding that a chart's a bit of a blunt instrument, the next section describes how to recognise a range of patterns and, more importantly, how to interpret them.

Stockcharts (www.stockcharts.com) is probably the most useful technical analysis forum on the web. You can find a very comprehensive rundown on the theoretical basics at the so-called Chart School on this site, and a useful comparison between the principles of technical analysis and its arch enemy, fundamental analysis.(That's where you value a share the 'rational way', according to how its market position, its share price and its financial performance stack up.)

# Looking for Patterns

The range of patterns that technical analysts look for is almost limitless. Some hardliners think that their science is pure and eternal, and that therefore it has no need to consider the effects of outside influences like changeable economic conditions. Others, perhaps more sensibly, prefer to regard the charts, and the underlying psychology they represent, as just one of the factors to examine when you look at a share. As you can probably guess, I'm one of the latter group.

## Double tops

A *double top* is what you get when a share reaches a peak and falls back by 10–20 per cent, and then does exactly the same again some time later: hitting exactly the same top price the second time round and falling away at the same rate. In effect, the chart describes an inverted W, as shown in Figure 10-1.

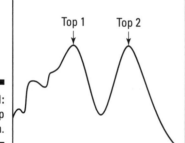

**Figure 10-1:**
A double top
pattern.

What a double top says to an investor is that this stock probably doesn't have very much growth potential left and the time's come to sell. The market's made two attempts to beat a particular price level, but somehow just not enough people are willing to give it their backing. The share has hit a ceiling – that is, a 'resistance level', described in 'Rising floors, support levels, and resistance levels', later in this chapter.

The decline that follows this second peak may be very sharp indeed, but a few small rallies probably occur along the way, during which cannier investors may manage to offload some of their holdings.

I hardly need to tell you that almost nobody's thinking about the company itself – only about the curve! That's how technical analysis works, at least in its purest form. You may say it isn't very analytical at all. And it drives

'fundamentals' investors to distraction. I've seen quite a few serious alterca-
tions on Internet discussion forums between TA fans and 'fundies', and as a
rule the TA fans end up retreating into their own little corners where they
all speak the same language. I think this is rather a shame, because the best
results by far are obtained by comparing and then synthesising the strengths
of the two approaches. Your views might vary, of course.

## Head and shoulders

A *head and shoulders* pattern is what you get when a share rises, dips, rises
to a peak, then falls back and has another go at reaching the peak – but fails.
What you're left with is a pattern that looks, well, like a head and shoulders.
And this is the surest sign you're likely to get that the share's reached its
sell-by date. See Figure 10-2.

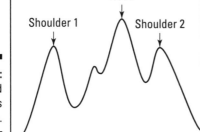

**Figure 10-2:**
A head and
shoulders
pattern.

But what's interesting is that head and shoulders patterns come in an inverse
formation too. In this example, a share's fallen, recovered, fallen to an even
deeper depth, and then started a bigger recovery that takes it pretty much
back to its starting level. But as soon as it dips for a third time, a body of
investors think 'hang on, this share isn't as bad as the pessimists have
been making out'. A renewed buying push starts, and eventually you get to
something called a breakout.

A *breakout* is what every TA investor dreams of spotting. That's when all the
previous assumptions about what the market can and can't bear go out of
the window, and some pent-up trend gets unleashed as the magic spell of the
resistance level gets broken. (I cover resistance levels in the section 'Rising
floors, support levels, and resistance levels' later in this chapter.) You're
more than welcome to tell me that the whole idea of having floors and
ceilings to a share price is strictly for the fairies in the first place. But wearing
my TA hat just for now, a sizeable number of people think that a breakout's
a development on the general scale of Jupiter and Mars aligning with each
other. A breakout is a big event.

Being a bit less sceptical, just for once, you can reason that a breakout signifies that something has indeed changed in the psychology of the market. People have suddenly abandoned whatever was holding them back. And if you're quick enough, you can profit from the emerging change in the conditions. Figure 10-3 illustrates a breakout.

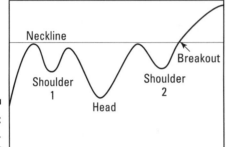

**Figure 10-3:**
A breakout.

In the same way, a double bottom (no, really), looks like a normal W. In a *double bottom*, the share price has tried twice to plunge below a certain level, but the market isn't playing ball and the price has rebounded strongly. Once the price has recovered for the second time to the level that prevailed at the start of the W, a TA investor feels pretty sure that another breakout has happened, and the likelihood is that the share is now free to rise much more quickly.

## Rising floors, support levels, and resistance levels

Look at a typical TA chart and you're likely to notice that it's covered with straight diagonal lines that run roughly in parallel with the main trends over a given period. One soars above the curve and one's below it, so that the actual share price line is sandwiched between the two.

Why? TAs believe that at any one time the market includes a fairly fixed level of tolerance that dictates just how high a share's price can reasonably be allowed to go, and another level of tolerance for how low it can go. In other words, if a share goes outside those limits, a fair number of investors say no thanks. The share has hit an invisible wall.

You're probably thinking that this is close to mumbo-jumbo. Why on earth should the 'collective psychology' of the market decide, all at once, that an absolute ceiling applies to a share's price beyond which it can't go? And an absolute floor (the 'support level') below which nobody's tempted to sell it?

These are good questions, and I honestly can't answer them. But sheer experience dictates that a great many shares seem to run into these frustrating barriers, so maybe they do exist after all.

I can suggest rational reasons for some of these phenomena, but not all. If a share has been floated on the stock market at 200p but then drops alarmingly back to 100p, a lot of investors may say, 'Yes, I made a mistake, but I'm jolly well not going to sell that share until it reaches the price I bought it at – and then I'm out of here.' So the price hits an invisible wall at 200p.

Other investors may leave instructions with their broker to sell if ever the dividend yield goes lower than the bank rate, or if the price/earnings ratio (see Chapter 2 for more on these) gets to be more than 50 per cent above the sector average. You can't ever really know, which is why the mumbo-jumbo accusations don't stop coming.

What you can say, though, is that if (big *if*) these ceilings and support levels are genuine, their very consistency suggests that the market's a bit more logical than some people suppose. Not every day does a fundie accuse a TA devotee of being excessively logical, but these things do happen.

# Triangles

The apotheosis of the support and resistance line theory (see the preceding section) comes when an investor reckons that these two lines are converging. As a general rule they tend to hover around in parallel to each other like the outer layers of a sandwich. But when you get a chart like Figure 10-4, a TA specialist says, 'Whoa, this market is getting surer about exactly what it wants.'

And indeed it is. The chart shows a share that's got hardly any more room for manoeuvre. The market's ideas about its top and bottom price are converging so progressively that all the doubt is being squeezed out as the weeks go by. Perhaps the company's in the final stages of a takeover bid, and everyone's pretty sure what the final price may be?

**Figure 10-4:**
A triangle
pattern.

Source: Chart by MetaStock

More types of triangles exist than I have the patience or the room to describe in this chapter. You can get soft bottoms, triple bottoms, flags, pennants, wedges, and cups and handles. If you've got the time and the inclination, you can find plenty of information about these TA trends (try the Stockcharts website, www.stockcharts.com). Whether you choose to believe in them or not is entirely up to you. But at least now you understand what people are yakking on about in the discussion forums. That's good enough for me, because by bringing them to your attention I've primed you for the day you meet these peculiar terms in the flesh.

## The Elliott Wave theory

Forget about watching tiny share price movements over short spaces of time, and turn your gaze to the heavens instead for the bigger picture. The giant of TA theories is the Elliott Wave.

The *Elliott Wave* is half-philosophy, half-superstition. It dictates that nearly all really important stock market developments come in predictable waves. And that something mystically called Fibonacci numbers determine these waves.

Bull markets (long-term trends of stock market growth) are characterised by five major waves, according to Elliott Wave theorists: a first wave, followed by a small relapse, then a third wave and another fallback, and then the fifth really big wave where all the action really happens. You may hear TA enthusiasts arguing for months on end as to whether the fifth wave has really started, or whether the third wave has merely had a fit of indigestion and thrown a minor wobble that makes you think the first wave has started. Chapter 4 covers bull markets.

But bear markets (longish periods of stock market decline) give you less warning. They have only three waves, according to Elliott Wave followers: a first falling wave, then a small recovery, then the *big* drop! See Chapter 4 on bear markets.

I'm oversimplifying this theory quite horribly, and I apologise to all genuine Elliott Wave people for my unforgivable heresy. If you want the real lowdown, the information section on the Stockcharts website (www.stockcharts.com) gives you plenty to think about.

## Using Charts to Check Your Decisions

I don't ever buy a share, or a tracker, or a commodity, without taking a good look at the historical charts – maybe going back three years, or maybe even five or ten years. Until I've seen with my very own eyes how the share's behaved in the past, I don't feel I have a proper understanding of it.

Knowing that a company has recently announced a bright new trading statement isn't much consolation to me if the stock market turns out to have marked its share price down as soon as the news became public. Either that optimistic announcement wasn't quite as straightforward as it appeared (that is, the market flatly refused to believe it), or else the market was expecting the news to be even better, so the price fall signifies its disappointment. These things really do happen, and a chart gives me a picture in a split second that can be more useful than the proverbial thousand words.

Conversely, I may be very impressed by the news that a share has put on a lot of money in the last year. And rather less impressed by the discovery that it used to be four times as high.

Increasingly, a new kind of interactive share chart is appearing that allows you to grab a 'time slice' from the chart with your mouse and then home in on the fine detail. If commodities like oil or metals are your thing, you can get excellent free charts from the likes of Kitco (www.kitco.com) or TFC (www.tfc-charts.com). I like the currency charts from X-Rates (www.x-rates.com) and HiFX (www.hifx.co.uk), but you've plenty of choice, so do take the time to find the ones that suit you best.

Figure 10-5 shows an example, a five-day chart for British Telecom that looks rather tasty. Goodness, the share price is up by 14 per cent in three days. Talk of a major cost-cutting exercise is in the papers, and the management's making positive noises about turning the company round after a disastrous run of bad publicity caused by some frankly unforgivable management failings. So far, so good. This is looking promising.

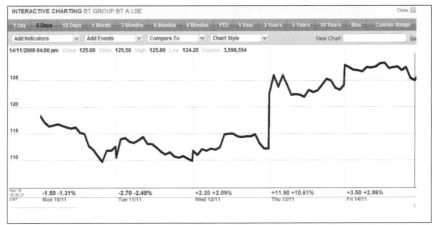

**Figure 10-5:** Five-day chart for British Telecom.

But oh dear, Figure 10-6 shows what the same chart looks like if you take the five-year view. The share has lost nearly two-thirds of its value in the space of

12 months, and you suddenly start to see that 14 per cent share price rally in a completely different context. So is the share still such a bargain?

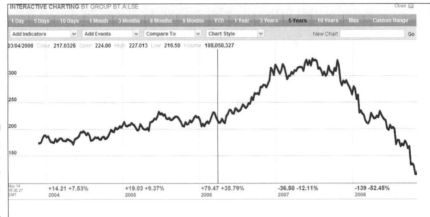

**Figure 10-6:** Five-year chart for British Telecom.

Don't get me wrong here. Like a lot of long-term investors, I don't mind if a share's fallen by quite a bit in the last few years, just as long as I understand why. After all, the time to buy a share is when it's cheap. But I do like to see a share that's starting to stage a bit of a comeback before I lay down my money. And a rally that's so badly counter to the trend is a bad enough omen to make me very suspicious.

Armed with this information, I now go in hard with some thorough research that tells me whether I can really believe in this company. Maybe this research convinces me, and maybe it doesn't. But can you think of any other way to assemble so much information in such a short space of time?

Whatever you happen to think about the strengths and weaknesses of using charts for predicting the market's psychology, they do come up trumps for spotting trends and generally looking out for candidates – and for weeding out the duds, too.

# Part IV
# Using the Pages for More Advanced Investments

'Your stock market investments, at this very moment, are being chosen with meticulous care by our team of approved experts.'

# In this part . . .

*W*e start to get into slightly racier territory in this section of the book. Chapter 11 explores the many advantages of broadening out your horizons to include foreign shares as well as British ones. Then we discuss the so-called derivatives market – futures, options and so forth – and we take a long look at the fast-growing commodities sector. I show you how to use the new generation of exchange traded funds, which are a cheap and flexible way of backing your hunches on gold, oil and other basic items.

Finally we move on to managed funds – unit trusts, investment trusts, guaranteed income bonds (a kind of stock market tracker), and hedge funds. What do they do? How do they calculate their prices? Why are some riskier than others? And where do you get up-to-date information about them?

# Chapter 11

# Going International

· · · · · · · · · · · · · · · · · · · · · · · · · · · · · · · · · · · · · · · · · · · · ·

## In This Chapter

▶ Getting the international mix right

▶ Making the most of national differences

▶ Finding the information you need

▶ Using currency differentials

· · · · · · · · · · · · · · · · · · · · · · · · · · · · · · · · · · · · · · · · · · · · ·

*W*e've got a global economy in which every country's fortunes are linked in some way or other with all the others. And a global electronic investment structure which allows you to put your money into almost any company of your choice, no matter where it might be. Not to mention a tax regime in Britain which is being steadily loosened up so as to let you get the full benefit of tax-efficient investment in a growing number of countries. So what could be more natural than to feel like spreading your wings and investing a little of your cash in some of these less familiar places? Even a beginner can do it.

But first, let's put your mind at rest on one important point. You don't need to have any special language skills to buy foreign investments these days. The chances are that every company you're likely to be interested in has an English-language section on its website – and if you buy its shares through the London Stock Exchange (which is often possible), you get the same transparency and investor protection as for any UK share.

If you still don't feel up to the task of going international alone, hundreds of managed funds enable you to take a stake in another country without getting up to your neck in complications. And these days, London-listed Exchange-Traded Funds (ETFs) make international investing twice as easy because they're just like shares – but with no stamp duty!

# Why You Need Foreign Shares in Your Portfolio

You don't have to think too much to realise that pegging your investment fortune to the fate of the London Stock Exchange (LSE) is limiting yourself just a little. You must have noticed that countries' economies often move at different rates. So doesn't the logic follow that, by taking an interest in a few items from those countries, you can insulate yourself from some of the ups and downs of the British market?

Besides, as I've said, investing in foreign stock markets is such a simple matter these days. All you need is a suitable kind of trading account with one of the main *execution-only* stockbroking firms (that's a broker that doesn't actually give you advice, just buys and sells things when you tell it to). Running the account may typically cost you £30 a year in charges, although at the moment you can get an account for nothing with some of the online brokers.

A lot of the time, you don't need to set up anything so complicated. The range of foreign-company stocks that you can buy into in London may amaze you, because they have dual or multiple listings that make them available on more than one market at a time. So although the shares you see in the *Financial Times* or on the London Stock exchange website are listed in euros, or dollars, or whatever, the price you pay is in sterling. And because the shares are listed according to London's rules, the level of investor protection you get is just the same as if you're buying ICI.

You're more or less forced to go 'offshore' if your interests extend to certain types of company. You don't find very many gold and diamond mining companies in the LSE's main-market listings, because most of the best and most interesting ones are listed only in Canada, America, Australia, or South Africa. (Although the higher-risk Alternative Investment Market, or AIM, will give you a fair selection of the racier companies.) If you're looking for clothing manufacturers or sugar producers or alternative energy companies, you're probably going to struggle to come up with many leading names in London, because they tend to be based in low-cost manufacturing centres. (Some clothing companies are on AIM, but otherwise you're restricted to top-end producers like Burberry if you don't fancy going offshore.)

Don't forget, too, that even if you don't feel like going the whole hog and buying shares directly, you can get some exposure to foreign stock markets by buying either investment trusts with a regional bias, or perhaps Exchange-Traded funds. ETF operators like Lyxor (a subsidiary of the French AXA group) or iShares (part of Barclays International) can sell you what is effectively a tracker fund that shadows the movement of a foreign stock market's main indices. I examine tracker funds in more detail in Chapter 14.

I describe ETFs in more detail in Chapters 13 and 14. For the moment, though, all you need to know is that you buy and sell an ETF on the London Stock exchange, just like any other share. You can put it into a tax-efficient savings plan like an Individual Savings Account (ISA) or a Self-Invested Pension Policy (SIPP). Unlike the unit trusts and investment trusts (Chapter 14 covers these) that you may be using already for your pension and savings funds, you don't pay any joining fees or management fees. You also don't have any problems selling an ETF, even on the spur of the moment, because the ETF markets are very liquid (that is, enough people are always out there ready to buy ETFs, so you never need to worry about getting stuck with them). And, perhaps best of all, you don't pay any stamp duty when you buy an ETF – just the dealer's commission, which may be as low as £5, and a very small 'spread' between the buying and selling price that's rarely as much as 0.1 per cent.

# Riding the Macro Waves

The main reason I enjoy trading in foreign shares is that they offer me a way of escaping the strictures of the UK investment scene. There have been so many times in recent decades when Britain's economy has seemed to be falling while America's has been soaring – or vice versa! So many occasions when the euro has seemed so cheap that it was bound to rebound, with massively beneficial effects on my European shareholdings. Not that we should try and draw up any hard and fast rules about this, of course, because one year's growth market can all too quickly become the next year's problem area. But you get my point.

In short, I'm convinced that a judicious mix of international stocks can provide your portfolio with shock absorbers to help it weather a bout of stormy weather at home.

What sort of storms am I thinking of? Well, I talk in Chapter 3 about the way in which economic cycles affect whole economies, and in Chapter 13 you can also find a brief analysis of how these cycles work on the commodities markets that supply raw materials to the world's manufacturers. What I'm driving at is that the various markets and economies of the world are never in completely stationary relationships to each other. Instead, they rub up and down against each other as their various fortunes improve and deteriorate – and, with only a little guesswork, you can often figure out which ones may be in the ascendant next.

All well and good. But this is sweeping stuff. How can you get all this underlying economic information, ideally in a format that applies regular statistical criteria across a range of countries? Probably the best place to start is business magazines like *The Economist*, whose back pages are filled with cross-border comparative material (also available at www.economist.com).

But if you don't have an *Economist* subscription and you need a free supply of carefully crafted information, try the IMF website (www.imf.org) or the Organisation for Economic Co-operation and Development (www.oecd.org) for the latest on economic trends.

# Investing in Emerging Markets

You may, not surprisingly, decide to keep your foreign investments safely restricted to the very big stock markets – America, Germany, Canada, Australia, or perhaps Japan. After all, those are the countries where you probably feel safest. They have their share of problems, of course, but what they also have are very large domestic shareholder bases – that's to say, very large numbers of their own citizens are direct investors, so you know that there's always likely to be enough market activity going on to avoid big 'liquidity squeezes' – the times when nobody is either buying or selling shares, and when share prices can go a little stir-crazy as a result.

You probably don't fancy the idea of stock-picking in a country whose language you don't speak. (Although, in practice, you may be amazed at how many emerging-market companies have English-language sections on their websites.) And you're probably feeling rather wary of investing your money in a country where the stock market rules may not be the same as yours.

Rightly so! How would you feel if it turned out that insider trading was tolerated in the country you'd just bought into? Or if you didn't get your dividends because you were a foreigner? Or simply that you didn't know the 'inside track' of the business environment, so that your chosen company came off worse in a race with one of its rivals?

For all of these reasons, you're better off investing through a fund rather than going international yourself, if it's the less-developed stock markets that especially interest you. Even in today's electronically linked markets, the chances are that you'll be at a disadvantage to the locals at least some of the time.

# Finding Information on International Investments

Inevitably you want to keep track of your foreign investments. If you don't have time to regularly read one of the financial heavyweight newspapers, or to keep your nose permanently pressed to your computer screen, you need to look elsewhere for the information you want.

# *Using comparison charts*

The *FT* online (`markets.ft.com/markets/overview.asp`) is one of the very best comparison sites. It allows you to survey a range of big-picture economic and investment criteria and provides breakdowns for stock markets, currencies, bonds, and commodities.

You can, for instance, get a daily facsimile of the *FT*'s listings of all the dominant stock market indices of the world (see Chapter 3 on indices), showing you where those indices have been heading over the last few days and telling you what the 12-month highs and lows have been — see Figure 11-1.

But Figure 11-1 is a strangely unhelpful chart, considering the amount of detail it contains. It only really helps you if you're already familiar with each of the indices you're interested in, and if you've been following them really closely. My personal choice instead is the chart in Figure 11-2, which shows you the key ratios for each of the most important global markets: the price/earnings ratio and the dividend yield.

Oddly, this chart doesn't specify which of the various stock market indices for each country it's actually talking about. Instead, it describes its content simply as 'a sample of stocks that cover at least 75 per cent of each market's capitalisation' (that is, at least three-quarters of the total value of the stock markets concerned).

**Figure 11-1:** World equity market summary from the Financial Times.

| WORLD EQUITY MARKETS AT A GLANCE | | | | | | | |
|---|---|---|---|---|---|---|---|
| Country | Index | Oct 15 | Oct 14 | Oct 13 | 2008 High | | 2008 Low | |
| **Argentina** | Merval | 1185.73 | 1349.69 | (c) | 2248.63 22/5/08 | 1185.73 15/10/08 |
| | General | 68261.31 | 77044.91 | (c) | 128072.40 22/5/08 | 68261.31 15/10/08 |
| **Australia** | S&P/All Ordinaries | 4272.5 | 4311.5 | 4141.9 | 6434.10 2/1/08 | 3939.50 10/10/08 |
| | S&P/ASX 200 Res | 4055.6 | 4219.4 | 3999.5 | 7145.20 19/5/08 | 3782.40 10/10/08 |
| | S&P/ASX 200 | 4300.0 | 4335.2 | 4180.7 | 6353.20 2/1/08 | 3960.70 10/10/08 |
| **Austria** | ATX | 2270.20 | 2394.35 | 2257.78 | 4532.10 19/5/08 | 2002.05 10/10/08 |
| **Belgium** | BEL 20 | 2082.59 | 2213.87 | 2324.80 | 4117.49 3/1/08 | 2082.59 15/10/08 |
| | BEL Mid | 2461.42 | 2612.41 | 2481.86 | 4026.51 2/1/08 | 2312.25 10/10/08 |
| | Brussels Cash | 17937.72 | 19175.82 | 19442.59 | 33984.21 3/1/08 | 17535.63 10/10/08 |
| **Brazil** | Bovespa | 36667.60 | 41569.03 | 40829.13 | 73516.80 20/5/08 | 35609.54 10/10/08 |
| **Canada** | S&P/TSX Met & Min | 369.98 | 401.93 | (c) | 888.96 16/5/08 | 365.31 10/10/08 |
| | S&P/TSX 60 | 562.16 | 602.65 | (c) | 900.93 18/6/08 | 546.25 13/10/08 |
| | S&P/TSX Comp | 9323.83 | 9955.66 | (c) | 15073.13 18/6/08 | 9065.16 10/10/08 |
| **Chile** | IGPA Gen ♥ | 11648.23 | 11705.06 | 11398.75 | 14933.86 25/6/08 | 10411.65 10/10/08 |
| **China** | Shanghai A | 2095.04 | 2118.79 | 2177.92 | 5770.53 14/1/08 | 1990.90 18/9/08 |
| | Shanghai B | 111.19 | 113.09 | 115.43 | 373.14 4/1/08 | 110.70 10/10/08 |
| | Shanghai Comp | 1994.67 | 2017.32 | 2073.57 | 5497.90 14/1/08 | 1895.84 18/9/08 |
| | Shenzhen A | 551.01 | 556.12 | 568.58 | 1659.61 15/1/08 | 551.01 15/10/08 |
| | Shenzhen B | 268.53 | 272.59 | 274.06 | 724.49 14/1/08 | 265.28 10/10/08 |
| | FTSE/Xinhua A200 | 5361.00 | 5416.78 | 5559.47 | 16167.93 14/1/08 | 5287.45 18/9/08 |
| | FTSE/Xinhua B35 | 3998.58 | 4074.57 | 4130.50 | 12090.30 4/1/08 | 3951.76 10/10/08 |
| | FTSE/Xinhua B All Share | 3013.87 | 3062.90 | 3104.97 | 9243.96 4/1/08 | 2988.00 10/10/08 |
| **Colombia** | CSE Index | 7666.79 | 8192.50 | (c) | 10868.78 30/6/08 | 7502.73 10/10/08 |
| **Croatia** | CROBEX | 2542.26 | 2762.62 | 2561.37 | 5279.14 4/1/08 | 2209.47 10/10/08 |
| **Cyprus** | CSE M&P Gen | 1934.84 | 2066.75 | 1941.00 | 4880.97 2/1/08 | 1719.38 10/10/08 |
| **Czech Republic** | PX | 998.8 | 1085.1 | 981.5 | 1808.60 2/1/08 | 888.50 10/10/08 |
| **Denmark** | OMX Copenhagen 20 | 298.57 | 317.59 | 308.63 | 468.66 19/5/08 | 280.67 10/10/08 |
| **Egypt** | CASE 30 | 5972.59 | 6138.19 | 5760.90 | 11935.67 5/5/08 | 5478.55 8/10/08 |
| | CMA General | 2072.52 | 2112.77 | 2012.92 | 3889.17 5/5/08 | 1993.78 8/10/08 |
| **Estonia** | OMX Tallinn | 399.10 | 409.62 | 399.00 | 744.22 3/1/08 | 387.75 10/10/08 |
| **Finland** | OMX Helsinki General | 6039.12 | 6450.62 | 6193.69 | 11506.04 3/1/08 | 5799.43 10/10/08 |
| **France** | CAC 40 | 3381.07 | 3628.52 | 3531.50 | 5550.36 2/1/08 | 3176.49 10/10/08 |
| | SBF 120 | 2436.40 | 2612.61 | 2540.09 | 4015.90 2/1/08 | 2291.04 10/10/08 |
| | SBF 250 | 2380.98 | 2551.10 | 2480.11 | 3913.71 2/1/08 | 2239.14 10/10/08 |
| **Germany** | M-DAX | 5657.63 | 6052.04 | 5962.49 | 10068.96 19/5/08 | 5325.60 10/10/08 |
| | XETRA Dax | 4861.63 | 5199.19 | 5062.45 | 7949.11 2/1/08 | 4544.31 10/10/08 |
| | TecDAX* | 553.00 | 585.97 | 584.64 | 970.51 2/1/08 | 516.75 10/10/08 |
| | FAZ Aktien | 1450.25 | 1496.47 | 1385.25 | 2217.48 2/1/08 | 1301.91 10/10/08 |
| **Greece** | Athens Gen | 2381.57 | 2561.80 | 2506.45 | 5207.44 2/1/08 | 2372.09 10/10/08 |
| | FTSE/ASE 20 | 1314.90 | 1421.93 | 1384.62 | 2762.60 2/1/08 | 1308.98 10/10/08 |
| **Hong Kong** | Hang Seng | 15998.30 | 16832.88 | 16312.16 | 27615.85 9/1/08 | 14796.87 10/10/08 |
| | HS China Enterprise | 7894.06 | 8435.46 | 8083.43 | 16139.46 9/1/08 | 7135.80 10/10/08 |
| | HSCC Red Chip | 3174.45 | 3364.65 | 3185.92 | 6055.82 4/1/08 | 2854.83 10/10/08 |
| **Hungary** | Bux | 14484.10 | 16437.10 | 15387.80 | 26111.36 8/1/08 | 14484.10 10/10/08 |
| **India** | BSE Sens | 10809.12 | 11483.40 | 11309.09 | 20873.33 8/1/08 | 10527.85 10/10/08 |
| | S&P CNX 500 | 2553.30 | 2685.05 | 2654.35 | 5502.60 4/1/08 | 2507.55 10/10/08 |

(c) Closed. (u) Unavailable. † Correction. ♥ Subject to official recalculation.

## RATIOS

| | Oct 14 | | Oct 13 | | Week ago | | | Oct 14 | | Oct 13 | | Week ago | |
|---|---|---|---|---|---|---|---|---|---|---|---|---|---|
| | Yield | P/E | Yield | P/E | Yield | P/E | | Yield | P/E | Yield | P/E | Yield | P/E |
| Argentina | 6.2 | 9.1 | 6.4 | 8.7 | 6.1 | 9.2 | Mexico | 2.9 | 9.8 | 2.9 | 9.7 | 3.0 | 9.5 |
| Australia | 5.3 | 11.5 | 5.5 | 11.0 | 5.0 | 12.2 | Netherlands | 6.1 | 5.0 | 6.1 | 5.0 | 5.7 | 5.3 |
| Austria | 4.0 | 7.7 | 4.2 | 7.2 | 3.9 | 7.8 | †AEX | 6.4 | 4.6 | 6.3 | 4.7 | 5.8 | 5.1 |
| Belgium | 8.2 | 6.1 | 7.8 | 6.3 | 7.2 | 6.9 | New Zealand | 5.9 | 13.7 | 6.3 | 13.0 | 5.8 | 13.9 |
| Brazil | 4.4 | 10.5 | 4.5 | 10.3 | 4.5 | 10.3 | Norway | 5.1 | 5.3 | 5.4 | 5.0 | 4.8 | 7.1 |
| Canada | 3.8 | 11.7 | 4.2 | 10.7 | 3.8 | 11.6 | Pakistan | 5.5 | 8.4 | 5.5 | 8.4 | 5.5 | 8.4 |
| †S&P/TSX Cmp | 4.3 | 11.0 | 4.7 | 10.1 | 4.3 | 10.9 | Peru | 6.3 | 30.5 | 6.4 | 29.6 | 6.1 | 27.5 |
| Chile | 4.7 | 13.8 | 4.8 | 13.4 | 4.8 | 13.4 | Philippines | 1.9 | 14.5 | 1.9 | 14.5 | 1.9 | 14.5 |
| China | 2.6 | 10.6 | 2.7 | 10.2 | 2.6 | 10.5 | Poland | 5.0 | 8.9 | 5.2 | 8.5 | 4.8 | 9.1 |
| Colombia | 0.9 | 21.9 | 1.0 | 20.5 | 0.9 | 22.4 | Portugal | 5.2 | 10.2 | 5.5 | 9.8 | 5.6 | 9.6 |
| Cyprus | 8.0 | 4.9 | 8.6 | 4.5 | 8.6 | 4.7 | Romania | 4.9 | 7.2 | 5.5 | 6.4 | 4.9 | 7.6 |
| Czech Rep | 5.1 | 13.6 | 5.5 | 12.6 | 5.2 | 13.4 | Russia | 3.1 | 5.8 | 3.2 | 5.5 | 3.1 | 5.8 |
| Denmark | 2.4 | 11.0 | 2.5 | 10.6 | 2.5 | 10.5 | Singapore | 4.3 | 6.1 | 4.4 | 6.0 | 4.2 | 6.3 |
| Finland | 6.7 | 8.8 | 7.0 | 8.5 | 6.8 | 8.7 | South Africa | 4.6 | 10.0 | 4.8 | 9.6 | 4.8 | 9.5 |
| France | 4.8 | 9.2 | 4.9 | 9.0 | 4.7 | 9.4 | South Korea | 2.1 | 9.9 | 2.1 | 9.9 | 2.0 | 10.1 |
| Germany | 4.0 | 10.8 | 4.1 | 10.7 | 4.0 | 10.8 | Spain | 5.0 | 8.4 | 5.0 | 8.2 | 4.7 | 8.9 |
| †Dax 30 | 4.7 | 10.5 | 4.8 | 10.2 | 4.6 | 10.7 | †Ibex 35 | 5.4 | 9.0 | 5.6 | 8.7 | 5.1 | 9.5 |
| Greece | 4.2 | 9.5 | 4.3 | 9.3 | 4.2 | 9.7 | Sri Lanka | 4.2 | 7.6 | 3.9 | 8.1 | 4.1 | 8.3 |
| Hong Kong | 2.8 | 10.6 | 2.9 | 10.1 | 2.8 | 10.5 | Sweden | 5.8 | 7.9 | 5.9 | 7.7 | 5.7 | 7.9 |
| †Hang Seng | 4.1 | 10.2 | 4.3 | 9.9 | 4.1 | 10.2 | Switzerland | 2.8 | 13.5 | 2.9 | 12.9 | 2.7 | 13.9 |
| Hungary | 4.5 | 9.7 | 4.8 | 9.1 | 4.2 | 10.4 | Taiwan | 6.6 | 8.7 | 6.6 | 8.7 | 5.3 | 11.2 |
| India | 1.5 | 14.3 | 1.5 | 14.1 | 1.4 | 14.6 | Thailand | 6.0 | 7.0 | 6.3 | 6.6 | 5.8 | 7.2 |
| Indonesia | 1.9 | 21.2 | 1.9 | 21.2 | 1.9 | 21.2 | Turkey | 3.2 | 6.6 | 3.4 | 6.3 | 3.1 | 6.8 |
| Ireland | 6.5 | 4.7 | 6.7 | 4.5 | 6.1 | 5.1 | UK | 6.0 | 8.3 | 6.2 | 8.1 | 5.8 | 8.7 |
| Israel | 5.3 | 9.0 | 5.3 | 9.0 | 5.1 | 9.2 | USA | 3.1 | 12.2 | 3.1 | 12.3 | 3.1 | 12.3 |
| Italy | 7.8 | 7.2 | 8.1 | 6.9 | 7.8 | 7.2 | †Dow Jones | 3.3 | 11.4 | 3.3 | 11.5 | 3.3 | 11.6 |
| Japan | 2.3 | 11.5 | 2.6 | 10.1 | 2.2 | 12.3 | †S&P 500 | 3.2 | 12.1 | 3.2 | 12.3 | 3.2 | 12.2 |
| †Topix | 2.4 | 11.3 | 2.7 | 10.0 | 2.3 | 11.6 | Venezuela | 10.3 | 2.1 | 8.5 | 2.1 | 7.5 | 2.2 |
| Luxemburg | 3.5 | 6.1 | 3.5 | 6.1 | 3.4 | 6.2 | | | | | | | |
| Malaysia | 3.3 | 15.3 | 3.3 | 15.3 | 3.3 | 15.3 | | | | | | | |

**Figure 11-2:** Key ratios chart from the *Financial Times*

Country Yields and P/E's relate to a sample of stocks that cover at least 75% of each markets capitalisation.
† Losses are excluded from the P/E calculation on country indices.　　　Source: Thomson Reuters.

I have no idea how many individual calculations go into those daily computations of the average price/earnings ratios and dividend yields in all those countries, but the number must be absolutely mind-boggling. The effort required to research and calculate the average p/e from 75 per cent of the London Stock Exchange's shares (by size) every day stretches anyone's computer skills; but to do it for 60 or so different markets, many of which don't record their results in anything like the same degree of detail as London, is a mighty achievement.

## *Locating information on individual companies*

Comparison charts are a reasonable start for monitoring your foreign investments. But unless you're investing in a tracker that shadows a whole stock market index, such a chart isn't exactly going to give you everything you want. Where are you going to get the information you need about individual companies?

Unfortunately, for companies with foreign bases, the *FT*'s excellent online resources don't always do the job. If you look up the *FT*'s news reports for even a German company, let alone a Chinese one, you might very well draw a blank because often the information's not there. Nor do you find very much recent news on the London Stock Exchange website (www.londonstock exchange.co.uk), although you can find good charts that go back five years. (To go even further back, you're probably better off with the *FT*'s 'interactive charting' facility, which reaches as much as 20 years into the past, even for non-UK companies.)

Yahoo!'s UK finance site (http://uk.finance.yahoo.com) gives you a complete company profile, together with news, charts, recent trade prices, and quite often a message board containing views from other investors.

Also scour the newspaper files for news of any sort about the company you're interested in. The *FT*'s premium-priced 'Level 2' searches provide access to possibly the best background information you can get, because they bring in updates and news from more than 100 news sources. (By the way, you can often get a limited use of this amazing facility for free.) The information exists – you just need to do a bit more legwork with a foreign company than you would with a comparable British one.

## Overlooking structural differences

Occasionally, you run into a genuine structural mismatch. Some eastern economies measure their progress in terms of gross national product (or national production), instead of gross domestic product as in Britain. Their employment statistics may be based on different parameters, their idea of inflation may be calculated differently, and – in extreme cases – their profit and loss calculations may classify some things differently. Even within Europe, the accounting conventions that apply to various classes of company differ across European boundaries.

Ignore all these differences. Unless you're looking at a huge deficit in a place where most people expect a surplus, the best approach is to take a deep breath and mutter a prayer to the effect that if those accounts are good enough for the country's own stock market analysts, they're probably good enough for you. Trying to insist on more conformity with the UK than this just frustrates you and serves no point.

# Understanding Currency Risks and Using Them to Your Advantage

Making 25 per cent on the Indian stock market is a waste of time if the rupee falls by 25 per cent against the pound and leaves you right back where you started. Obviously that's an extreme example of currency movements, but you get my point.

Fortunately this argument has an upside as well. If you can anticipate the general trend of a currency's movements over the next few months or years, then you can add to your gains. What's especially gratifying is that often the economies that are on the up have the currencies in demand. That isn't so surprising, really, when you consider that a country experiencing lots of growth attracts other foreigners besides you, all of whom want to buy that currency to gain their stake in the country's future.

But how do you get a handle on which way the currency markets are going? If I knew all the answers to that one, I wouldn't need to work for a living. The shifting currency scene has caught so many investors out over the last 50 years – including some very rich and powerful people – that the consensus view among professionals is that currencies adopt a 'random walk' that's always unpredictable in the short term, but generally pretty reliable in the medium term.

No one can really be certain about these trends, and the cost of getting them wrong can be quite horrendous. But here are a few things that the currency market really, really hates:

- ✔ A sharply slowing economy, especially if it causes companies in the target country to go bust.

- ✔ A steep increase in inflation, because inflationary pressures in the future make the fixed-interest returns from government bonds look pretty silly. (I explain this principle in Chapter 6.) In this situation, foreign investors are likely to try to pull out their cash investments, which only makes the situation worse and damages the currency still further.

- ✔ A weakening interest rate policy, especially when other countries are raising their own bank rates. The only exception is if the markets think that lower interest rates may spark stronger economic growth.

- ✔ A big foreign trade deficit, especially on top of a heavy foreign debt that may make international investors try to pull out their investment stakes at short notice. A big pull-out of foreign money always hurts a currency.

My own, rather unscientific, view is that although finding a first-world currency moving by more than 10 per cent compared to its historical average against other first-world currencies is common, for those deviations to go beyond 25 per cent is pretty rare.

Which is not to say that it can't happen, however. The pound lost 25 per cent of its value against the dollar between April and November 2008 – which was pretty good going considering that the US economy itself was suffering. But it was an ill wind that brought nobody any good. Anyone in Britain who'd invested in a commodity like gold, that was denominated in dollars, would have made a big profit even though the price of bullion was itself in decline at the time.

Here's another example of how currency movements can work in your favour. A few years ago, I was able to save quite a lot of money off the price of my new German car by buying my euros while the pound was relatively strong and then paying the supplier in euros. If you're buying a house in France or a boat in Italy, the same logic can apply. And the German shares I bought during the trough at the end of 2005 have rewarded me in two ways – first because of their strong growth and secondly because of the beneficial following tailwind they got from the currency markets at a time when the British markets were going nowhere fast.

Looking outside your own country's shores can be worth the effort.

So let's summarise. If you're willing to go that extra mile (or should that read kilometre?), and if you can locate and research investments that aren't tightly tied to the United Kingdom itself, you can improve your portfolio in three different ways. You can dilute the risk of your overall portfolio by spreading it between a range of economies, some of which will be coming up while others are going down. You can benefit from changes in currency exchange rates that will sometimes be so big that they outweigh any downward movement in those foreign markets – assuming that you're a sterling-based investor, of course – and you can more generally get a feel for the character of an investment world that's becoming more global as time goes by. And which won't ever go back to the way it was 20 years ago.

Are you ready for the challenge? In Chapters 14 and 15 we look at related questions, such as how to read the international environment in the first place, and where to find the information you need.

# Chapter 12

# Delving into Derivatives

*In This Chapter*

▶ Considering futures

▶ Deciding on warrants

▶ Recognising your options, your choices, and your responsibilities

*I*'m going to start this Chapter by saying that derivatives are probably the deepest water you're ever likely to get into as an amateur investor. No, actually, I'm going to go even further than that. Don't get into derivatives at all until you're good and ready, because they can really be far too dangerous for a beginner. A wrongly placed futures contract can leave you worse off than when you started. You can indeed lose much more than your original stake with some kinds of derivatives, and no-one wants to see that happening.

But the dangerous nature of derivatives doesn't mean that you don't need to understand at least a little bit about them. The more you get interested in the commodities market (oil, gold, copper, wheat, and all that), the more often you're going to come across mentions of derivatives in the newspapers, because derivatives really are what drive the raw materials industry. And the more sophisticated hedge funds (Chapter 15 deals with these) get in the next few years, the more likely you are to find yourself reading articles that demand at least a limited amount of knowledge about this peculiar business. So I wouldn't be doing my job if I didn't at least give you a feel for what they are.

*Derivative* is rather a broad piece of terminology that covers an awful lot of ground, so I need to simplify things a bit. A *derivative* is a financial product that's *derived* from a share, or maybe a commodity, or maybe even an index of some sort. And a derivative is all about managing financial risk. You're unlikely to come across derivatives in the course of your normal life – except for a type called *options* (see the 'Options' section later in this chapter). If you work for a fast-growing company that has more prospects than cash, you may well be offered these. Back in the crazy 1990s, many companies paid their key personnel partly in stock options that made them rich if everything worked out well for the company.

Some stock options did do well, of course, and some didn't. Some options schemes evolved into employee share ownership schemes, although with slight differences. But full-on options mania may very well strike again one day, when everyone's feeling a bit more optimistic about the future. So I think you'll agree that knowing at least a little bit about derivatives does no harm.

# Finding Out about Futures

Futures are really quite a simple concept to grasp, once you've got a few basics sorted out. A properly used futures contract is a thoroughly useful and valuable thing, which can help to protect the interests of just about everyone whenever people are dealing with a situation in which nobody really knows what the future will bring. Used wisely, futures can even out the bumps when the going gets rough. But futures can also be used in a different, more dangerous way – which is where they get their bad reputation. If you set out to use them speculatively, rather than for safety, they can make you very rich, or very poor, in a remarkably short space of time.

I suppose I could always start with the formal explanation. I could tell you that a futures contract is an agreement between two parties to exchange a specific type of goods, in a specific quantity, and at a specific time in the future. And that the contract they draw up between them is set up in such a way that either of them can back out of it (with a suitable cash adjustment), or sell it on to somebody else, or just go through with the deal as planned. But the chances are that you wouldn't find that very easy to understand.

So, rather than heading straight into the complicated nuts and bolts of a futures strategy, I'm going to start this section with a fictional analogy that I hope will give you a rough idea of how the principle of futures trading works. Then I'm going to translate this analogy into how things operate in the real world. Ready?

Say I'm a ticket tout and I've got a stack of £100 tickets to watch the quarter-finals of the European Championship in two months' time. You're interested in buying one of them, because you reckon a 75 per cent chance exists that your national team's playing in the match.

But neither of us knows what the street value of a ticket for the match is likely to be in two months' time. What we probably do know is that, if the national squad's playing, the ticket will be worth the £100 I'm asking for it, and maybe more. But if our boys get knocked out during the qualifiers, the chances of anybody wanting to buy the tickets are sharply reduced. Their value may quite possibly fall sharply. Indeed, maybe I won't manage to sell any of my tickets at all.

I can, of course, sell you the ticket now for £100 and say take it or leave it. But that doesn't really work for you. In an ideal world, you want to wait until the qualifying rounds are over, because if the national squad gets knocked out you might decide to walk away and not buy the ticket at all.

But those aren't the terms I'm offering. I can't afford to let you wait that long, because then I may end up with nothing at all. So I need to reach a deal with you whereby we both get roughly what we want. And I also promise you to deliver the ticket to you on the day of the match. (Yes, I know that's a bit improbable, but bear with me.)

In effect, as far as you're concerned, the value of my £100 ticket is £75 right now, because the national team has a 25 per cent chance of being knocked out. So, by committing yourself to buying my ticket now for £75, you're taking a gamble on our boys getting lucky. If they do get through to the quarter-finals, you may even be able to sell the ticket on to somebody else for £100 or even more. But if we don't get through, then nobody you know's likely to buy the ticket from you, and you're anything up to £75 out of pocket.

Remember, however, that I've taken a gamble as well, because I may have forgone £25 by selling the ticket to you for £75 now when I may get £100 later on.

I have, in effect, sold you the right to attend a £100 event for £75, if everything works out well in the near future and England does get to play in the quarter-final. And you for your part have insured yourself against the risk of not getting a ticket to the match, by agreeing to pay me 75 per cent of the full £100 asking price. We've arranged a *futures contract*, in which we've both taken a risk but we're both a bit safer.

## *The perils of leverage*

So far, so good. But actually futures contracts involve a bit more than I've suggested so far. In a real-world situation, you might say to me: 'Look, I'm not getting paid until the end of the month and besides, I don't see why I should pay you now for a match that I'm not attending until next month.'

'Fine,' I say, 'pay me 10 per cent of the £75 now (£7.50) and we can settle up the remaining £67.50 on the day of the match. Of course, if you manage to sell the ticket on to somebody else by that date, you're quids in. But remember, you still owe me the £67.50 even if you don't attend the match and you can't find anybody willing to buy the ticket. Can we shake hands on that?'

In the market's own lingo, I'm allowing you to trade *on margin*. I only do that because I trust you, and I'm probably not doing it at all unless I've already got your credit card details in case you mysteriously flee the country.

But you don't mind. 'That's great,' you think. 'I'm on to a good thing here, because I've got a ticket worth £100 that's going to be delivered to me on the day of the match, and I've only put down £7.50 up front. Now, I wonder what happens if I buy another nine tickets with the £67.50 that's still sitting here in my pocket? I'm buying £1,000 worth of tickets for only a £75 down-payment! (Or £750 by the time I finally settle up with the ticket tout.) Why, I can clear an easy £250 profit on this deal if England goes through and I can sell them all to my mates for £100 apiece. And all I've got to pay the ticket tout this afternoon is £75!'

At this point you might come unstuck. Putting down the £75 on margin is the easy bit. The tricky part will be explaining to your partner on the day of the match why you've now got ten useless tickets and owe me £750, because the national squad lost the qualifiers and nobody wants to buy them from you.

£750 is your total *exposure* on this contract, even though you only lay down £75. And you can be quite sure that I'll be sending the boys round to collect the missing £675!

This is an extreme scenario, of course, and in real life things don't often work out quite as badly as that. Even if your gamble doesn't come off, the chances are that you can still sell your tickets to some other country's supporter (or whatever) for £50 each, so that your losses on each ticket are only £17.50, plus the £7.50 you paid me on margin. But even then, you still lose £250 on the deal. Silly you.

I might also be able to sell the tickets on to somebody else, or get my supplier to take them back so that I can negotiate a mutually satisfactory exit from my futures deal with you, if that's what you request. (Who knows, maybe I never even had the tickets in the first place, but was just planning to get them from a mate if you agreed to go through with the deal and actually buy them from me?) One way or another, only a small proportion of futures contracts ever get to the stage of physical delivery (which in this case is when I hand you the tickets on the day of the match). Most contracts, in practice, are settled amicably or cancelled by mutual agreement before their expiry date comes up, so no goods ever actually change hands.

Another thing that wouldn't happen in real life is that I wouldn't simply take your credit card details. Instead, I'd ask you to set up an account with me, and to put enough money into the account to make sure that you'd covered at least a decent proportion of your exposure. Maybe I'd even let you have some interest on the account balance if I was feeling particularly kindly disposed toward you. But if I ever started getting anxious about the risks you were running – for instance, if our squad's star striker broke his leg and couldn't play – I'd be on the phone to you making a *margin call*. Which is to say, I'd insist that you put some more money into that account quick-sharp, or the deal's off.

## Whose bright idea was this futures business anyway?

In the American Midwest, some time around the arrival of the railroads, the grain merchants and flour millers found they needed to find a way of ensuring that they didn't pay too much or too little for the grain they were getting in the autumn – even though they had no idea yet what the harvest was going to be like.

Were the fields likely to be so full of golden grain that wheat prices plummeted? Or might storms and drought and pestilence drive up the grain prices to absurd levels? By agreeing a futures price with the farmers, the grain merchants insulated themselves from the fluctuating prices and kept their customers happy.

The deal also looked good from the farmers' point of view. Okay, by fixing their autumn sale prices with the millers in advance, they were taking a risk on the possibility that it might actually be a terrible summer in which prices are much higher than the prices they've already agreed. But you know what they say about a bird in the hand being better than two in the bush. Having a deal with the millers and grain merchants allowed everybody to sleep better at night.

Thus, by no coincidence at all, the American Midwest became the world's busiest centre for commodity futures trading, and the Chicago commodity houses gained a dominant position that they've never relinquished. Every major country in the world trades food commodity futures now – including China, which doesn't really like them but can't manage without them.

## *Hedging with futures contracts*

Okay, our analogy with the football tickets has got us this far. And it's not so very far from reality, in fact, because people really do run futures on the price of tickets for the Wimbledon tennis tournament. But in the real world of business you don't deal in football tickets. Instead, you take calculated bets on other unknowables, such as the direction the stock market's likely to take, or the direction of the dollar. At this point I return to the question of leverage, or 'trading on margin' as it's also called.

The thing is, you can use a futures contract in two very different ways. You can either use it as a 'hedge', to reduce your risk, the way the Midwest grain merchants used to. Or else you can exploit the 'margin trading' principle, and the leverage it gives you, to take aggressively large speculative positions on the way you think things are going to go.

In the example of the football ticket, you decided to go for the aggressive approach and you acquired a £750 exposure by using your leverage on what was effectively a £75 bet (that is, a £75 margin payment). If your gamble works out and you get your ten £100 tickets for a final amount of £750, then you make an easy £250, a 333 per cent return on your margin stake! But if it fails, you've made a dreadful mistake. Your unsaleable tickets have left you £750 out of pocket. Ouch!

A wiser technique would have been to buy just the one ticket, lay down the £7.50 margin payment, and put the rest of the money in the bank where it would earn a bit of interest. But you wouldn't listen, would you? You might also have found some other way to balance your futures contract – for instance, by taking out a different bet against the chances of a Germany versus Italy clash in the same quarter finals, that would have paid out if you'd lost on your main contract. But instead of balancing your contracts sensibly against each other, you had to go and spoil it by 'going naked', as it's known. You didn't cover yourself against disaster!

A futures contract is like a box of matches. Used sensibly, it can warm your home and keep you secure. Used recklessly, however, it can burn the whole place down.

What about hedge funds? Well, you've probably heard a lot of bad things about hedge funds in the last few years. They've been accused of creating the credit crunch of 2007 and 2008, by taking big risks on commodity prices and by playing all sorts of risky games with the shares of companies that are only important to them as pawns in a very complicated game. And then by selling them all off again, creating panic and disorder in the financial markets because nobody could really see what they were doing until it was too late and the crash had already started happening. They are, as the market says, 'lacking in transparency'. And that's putting it mildly.

I say in Chapter 14 on managed funds that these exotic funds have the freedom to invest in absolutely anything they like – stocks, bonds, cash, commodities – and that nobody can call them to account because they don't leave clear audit trails behind them. But hedge funds have been getting the blame for quite a lot of the volatility in commodities prices recently.

'Hedge? What hedge?' I hear you ask. 'No proper hedging's going on here, just out-and-out naked speculation, which is sending the markets into a real spin because nobody really knows how many of these contracts are just being drawn up for the sake of pushing prices up and down, instead of seeking safety and security.'

To that I can only say amen. If the 2007/2008 stock market panic didn't convince you that speculative futures activity from hedge funds is a dangerous thing, then I don't know what will. But then, stable markets aren't much use to a hedge fund manager. He makes her money by exploiting the twists and turns of the market, and she thrives on volatility. If everybody's settled into the status quo, then no trading's going on. And if no trading's happening, then no opportunities exist to turn a profit on a deal.

# *Companies that hedge their own prices!*

The nearby sidebar concerns the grain farming trade, where futures started out. But in time, the American futures trading business spread to include other types of commodities: oil, copper, gold, and all sorts of highly price-volatile things. When you look at the oil or metals prices listed in the papers, the chances are that they say something like 'tin for November 2011 delivery' (or some date in the future). That is, somebody's offering a futures contract that effectively sets out what the expected tin price is in the future, and asks you to take a gamble on whether the guess is right or not.

Except that the gamble isn't quite as big as it may appear. By fixing the future price at which you're going to buy that tin, you're protecting yourself and using the futures contract as a tool to stabilise your business.

Airlines and bus companies use futures contracts to protect themselves against sharp fluctuations in fuel costs. Doing so helps them keep their books on an even keel while prices are swooping about, and that in turn helps their investors stop worrying about the volatility of the companies' cost bases.

Things get even more interesting in the mining industry. Gold producers, who have seen the value of their output shooting up and down in recent years, are increasingly using the futures business to bet against falls in the gold price! Yes, they can and they do. If a company suspects that the price may go down, it might take out contracts that will produce disproportionately large returns if its worst fears are realised. These returns will then help to repair the damage to its bottom line. The company's said to be *fully hedged* (or '80 per cent hedged', or whatever.)

# *Why you don't find many futures prices in the papers*

Open a typical paper and you'll search in vain for the details of all the thousands of futures contracts that are set up and traded every day. And no wonder. There are simply too many of them to be worth listing, even if anybody were interested in reading them. Instead, you're more likely to learn something from the lists of indices that commodity exchanges like the Chicago Board of Trade or the New York Nymex posts up. These will give you the flavour of the trades that are happening right now, but not the details, which are crashingly boring. You can find some links to these price lists, and some illustrations of what they look like, in Chapter 13.

As a general principle, the further ahead a futures contract is set to expire, the greater the uncertainty about the underlying prices that are being bet on. So a one-month futures contract is probably rather closer to the current price than a six-month contract, where much more guesswork's involved.

# Weighing Up Warrants

Warrants are rather safer than the futures contracts the preceding section describes. With a futures contract, you can lose more than your original stake if your bets come seriously unstuck. But with a warrant you can just walk away, take your losses, and chuck your betting slip in the bin.

A warrant is a special kind of security that a company issues in order to raise money. It isn't a share as such, but you can convert it into a share if that's what you decide to do. Your decision's likely to depend on how high the share price has gone.

With a warrant, the deal is that you pay a fairly modest amount of money for a piece of paper that entitles you, for example, to buy a fixed number of company ABC's shares at a price of 200p each, by a certain date (the *expiration date*). This is called *exercising the warrant*. And if the share price doesn't reach that level by the expiration date, you simply walk away and write off your loss.

That may not sound like a very attractive prospect if the 'target' share price is only 100p at the moment; but as ABC's share price rises, so does the value of the warrant – disproportionately so, in fact, and not surprisingly too. If the going rate for the share is, say, 25 per cent of the warrant price, then the chances of the warrant ever being worth anything can be considered minimal; but by the time it reaches 80 per cent of the warrant price, the odds are more heavily stacked in your favour.

Why would any company want to issue a warrant in the first place? Usually, it issues a warrant as an attachment to a corporate bond or a preference share (see Chapters 6 and 9 on these), as compensation for the fact that the bond or preference share carries a fairly low rate of interest (or dividend). However, because the warrant can then be 'stripped' from the share and sold to somebody else, it then becomes a marketable security in its own right.

Next question. When you exercise your warrants and convert them into shares, where do those shares come from? Does the company fish them out of a sack that it keeps topped up for the purpose and hand them to you? Sadly, no. When you exercise a warrant, the company issues brand new shares to run alongside the existing shares. And since the company hasn't grown in size to match the emergence of the new shares, warrants are therefore *dilutive* of the company's equity. So they're not popular with the other shareholders whose own shares are being diluted. All companies are required to officially declare it when warrants are redeemed, by issuing a Regulatory News Service statement, just so that everybody knows what's going on. (I discuss RNS statements in Chapter 8)

Quite a few different types of warrant exist:

- ✔ **Call warrants:** which allow you to buy the underlying shares.

- ✔ **Put warrants:** which let you sell the underlying shares.

- ✔ **Covered warrants:** which means the company's put up some independent financial backing for the warrants, so that they don't dilute the equity. Often it achieves this by using cash, not equity, to cover the value of the warrant.

- ✔ **Basket warrants:** which track an entire group of shares, or indeed an entire industry sector rather than just one company's shares.

Where do you find warrants? Not on the main stock market, as a rule, although exceptions apply. You're more likely to track them down on the *over-the-counter* market (OTC), which is more lightly regulated than the main stock market. You won't find much information on the OTC market in the papers or on the Web, but a good stockbroker should be able to help you research and trade this market. It's not the safest of activities for a raw beginner, though, because of the lack of regulation, so be very careful.

# Casting an Eye Over Options

Options are another kind of derivative that you'll often read about in the financial pages, so it's important to have a working understanding of what they are even if you're never actually going to need to trade them. I want to say straight away that options are slightly less dangerous beasts than futures, for the very good reason that you don't run the risk of losing more than your original stake if things go wrong. But at the same time they're more likely to come your way than warrants (see the preceding section).

Why? Because options are often handed out to a company's staff, as part of a pay package. Especially if you're a director or a senior employee. They're a bit similar to the employee share schemes that your employer may make available to you, but without the tax advantages, because your gains are taxable under all circumstances if you make a profit when you exercise them. Moreover, unlike conventional options, employee share schemes don't generally have an expiration date by which they must be exercised.

What are options? Well, let's start out with the formal definition, the same way that we did when we considered futures, and then we'll take it from there. An option is a piece of paper that gives its holder the right to buy (or sell) a share, or a bond, or any other security, at a fixed price (which is usually called the 'strike price'), at any time up to a particular date in the future. As with warrants, the holder of the option isn't obliged to go throught with the deal - instead, he or she can simply walk away if the price doesn't look attractive when the expiry date (or 'maturity date') approaches. So there's a definite floor to how badly off you can end up.

Options come in two flavours. A *call option* entitles you to buy the underlying shares, bonds or whatever, at the agreed price, and a *put option* entitles you to sell it, also at the agreed price. But you'll also find that options are available for entire stock market indices, or for currencies (you can get a call option on the dollar, for instance).

Assuming that we're talking about a share, you can exercise the option at any time up to the expiration date. (Unless it's something called a 'European option', in which case you can only exercise it on the expiration date, and at no other time.) You can also sell your options to a third party.

As with a warrant, the company will need to issue some new shares with which to redeem your options when you exercise them – and this doesn't go down at all well with shareholders, who once again see their equity being diluted by the new issues.

Beyond this brief overview, I'm afraid the subject is veiled in complexity. A whole convoluted vocabulary is associated with options investing, and I don't propose to take you into it. Strangles, straddles, butterfly spreads, and iron condors are just the start of it. When you're ready for that sort of heavy talk, you won't need this book any more. And good luck to you.

# Chapter 13

# Making Money from Commodities

## In This Chapter

▶ Understanding how commodity markets work

▶ Making sense of the statistics

▶ Investing in oil, food, copper – and uranium!

*A* few years ago, only the very bold, the very skilled, and the slightly unstable ventured into the commodities markets. Their pricing patterns were so hard to forecast (or so some people believed) that they could spell death to any portfolio that was unwise enough to include them.

These days the commodities markets have been tamed to the extent where they can provide a useful counterpoint to the hurly-burly of the stock markets. And the arrival of new investment tools such as Exchange-Traded Funds has made it as easy to invest in copper as in Marks & Spencer.

## Introducing Commodities

Companies are familiar, because everyone knows what they do, and pretty well anyone can see what makes a good one different from a bad one. Savings accounts are the same: you can feel reasonably sure that what you see is what you're going to get. You're going to lend somebody your money, and he's going to return it with interest, or some other form of agreed payback.

But you enter a different sort of game when you start working with commodities. Put simply, one pile of iron ore looks very much like another pile of iron ore, and surely only an expert can tell you which one's worth a lot of money and which one's just so much scrap? Since I'm not a geological expert, and probably neither are you, surely you're going to be on your own in the company of thousands of people who actually know what they're doing?

Relax. I'm not going to ask you to pick out the good stuff from the bad. Nor, for the most part, am I going to ask you to choose the companies that produce the best commodities. Instead, I'm going to ask you to believe me when I say that there are very reliable grading systems for minerals and foodstuffs and so on – and that unless you're really determined to hand-pick your own mining companies, you can safely ignore the worry that you're buying a pup.

That's because the commodities market would be nothing without its system of product standardisation. If I phone a corn dealer in Australia with an order for 20,000 tonnes of wheat, I don't want to go and see it in person – although I suppose I might want to see the certification that it's good stuff with not too many nasties. And he for his part knows that if he ships me a consignment of poor-quality goods we both end up in court, so he has no incentive to lie to me.

The same principle goes for coal or oil or copper or gold. The business world works on the assumption that one pile of copper is the same as any other pile that carries the same quality classification. And one gold ingot from Australia is worth the same as a similar ingot from South Africa, providing that it's properly certified. The commodity business is *commoditised*. That's what enables someone like me to invest in raw commodities even though I don't know much about the technicalities of the industry.

A lot of the time, I never see the product at all – instead, I just take a gamble in the industry by buying some sort of 'tracker' investment that follows the prices of oil or coal or gold, or whatever. Chapter 14 covers the growing popularity of Exchange-Traded Funds, which are just like trackers except that you can buy and sell them on the spur of the moment exactly like shares. And these ETFs are springing up all over the place, in London and elsewhere, allowing you to 'buy into' the price of a commodity and then sell it out when you've made a profit on it. ETFs are clever things.

What's an ETF? In its simplest terms, it's a kind of tracker fund that will enable an ordinary investor like you or me to 'take a stake' in some large and intangible investment like gold or oil or Chinese shares, without necessarily knowing anything about the ins and outs of that market. ETFs are a major advance for people who like to follow their noses and their instincts.

ETFs aren't shares, strictly speaking, but they behave exactly like shares or investment trusts because you can buy them from your stockbroker like a share, in any quantity you like – for instance, there's no other way that you could buy £500 worth of oil (as distinct from oil producing companies)! You can then sell your ETFs whenever you're ready, exactly as if they were shares, and you'll find that you get a sale price that's very close to the buy price that you'd been the buyer. (The City would say that the 'spread' is very small.) Best of all, you don't pay stamp duty on ETFs!

So, as I hope I've made clear, the advent of ETFs just about does away with the idea that pure commodity trading (as distinct from buying commodity producers) is only for the professionals. Until ETFs were launched a few years ago, the idea that the only people able to trade effectively in commodities were those able to lay down hundreds of thousands of pounds at a time contained some truth. (And stand around in a bear-pit wearing silly blazers and waving their arms around.) These days, as I've said, anyone can trade in commodities – and frankly, most of us probably should sometimes.

## *Understanding the long-term argument for minerals*

I'd be the first to agree that commodities can be a bit daunting for a beginner, because you're not looking at individual companies but at big macro-economic trends instead. And many non-food commodities do something rather wonderful. They move in long-term price cycles, often lasting a decade or more, which are *largely independent of whatever the stock market happens to be doing* at the time. And that makes them especially interesting for an investor who's looking to mitigate some of the risks involved in equity investing.

Indeed, some very experienced investors claim that commodity prices habitually rise when share prices are falling. I'm a bit wary of agreeing with that theory myself, because it seems too simplistic and too counter-intuitive to be really likely. All right, I can't deny that the terrific price rises in oil and copper and gold during 2007 and early 2008 were happening at a time when world stock markets were undergoing their worst crisis in a decade. But the stiff price falls that followed as the credit crunch of 2008 got under way do raise some serious questions about just how wise these 'experienced' commodity investors really were?

The professionals spent the second half of the credit crunch trying to convince us that 2008 was an exceptional situation for the commodity ,markets. Ordinarily, they said, the commodity producers don't really care whether or not their customers can afford to buy their products. They cost what they cost, and that's that. Like it or lump it.

Well, that argument didn't stand the test of time particularly well, because the market prices of most major commodities fell pretty sharply during late 2008. The traders mostly spent those months trying to defend their idea with the claim that commodity prices were being driven up, and then sharply down, by hedge funds which had taken up vast speculative positions in gold, copper, oil and other minerals, and which had then dumped them all when the credit crunch of 2008 got started. It was all getting a bit much to swallow by the time the end of 2008 approached and the oil price was still down at about a third of what it had been just six months earlier. Ouch!

But even so, the commodity bulls' argument has a kind of logic, at least as far as energy and base metals are concerned. The thing is, building a copper smelter or digging a copper mine costs an awful lot of time and money – and that creates a very dangerous time lag between the supply and the demand. That's where the real tensions in the commodity markets start to kick in. So let me see whether I can explain this very simply.

### Describing how the cyclical process works

Suppose you're a big mineral company. By the time you've spotted a rising global demand for copper and dug your mine, or built your brand-new smelter, you're already five years too late and everybody else in the world has been doing the same thing. All of a sudden the world has too many copper smelters and they're all having to sell their copper very cheaply just to keep going. That's when the copper price collapses, the surplus copper smelters get put into mothballs, and the industry goes into a cyclical slump. This isn't anything to do with the state of the stock market at all, is it?

The situation's pretty much the same with forestry products such as timber, cardboard, and paper, except that the commodity cycles last much longer. A tree takes 20 years to grow, and by the time you've planted your forests and waited patiently to fell them, a good chance exists that the wave has passed and nobody wants your wood pulp any more. So you lose interest, and planting slows down or stops, and the next thing you know there isn't enough timber to go round and prices start to soar again.

Or suppose you run a rubber plantation, and you suddenly notice that other people are getting good prices for growing coffee or bananas or coconuts. You dig up your trees, and with a bit of luck you're in business within five years. The trouble is, so's everybody else! The whole commodities world is running on what my dad used to call kangaroo petrol – it's either lurching forward or stuttering and stalling, and because of those time lags no easy way exists of smoothing out the periods in between. Commodity prices are constantly soaring and nose-diving, according to these cyclical patterns. Read the patterns correctly, and you can get rich – in theory, anyway.

### Considering exceptions to the cyclical process

But you need to be aware of two big exceptions to this cyclical principle. One is annual food crops. Often a farmer only requires a year to switch from rapeseed to wheat, or from cabbages to soya beans, or even from cattle to pigs. So the commodity cycle here is so short that it's not really a cycle at all.

Instead, unpredictable things like floods, droughts, bird flu, and late frosts throw food commodity prices about. All those things mean that food crops are generally far too dangerous for a beginner to get involved in. Unless you can see a big long-term global trend coming up, such as an exploding Chinese demand for imported soya beans, avoid tangling with food commodities.

The other big commodity exception is in the field of gold, gemstones, and precious metals, and they can be just as dangerous for an unlucky amateur investor. You can't build a gold factory or a diamond manufacturing plant, much as you'd like to – instead, the value of these commodities is determined precisely by their scarcity, and by the absolutely limited supply of new gold and diamonds that comes onto the market every year.

This extreme scarcity makes gold and silver and platinum so precious – and so volatile when the rest of the world suddenly decides to buy them! Temporary scares about the dollar make investors rush to pay absurd amounts for bullion. And then, as likely as not, they're able to repent at leisure.

Is gold too expensive? Not if you compare the historical price trends. Back in 1980, worries about rising oil prices and an impending war between Iran and Iraq sent the price above $850 per troy ounce – which doesn't sound so crazy compared with today's prices until you allow for the costs of inflation. In real (inflation-adjusted terms), you'd have to be paying way in excess of $2,500 per ounce before you beat the 1980 price.

# Getting started on commodity investing

To make a success of a commodity portfolio, you need to have a reasonably good grasp of which products are being bought by which parts of the world, and which ones are rising or falling in popularity. In fact that's not as hard as it sounds. Gaining this information is largely a matter of reading the papers and using your common sense. If your Sunday paper tells you that China and India are going full tilt with their manufacturing industries, then you've got a pretty good idea that they're going to be buying all the iron ore and copper and oil they can lay their hands on. If you read that Australia or South America is expecting a bad harvest, you can probably figure out for yourself that wheat prices are likely to be on the rise soon. But conversely, if you hear that big companies in those countries are falling on hard times, or that Japan's export industries are flagging, or that America has just slapped an embargo on Chinese chemical exports, then you can logically expect commodity prices to have a harder time.

This principle is often described as the *commodities super-cycle*. According to the current theory, the world has always moved between over-production and under-production in great long waves, just the way I've described it. But with an added twist. The huge levels of demand from the developing asian economies – china in particular – means that we have entered a new era with regard to commodity demand, the like of which humanity hasn't seen before.

Essentially, the 'supercycle' theory has it that virtually commodity prices will continue to trend strongly upwards as Chinese and Indian industries keep churning out consumer goods for export, and as the population of the two countries leaves the countryside and heads for the cities. For instance, it's currently estimated that this urbanisation trend is seeing 13 milion people flood into Chinese cities each year – that's the equivalent of creating a new city the size of London each year. With such massive energy and commodity consumption, the super-cycle theory isn't exactly easy to ignore.

So the supercycle theorists reckon that the steep commodity price falls we saw in 2008 don't amount to a hill of beans in comparison with the crushing inevitability of global economic development. Are they right? I don't really know, and nor does anybody else – but it would take a real diehard to suppose that we in the West could argue with three billion people in the developing countries of Asia!

As a general rule, the wider your reading, the better informed you are. If you have the appetite for vast amounts of detailed information, look at the second section of the *Financial Times*, where the commodities coverage is especially good in the midweek editions. Broadsheets like *The Times* or the *Daily Telegraph* do a decent job of reporting the major trends but don't give you the same sort of detail. Also read *The Economist* for an informed and sensitive analysis of where the overall supply and demand trends are heading, especially on energy matters. No magazine handles the political aspects of trade better.

Don't get too bogged down in detail, in spite of all that reading. Focus instead on the 'top-down' aspects of the commodities trade (i.e. start by looking at the big 'macro-economic' realities facing the globe) and take your research downward from there. You'd soon start to drown in the small print if you tried to follow every one of the thousands of news threads, most of which are deeply boring!

## Finding price information

As you'd expect, there's plenty of good online information out there on the shape, structure and pricing history of the mining industry. Some of it, like the information published by the World Gold Council, is hardly impartial, because it represents the views of a set of interested parties (mainly gold producers and users); other sources, such as Kitco (www.kitco.com), adopt an impartial approach which simply gives you the prices and shows you charts that illustrate the trading patterns of the past.

But as a general guide to the metals industry in particular, I'd like to point you toward a new web site which is currently being put together by the United Nations Conference on Trade and Development (Unctad), and which will eventually provide information on prices, industrial usage, mining details and a host of other related matters. You'll find it at www.unctad.org/info comm – you'll need to click the 'English' tab and then select from the 'Metals and Minerals' menu. Worth keeping an eye on.

Figure 13-1 shows what's available from the online edition of the *Financial Times*, practically the only British paper that covers a reasonably broad daily range of the commodities sold on various markets around the world.

I'll admit that this table is bound to look rather daunting to somebody just starting out in investing. And frankly, you're not ever likely to tangle with the commodities industry in the way the people who put this page together imagine. Instead, you're going to want to invest in commodities through ETFs and other types of tracker instruments. But I'm not doing my job if I don't at least give you a glimpse of what the underlying market looks like.

The 'basic metal' prices supplied in Figure 13-1 come from the London Metal Exchange, still the world's foremost authority on the subject. Gold prices come from the London Bullion Market. Oil figures come from the International Petroleum Exchange (also in London); and wheat, white sugar, cocoa, and rapeseed come from the London International Financial Futures Exchange (LIFFE).

But it may not escape your notice that most of the other statistics quoted here are based on data from the North American commodity exchanges: Comex (the New York Mercantile Exchange and Commodities Exchange), Nymex (the New York Metals Exchange), Nybot (the New York Board of Trade), the New York Commodities Exchange, the Chicago Mercantile Exchange, and the Chicago Board of Trade. The nearby sidebar, 'Why everything's priced in dollars', explains why America's so dominant in the commodities trade.

One thing you may notice straight away in Figure 13-1 is that the market provides 'cash official' prices, '3 month official' prices, and 'kerb PM 3 month closes' for all the basic metals listed at the top of the page (copper, aluminium, lead, nickel, and the like). This is because heavy and bulky commodities are often bought well ahead of the date they're actually required for delivery, so the market has adapted to allow for this need by providing 'forward pricing'. Manufacturers can't survive without them.

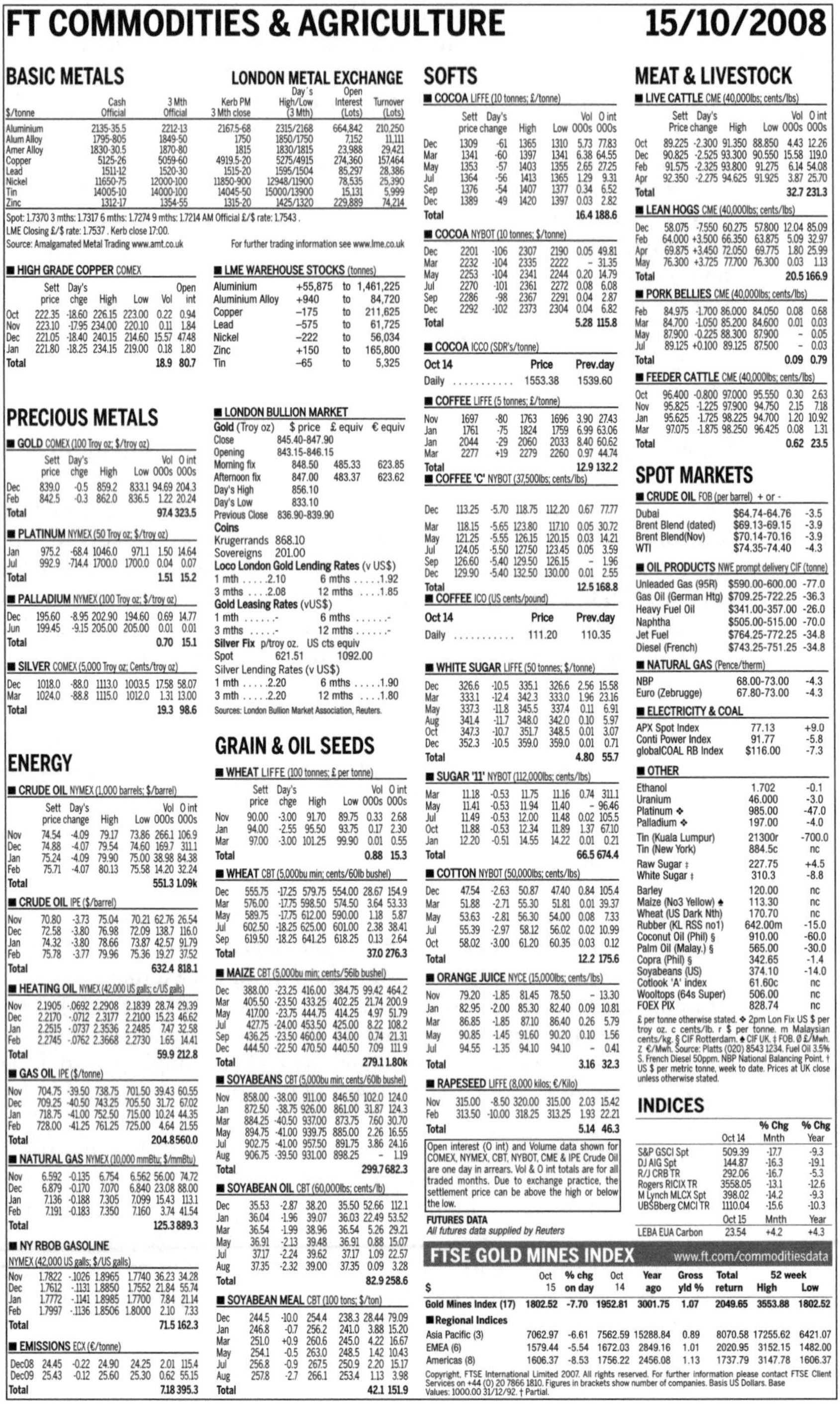

# FT COMMODITIES & AGRICULTURE 15/10/2008

## BASIC METALS

### LONDON METAL EXCHANGE

| $/tonne | Cash Official | 3 Mth Official | Kerb PM 3 Mth close | Day's High/Low (3 Mth) | Open Interest (Lots) | Turnover (Lots) |
|---|---|---|---|---|---|---|
| Aluminium | 2135-35.5 | 2212-13 | 2167.5-68 | 2315/2168 | 664,842 | 210,250 |
| Alum Alloy | 1795-805 | 1849-50 | 1750 | 1850/1750 | 7,152 | 11,111 |
| Amer Alloy | 1830-30.5 | 1870-80 | 1815 | 1830/1815 | 23,988 | 29,421 |
| Copper | 5125-26 | 5059-60 | 4919.5-20 | 5275/4915 | 274,360 | 157,464 |
| Lead | 1511-12 | 1520-30 | 1515-20 | 1595/1504 | 85,297 | 28,386 |
| Nickel | 11650-75 | 12000-100 | 11850-900 | 12948/11900 | 78,535 | 25,390 |
| Tin | 14005-10 | 14000-100 | 14045-50 | 15000/13900 | 15,131 | 5,999 |
| Zinc | 1312-17 | 1354-55 | 1315-20 | 1425/1320 | 229,889 | 74,214 |

Spot: 1.7370 3 mths: 1.7317 6 mths: 1.7274 9 mths: 1.7214 AM Official £/$ rate: 1.7543 .
LME Closing £/$ rate: 1.7537 . Kerb close 17:00.
Source: Amalgamated Metal Trading www.amt.co.uk
For further trading information see www.lme.co.uk

### HIGH GRADE COPPER COMEX

| | Sett price | Day's chge | High | Low | Vol | Open int |
|---|---|---|---|---|---|---|
| Oct | 222.35 | -18.60 | 226.15 | 223.00 | 0.22 | 0.94 |
| Nov | 223.10 | -17.95 | 234.00 | 220.10 | 0.11 | 1.84 |
| Dec | 221.05 | -18.40 | 240.15 | 214.60 | 15.57 | 47.48 |
| Jan | 221.80 | -18.25 | 234.15 | 219.00 | 0.18 | 1.80 |
| **Total** | | | | | **18.9** | **80.7** |

### LME WAREHOUSE STOCKS (tonnes)

| | | | |
|---|---|---|---|
| Aluminium | +55,875 | to | 1,461,225 |
| Aluminium Alloy | +940 | to | 84,720 |
| Copper | –175 | to | 211,625 |
| Lead | –575 | to | 61,725 |
| Nickel | –222 | to | 56,034 |
| Zinc | +150 | to | 165,800 |
| Tin | –65 | to | 5,325 |

## PRECIOUS METALS

### GOLD COMEX (100 Troy oz; $/troy oz)

| | Sett price | Day's chge | High | Low | Vol 000s | O int 000s |
|---|---|---|---|---|---|---|
| Dec | 839.0 | -0.5 | 859.2 | 833.1 | 94.69 | 204.3 |
| Feb | 842.5 | -0.3 | 862.0 | 836.5 | 1.22 | 20.24 |
| **Total** | | | | | **97.4** | **323.5** |

### PLATINUM NYMEX (50 Troy oz; $/troy oz)

| | | | | | | |
|---|---|---|---|---|---|---|
| Jan | 975.2 | -68.4 | 1046.0 | 971.1 | 1.50 | 14.64 |
| Jul | 992.9 | -714.4 | 1700.0 | 1700.0 | 0.04 | 0.07 |
| **Total** | | | | | **1.51** | **15.2** |

### PALLADIUM NYMEX (100 Troy oz; $/troy oz)

| | | | | | | |
|---|---|---|---|---|---|---|
| Dec | 195.60 | -8.95 | 202.90 | 194.60 | 0.69 | 14.77 |
| Jun | 199.45 | -9.15 | 205.00 | 205.00 | 0.01 | 0.01 |
| **Total** | | | | | **0.70** | **15.1** |

### SILVER COMEX (5,000 Troy oz; Cents/troy oz)

| | | | | | | |
|---|---|---|---|---|---|---|
| Dec | 1018.0 | -88.0 | 1113.0 | 1003.5 | 17.58 | 58.07 |
| Mar | 1024.0 | -88.8 | 1115.0 | 1012.0 | 1.31 | 13.00 |
| **Total** | | | | | **19.3** | **98.6** |

### LONDON BULLION MARKET

| Gold (Troy oz) | $ price | £ equiv | € equiv |
|---|---|---|---|
| Close | 845.40-847.90 | | |
| Opening | 843.15-846.15 | | |
| Morning fix | 848.50 | 485.33 | 623.85 |
| Afternoon fix | 847.00 | 483.37 | 623.62 |
| Day's High | 856.10 | | |
| Day's Low | 833.10 | | |
| Previous Close | 836.90-839.90 | | |

**Coins**
Krugerrands 868.10
Sovereigns 201.00

**Loco London Gold Lending Rates** (v US$)
1 mth .....2.10 6 mths .....1.92
3 mths ....2.08 12 mths ....1.85

**Gold Leasing Rates** (vUS$)
1 mth ......- 6 mths ......-
3 mths .....- 12 mths ......-

**Silver Fix** p/troy oz. US cts equiv
Spot 621.51 1092.00

Silver Lending Rates (v US$)
1 mth .....2.20 6 mths .....1.90
3 mth .....2.20 12 mths ....1.80

Sources: London Bullion Market Association, Reuters.

## ENERGY

### CRUDE OIL NYMEX (1,000 barrels; $/barrel)

| | Sett price | Day's change | High | Low | Vol 000s | O int 000s |
|---|---|---|---|---|---|---|
| Nov | 74.54 | -4.09 | 79.17 | 73.86 | 266.1 | 106.9 |
| Dec | 74.88 | -4.07 | 79.54 | 74.60 | 169.7 | 311.1 |
| Jan | 75.24 | -4.09 | 79.90 | 75.00 | 38.98 | 84.38 |
| Feb | 75.71 | -4.07 | 80.13 | 75.58 | 14.20 | 32.24 |
| **Total** | | | | | **551.3** | **1.09k** |

### CRUDE OIL IPE ($/barrel)

| | | | | | | |
|---|---|---|---|---|---|---|
| Nov | 70.80 | -3.73 | 75.04 | 70.21 | 62.76 | 26.54 |
| Dec | 72.58 | -3.80 | 76.98 | 72.09 | 138.7 | 116.0 |
| Jan | 74.32 | -3.80 | 78.66 | 73.87 | 42.57 | 91.79 |
| Feb | 75.78 | -3.77 | 79.96 | 75.36 | 19.27 | 37.52 |
| **Total** | | | | | **632.4** | **818.1** |

### HEATING OIL NYMEX (42,000 US galls; c/US galls)

| | | | | | | |
|---|---|---|---|---|---|---|
| Nov | 2.1905 | -.0692 | 2.2908 | 2.1839 | 28.74 | 29.39 |
| Dec | 2.2170 | -.0712 | 2.3177 | 2.2100 | 15.23 | 46.62 |
| Jan | 2.2515 | -.0737 | 2.3536 | 2.2485 | 7.47 | 32.58 |
| Feb | 2.2745 | -.0762 | 2.3668 | 2.2730 | 1.65 | 14.41 |
| **Total** | | | | | **59.9** | **212.8** |

### GAS OIL IPE ($/tonne)

| | | | | | | |
|---|---|---|---|---|---|---|
| Nov | 704.75 | -39.50 | 738.75 | 701.50 | 39.43 | 60.55 |
| Dec | 709.25 | -40.50 | 743.25 | 705.50 | 31.72 | 67.02 |
| Jan | 718.75 | -41.00 | 752.50 | 715.00 | 10.24 | 44.35 |
| Feb | 728.00 | -41.25 | 761.25 | 725.00 | 4.64 | 21.55 |
| **Total** | | | | | **204.8** | **560.0** |

### NATURAL GAS NYMEX (10,000 mmBtu; $/mmBtu)

| | | | | | | |
|---|---|---|---|---|---|---|
| Nov | 6.592 | -0.135 | 6.754 | 6.562 | 56.00 | 74.72 |
| Dec | 6.879 | -0.170 | 7.070 | 6.840 | 23.08 | 88.00 |
| Jan | 7.136 | -0.188 | 7.305 | 7.099 | 15.43 | 113.1 |
| Feb | 7.191 | -0.183 | 7.350 | 7.160 | 3.74 | 41.54 |
| **Total** | | | | | **125.3** | **889.3** |

### NY RBOB GASOLINE
NYMEX (42,000 US galls; $/US galls)

| | | | | | | |
|---|---|---|---|---|---|---|
| Nov | 1.7822 | -.1026 | 1.8965 | 1.7740 | 36.23 | 34.28 |
| Dec | 1.7612 | -.1131 | 1.8850 | 1.7552 | 21.84 | 55.74 |
| Jan | 1.7772 | -.1141 | 1.8985 | 1.7700 | 7.84 | 21.14 |
| Feb | 1.7997 | -.1136 | 1.8506 | 1.8000 | 2.10 | 7.33 |
| **Total** | | | | | **71.5** | **162.3** |

### EMISSIONS ECX (€/tonne)

| | | | | | | |
|---|---|---|---|---|---|---|
| Dec08 | 24.45 | -0.22 | 24.90 | 24.25 | 2.01 | 115.4 |
| Dec09 | 25.43 | -0.12 | 25.60 | 25.30 | 0.62 | 55.15 |
| **Total** | | | | | **7.18** | **395.3** |

## GRAIN & OIL SEEDS

### WHEAT LIFFE (100 tonnes; £ per tonne)

| | Sett price | Day's chge | High | Low | Vol 000s | O int 000s |
|---|---|---|---|---|---|---|
| Nov | 90.00 | -3.00 | 91.70 | 89.75 | 0.33 | 2.68 |
| Jan | 94.00 | -2.55 | 95.50 | 93.75 | 0.17 | 2.30 |
| Mar | 97.00 | -3.00 | 101.25 | 99.90 | 0.01 | 0.55 |
| **Total** | | | | | **0.88** | **15.3** |

### WHEAT CBT (5,000bu min; cents/60lb bushel)

| | | | | | | |
|---|---|---|---|---|---|---|
| Dec | 555.75 | -17.25 | 579.75 | 554.00 | 28.67 | 154.9 |
| Mar | 576.00 | -17.75 | 598.50 | 574.50 | 3.64 | 53.33 |
| May | 589.75 | -17.75 | 612.00 | 590.00 | 1.18 | 5.87 |
| Jul | 602.50 | -18.25 | 625.00 | 601.00 | 2.38 | 38.41 |
| Sep | 619.50 | -18.25 | 641.25 | 618.25 | 0.13 | 2.64 |
| **Total** | | | | | **37.0** | **276.3** |

### MAIZE CBT (5,000bu min; cents/56lb bushel)

| | | | | | | |
|---|---|---|---|---|---|---|
| Dec | 388.00 | -23.25 | 416.00 | 384.75 | 99.42 | 464.2 |
| Mar | 405.50 | -23.50 | 433.25 | 402.25 | 21.74 | 200.9 |
| May | 417.00 | -23.75 | 444.75 | 414.25 | 4.97 | 51.79 |
| Jul | 427.75 | -24.00 | 453.50 | 425.00 | 8.22 | 108.2 |
| Sep | 436.25 | -23.50 | 460.00 | 434.00 | 0.74 | 21.31 |
| Dec | 444.50 | -22.50 | 470.50 | 440.50 | 7.09 | 111.9 |
| **Total** | | | | | **279.1** | **1.80k** |

### SOYABEANS CBT (5,000bu min; cents/60lb bushel)

| | | | | | | |
|---|---|---|---|---|---|---|
| Nov | 858.00 | -38.00 | 911.00 | 846.50 | 102.0 | 124.0 |
| Jan | 872.50 | -38.75 | 926.00 | 861.00 | 31.87 | 124.3 |
| Mar | 884.25 | -40.50 | 937.00 | 873.75 | 7.60 | 30.70 |
| May | 894.75 | -41.00 | 939.75 | 885.00 | 2.26 | 16.55 |
| Jul | 902.75 | -41.00 | 957.50 | 891.75 | 3.86 | 24.16 |
| Aug | 906.75 | -39.50 | 931.00 | 898.25 | - | 1.19 |
| **Total** | | | | | **299.7** | **682.3** |

### SOYABEAN OIL CBT (60,000lbs; cents/lb)

| | | | | | | |
|---|---|---|---|---|---|---|
| Dec | 35.53 | -2.87 | 38.20 | 35.50 | 52.66 | 112.1 |
| Jan | 36.04 | -1.96 | 39.07 | 36.03 | 22.49 | 53.52 |
| Mar | 36.54 | -1.99 | 38.96 | 36.54 | 5.26 | 29.21 |
| May | 36.91 | -2.13 | 39.48 | 36.91 | 0.88 | 15.07 |
| Jul | 37.17 | -2.24 | 39.62 | 37.17 | 1.09 | 22.57 |
| Aug | 37.35 | -2.32 | 39.00 | 37.35 | 0.09 | 3.28 |
| **Total** | | | | | **82.9** | **258.6** |

### SOYABEAN MEAL CBT (100 tons; $/ton)

| | | | | | | |
|---|---|---|---|---|---|---|
| Dec | 244.5 | -10.0 | 254.4 | 238.3 | 28.44 | 79.09 |
| Jan | 246.8 | -0.7 | 256.2 | 241.0 | 3.88 | 15.20 |
| Mar | 251.0 | +0.9 | 260.6 | 245.0 | 4.22 | 16.67 |
| May | 254.1 | -0.5 | 263.0 | 248.5 | 1.42 | 10.43 |
| Jul | 256.8 | -0.9 | 267.5 | 250.9 | 2.20 | 15.17 |
| Aug | 257.8 | -2.7 | 266.1 | 253.4 | 1.13 | 3.98 |
| **Total** | | | | | **42.1** | **151.9** |

## SOFTS

### COCOA LIFFE (10 tonnes; £/tonne)

| | Sett price | Day's change | High | Low | Vol 000s | O int 000s |
|---|---|---|---|---|---|---|
| Dec | 1309 | -61 | 1365 | 1310 | 5.73 | 77.83 |
| Mar | 1341 | -60 | 1397 | 1341 | 6.38 | 64.55 |
| May | 1353 | -57 | 1403 | 1355 | 2.65 | 27.25 |
| Jul | 1364 | -56 | 1413 | 1365 | 1.29 | 9.31 |
| Sep | 1376 | -54 | 1407 | 1377 | 0.34 | 6.52 |
| Dec | 1389 | -49 | 1420 | 1397 | 0.03 | 2.82 |
| **Total** | | | | | **16.4** | **188.6** |

### COCOA NYBOT (10 tonnes; $/tonne)

| | | | | | | |
|---|---|---|---|---|---|---|
| Dec | 2201 | -106 | 2307 | 2190 | 0.05 | 49.81 |
| Mar | 2232 | -104 | 2335 | 2222 | - | 31.35 |
| May | 2253 | -104 | 2341 | 2244 | 0.20 | 14.79 |
| Jul | 2270 | -101 | 2361 | 2272 | 0.08 | 6.08 |
| Sep | 2286 | -98 | 2367 | 2291 | 0.04 | 2.87 |
| Dec | 2292 | -102 | 2373 | 2304 | 0.04 | 6.82 |
| **Total** | | | | | **5.28** | **115.8** |

### COCOA ICCO (SDR's/tonne)

| Oct 14 | Price | Prev.day |
|---|---|---|
| Daily ........... | 1553.38 | 1539.60 |

### COFFEE LIFFE (5 tonnes; £/tonne)

| | | | | | | |
|---|---|---|---|---|---|---|
| Nov | 1697 | -80 | 1763 | 1696 | 3.90 | 27.43 |
| Jan | 1761 | -75 | 1824 | 1759 | 6.99 | 63.06 |
| Jan | 2044 | -29 | 2060 | 2033 | 8.40 | 60.62 |
| Mar | 2277 | +19 | 2279 | 2260 | 0.97 | 44.74 |
| **Total** | | | | | **12.9** | **132.2** |

### COFFEE 'C' NYBOT (37,500lbs; cents/lbs)

| | | | | | | |
|---|---|---|---|---|---|---|
| Dec | 113.25 | -5.70 | 118.75 | 112.20 | 0.67 | 77.77 |
| Mar | 118.15 | -5.65 | 123.80 | 117.10 | 0.05 | 30.72 |
| May | 121.25 | -5.55 | 126.15 | 120.15 | 0.03 | 14.21 |
| Jul | 124.05 | -5.50 | 127.50 | 123.45 | 0.05 | 3.59 |
| Sep | 126.60 | -5.40 | 129.50 | 126.15 | - | 1.96 |
| Dec | 129.90 | -5.40 | 132.50 | 130.00 | 0.01 | 2.55 |
| **Total** | | | | | **12.5** | **168.8** |

### COFFEE ICO (US cents/pound)

| Oct 14 | Price | Prev.day |
|---|---|---|
| Daily ........... | 111.20 | 110.35 |

### WHITE SUGAR LIFFE (50 tonnes; $/tonne)

| | | | | | | |
|---|---|---|---|---|---|---|
| Dec | 326.6 | -10.5 | 335.1 | 326.6 | 2.56 | 15.58 |
| Mar | 333.1 | -12.4 | 342.3 | 333.0 | 1.96 | 23.16 |
| May | 337.3 | -11.8 | 345.5 | 337.4 | 0.11 | 6.91 |
| Aug | 341.4 | -11.7 | 348.0 | 342.0 | 0.10 | 5.97 |
| Oct | 347.3 | -10.7 | 351.7 | 348.5 | 0.01 | 3.07 |
| Dec | 352.3 | -10.5 | 359.0 | 359.0 | 0.01 | 0.71 |
| **Total** | | | | | **4.80** | **55.7** |

### SUGAR '11' NYBOT (112,000lbs; cents/lbs)

| | | | | | | |
|---|---|---|---|---|---|---|
| Mar | 11.18 | -0.53 | 11.75 | 11.16 | 0.74 | 311.1 |
| May | 11.41 | -0.53 | 11.94 | 11.40 | - | 96.46 |
| Jul | 11.49 | -0.53 | 12.00 | 11.48 | 0.02 | 105.5 |
| Oct | 11.88 | -0.53 | 12.34 | 11.89 | 1.37 | 67.10 |
| Jan | 12.20 | -0.51 | 14.55 | 14.22 | 0.01 | 0.21 |
| **Total** | | | | | **66.5** | **674.4** |

### COTTON NYBOT (50,000lbs; cents/lbs)

| | | | | | | |
|---|---|---|---|---|---|---|
| Dec | 47.54 | -2.63 | 50.87 | 47.40 | 0.84 | 105.4 |
| Mar | 51.88 | -2.71 | 55.30 | 51.81 | 0.01 | 39.37 |
| May | 53.63 | -2.81 | 56.30 | 54.00 | 0.08 | 7.33 |
| Jul | 55.39 | -2.97 | 58.12 | 56.02 | 0.02 | 10.99 |
| Oct | 58.02 | -3.00 | 61.20 | 60.35 | 0.03 | 0.12 |
| **Total** | | | | | **12.2** | **175.6** |

### ORANGE JUICE NYCE (15,000lbs; cents/lbs)

| | | | | | | |
|---|---|---|---|---|---|---|
| Nov | 79.20 | -1.85 | 81.45 | 78.50 | - | 13.30 |
| Jan | 82.95 | -2.00 | 85.30 | 82.40 | 0.09 | 10.81 |
| Mar | 86.85 | -1.85 | 87.10 | 86.40 | 0.26 | 5.79 |
| May | 90.85 | -1.45 | 91.60 | 90.20 | 0.10 | 1.56 |
| Jul | 94.55 | -1.35 | 94.10 | 94.10 | - | 0.41 |
| **Total** | | | | | **3.16** | **32.3** |

### RAPESEED LIFFE (8,000 kilos; €/Kilo)

| | | | | | | |
|---|---|---|---|---|---|---|
| Nov | 315.00 | -8.50 | 320.00 | 315.00 | 2.03 | 15.42 |
| Feb | 313.50 | -10.00 | 318.25 | 313.25 | 1.93 | 22.21 |
| **Total** | | | | | **5.14** | **46.3** |

Open interest (O int) and Volume data shown for COMEX, NYMEX, CBT, NYBOT, CME & IPE Crude Oil are one day in arrears. Vol & O int totals are for all traded months. Due to exchange practice, the settlement price can be above the high or below the low.

**FUTURES DATA**
*All futures data supplied by Reuters*

## MEAT & LIVESTOCK

### LIVE CATTLE CME (40,000lbs; cents/lbs)

| | Sett Price | Day's change | High | Low | Vol 000s | O int 000s |
|---|---|---|---|---|---|---|
| Oct | 89.225 | -2.300 | 91.350 | 88.850 | 4.43 | 12.26 |
| Dec | 90.825 | -2.525 | 93.300 | 90.550 | 15.58 | 119.0 |
| Feb | 91.575 | -2.325 | 93.800 | 91.275 | 6.14 | 54.08 |
| Apr | 92.350 | -2.275 | 94.625 | 91.925 | 3.87 | 25.70 |
| **Total** | | | | | **32.7** | **231.3** |

### LEAN HOGS CME (40,000lbs; cents/lbs)

| | | | | | | |
|---|---|---|---|---|---|---|
| Dec | 58.075 | -7.550 | 60.275 | 57.800 | 12.04 | 85.09 |
| Feb | 64.000 | +3.500 | 66.350 | 63.875 | 5.09 | 32.97 |
| Apr | 69.875 | +3.450 | 72.050 | 69.775 | 1.80 | 25.99 |
| May | 76.300 | +3.725 | 77.700 | 76.300 | 0.03 | 1.13 |
| **Total** | | | | | **20.5** | **166.9** |

### PORK BELLIES CME (40,000lbs; cents/lbs)

| | | | | | | |
|---|---|---|---|---|---|---|
| Feb | 84.975 | -1.700 | 86.000 | 84.050 | 0.08 | 0.68 |
| Mar | 84.700 | -1.050 | 85.200 | 84.600 | 0.01 | 0.03 |
| May | 87.900 | -0.225 | 88.300 | 87.900 | - | 0.05 |
| Jul | 89.125 | +0.100 | 89.125 | 87.500 | - | 0.03 |
| **Total** | | | | | **0.09** | **0.79** |

### FEEDER CATTLE CME (40,000lbs; cents/lbs)

| | | | | | | |
|---|---|---|---|---|---|---|
| Oct | 96.400 | -0.800 | 97.000 | 95.550 | 0.30 | 2.63 |
| Nov | 95.825 | -1.225 | 97.900 | 94.750 | 2.15 | 7.18 |
| Jan | 95.625 | -1.725 | 98.225 | 94.700 | 1.20 | 10.92 |
| Mar | 97.075 | -1.875 | 98.250 | 96.425 | 0.08 | 1.31 |
| **Total** | | | | | **0.62** | **23.5** |

## SPOT MARKETS

### CRUDE OIL FOB (per barrel) + or -

| | | |
|---|---|---|
| Dubai | $64.74-64.76 | -3.5 |
| Brent Blend (dated) | $69.13-69.15 | -3.9 |
| Brent Blend(Nov) | $70.14-70.16 | -3.9 |
| WTI | $74.35-74.40 | -4.3 |

### OIL PRODUCTS NWE prompt delivery CIF (tonne)

| | | |
|---|---|---|
| Unleaded Gas (95R) | $590.00-600.00 | -77.0 |
| Gas Oil (German Htg) | $709.25-722.25 | -36.3 |
| Heavy Fuel Oil | $341.00-357.00 | -26.0 |
| Naphtha | $505.00-515.00 | -70.0 |
| Jet Fuel | $764.25-772.25 | -34.8 |
| Diesel (French) | $743.25-751.25 | -34.8 |

### NATURAL GAS (Pence/therm)

| | | |
|---|---|---|
| NBP | 68.00-73.00 | -4.3 |
| Euro (Zebrugge) | 67.80-73.00 | -4.3 |

### ELECTRICITY & COAL

| | | |
|---|---|---|
| APX Spot Index | 77.13 | +9.0 |
| Conti Power Index | 91.77 | -5.8 |
| globalCOAL RB Index | $116.00 | -7.3 |

### OTHER

| | | |
|---|---|---|
| Ethanol | 1.702 | -0.1 |
| Uranium | 46.000 | -3.0 |
| Platinum ❖ | 985.00 | -47.0 |
| Palladium ❖ | 197.00 | -4.0 |
| Tin (Kuala Lumpur) | 21300r | -700.0 |
| Tin (New York) | 884.5c | nc |
| Raw Sugar ‡ | 227.75 | +4.5 |
| White Sugar ‡ | 310.3 | -8.8 |
| Barley | 120.00 | nc |
| Maize (No3 Yellow) ♠ | 113.30 | nc |
| Wheat (US Dark Nth) | 170.70 | nc |
| Rubber (KL RSS no1) | 642.00m | -15.0 |
| Coconut Oil (Phil) § | 910.00 | -60.0 |
| Palm Oil (Malay.) § | 565.00 | -30.0 |
| Copra (Phil) § | 342.65 | -1.4 |
| Soyabeans (US) | 374.10 | -14.0 |
| Cotlook 'A' index | 61.60c | nc |
| Wooltops (64s Super) | 506.00 | nc |
| FOEX PIX | 828.74 | nc |

£ per tonne otherwise stated. ❖ 2pm Lon Fix US $ per troy oz. c cents/lb. r $ per tonne. m Malaysian cents/kg. § CIF Rotterdam. ♠ CIF UK. ‡ FOB. Ø £/Mwh. Z €/Mwh. Source: Platts (020) 8543 1234. Fuel Oil 3.5% S. French Diesel 50ppm. NBP National Balancing Point. † US $ per metric tonne, week to date. Prices at UK close unless otherwise stated.

## INDICES

| | Oct 14 | % Chg Mnth | % Chg Year |
|---|---|---|---|
| S&P GSCI Spt | 509.39 | -17.7 | -9.3 |
| DJ AIG Spt | 144.87 | -16.3 | -19.1 |
| R/J CRB TR | 292.06 | -16.7 | -5.3 |
| Rogers RICIX TR | 3558.05 | -13.1 | -12.6 |
| M Lynch MLCX Spt | 398.02 | -14.2 | -9.3 |
| UBSBberg CMCI TR | 1110.04 | -15.6 | -10.3 |
| | Oct 15 | Mnth | Year |
| LEBA EUA Carbon | 23.54 | +4.2 | +4.3 |

## FTSE GOLD MINES INDEX

www.ft.com/commoditiesdata

| $ | Oct 15 | % chg on day | Oct 14 | Year ago | Gross yld % | Total return | 52 week High | 52 week Low |
|---|---|---|---|---|---|---|---|---|
| **Gold Mines Index (17)** | **1802.52** | **-7.70** | **1952.81** | **3001.75** | **1.07** | **2049.65** | **3553.88** | **1802.52** |
| **Regional Indices** | | | | | | | | |
| Asia Pacific (3) | 7062.97 | -6.61 | 7562.59 | 15288.84 | 0.89 | 8070.58 | 17255.62 | 6421.07 |
| EMEA (6) | 1579.44 | -5.54 | 1672.03 | 2849.16 | 1.01 | 2020.95 | 3152.15 | 1482.00 |
| Americas (8) | 1606.37 | -8.53 | 1756.22 | 2456.08 | 1.13 | 1737.79 | 3147.78 | 1606.37 |

Copyright, FTSE International Limited 2007. All rights reserved. For further information please contact FTSE Client Services on +44 (0) 20 7866 1810. Figures in brackets show number of companies. Basis US Dollars. Base Values: 1000.00 31/12/92. † Partial.

**Figure 13-1:** The commodities and Agriculture listings from the Financial Times.

*Source: FT.com*

For other sorts of commodities, such as various oil blends, farm products, and meat and livestock, the *FT*'s listings set things out in a different way that provides rather more information. Instead of simply giving you a three-month delivery price for each commodity, in the volumes of goods listed at the top of each sub-table the statistics offer you price data for many months ahead. Grain crops like maize are quoted almost a year ahead! And coffee, orange juice, cotton, and various other commodities are listed even further ahead than that.

On the other hand, Figure 13-1 also gives 'spot market' prices for oil, gas, and energy commodities, plus a handful of miscellaneous farm products. The *spot price* is the price at which you shake hands on the deal today and sort out the delivery arrangements afterwards. This isn't as sophisticated as having forward prices for a year next month, but it gets the job done.

You can get also get detailed breakdowns of daily commodity prices by looking at *Lloyd's List* (www.lloydsshipmanager.com), a specialist paper that caters for the international shipping community. Because its readers have so much riding on the state of the commodities scene – and so much more money to make if they can get their ships into the right ports at the right times – the intelligence in *Lloyd's List* is right up with the very best. You can get a free trial to *Lloyd's List*, but once that runs out you need to subscribe to get your hands on the data.

Finally, I should mention a company called Platts (www.platts.com), reckoned to be one of the world's most authoritative sources on anything relating to energy. It's pretty good on shipping too! But again, the company charges quite a stiff subscription for accessing the data.

## Why everything's priced in dollars

No matter where you look in the financial pages, the one thing you always notice is that the vast majority of commodity prices are quoted in US currency. They always have been, and if Washington had its way they always would be. As long as commodities are priced in dollars, Americans don't have to worry about whether the dollar happens to be riding up or down at the time. What they see is what they get.

For other nationalities, however, the situation's a little more complicated. You need to make allowances for the fluctuating dollar whenever you look at buying gold or grain or petroleum, because shifts in the greenback can spell the difference between success and disaster. For a German investor, the steep fall in the dollar–euro exchange rate between 2006 and 2008 completely wiped out any gains he made on gold bullion during those years.

So you might be wrong to expect that a Frenchman or a Spaniard would always be as interested in gold – or many other commodities, for that matter! – as an American. This is important information that you ignore at your peril.

One of my favourite sources of online information on all kinds of commodity contracts is TFC Charts (www.tfc-charts.w2d.com). It isn't going to win any prizes for the attractiveness of its website, but it's reliable, flexible, updated daily – and free.

But equally good, in my view, is the wealth of price information you can obtain from a company called Kitco (www.kitco.com), which supplies data to many of the world's most prominent investment houses. A lot of the time, you'll notice that the Kitco charts are going rather further than simply supplying you with 'spot' information. Instead, you'll find that they give you forward (or futures) prices for a range of different dates in the future. As we noted earlier when we looked at the FT chart, you'll find that these prices might be quite a lot higher or lower than today's 'spot' price. But having them expressed in a chart format rather than just a table of figures is a big help when it comes to getting a picture of the global trend.

# Investing in Oil

The discreet charm of a fast-disappearing asset makes the investment world sit up and take notice. You can hardly open a newspaper these days without somebody telling you that we're living in the age of Peak Oil. They mean that the world's consuming more and more of the stuff, at the exact same time as oil resources are beginning to tail off. And therefore that you can make money by buying into oil stocks now, because oil's never going to get any cheaper and can only get more expensive. Why, you only have to look at the falling levels of new oilfield discoveries to realise that the world's living on borrowed time.

Is that actually true, though? Many people in the oil extraction industry say that, although they're getting less successful at finding new oilfields, they're getting much better at extracting every last drop of oil from the wells that already exist, and that therefore the rate of oil depletion may be a bit slower than the pessimists expect.

Every time the oil price rises, oil experts say, it becomes viable to spend a little more money on giving all the depleted oilfields a thorough work-over. And at the same time, whole new oil extraction possibilities come into view. I'm not just talking about spending money on converting grain into bioethanol; the Canadian Oil Sands project has billions of tonnes of crude locked up in a series of ancient bituminous lakes. As long as crude oil was $40 a barrel, the Oil Sands' fixed extraction costs of around $35 weren't worth bothering with; but now that a barrel frequently fetches $55 and often more, the economics have been transformed.

If you're looking for long-term information on the world's energy situation, you can't do much better than the annual BP Statistical Review of World Energy, available through the BP web-site (`www.bp.com`). Hundreds of pages of information are available on oil, natural gas, coal, electricity, and so on – both production and consumption – and you can download the data either as a PDF file (for use with Adobe Acrobat), or as an Excel chart if you don't mind not having the very latest information.

Alternatively, a free 80-page download, 'Key World Energy Statistics', is available on the International Energy Agency's website (`www.iea.org/Textbase/stats/index.asp`), together with a daily oil market report (`http://omrpublic.iea.org`).

## Getting started

How do you invest in oil? Well, you can buy shares in Shell or BP or any of the other companies that actually produce, process, and distribute the stuff. If you fancy the added excitement of an emerging market situation, a Chinese company like PetroChina (available on the New York Stock Exchange, and listed in US dollars) ought to give your heart that extra tweak when the exchange rate shifts. But that route's full of risks. Instead, the main objective here is to look for 'pure' investments instead. So the main options consist of the following:

- ✔ Using Exchange-Traded Funds, which behave exactly like shares but track the underlying prices of oil.

- ✔ Investing directly in government oil funds like the US Oil Fund, which track the oil price and charge a modest management fee.

- ✔ Buying a UK-based energy trust such as the Investec Global Energy Fund or the ABN AMRO Energy Fund, both of which invest in oil companies but tend to shadow the prices of the raw commodity itself.

- ✔ Buying oil derivatives with the aim of second-guessing the markets.

I honestly can't recommend the derivatives option, because it's just too tough and too dangerous for a beginner. Not only are you in the company of experts when you trade derivatives – you also run the risk of potentially unlimited losses if your bet goes wrong (take a look at Chapter 12 for more on derivatives).

As for using government oil funds, that's a rather old-fashioned approach for a private investor these days, and it may turn out to be unfeasibly expensive and awkward. Why bother with all that hassle when you can buy a UK-listed ETF that goes straight into your Individual Savings Account (ISA) and gives you tax efficiency too? (ETFs are currently exempted from stamp duty on purchases.)

# Finding an oil or gas ETF

The number of commodity ETFs available on the London market has exploded into the dozens over the last few years, so practically anything I write here may soon be out of date. You can get an up-to-date list either from the London Stock Exchange or from independent sources such as `http://etf.stock-encyclopedia.com`.

Barclays Global Investors run a series of ETFs under the iShares label, although at the moment they don't include many direct energy plays. You may like to check the current range of iShares ETFs at `www.ishares.eu`. The French banking and insurance giant AXA operates a range of commodity ETFs under the Lyxor brand. Currently, the dominant source of energy-related ETFs in London is an American company called ETFS. All of its ETFs are listed below, together with their TIDM identifying codes (which used to be known as EPICs, and still are in some quarters):

- ETFS Brent Oil ETF (OILB)
- ETFS Crude Oil ETF (CRUD)
- ETFS Energy ETF (AIGE)
- ETFS Gasoline ETF (UGAS)
- ETFS Heating Oil ETF (HEAT)
- ETFS WTI Oil ETF (OILW)
- ETFS Natural Gas ETF (NGAS)
- ETFS Petroleum ETF (AIGO)

The nearby sidebar, 'Finding an oil or gas ETF', provides some useful sources.

You can get daily price quotes for all ETFs from the London Stock Exchange, or from your usual stockbroker. If you have a nominee account with an online (execution-only) broker, you should be able to buy, sell, and price any of these without any difficulty at all. See Chapters 2 and 3 for more on dealing with brokers.

## Finding price information

Once you've decided what sort of oil you're interested in, laying your hands on the price information you need should get a little easier. You can find a comprehensive range of price information in every kind of online publication (rather fewer from the printed media). The list, in fact, is daunting. But here are a few of my favourites:

- Bloomberg: `www.bloomberg.com/markets/commodities/energyprices.html`
- *Financial Times*: `http://markets.ft.com/ft/markets/commodities.asp`

✔ The good old BBC: `http://newsvote.bbc.co.uk/1/shared/fds/hi/business/market_data/commodities`

I rather like the approach at WTRG Economics, (`www.wtrg.com`), an American website that contains a pretty good run-down of the major issues facing the oil industry together with some in-depth analysis of the current major news stories.

## Can anyone forecast the oil price?

Can you possibly tell how much more expensive oil is going to be in twelve months' time? No, is the short answer, but you can get a very good feel for how the market regards its own prospects by tuning into the oil futures market.

What's the oil futures market? If you're running a bus company and you're worried that rising diesel prices may put you out of business by Christmas, you can protect yourself by 'hedging' your future diesel requirements. That is, you do one of two things:

✔ You make an agreement with a supplier whereby you pay him an agreed price for the fuel he's going to deliver to you in a year's time. That price is probably higher than the going rate in today's marketplace because the supplier's taking a gamble on the possibility that he may need to sell you the oil for less than he can get for it from somebody else, so you're paying him a bit over the odds to keep him sweet.

✔ You take out a bet on the futures market, whereby you 'win' a lot of money if the oil price rises between now and Christmas. Your winnings compensate you at least partially for the burden of the higher fuel bills that you're paying by then. (In fact, the same principle of using futures for a hedging strategy applies to all types of commodities, from gold right the way through to wheat or even currencies. Unsurprisingly, commodities and futures markets always go together, even in Communist China, which doesn't really approve of them.)

What all this tells you is that, if you can find out what the hedging markets are saying right now, you can figure out whether the market thinks the price is likely to rise or fall. You often find a news report that says something like 'Brent crude for December delivery rose by $3 to $150 per barrel on fears of an escalation of tension between Iran and Israel'.

Whoops, you've just tripped over another hidden wire in the grass. You probably don't need me to tell you that real, physical, and political events can send the oil price all over the place. And no real substitute exists for keeping yourself informed about the global trade economy if you want to play the oil markets effectively.

# Understanding petroleum grades

You may not be surprised to hear that different parts of the world produce different qualities of oil. The varying geology means that differences are inevitable, and they can make quite a differenceto the usability of crude petroleum.

For instance, China has a fair amount of oil in its coastal waters, but it tends to be rather heavy stuff with a lot of waxy substances that are better suited to making plastics, when what the refiners really need is a large proportion of fuel-grade material. In contrast, Bonny Light is a Nigerian oil with low sulphur characteristics and a high proportion of fuel-grade components that produces more gallons of petrol or kerosene for every barrel.

Surprise, surprise, Bonny Light fetches a higher price than Chinese crude. And dozens of other grades of oil are classified mainly according to the regions where they're drilled. Indeed, the *International Crude Oil Market Handbook*, published by the American Energy Intelligence Group, lists around 160 different internationally traded crude oils.

But the chances are that you don't want to bother with all this. Instead, you can fix your gaze on two or three of the so-called benchmark petroleum types that have a low density, and therefore produce high proportions of 'light' fuel oils. You can find the prices for all (or most) of these benchmark oils in any serious business publication:

✓ **West Texas Intermediate (also known as WTI)** is generally reckoned to have the best combination of grades, with an API gravity rating of 39.6 degrees (meaning that it's very light indeed) and a low level of sulphur, meaning that it's considered to be a 'sweet' oil. Highly desirable.

✓ **Brent Blend,** Britain's very own product, is actually a blend of 15 different crudes from the North Sea. Its API gravity of 38.3 degrees makes it a bit heavier than WTI, and its sulphur rating is slightly less good. It usually sells for around $2 a barrel less than WTI.

✓ **OPEC basket price** is a rather clumsy name for an even clumsier mix of seven different crudes from around the world, including Nigeria's Bonny Light, Saudi Arabia's Arab Light, Venezuela's Tia Juana Light, and Indonesia's Minas. It sells for about $4–6 per barrel less than WTI.

And how much, exactly, is a barrel of oil? It's 42 US gallons, which is equivalent to 34.972 imperial gallons or 158.987 litres. An imperial gallon is almost exactly 1.2 US gallons. An American measure is not often smaller than everybody else's, but this is the exception that proves the rule.

To explain more, if the slightest chance exists of armed conflict, or sabotage to a pipeline, or even just a political stand-off (reports like 'Moscow today suspended shipments to Western Europe because of disputes over its human rights policy'), it can send the oil price soaring.

The oil industry has seasons! Oil prices commonly dip a bit during the late spring when the central heating systems in the northern hemisphere go off, and then rise again when America's 'driving season' gets under way in May.

## Drillers, explorers, and producers

Taking a 'pure' investment in oil is very different from investing in the production company that drills it and produces it.

You don't need me to tell you why oil producers' fortunes go up and down at a different rate from the prices of the goods they produce. Having a barrel of oil in a tank and selling it to someone is one thing; having it sitting a mile underground, or perhaps underwater, under a chunk of land that belongs to a foreign government is quite another. The oil companies have to cope with a welter of different risks, from technical issues and transport problems to manpower shortages, environmental issues, and – not least – the sheer political risk of trading in a sensitive commodity under a foreign government's nose, which isn't always easy.

So much for the companies that produce the oil when an exploration company's located it. But the explorers who drill for the stuff in the first place are a different breed altogether. Obviously, the oil majors themselves do a lot of exploration, but a small army of independent explorers also work the oilfields of the world – many of them tiny little outfits with market capitalisations that barely make it into the millions. These independents know that they stand to make big money if they ever hit a really large deposit – which is why so-called 'value investors' and other adventurous types who like to buy risky things at cheap prices love them so much.

Don't touch independent explorers if you haven't got a higher than average appetite for risk – they have a habit of going bust. That said, more than 90 of them are in the Alternative Investment Market (AIM) listings at the back of the *Financial Times* or on the London Stock Exchange's website (www.london stockexchange.co.uk).

# Investing in Food Commodities

Food commodities (often called 'soft commodities') are a bit different from mainstream commodities, for a number of reasons. They don't conform to the usual long-term cycles that dominate the metals industry, say, or the oil industry. That's because for a farmer to switch from coffee to soya (and back again, if need be) takes such a short time that predicting which way things are likely to turn in the next twelve months is incredibly hard.

A frost, drought, or flood will open up the possibilities for big price swings at very short notice. That's why you should never regard food commodities as anything other than a tough gamble, unless you're absolutely cast-iron certain that a particular trend's going to happen over a number of years. And even then, you'll be sharing the bear pit with thousands of dedicated experts, many of whom have their own intelligence operations running in various parts of the world. The big boys use aerial photography to tell them how the crops are coming on in Russia or Brazil – and if you haven't got that information too, you're going to be at a competitive disadvantage!

If that thought doesn't scare you off, then good luck to you. You can always buy shares in a major agribusiness company like America's Bunge, but once again I advise you to use an ETF every time. An ETF is flexible, fast, liquid, and doesn't incur stamp duty. The nearby sidebar, 'Finding a food products ETF', lists the relevant codes.

## The DJ-AIG commodity indices

Before very long you will notice that many of the world's most prominent food ETFs track a series of price indices (see Chapter X on indices) run by the Dow Jones organisation in New York, in collaboration with the American International Group, and usually known as the DJ-AIG indices. This transatlantic predominance is for a reason.

America, and more specifically Chicago, is the spiritual home of all the world's biggest agricultural derivative industries. America's Midwest farming industries first felt the need to have a futures system way back in the nineteenth century, to insulate themselves from unexpected fluctuations in the grain prices and 'hedge' against crop disasters that may wipe out either the farmers or the food merchants, or both. (See Chapter 12 for the lowdown on derivatives.) So, by no particular coincidence, Chicago quickly became the centre for hard-headed folk who understood enough about agricultural risk to create what became the world's premier farm derivatives market. It's still the dominant worldwide centre today.

That's where ETFs come into the picture. ETF providers don't actually buy grain, or oil, or whatever. Instead, they keep some of their money in cash and trade the rest of it in futures contracts and so forth – things that bring them disproportionately large gains or losses according to which way the markets move as time goes on. And those are the gains and losses that get passed back to you in the form of the profits or losses you make on your ETFs.

I'm over-simplifying the situation quite outrageously here, but as a working explanation of a very complicated financial product, I'm at least pointing you in the right direction. ETFs are very tightly regulated, and a welter of protective legislation secures your money, so you've no reason to feel that ETFs are any less secure than ordinary shares.

## Finding a food products ETF

Food product ETFs in London include the following, listed together with their TIDMidentifying codes:

- ✔ ETFS Agriculture ETF (AIGA)
- ✔ ETFS Grains ETF (AIGG)
- ✔ ETFS Wheat ETF (WEAT)
- ✔ ETFS Soybeans ETF (SOYB)
- ✔ ETFS Soybean Oil ETF (SOYO)

- ✔ ETFS Sugar ETF (SUGA)
- ✔ ETFS Coffee ETF (COFF)
- ✔ ETFS Livestock ETF (AIGL)
- ✔ ETFS Live Cattle ETF (CATL)
- ✔ ETFS Lean Hogs ETF (HOGS)

I anticipate a major expansion of food ETFs from other suppliers in the near future, so check to see what's currently available.

## Finding price information

Daily prices for food products ETFs are listed on the London Stock Exchange (www.londonstockexchange.co.uk).

Go to www.djindexes.com/aig for everything you need to know about DJ-AIG commodity indices, including all the current price quotes and enough charts to keep you busy for years.

# Investing in Gold and Other Precious Metals

And so to the gold market, perhaps the most darkly fascinating area of the whole investment scene. Gold's value can soar and then plummet, often within a matter of months (see 'Considering exceptions to the cyclical process', earlier in this chapter), and must make more people unhappy with its long-term performance than almost any form of investment because:

- ✔ It doesn't pay interest or dividends.
- ✔ It doesn't have many industrial uses.

✔ It's expensive to store, transport, and insure.

✔ It lost half its value in the early 1980s, and then took 27 years to regain even its nominal value! (Gold was still 60% down on 1980 in real terms at the time of writing.)

The reason gold's value is so unpredictable is simply that a finite amount of the stuff exists, and when everybody decides they want to have some a scramble always takes place for the short available supply.

Gold also has a few industrial uses, despite everything. For example, it's an excellent electrical conductor, which is why many of the chips and memory cards in your personal computer have gold-plated edges. It's used in certain types of electroconductive paint, and it turns up in the devices that scrub the exhaust systems of big industrial plants. Oh, and Japanese restaurants serve it to their customers with the flaked chocolate toppings on their desserts.

But all these applications put together can't make much of a destructive dent in a global market that prizes the indestructibility of gold. Gold doesn't rot, it doesn't rust, and although it's soft it can be melted down and reclaimed easily. Estimates are that 90% of the gold that's ever been mined is still in existence. A sobering thought.

## *Finding price information*

You're going to want to know many things when you buy a gold investment, but perhaps the most obvious is the one you may well miss. Gold's value is the combined result of its scarcity and its ability to make people feel safer when they experience greed or fear – but how exactly are you going to measure that scarcity and make sure that it's still there?

The best information source is the World Gold Council, a private consortium of gold producers around the world that has a vested interest in selling you gold. It publishes regular surveys of the amounts of gold being dug out of the ground, together with the shape and structure of demand from jewellers, manufacturers, and of course the central banks who like to keep gold as a reserve currency. You need a free subscription to read the online reports, but logging on to www.gold.org is worthwhile if you're at all serious about gold investing.

Gold mining production has been falling well short of global demand during the last five years or so, which is why prices have risen so much. Every gold mining company worth its salt has been digging new mines as fast as it can, but with little likelihood of any of them beginning to produce gold until at least 2010. You must decide for yourself whether that means gold has a secure future, but to me the indicators are looking good so far. Figure 13-2 shows the generally upward price movement for gold since January 2000.

Round-the-clock 'spot' gold prices are quoted in the daily papers and on the Internet. But you may not know that the global price is fixed twice a day in Britain, by the so-called London Gold Pool, whose five members hold a telephone conference at 10.30 a.m. and 3 p.m. Dealers all over the world then use those prices as a benchmark for fixing spot prices. But serious traders can also get 'forward' gold prices, which effectively fix a sale price for some future date and are used in hedging arrangements.

**Figure 13-2:**
Gold prices
over an
8-year
period.

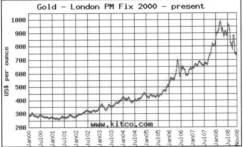

# Choosing gold certificates and Exchange Traded Funds

The trouble with gold is that it's so awkward to have around the house. If you buy gold abroad you need to ship it, insure it, and possibly face a lot of wrangles about value added tax (gold is VAT free in the UK, but not in every other country).

Small wonder, then, that investors go out looking for more convenient ways to own gold bullion. One way is through a 'proxy gold' scheme such as the one the government of Western Australia runs. You buy your gold from the Perth Mint (`www.perthmint.com.au`) and instead of posting it to you, they keep it in a vault and send you a certificate from the government and accredited by the London Bullion Market Association (LBMA), the New York Commodities Exchange (Comex), and the Tokyo Commodities Exchange (Tocom). That's a pretty high level of investor protection. And if you prefer to take physical delivery of your gold, they can arrange that as well.

This still sounds like too much trouble to most people, though. Now that Exchange-Traded Funds (ETFs) have become commonplace among commodity investors, you can simply buy one of the many bullion and precious metal ETFs. I use ETFS Gold Bullion and I can buy it and sell it on the spur of the moment through my online ISA account, just like a share. But the Lyxor Gold Bullion Securities ETF is also very popular and very liquid.

Both of these ETFs are denominated in US dollars, so make some allowance for the possibility of currency movements affecting your returns.

## Investing in silver, platinum, palladium, and the rest

Silver, platinum, palladium, and a host of other precious metals are traded on the commodities markets. The only thing I'm going to say is that, although silver is often regarded as a 'poor man's gold', involving lower-cost transactions than its bigger brother, it doesn't have the same characteristics.

For one thing, rather a lot of silver exists. Almost every mine that produces lead, nickel, or tin has deposits of the stuff mixed in with its seams, as a natural result of the volcanic geology that creates all metal deposits in the first place. This means that the key attribute of gold – its tightly limited availability – simply doesn't apply to silver. There are vast quantities of the metal out there.

That's not quite so bad as it might seem, actually, because silver is used quite a lot in industry. Its good conducting qualities, its chemical sensitivity to light and its ability to withstand extremes of temperature have created a vast number of applications in medicine, in electronics manufacturing, and of course in photography, where it's a basic component of film. It does of course have a major role to play in the jewellery industry, and in coins, cutlery and tableware. But a growing proportion of the world's output – maybe 10% – is now going straight into silver bullion bars for sale to investors whose finances can't quite stretch to gold ingots.

The good news, for an investor, is that the silver price improved massively in the first seven years of the 21st century, rising from just $5.25 at the start of the decade to $10 in November 2008. That's double what you'd have got from either the London stock market or the American S&P 500 index. The bad news is that it has also seen prices as low as $4 and as high as $21 along the way! Figure 13-3 shows you fluctuations in the price of silver during the course of 2008.

Platinum is another ball game entirely, however. On the one hand it's in very limited supply: there are only about ten major producers in the world, and 90% of global production comes from just two countries, Russia and South Africa. On the other hand, it has quite a number of industrial uses, which means that, unlike gold, it tends to get used up.

**Figure 13-3:**
Silver prices
over 11
months.

It might surprise you to know that only about 25% of the world's platinum production goes into jewellery. 5% goes into glass manufacturing, 6% goes into electrical goods, 3% is used in generating energy, and another 5% is bought by the chemicals industry for amalgamation into other products.. Perhaps most importantly, more than 50% or the world's platinum production is used to make the catalytic converters that are used in the exhaust systems fitted to nearly every car on the planet. When you think about how many new cars are being sold every year in China or India, it's clear that the prospects for this scarce metal are probably more secure than gold itself.

What's more, it takes a lot more technology to extract platinum from its ore than would normally be the case with gold – a popular estimate is that it takes 12 tonnes of ore to produce a single ounce of gold, and the extraction process may well take six months to complete. What does that mean for investors? It means it's pretty unlikely that new rivals will be able to spring up and contest the dominance of the existing major players. In the City's jargon, the entry barriers are very high.

Palladium, another "rich man's gold", is also finding favour these days among investors who are looking for a rare metal to back. Like platinum, it comes largely from Russia and South Africa (with some also from North America), and like platinum it's used in car exhaust systems, jewellery and electronics. Also in dental applications, where its malleability and adaptability have made it very popular metal.Palladium is the metal that's used in making 'white gold', by melting it in with conventional gold – a process which makes the yellow in the gold fade away.

But if you've been expecting that palladium prices would mirror the soaring cost of gold you're likely to be disappointed. From a price of barely $150 per counce in 1996, the metal soared to nearly $750 in early 2000 – only to fall back steeply to $200 by 2003. Then up to nearly $600 in May 2008, before dropping below $185 as December approached. That's a pretty scary rate of fluctuation, and it should give you all the warning you need not to mess with this most speculative of metals unless your tolerance for risk is exceptionally high. Enough said, I hope.

## Finding a precious metals ETF

Precious metal ETFs in London include the following, listed together with their TIDM identifying codes:

- ETFS Precious Metals ETF (AIGP)

- Lyxor Gold Bullion Securities ETF (GBS)

- ETFS Gold ETF (BULL)

- ETFS Silver ETF (SLVR)

## *Discovering gold collectable coins*

You don't get a lot of pleasure out of looking at a bar of gold even if you go out and buy one. Gold's inconvenient, hard to insure against loss or theft, and having it lying around the house is a constant worry. Small wonder, then, that most people who buy physical bullion decide to store it in a safe deposit box where it brings them no aesthetic joy at all.

That's just one of the reasons people often prefer to hold their gold in the form of either jewellery or gold coins.

One thing that may well surprise you is how little most sovereigns are worth. Britain has issued so many gold coins over the last century and a half that most of them command only a fairly small premium over the bullion value of the gold they're made from. An inherited gold sovereign in my sock drawer is worth only marginally more than when my father bought it in the 1980s. You can find the same lack of price appreciation happening with South African Krugerrands and Eurozone gold coins. But American gold coins can be worth much, much more because none was issued for a long period, so the scarcity value attached to them is much higher.

Be prepared to pay some pretty breathtaking commissions when the time comes to sell. The dealer or the auctioneer wants a goodly slice of the action if you're selling through any expert channel (and face it, who in their right mind is going to buy gold from you any other way?). And of course, any dealer who sells you a newly minted gold coin in a presentation box is going to be looking for a so-called 'coin premium' to cover his extra costs. So you need to factor this into your cost calculations. Gold coins are more likely to make your dealer rich than you! But if you're undeterred, do at least think of your gold coin investments as long-term purchases.

## Finding prices information

My favourite site for bullion and precious metal prices is Kitco (www.kitco.com), which gives up-to-the-moment price information in a range of different formats. The fact that it's US based isn't a problem as long as the world's bullion reserves continue to be valued in US dollars.

Things tend to go awry at weekends, however, because Kitco often switches off its charting updates between Friday night and Monday lunchtime (for Brits) when the US markets finally open. At these times you may get on better with the live-action interactive charts from GalMarley (www.galmarley.com), which are open all hours.

If you're after gold coins and physical bars, your best bet in Britain is probably the country's biggest independent dealer, Chard, which has the rather unappealing-sounding website www.taxfreegold.co.uk. This is an out-and-out sales site, of course, so don't expect impartial advice. But as a general guide to what you're likely to pay for top-quality coins, it's hard to beat.

# Investing in Less Glamorous Commodities

For every headline that gold, silver, oil, and all the rest of them make, thousands upon thousands of unsung heroes are digging up base metals such as copper, tin, aluminium, and iron ore, and negotiating contracts for millions of tonnes of these indispensable industrial staples. The only time these Plain Janes of the investment world show their faces is when China or India agrees to pay double the price it paid last year for top-grade Australian iron ore.

You can't make high-grade specialist steel out of any old raw materials. Those companies with deposits of the finest mineral grades – and I'm thinking of BHP Billiton, Vale, and Rio Tinto – can virtually command their own prices. That's why the giants of the mining sector are continually on the lookout for new sources of these metals.

---

## Finding a base metals ETF

Base metal ETFs in London include the following, listed together with their EPIC identifying codes:

✔ ETFS Industrial Metals ETF (AIGI)

✔ ETFS Aluminium ETF (ALUM-LSE) ETFS Copper ETF (COPA)

✔ ETFS Zinc ETF (ZINC)

✔ ETFS Nickel ETF (NICK)

## Uranium

Don't forget the stock market power of one of the most toxic metals on earth. As the demand for nuclear energy heats up in the coming decades, so will the need for regular supplies of high-quality uranium deposits.

Uranium ore is actually an amazingly common mineral. Large parts of northern Africa and Australia are strewn with the stuff, and in Europe it turns up in unexpected places: several open-cast uranium mines used to exist in France, although most of them have gone now.

The point is that uranium ore needs an awful lot of processing before you can extract anything you can use in a nuclear reactor. The better the ore quality, the fewer trainloads of rock you need to transport in order to get a kilogram of fuel.

And don't forget the political dimension. Many people are afraid of nuclear power, but now that the oil price seems to have hit higher long-term average levels, the advantages of this energy source are again becoming apparent. Building a new reactor takes eight to ten years, so the physical demand for uranium isn't going to heat up for a long time even if every country in the world starts construction today. But the sheer shortage of suitable ore suppliers in the world has created a nasty bottleneck, which has been doing explosive things to the uranium price.

Good heavens, what a lurching price trend. Between January 2006 and January 2008 you could have quadrupled your money and then lost half of it again. Uranium may be the word on every speculator's lips these days, but it isn't for the faint-hearted.

## Finding price information

To locate sources of information on uranium, start with the TFC Charts (http://tfc-charts.w2d.com), and continue through the Kitco base metals site at www.kitcometals.com. And definitely take a look at Infomine (www.infomine.com), which carries charting and price information for nearly 30 different minerals – and in around 50 currencies!

# Chapter 14

# Investing in Funds and Trusts

## In This Chapter

▶ Handing things over to an expert

▶ Locating information on trusts and funds

▶ Differentiating between unit trusts and investment trusts

*N*o matter how good your own stock-picking skills may be, there are probably going to be some times and some situations where you'll probably want to leave the choices to somebody else. Leaving another person in charge of your savings means that you're free to get on with your life and do the things you want to with your time, instead of spending every waking moment wondering whether the Nikkei is heading down the tubes or the FTSE's being overvalued.

Anyway, of course, you already do employ professional fund managers to run your investments on your behalf. Your pension funds are a prime example of letting somebody else do the legwork – and let's remember that, even if your employer runs your pension scheme, it's a professional manager who's actually investing your cash. As for those guaranteed income bonds you bought last year – to say nothing of your endowment mortgage – none of them would function at all without somebody at the controls to get on with the daily grind of selecting and monitoring the things that will go into your portfolio.

# Employing a Professional Pilot

But I'm assuming, for the moment, that you rather enjoy the thrill of the chase, and that your investing record so far hasn't been so terrible as to make you think that you really ought to give up and do something different. What, you ask, is so wrong with your own stock-picking that you should feel the need to bring in a hired hand?

Nothing at all, probably. I thoroughly enjoy picking the stocks that have brought me a modestly successful result over the years. But there are some areas where I know that I'm in right over my head, and where I really do prefer to let somebody else take control of the tiller.

## Utilising expert knowledge

If you're investing in a country whose local language you don't speak, employ someone who does. If your Japanese isn't up to much, you don't gain much from trying to invest in the small companies that are making so much of the running in Tokyo these days, because so few of them disseminate any of their shareholder information in English. Then again, if you don't know how a Chinese company likes to treat its investors and its business partners, you may be in for a few shocks when little things like business protocol start to get in the way of what you may think are cut-and-dried deals.

If you're investing in the Middle East, you need somebody who understands the ways of Islam. If you want to run a few Russian investments, a manager who knows her way round the silent hierarchy of powerful people who control so much in the Russian business world is a real help.

Another situation where a good pilot can make all the difference is when the technical aspects of the industry in question go right over your head. Only an analyst with the right blend of investment skills and an in-depth knowledge of the sector can get you the right results when the little details count. Is the plusfix matrix count system really going to revolutionise the home security system, or will the regenerative synastic loop knock it out of contention? (All right, I confess, I made up both of these innovations, but you get the idea.) Naturally, you can try to beat the experts by reading everything you can find about the companies and technologies you're interested in – that's one task the Internet's very useful for – but at the end of the day you're likely to find yourself reading the fund managers' commentaries in the newspapers and simply doing what they recommend anyway.

But perhaps the greatest joy of using a professional pilot instead of operating alone is that your manager can spread your money over a much wider range of stocks than you'll ever manage to do yourself. If you have £5,000 to invest and you buy ten different lots of shares in ten different companies, you'll probably end up spending £200 (4 per cent) on handling charges and stamp duty, plus another £10 in commissions when the time comes to sell any one of them. Your manager will probably scoop up all the charges for a flat initial fee of less than 1 per cent and a management fee of maybe 1 per cent a year, possibly even less.

## Considering the autopilot advantage

In aviation circles, the joke goes that if you look inside the cockpit of a modern passenger aircraft you'll find a pilot, a computer, and a big fierce dog. The computer's job is to fly the plane. The dog's job is to bite the pilot if he/she tries to touch the controls.

Most of the tracker funds you meet in the course of your everyday investing are a bit like that. With only rare exceptions, no humans are in charge of the investment process – instead, the computer takes all the decisions, and the human just does what he or she's told. Buy this, sell that, press this button to authorise the transaction, and I'll do the rest..

That's good news for everybody, of course. First, the pilot (sorry, I mean fund manager) doesn't make personal mistakes that reveal his human vulnerability to those good old emotions, greed and fear.

And secondly, an automated process means that the fund's much less likely to miss out on a trend because somebody just hasn't noticed it.

But for most other fund situations the pilot's still very much at the controls, and his knowledge makes an awfully big difference.

# Sourcing Information

The problem with looking up the latest information about managed funds is that there's so much of it , and none of it seems to go very deep. One glance at the back pages of the *Financial Times*, which lists *seven full pages* of listings in microscopic print every single day of the week, is enough to get you whimpering for the long-lost simplicity of your post office account.

I mean, who reads all that stuff? The experts. And are you an expert? Of course not. Surely you can find a better way of sifting through all that crashingly boring detail and selecting the best buys.

You can. Nearly every fund that this chapter considers has a unique identifying code that you can type into your computer and get all the useful information your heart desires. Plus graphs, sectoral weighting breakdowns that tell you which funds are investing in which companies, and much more besides.

## TIDMs, SEDOLs, and ISINs

Each fund is known by a three- or four-letter code called a TIDM (which used to be known as an EPIC), or an ISIN (if it's an investment trust or a foreign fund), or a SEDOL, which is the same as the ISIN, but without the GB800 code that tells you it's British. Often a fund has all three of these codes at once. For instance, the Blue Planet European Financials investment trust is known by the following:

   ✔ TIDM: BLP

   ✔ SEDOL: 0532707

   ✔ ISIN: GB0005327076

With the code information in your hot little hand, you can now call up masses of information by typing any of those identifiers into Google, or FT.com, or (my own favourite) Trustnet (`www.trustnet.com`). You're able to set up charts that compare how the fund's fared against the FTSE-100, or against the sector average for other funds of its own type, or simply against the market average for funds of that particular type.

Trustnet gives you an almost unlimited range of options for selecting your top performers. You can have them ranked in order of the funds that are doing best, or the fund providers that are getting the best results, or the geographical regions that are producing the best profits for the funds that invest in them, or the industry sectors that are performing best.

And in case all that's not enough, you can choose which time span you want your performance leagues to cover. Do you want to know the top performers over the last year? Or the last three years? Or the last five? And do you want your information sorted according to how the funds' own values performed, or are you more interested in the growth in their underlying assets, the so-called net asset values? (See 'Understanding discounts and premiums', later in this chapter, for more on these.)

Monthly investment magazines also provide listings showing which funds have been turning in the best performances over the last couple of years. You can dump your money into these funds before walking away whistling. Job done. These magazines also provide details of how to contact the various sales offices once you've made your decision. *Investors Chronicle*, *Money*, *Shares*, and *What Investment?* are just four of the names that spring to mind.

## Where's your manager gone?

If you put your money away for the long term you need to keep an eye on your fund manager. Often, a fund achieves a glittering performance under one particularly talented manager, only to plummet when she leaves the fund provider in search of a better future with another company.

Does your fund provider tell you when its star manager jumps ship? Not likely. If it thinks you're going to sell off all your funds and move your money to the manager's new company, it does everything in its power not to let you know.

# Pedigree pooches versus the dogs of the Dow

Resist the temptation always to go for the funds that happened to perform best last year. A fund holding a top-ten position in the rankings for more than a couple of years in a row is really very rare – and if you do decide to plump for a top performer, you have a good chance of paying top whack for something that's only going to disappoint you.

Why's that? Firstly, because if a successful fund has been getting lots of mentions in the Sunday papers for a long time, the chances are that other investors have seen it long before you do. In their wild enthusiasm to bundle into this one account, they can hardly help but price it upwards towards the upper reaches of what you or I regard as sensible. Then you're in a situation where not very much upside is left even if everything goes well – but plenty of downside if something goes wrong.

Secondly, and more importantly, because last year's big growth market was probably playing a game of catch-up which meant that it was growing unusually fast in relation to the overall market. The chances of it being able to repeat that trick for a second year are slim indeed. So if you're investing in a fund that specialises in one particular area of business, or one part of the world, you're likely to come a cropper by backing last year's winner.

Thinking about it more broadly, so-called cyclical factors are also bound to come into play when you're talking about anything as broadly spread as a themed trust. Chapter 13 covers cyclical factors, as does Chapter 3, so all I'm going to say here is that financial markets in various parts of the world often move according to their own sweet rhythms, which may be well out of sync with each other. So if South

Asia's been this year's big growth story, a very good chance exists that next year the crown passes to Latin America, simply because India and Pakistan have been getting a bit overpriced and the world's looking for the next bargain-basement location. Any funds that were in India this year may be eclipsed, and they may well fall quite sharply as the smart money moves out in search of pastures new.

But at the other extreme of the range, there's a rather interesting theory that says you should always pick the funds that have been performing the least well recently, because they're the funds that are likely to pick up the fastest in the future. The theory originated on the New York Stock Exchange, where the 'Dogs of the Dow', the worst large-company performers of all, were found to beat the stock market by a reliable margin even if you allowed for the fact that a few got into serious trouble.

Do I think the Dogs of the Dow approach is a good way to buy funds? No, not in its most extreme form, because certain sectors are always in long-term or even terminal decline. There's no point in hitching your star to a whole industry sector that modern life has superseded, like bulk chemicals or department stores or old-fashioned record shops. And, by the same token, just because financial uncertainty has battered some parts of the world, you've no automatic reason to think that their turn to flourish is coming up. For all you know, they might have regimes that stamp on any growth prospects.

The answer, then, is to seek a middle path. When you look at fund rankings, remember to look not just at the one-year performances but the five-year records as well.

The serious financial papers often tell you when somebody changes jobs, but if you want a really comprehensive run-down of job moves you can find one at Trustnet (`www.trustnet.com`), which has a section called Fund Manager News in its News Archive section. Keep an eye on it.

# Unit Trusts

The basic idea behind a unit trust is incredibly simple. You give your money to a fund provider, and she puts it into a big bag with other people's money and uses it to buy a portfolio of shares. You buy so-called units, each of which represents your fair share of all the value in the portfolio, and the fund provider publishes an update on the value of the portfolio every few days, quite often every single day.

Until the 1930s no pooled investments existed – and even up to the 1960s they were pretty thin on the ground. Instead, you either bought dozens of shares in order to give you a safely diversified coverage of the sector you were interested in – a very expensive process in those days – or else you bought one or two and crossed your fingers.

It's probably fair to say that unit trusts are going slightly out of fashion these days. Investors don't like being charged all the fees that unit trusts almost invariably entail – and they certainly don't like the idea of being forced to sell their units back to the original vendor when they're ready to move on. That's because selling unit trusts back to the vendor creates a situation where he can suck her teeth like a used car dealer and offer the seller a much lower price than he's going to charge the next punter who wants to buy them. (The gap between the buying and selling price is known as the bid–offer spread, or occasionally the bid–ask spread).

Besides, now that we've all got Internet trading and Trustnet, and investment trusts and Exchange-Traded Funds (ETFs), amateur investors have much better access to the tools they need in order to make their own decisions. Some day, unit trusts are going to disappear completely.

Or are they? You probably don't see the full advantages of unit trusts until you see the big downside in the investment trust idea. They may be more expensive than investment trusts, but they're a lot more stable over the long term. And surely, peace of mind is one of the things that you're trying to achieve?

# *Understanding unit trusts*

The unit trust manager never quite knows how much of her investors' money is going to be in the bag at any one time, so she can increase or decrease the number of units in circulation to suit the mood of the moment. In effect, the fund can shrink or grow in response to the need. Unit trusts are an 'open-ended' investment vehicle (in contrast to investment trusts, which can't expand or contract and are therefore 'closed-ended').

The fees involved in unit trusts can be steep. The example in Table 14-1 has a 5.25 per cent initial charge, which is going to knock quite a big hole in your capital, and thereafter you're charged 1.5 per cent a year just for managing it. That's because the unit trust really is being managed by a real live human being, not a computer, and she needs to be paid.

You can often reduce these initial fees by buying your unit trusts through a fund supermarket rather than getting them directly from the fund provider. Sometimes you can get the fees right down to zero.

But you may also come up against a hidden catch when the time comes to sell. The provider sells you the fund at the 'offer' price, which is likely to be rather higher than the 'bid' price at which she's prepared to buy it back from you if you're selling rather than buying.

Table 14-1 shows how one website lists the daily bid and offer prices for a popular unit trust, the Jupiter Merlin Growth Portfolio. As you can see, the bid's more than 5 per cent less than the offer, which is a nice way of saying that the provider's creaming off another 5 per cent of your money at the end of your relationship. That's 5 per cent that you don't have to pay with an investment trust!

| Table 14-1 | Prices for a typical unit trust |
|---|---|
| Bid (GBX) | 186.42 |
| Offer (GBX) | 196.47 |
| Change (Bid) | + 0.41 |
| Per cent change** | + 0.22 |

The unit trust manager probably only buys additional shares for her portfolio once a day, so you can forget any ideas you may have about being able to catch the market in mid-afternoon, the way you can if you're buying the shares directly. In effect, the prices are set once a day, and the unit price you're likely to pay is whatever price prevails at the close of play.

## Finding unit prices

You don't have any trouble getting daily prices for unit trusts. The *FT* does a good job of providing daily prices, as well as the net asset value information that underpins the daily unit valuation (turn to 'Understanding discounts and premiums', later in this chapter, for more on net asset values).

But for a deeper analysis, Figure 14-1 shows Trustnet's evaluation of the same unit trust as in Table 14-1. As you can see, the unit trust comes with its own optional 'ISA wrapper', meaning that you can buy it in a tax-efficient form if you want to. You have to buy a minimum £500 worth, or commit to at least £50 a month if you're buying it through a savings builder plan.

The fund's been going since September 1992, and the last time it released any information about its size, in August 2008, it was worth £738 million.

This particular unit trust issues a dividend twice a year, which is payable in April and October. Many unit trusts don't provide dividends, however.

**Figure 14-1:**
Trustnet's evaluation of the Jupiter Merlin Growth Portfolio.

| Detailed fund information | | | |
|---|---|---|---|
| Fund type | UK Unit Trust | | |
| Own ISA wrapper | ✓ | Fund size | £738.0m / $1,202.9m (31-Aug-08) |
| Savings plan | ✓ Minimum: £50 monthly | Launch | 14-Sep-1992 |
| PEP transfer | ✓ | Pricing method | Forward |
| CAT standard | | Pricing times | 12:00 Daily |
| Minimum initial | £500 | Dealing frequency | Daily |
| Minimum additional | £250 | Dealing times | Mon-Fri 09:00 to 17:30 |
| Initial charge | 5.25% | | |
| Annual management charge | 1.50% | | |
| Note to charges | n/a | | |
| Trustee / Depositary | Royal Bank of Scotland Plc | | |
| Registrar | Jupiter Unit Trust Managers Ltd | | |
| Dividend policy | Income distributed 30 April and 31st October with ex-dividend dates a month prior. | | |

## Choosing between a business sector and a geographical sector

Trusts come in all shapes and sizes to suit all sorts of needs. If you want to get some easy exposure to the oil industry, you'll have no difficulty finding a trust to suit your tastes. Or if you fancy buying into the East European property markets, suitable candidates are bound to exist.

The great joy of unit trusts is that the presence of an experienced manager gives you an important safety net when you're venturing into unknown areas. And the relative price stability of the funds helps you sleep at night.

# *Introducing UCITS and OEICs*

]UCITs and OIECs may sound like some fearsome kind of monsters from a Tolkein story, but in practice they're a lot more friendly and rather less likely to turn round and bite you without warning. Especially if you give them the capitalisation they deserve. They are a relatively recent invention set up at the instigation of the European Union in an effort to make trusts more freely available across the national borders of the European financial area.

*OEICs* ('open-ended investment companies') are a first cousin to unit trusts, in that they're open-ended funds where the provider can create as many units as it likes, or cancel them when demand shrinks. As such, the unit price always reflects the value of the underlying investment assets, rather than shooting up and down with the fluctuating rate of investor demand.

But one very important difference with an OEIC is that it's a limited company or plc in its own right, just like an investment trust (see 'Investment Trusts', later in this chapter), rather than merely being a division of a big fund provider. That's bound to seem rather strange, given that the OEIC can shrink or grow at will.

Another very attractive difference with an OEIC is that it doesn't have 'dual pricing' like a unit trust. Instead of having a wide difference between the bid price and the offer price, as shown in Table 14-1 and Figure 14-1, an OEIC has just one central price for both buyers and sellers. What you see is what you get.

So you don't need to go looking for bid and offer prices with an OEIC, because there aren't any. What you do need to watch, though, is the steeper level of fees. Initial charges are frequently higher than for unit trusts, and so are the annual management charges.

The very name *UCITS* (Undertakings for Collective Investment in Transferable Securities) has that unmistakeable dead hand of European bureaucracy about it. But UCITS mean well, honestly. The general idea is that any provider of either an existing unit trust or an investment trust can apply to Brussels for an approval note that will allow it to promote its products anywhere in the EU: the main point is that the approval gives you certain guarantees about the minimum standards of protection and the quality of the financial reporting. But Brussels also hopes that this initiative will enable the providers to reduce their hefty charges because they're able to address a much larger target audience than before.

These days, about 70 per cent of all European trusts have been successfully registered as UCITS. In time, all of them are presumably going to follow suit.

# Investment Trusts

Investment trusts (ITs) are everything that unit trusts are not (see the previous sections). They're not 'open-ended' funds that can shrink or grow at will to accommodate the level of demand for their services. Instead, every IT is a limited company, with a once-and-for-all initial budget that's all gone when it's all been invested in a suitable portfolio of investments.

After that initial buying phase – which may take months or even years to complete! – the trust's only way of growing any further is to increase the value of its underlying assets through successful stock-picking, and to get itself noticed by investors like you and me so that everyone wants to come and have a piece of its success.

Investment trusts can invest in any kind of portfolio they like, as long as it's within the limits of their statutes. For instance, a property IT isn't allowed to invest in food retailing companies, but it might be allowed to own pieces of the companies that buy the superstores and then lease them out to Sainsbury's and Morrisons. All ITs are allowed to hold cash, of course, because money's always rattling around when something's being bought and sold. But that's about as far as their leeway goes.

## Understanding discounts and premiums

And that's where the vexed question of discounts and premiums starts to come into the picture. As you saw with unit trusts, eEach trust has a *net asset value* (NAV) – which, in simple terms, represents the market value of all the investments in its portfolio.

Let's set up a rather simplistic example to illustrates this. If an IT owns 10 per cent of a company whose market capitalisation (that is, its current stock market value) is £500 million, and another 20per cent of a company that's worth £1 billion, then you'd say that its total net asset value iwas £250 million:

$$(£500 \text{ million} \times 10)/100 + (£1{,}000 \text{ million} \times 20)/100$$

$$= £250 \text{ million}$$

Supposing the fund has issued 100 million shares, its NAV is 250p per share. But if it's having a good year and the stock market's taken a particular shine to it, its actual share price may rise as high as 275p. The trust is then trading at a 10 per cent premium to its NAV.

Actually, this situation isn't very common. Normally when the stock market looks at an IT, it tries to calculate in all the costs that it incurs if it decides to get rid of all its holdings tomorrow. For instance, it probably has to sell its holdings at less than they're really worth, and it has dealing charges, experts' fees, and probably taxes to pay. So the market normally wants to knock off a fairly big chunk of the NAV when it tries to value the trust. All things being equal, the market's probably inclined to award the trust a value of (say) 237.5p, which is a 5 per cent discount to the NAV.

Many investors refuse point blank to buy an IT at a premium. The premium's a sure sign of irrational exuberance, they say, and the purchase is bound to end in tears.

## Finding information on the 'invisible' investment category

You don't hear very much about investment trusts in Britain. For reasons best known to themselves, the regulatory authorities regard ITs as too risky for the average investor to tangle with. Accordingly, advertisements for ITs are restricted to the trade press, and you almost never find them mentioned in the Sunday papers.

What's the problem? Officially, it's because ITs tend to be more volatile than some other types of investments. In practice, however, ITs incur much smaller fees and other charges than unit trusts, so fewer incentives exist for the trade to promote them.

Bearing this lack of information in mind, here are some facts about investment trusts:

- ITs are simply shares like any other. Each trust is a limited company or plc in its own right, and it has a unique EPIC or TIDM code that you can use at any time to track its performance (flip to 'TIDMs, SEDOLs, and ISINs', earlier in this chapter).

- Most of the ITs you come across in Britain are listed on the London Stock Exchange (LSE), just like any other share. You don't find them in most daily newspapers, but the online services at the FT or the LSE give you instant coverage.

- You can buy ITs in other countries besides Britain, but the paperwork can be a hassle. Try using Exchange-Traded Funds as an alternative (Chapter X has more on these).

- You can buy ITs through your Individual Savings Account, just like any other share – except for a few that list themselves on the Alternative Investment Market (AIM) and are banned from ISAs for that reason. This means, in effect, that you can buy as much as £7,200 worth a year .

- ITs are liquid, effective, and often very keenly priced.

## Realising why investment trusts are volatile

With a unit trust, the price of your investment is firmly fixed in relation to the net asset value ('Understanding discounts and premiums', earlier in this chapter, explains how to work out the NAV). With an investment trust, the price is determined by the underlying level of demand for the trust's shares, which is continually rising and falling. Unlike a unit trust, the IT can't just cancel some of its units if demand starts to drop off. Instead, its size is fixed, and so it has to weather the storm if demand drops away suddenly.

The premium or discount enters the picture at this point. If an IT's been successful for many years, a lot of people may have been happy to pay a premium to net asset value for its shares. But as soon as the price starts to fall, the investor's going to sit up and say:

'Oh no, I've been paying a 10 per cent premium to net asset value for those shares, and now the NAV has dropped by 5 per cent. That means I'm 15 per cent out of pocket! Better move fast before the situation gets any worse.'

That's nothing. Investor 2's going to say:

'Help, Investor 1's bound to sell her holdings now that she's 15 per cent over-exposed. I'm not quite that badly off, but I better get moving as well before she can phone her broker.'

Meanwhile Investor 3's been doing her sums. The falling NAV that frightened Investor 1 is starting to look decidedly shaky now that Investor 1 and Investor 2 have both decided to pull out. The racing certainty's that the NAV's going to fall even further once their sell trades hit the City's screens. 'Nothing for it but to beat them both to it' she says. 'I get my retaliation in first.'

The result? You have the makings of a mini-panic, which will drive prices down rather further than they really ought to go before eventually somebody sees reason and starts buying the ITs up again.

Investment trusts are always more volatile than the underlying securities they hold. And much more volatile than unit trusts, which aren't subject to the same exaggerated laws of supply and demand. None of this would happen if ITs could grow or shrink on demand, like unit trusts. In this respect, their similarity to shares is their great weakness. Except that, with shares, nobody ever pays a premium to the market price!

Do you see now why so many IT investors won't touch a premium?

# Chapter 15

# Discovering Hedge Funds, Bonds, and ETFs

### In This Chapter

▶ Understanding the mysteries of hedge funds

▶ Getting to grips with guaranteed income bonds

▶ Engaging with Exchange-Traded Funds

*I* was never noted for my prowess at science. In fact, I was thrown out of the lab at school for fighting with my best friend in class, because it seemed more fun than learning my atomic numbers. I'm reliably informed, however, that atomic scientists have spent a lot of their time scratching their heads over a strange type of atomic particle known as a Higgs boson, which is now the subject of a $9 billion experiment at the CERN laboratories in Lucerne. All of which is an act of faith, really, considering that the only way the scientists know these invisible atomic particles exist at all is that they can observe the effect they have on the things around them. Other particles dodge and swerve and do unexpected things whenever the Higgs bosons are in town. And, in a strange way, hedge funds bear a certain resemblance to these mysterious particles. Bear with me, it'll all become clear.

Investors might *think* they know what hedge funds are up to, most of the time, but they can never be completely sure. That's because hedge funds are secretive organisations that don't reveal what they're doing – and indeed, they often go to enormous lengths to cover their tracks. What I can say for certain, though, is that the role hedge funds play in the financial markets is simply enormous, and becoming more so with every passing year. I have to give hedge funds at least some sort of mention, because without them the daily behaviour of today's markets just doesn't make sense.

What you'll certainly have noticed, though, is that everyone seems to have heaped a lot of blame for the 2007/2008 global stock market crisis on the hedge fund managers. At a time when the stock markets were in desperate need of clarity and visibility, the hedge funds went about their business as usual in their own sweet way. They wouldn't tell anybody how many bonds or how much gold they'd bought, or how many shares they were short-selling (that's to say, how many shares they were gambling on to lose money rather than make it). And the result was that, when it all went wrong and the hedge funds' investors started to withdraw their cash, the funds found themselves locked into a devils' dance of more and more selling, which just heightened the general uncertainty and made everybody more panicky than ever, because you could only guess at what the hedge fund managers were selling – or what they'd be selling next. The result was chaos.

But I'm getting ahead of myself. This chapter covers the intricacies of three types of managed fund: hedge funds, guaranteed income bonds, and Exchange-Traded Funds, which are a whole lot less mysterious, and a bit less risky.

# Assessing Hedge Funds

Let's go back to basics here. Every time you read in the morning papers that the gold price has been boosted by hedge funds making speculative bullion buys in the Hong Kong market, you need to take the news with a big pinch of salt. What the reporter means is that the City's full of gossip that such-and-such a fund has been doing such-and-such a thing today. And although he may be able to name one or two funds, he's nothing much more than hearsay and apocryphal evidence to go on.

The reason this lack of information is a problem is that hedge funds are a $2.5 trillion industry (2007 estimate) that's attracting nearly $300 billion of new money every year. Now, $2.5 trillion is pretty close to the total gross domestic product of the United Kingdom. And, as I've said in my introduction, hedge funds leave no audit trails and no easy way of knowing exactly what they're doing. This elusiveness is a problem!

## Understanding why hedge funds are different

Hedge funds differ from ordinary managed funds in many ways, but to start with the basics:

  ✔ They're allowed to invest in anything they choose. A normal trust has statutes that define what sort of securities it can buy. But a hedge fund manager has no limits. If he thinks the time's come to swap diamonds for wheat, or biotechnology for property management, or bank certificates of deposit for carbon emission permits, he's free to do so.

✔ They're not required to post their results or their trading records. Indeed, since the majority of hedge funds are domiciled in tax hideaways like Bermuda or the British Virgin Islands, making them come clean's really quite hard, even if anybody wanted to. (Some movement's now occurring on this issue, however, as 'Considering if hedge funds are becoming respectable at last', later in this chapter, considers.)

✔ They adopt what's called an 'absolute return' policy. This means that they're committed to making a profit regardless of whether the market's moving up or down. Some of the time, this means using so-called long–short policies, under which the manager buys shares (or whatever) while simultaneously taking up complicated contrary positions through the derivatives markets (see Chapter 12 for more on these), to produce a win–win result. (This policy goes to the heart of why they're called hedge funds: the idea is that, by 'sitting on the fence', they ought to be able to make money out of any situation.)

✔ They also do a good deal of stock shorting (covered in Chapter 9) in an effort to make money out of even the most frighteningly bad markets. The general idea of shorting is that you aim to make money by borrowing shares from other people, then selling them – and hoping that the market will have fallen a long way by the time you need to buy the shares back again at a cheaper price, so that you can give them back to your lender. In the process, with a bit of luck, you'll have turned a profit on the difference between your sale price and your purchase price.your two transactions.

✔ Short selling doesn't necessarily deserve the bad press that it sometimes gets. Short sellers claim that they perform a useful service by drawing the market's attention to weak companies. But that hasn't stopped the market authorities from trying to tighten up the regulation of aggressive shorting by hedge funds, which they have accused of making wobbly market situations much worse. The chances are that this debate will run and run. . . .

✔ Hedge funds make extensive use of leverage; that is, they borrow money heavily in order to invest it in the hope of securing better returns. This 'gears up' the returns they can get, sometimes twenty-fold, but it also increases the risks to their fundholders if things ever go wrong. Many of the root causes of the 2007/2008 banking crises lie in leveraged hedge fund positions that went wrong.

✔ Hedge funds don't have fixed fees, or not large ones at any rate. Management fees are often pegged at 2 per cent of the funds under management. Instead, the vast bulk of the fee income derives from a hefty performance charge ('incentive fee') that the managers make on the profits they earn for their clients. Not untypically a manager charges 20 per cent of the amount by which he increases the net asset value of the funds under his control.

✔ You don't ever find out what hedge funds are up to from reading the financial pages in your newspaper. Or at least, not in any 100 per cent reliable way. You certainly can't find any statistical material there. But you do find plenty of informed guesses on the Internet – both on dedicated discussion forums and in subscriber newsletters (go to Chapter 16 for more on these information sources).

## Considering whether hedge funds are becoming respectable at last

You'll have noticed that I regard hedge funds with a certain amount of suspicion. Although I don't disagree that a well-placed 'short position' can put a very relevant question mark under a dodgy market situation, I do agree with those who say that the secrecy under which all this is going on is a problem for the financial markets at large. And that the more you can find out about a hedge fund in which you're considering investing, the better.

Oddly, for once I find myself in agreement with the US tax authorities, who've been clamping down on the whole offshore fund management industry in the aftermath of the 9/11 terrorist atrocities in New York and Washington. The Internal Revenue Service's claim that international terrorists are hiding behind the anonymity of these hedge funds may not have much substance, but if nothing else, the fear has forced Washington into seeking a sort of halfway house arrangement with the hedge fund managers.

Under a deal worked out a few years ago, the government of Bermuda has agreed to act as a kind of honest broker between the hedge funds and the US authorities. Basically, it inspects the affairs of the hedge funds in confidence, and then signals to Washington that all's well (or not), without giving details.

This deal marks progress. If it creates a greater atmosphere of trust between the cowboys and the lawmakers, and if it generates a less secretive atmosphere, then everyone should feel safer and the markets become more transparent. But, just in case I haven't said it loudly enough yet, the whole question of how to regulate hedge funds has been reopened in fine style by the credit crunch of 2007/2008, and it wouldn't surprise me at all if things started to get a lot more uncomfortable for the Higgs bosons of the investment world, some time very soon.

# *Gauging Guaranteed Income Bonds*

For many investors, a guaranteed income bond (GIB) sounds like the ideal way to cope with the uncertainties of a volatile stock market. You've probably seen these deals advertised in the Sunday newspapers, or in the windows of the banks and the building societies in the high street. For an unsophisticated investor who doesn't know much about the stock market but wants to have some of the benefits, they do have a certain appeal. Worse luck.

The usual deal with a guaranteed income bond (sometimes called a guaranteed equity bond) is that you commit your money to the provider for a fixed period of maybe five years. At the end of that time, if the stock market's fallen you get all your money back. But if it's risen you get a cash return on your money that's related to the growth in the market. Depending on the deal, you might get 100 per cent of the stock market's gains, although sometimes you only get 75 per cent . (The percentage terms are clearly set out in the offer document, so the provider can't change the ratio once you've signed up for it.)

One or two of these GIB deals have indeed been very good. National Savings ran one GIB a few years back that offered 115 per cent of the stock market's growth! But for all too many people, venturing into GIBs ends in tears and disappointment. Some real sharks are lurking in these sunny blue waters, and you need to know what their fins look like before you commit your money.

The following sections guide you through the pitfalls, and explain what some of the convoluted language connected with GIBs means. Until you've looked at those issues, you really don't have a clue exactly what sort of return you're really being offered.

## *Understanding how 'structured products' work*

I might confuse you by saying that although a GIB promises you a return that's linked to the stock market's growth, the GIB provider isn't going to invest your money in stocks and shares at all!

Instead, it's going to put most of the money into an interest-bearing account, where the money carries on earning a nice, reliable rate of interest until the five-year term (or whatever) is up. A small part of the money is then put to work in the derivatives markets (Chapter 12 covers these) and that's the part that brings in nearly all the income.

The details are complicated, but basically the fund manager takes out a series of futures contracts that will pay him a disproportionately large return in relation to any rise in the stock market. (A futures contract is an elaborate kind of bet on future trends, that can used to compensate the investor for any loses, whichever way the market might move. I talk more about this in Chapter 12.) The rest of the money sits in the bank account, effectively acting as collateral for the futures contracts. But these 'structured products' are 'hedged' in such a way that the overall result really can't deviate from the result that you'd get from investing directly in the stock market.

Your returns, then, are not stock market profits as such. Instead, they're a cash payment that imitates a stock market profit.

Most GIBs are run from bases outside mainland Britain (often in Ireland or the Channel Islands), where managers find wheeling and dealing at low cost easier. But don't worry about that. Because an accredited UK provider's selling you the product, you have full investor protection under UK law.

## Locking up your money for a fixed period

One of the important points about a GIB is that, once you've entered into it, you really can't back out of the deal before the fixed term's up. A few providers let you off the terms of the contract prematurely, subject to a heavy cash penalty that probably wipes out all your gains and damages your capital as well (especially if the stock market's fallen since you started the bond). But with most GIBs you quite literally have to be dead to get your money back! And that seems a rather excessive solution to the problem.

Never invest any money in a GIB unless you're absolutely certain that you don't need to get at it before the time's up.

## Taking those marketing claims with a pinch of salt

Newspapers don't like GIBs, and they tend not to be reticent about saying so. One reason they don't like them is that they think the providers are trying to hoodwink their customers! It's all very well getting 100 per cent of the capital return that you might have got from the stock market if you'd bought shares instead – but the fact is that you'd also have got a pile of dividends on your shares, which you won't be getting from your GIB. In other words, the GIB providers are hoping that you won't notice that you're being shrt-changed.

If you'd put £5,000 into real stocks and shares for five years at an average dividend yield of 4 per cent , you'd have amassed a rather amazing gross of £1,083 in dividends by the end of those five years (assuming that you left the dividends in the account to compound.) Even if you assumed that they were being taxed at source at the 20 per cent standard rate, your winnings would still be £852.

That's a 17% dividend return on your investment that you won't be seeing from your guaranteed income bond, which doesn't pay you any dividends at all! Of course, the capital gains from the bond is something that you'd have been getting from a stock market portfolio anyway.

Another reason the financial press isn't too keen on GIBs is that the marketing blurb often contains 'oversimplifications' about the way the return on your bond is calculated. Consequently, a lot of investors end up getting less than they expect at the end of the term.

Strangely enough, this practice isn't actually illegal, although it certainly ought to be. The companies that provide these bonds always take good care to make sure that the awkward truth's in the small print. The problem arises because the average high street investor doesn't read the small print at all.

These products are aimed at unsophisticated investors.

Here's an example. The headline on the GIB's blurb might say something like: 'You get 100 per cent of all the growth on the FTSE-100 index that happens between the start and finish dates.' But it ain't necessarily so. Often, when you look closely, you find that the starting price level for the FTSE-100 is actually a 'smoothed' level, which turns out to be *an average of the daily prices at each end of the first three months of the term* (that is, the FTSE-100 prices on Day 1 and Day 91).

What does that mean in practice? If the FTSE-100 happens to rise by 6 per cent during those first three months, from 6000 to 6360, the starting price the fund works from is 6180 – the average of those two daily prices – not the starting price of 6000 at all. That's 3 per cent of your growth that the company's just swiped!

The same thing might happen at the end of the term, so that the final value's actually an average of the last day's value and the value from 90 days earlier. If the markets are still rising at the time, the chances are that you've lost another 45 days' worth of growth there.

## Income Tax – are you liable?

The guaranteed income bond provider doesn't want you to know that chances are you have to pay income tax on the gains you make from your GIB, at your maximum marginal rate. So if you pay any income tax to HM Revenue and Customs at the higher rate, then that's what you pay on your GIB.

That's outrageous, you're probably thinking. My bond is linked to the growth in the stock market, so surely the gains it makes are classed as capital gains, not as income? Haven't I got an annual capital gains allowance of around £10,000 a year that I'm probably not using? What a swindle!

The sad fact is, however, that strictly speaking the GIB provider's absolutely correct. The gains you're making on the bond might be *calculated* according to the movement of the stock market, but they actually don't come from the stock market at all. Instead, they're earned in the cash and futures markets, where the earnings are most definitely income, and not capital gains.If you're a standard-rate taxpayer, you'll pay the standard rate of income tax unless the return from the GIB is big enough to tip you over into the higher rate band – in which case the higher rate applies on the excess amount. If you don't earn enough to pay income tax at all, you'll probably have to pay standard-rate tax on the GIB, although you should be able to get the tax back from the Revenue with a little effort.

Children under 18 aren't normally allowed to take out GIBs, so the question of letting them use their personal tax exemptions through a GIB doesn't apply in mainland Britain. However, some offshore providers based in the Channel Islands do offer GIB-type investments to minors.

The GIB provider will tell you that this is all for your own good. By 'flattening out the bumps' at the start and finish of the term, he claims that it's protecting you from any damaging volatility. In practice, however, it's giving you four-and-three-quarter years' stock market growth instead of the five you thought you were buying.

## *Avoiding precipice bonds*

I really hate to add yet another concern to your growing list of worries, but you do need to keep a sharp lookout for so-called 'precipice bond' clauses whenever you buy a GIB. These nasty little booby-traps can lie slumbering in the small print for years on end – and they very often don't wake up at all, which is a good thing because they can turn all your sweet dreams into nightmares if the worst should ever comes to the worst. But if you should ever get a particular combination of falling stock markets and sheer bad luck with your timing, precipice bond clauses can blow quite a large hole in the capital that you thought was 100 per cent safe.

If that sounds rather alarming, maybe I can say that the worst kinds of precipice bonds were outlawed nearly a decade ago, when the 2000 stock market crisis cost some GIB savers nearly all their money! But it looks as though they're now coming back in a slightly milder form. I was recently offered a bond with rather similar characteristics, so take great care.

The worst of the precipice bond deals used to have a little clause somewhere in the small print that said, in effect, that it wasn't entirely true that you'd get your money back if the stock market fell during the period of the term. If the investors had only read the terms and conditions carefully they'd have seen a line that said something like:

'If the FTSE-100 index falls by more than 20 per cent at any time during the five-year term, the value of the bond will be reduced by 3 per cent for every 1 per cent by which the fall exceeds 20 per cent.'

So if the stock market were to fall by 21 per cent at any time, you'd get only 97 per cent of your money back at the end of the five-year period. The other 3 per cent would have been snaffled by the penalty clause. If it fell by 30 per cent, you'd lose 30 per cent of your supposedly 'guaranteed' money.

Please note, incidentally, that the penalty still applies even if the stock market picks itself up and forges ahead strongly again after its 30 per cent setback. The clause says 'at any time', remember?

Things get even nastier with the new breed of GIBs that base their outcomes not on the FTSE-100 but on a hand-selected 'basket' of leading shares. I was offered a bond that promised to pay a big return on the strict condition that none of six UK banks in the portfolio saw its share price fall by more than 50 per cent during the five-year period. If it did, I'd suffer big penalties. I didn't touch that bond. Months later, a whole slew of British banks hit the skids, including Bradford & Bingley, whose shares lost nearly 80 per cent in two months, and eventually the bank was effectively nationalised by the British government. By the end of 2008 even giants such as Lloyds TSB, Barclays and Royal Bank of Scotland had their share prices trailing in the dust. And it was exactly the same story in America, France, Germany and even Switzerland. A bond based on their share prices would very probably have wiped me out completely.

Don't reject all GIBs on principle just because you're naturally risk averse. Many of them are worthwhile and trustworthy. The ones from National Savings & Investments have historically been clean and decent, although you have to make your own mind up about any future releases. And the regulator's cracking down much harder on transgressors these days.

However, don't sign up to any GIB contract without reading the small print in detail. Are you happy with the fixed term? Do you know how much tax you have to pay? Do you fully understand the date system by which the company calculates the amount it owes you?

# Exchange-Traded Funds

Exchange-Traded Funds (ETFs) are just one of a range of new fund products shaking up the London investment markets in fine style. They've been around in the United States for many years now, but in Britain they've only really had a proper presence since about 2006. Almost anything I say right now is going to be out of date within two years, because the rate of expansion's so fast. But you can keep up to date with the changing situation by checking with the London Stock Exchange (www.lse.co.uk) or independently run Internet sources such as the grandly named ETF Stock Encyclopedia (etf.stock-encyclopedia.com).

## Understanding how ETFs work

ETFs are probably unlike anything you've ever seen before. They're a kind of second cousin to the guaranteed equity bonds or guaranteed income bonds that your bank or building society tries to sell you in an attempt to ride on the back of the stock market 'without taking any risks'. (I look at GIBs in Chapter 14.)

Just like a GIB, an ETF is a 'structured product', which means that it isn't normally invested directly in the underlying shares. Instead, the ETF provider takes your money, sticks most of it safely in the bank (or in very secure bank securities), and then uses the rest to fund a convoluted system of betting on the derivatives markets (see Chapter 12 for more on these). The manager sets out to get a disproportionate return from this small part of your money, depending on which way the market moves – thus allowing it to give you a return that exactly matches the return you get from backing the underlying index directly. (At present, all ETFs in Britain are based on a public index of one sort or another.) Your gains on the ETF are paid for not by an increase in the market capitalisation of the underlying shares, but by a cash disbursement derived from the success of the 'bets'.

There are certain subtle differences in the way that ETFS and other 'structured products' are constructed in Europe and in America. I won't bore you with the fine details, but American funds are required to hold more shares and fewer derivative bets in their portfolios than their British and European counterparts. It isn't every day that the US version of an investment is less racy and risky than its European counterpart, but this is one of them.

Incidentally, why don't you pay stamp duty on ETFs? Because stamp duty only applies to shares and share-related products such as investment trusts. ETFs, however, are considered to be a different type of animal for stock market purposes: many of them belong to an exotic family of securities known as zero coupon bonds. But explaining that's going to take us rather a long way from the matter in hand, so let's keep it simple.

Things are moving on a little in America, where ETFs are now moving into new and exciting territory. Companies such as PowerShares are starting to ditch the underlying 'weighting' principle, whereby the biggest companies in an index automatically get the biggest cash weighting; instead, some of these ETFs give equal weighting to both the minnows and the whales. That produces some very interesting results in sectors such as biotechnology, where small biotech researchers are effectively driving growth in a market that big boys like Pfizer and Monsanto have always dominated.

Finally, I want to say a word about something called Exchange Traded Notes (ETNs), which are quite new on the scene in Britain but which are already becoming very popular in America. They're quite similar to ETFs in many ways, but instead of being structured as a share-type fund, they're actually a type of bond issued by a bank.

For technical reasons I won't go into, this makes ETNs slightly more exciting and rather more volatile than an ETF – meaning that if you get your guesses right you can make money faster. But there's a drawback with ETNs that you really ought to know about. Because ETNs are effectively bank bonds, their solidity and safety is effectively pinned to the stability of the issuing bank itself, and not to the stability of the underlying shares, as it would normally be with an ETF. This could mean, in theory, that if the bank itself should ever go bust, your investment might go with it. Take care!

This is probably more than you wish to know at this stage in the learning curve, and I apologise deeply for leading you so far up a very twisting path. But ETFs are the shape of tomorrow as far as UK fund investing is concerned, and I would have been failing in my duties if I hadn't shown you which way they're headed.

One very important point which I'll leave you with is that all London-listed ETFs are covered by the same investor protection regulations as normal stocks and shares. So there is no reason to suppose that the new kids on the block have brought any particularly dangerous risks with them.

## Finding out what's available in the UK

You'll find more about ETFs in Chapter 13, but for the time being let me just say once again that the situation is changing fast.

You will not find ETFs listed in any of Britain's newspapers – or not, at least, as far as I am aware. But the prices are always available from the FT or the LSE web sites, and from your online broker too.

## Buying foreign-listed ETFs

There are really no reasons why you shouldn't be able to buy a New York-listed ETF, or indeed any other of the many internationally traded funds. You may not be able to get all of them into your ISA – that will depend on who your account is with – but, on the whole, the much wider range of ETFs available in America makes it worth tackling a few little obstacles along the way.

ETFs are changing fast. They aren't listed in any UK newspapers, but you can find information on www.ft.com and the London Stock Exchange (www.lse.co.uk). Chapter 13 on commodities also briefly covers ETFs.

# Part V

# Other Places to Go for Financial Information

'The rose-tinted spectacles if you please, Miss Houndsfoot.'

## In this part . . .

This section takes a long look at the relative advantages of print media and internet-based information sources, and its conclusions might surprise you. Reports of the death of investment magazines are much exaggerated. Even though the sharpest, most up-to-date and most informative sources are online. I show you which sources you can trust and which ones are strictly bargepole territory.

The section concludes with a detailed look at listed company accounts.

# Chapter 16

# Using the Alternatives

*In This Chapter*

▶ Revealing the manifold delights of getting your information online

▶ Understanding why you shouldn't write off the printed media yet

▶ Reviewing discussion forums and blogs – the good, the bad, and the downright ugly

▶ Considering if analysts' opinions are worth having

*H*aving now run through all the traditional channels of investment research, I think we've safely established that investing involves a whole lot more than merely understanding the figures. If you're going to pick winners – and, just as importantly, avoid losers that simply look like winners – you need to cast your net a bit wider. What are other investors saying about those shares that you're considering buying? Can you learn something from somebody whose views you might completely disagree with? You'll never know until you find out for yourself.

And that's where we come up against the first obstacle. One real downside to this data-intensive age we live in is that the sheer mass of available information can get on top of you. There you are, trying to reach a clear decision in a reasonably civilised fashion, and suddenly you find yourself completely swamped by the sheer volume of stuff that's coming at you. Newspapers, computers, and television programmes are simply bombarding you with data. The trick is to work out which information sources you find the most reliable, and then discipline yourself to stick to them.

All the information sources this chapter discusses are worth taking seriously, because each one can give you a slightly different perspective on the market. Realistically, you don't have time to utilise them all. Choose, say, four sources to use regularly and others to dip into and out of.

# Online Resources

You might not be surprised if I say that the days are gone when you could do just as well as the experts by relying solely on the printed media. Now that we've got round-the-clock trading, web-based nominee share accounts, and the ability to react to information arriving from news sources all around the world, 24 hours a day, seven days a week, the whole pace of the business has increased. Now that you've got instant online access to every kind of statutory document, every set of accounts and every bit of the data you'll need to reach your decisions, the opportunities have really opened up wide for an investor who's really on the ball.

But there are other reasons why life is better online. Just as important, I think, is the ability to set up 'live' online graphs and comparisons that can show you in an instant how your shares are performing, and how they shape up against the competition. That's something no newspaper can ever give you. It was never more true than today that a picture is worth a thousand words.

## 'Official' websites

The following websites provide reliable, informative, and tightly regulated information.

### The London Stock Exchange

You may be surprised just how much information's on the London Stock Exchange's website (www.londonstockexchange.com), besides all the obvious things you normally expect to find there. Alongside the usual share price information, charts, official announcements, and information about how the various stock market indices are calculated, you find discussions, personal finance information sources, provocative opinions from senior investment figures, a useful finance glossary – and a surprising number of advertisements.

Now, maybe that idea shocks you. Isn't the London Stock exchange supposed to be a public body that tries to rise above the grubby forces of commerce? No, not really. The LSE is a private company with a share price of its own, and it needs to pay its way just like any other marketplace. What you're seeing when you look at the LSE's website is not just a repository of official information – it's also a gateway to the financial services industry in which various functions are subcontracted out to other firms.

Web sites are always changing as the demands of a changing marketplace meet with the periodic need for graphic redesign. Even the stock exchange has got to keep up with the times! So it wouldn't be very surprising if some of the things you find on the LSE web site differ from some of the things I describe here. But with a little perseverance you'll soon find your way around.

The first thing you find on the LSE's website is a general picture of where the most important indices have been going recently (Chapter 3 covers indices in detail). But much more's on offer. You can find links to a couple of hundred specialised FTSE indices from the Financial Times/Stock Exchange collaboration, that tell you how entire market sectors, or even whole stock markets, are moving. What's more, you'll also find links to other web pages that explain in detail exactly what these indices mean and how they're calculated.

The LSE offers some of the most comprehensive statistical information available on listed companies. At the press of a button, you can find out how many of a company's shares rare being bought and sold at the moment, and what the selling and buying prices are. (The 'spreads' between the selling and buying prices can tell you a lot about how the market's feeling today. A big difference between the two prices will often suggest that there isn't that much interest in a particular share, but a small one tells you that the sellers are keen to keep their prices very tight and competitive.) You need to register if you want access to the full range of services, but fortunately it's free.

You can also set up a personal 'dummy' portfolio via the LSE's website, and choose to add any share to your 'watch list' so that you can see at a glance whether it's risen or fallen. These services are free, though you do need to register, and you can run up to ten portfolios at once.

Make sure that you're really looking at the London Stock Exchange's web site! There's also an 'unofficial' web site which also bears the LSE name, but which is actually nothing at all to do with the London Stock Exchange itself. The London South East web site (www.lse.co.uk) is a fine and useful place to do your financial markets research – and in many ways it gives you useful services and information that the stock exchange itself doesn't provide – but it isn't 'the real thing', and I wouldn't be doing my job if I didn't alert you to this potential pitfall. I'll say more about www.lse.co.uk very shortly.

### RNS statutory announcements

Chapter 8 talks about the crucially important role that the RNS (Regulatory News Service) at the London Stock Exchange plays in the running of a fair stock market for Britain as a whole. Not just the LSE itself, incidentally, but the whole gamut of financial services (because the LSE is only one of the places where investments are traded). If you need to know precisely what a company's said publicly, then the RNS reports are the place to go for information. You can get RNS reports online, and they're free.

The reason RNS announcements are so important is that they're the official route by which 'price-sensitive' information is carefully metered out to the world at large. And the Financial Service Authority's fact-checkers police them rigorously.

Here's one reason why the RNS announcements system is so important. Imagine for a moment that you're running a large company and somebody's just built up a sizeable stake in your company. You think a possibility exists that they're about to make a takeover offer. The law requires you to publish this information immediately, as soon as the shareholding goes above a certain level. But the news has to go out to everybody *simultaneously*, so that you don't get a situation where the first person to read your announcement goes out and buys a load of your shares before everybody else has even had the chance to read the news. Remember, for a professional investor, seconds can count in grabbing a bargain. And if she has to wait even an hour, she faces a good chance that the best of the pickings are already taken.

Consequently, if your company's been approached then you're not allowed to breathe a single word to anybody about it. Not until the RNS has received your draft submission of the news, and gone right through it with a fine-toothed comb to look for errors, and then finally passed it for publication. The RNS report then goes out on the RNS's own computers, stock market tickers, and so forth, at exactly the same instant, so that everybody gets the same chance to read it first. And after that the shares are first come, first served.

I talk about a takeover situation here, but the same rules apply to share issues, changes of directorships, interim financial reports, end-of-year reports, dividend announcements, and any occasion when the company or a director appears to have bought some of its own shares. (A fuller list of these conditions is to be found in Chapter 8.) In nearly every case, the announcements have standardised headings that leave you in no doubt as to what they're announcing.

You can find the RNS announcements online at `www.londonstockexchange.com`, hidden away in the section labelled Information Products and Services. But you can also get the information from Citywire (`www.citywire.co.uk`), the *Financial Times*, the Motley Fool's UK Wire service (`http://fool.uk-wire.com`), Investegate (`www.investegate.co.uk`), or financial news agencies like AFP, Reuters, or Bloomberg.

## *'Unofficial' Websites*

When you get past the official websites, information can get interesting. You start to leave the bare bones of the legal requirements behind and flesh a situation out with more informative details. This is also the point at which you can enter the realms of speculation, misinformation, and misunderstanding!

Take care when you read these non-official websites. And remember, if you see something that really surprises you, check the information out elsewhere before you act on it. The financial markets aren't particularly complicated, but somebody always adds up two and two and comes up with five for an answer.

One kind of statement that catches people out with surprising regularity is 'Lloyds launches inquiry after record losses'. Now, is that Lloyds TSB the bank, or Lloyd's of London the insurance company? Americans regularly get them mixed up. So do some Britons – which can be really embarrassing.

Here's another trap: 'Red faces at NXT.' Is that Next the fashion chain, which goes by the identifier code NXT? Or is it the technology outfit NXT, which uses the code NTX on the London Stock Exchange? What do you mean you don't know?

- ✔ If in doubt, seek corroboration.

- ✔ Before you invest, seek corroboration (or at least a chart).

- ✔ Before you believe the worst, seek corroboration.

### *FT.com*

For an investor who's still new to the game, working out exactly where the *Financial Times* stands in the pecking order can be confusing. On the one hand, as I point out in Chapter 3, most of the stock market's most important indices – the FTSE-100, the All-Share index, and so forth – are collaborative projects between the Stock Exchange and the Financial Times. And only in the FT do you find incredibly detailed performance data that tells you how thousands upon thousands of managed funds are performing.

But with the *FT*'s other types of coverage the situation's a little different. Despite appearances, the *FT*'s not the official mouthpiece of the London Stock Exchange, or of any other institution for that matter.

The *FT*'s journalists are probably among the best in the world, but they're on the same footing as those at *The Times* and the *Daily Telegraph* and everybody else in sniffing out news stories. They don't get preferential access to information from the Stock Exchange.

But with its online presence (www.ft.com), the *FT* does do better than anybody else. The paper's spent many tens of millions on a huge database operation, which now encompasses not just its own news archives but also a vast range of rival news sources. The snag is that you need to be registered to be able to take advantage of the full online search facility, and you may find a paid-for membership (around £100 a year for extra 'stage 2' services) worthwhile if you want to go deep on the news stories. As a journalist, I couldn't manage without it.

The real power of the *FT*'s online presence is right at its heart. No matter whether you're looking at the main news page or the Markets page where the financial stuff is stored, just start to type in the name of a company (or its stock market identifier) in the 'Quotes' box, and the website offers to take you straight to information about the company. No other independent online source is this good.

 Click on 'Interactive Charting' from the company information page and prepare to be amazed. You get a chart that you can zoom into (or out of) to cover any period you care to select with your mouse, together with giving you information about share transaction volumes, high and low thresholds, and all kinds of useful stuff.

The *FT* website isn't without its faults, however. Because the company statistics pages and the online portfolio facilities are automatically computed, the occasional huge blooper creeps in. For instance, if nobody's told the *FT* that a share's switched its denomination from sterling to euros, the results can be odd for several months.

And some infuriating teething troubles have occurred, including service time-outs that make you tear your hair with frustration. But for an all-round service, nothing else comes close to the *FT*.

### London South East

This is the web site at www.lse.co.uk that I mentioned earlier when I said that it could easily be confused with the London Stock Exchange's own site (www.londonstockexchange.co.uk). Since it's mainly a financial services web site, I'd be surprised if the use of the LSE name was a complete coincidence. . . .

The London South East web site is an invaluable resource, just as long as you don't confuse it with its official near-namesake. It contains up-to-the-minute news reports, company information, share price information (including more detail on buy and sell prices than the London Stock Exchange itself), and RNS news releases.

There's also a chat forum which can perhaps best be described as 'robust'. Don't expect gentle treatment here!

### Thisismoney

The *Daily Mail*'s financial website (www.thisismoney.co.uk) deserves a special mention for its all-round user-friendliness. Like both the London Stock Exchange and the the LSE's websites, Thisismoney is effectively a portal of links to other companies' financial products – it also provides specialist sections on no-nonsense subjects such as making a will, dealing with debt, or getting the best out of credit cards. Its journalists and features writers are of the highest calibre.

Thisismoney also provides a discussion forum, but that's rather poorly organised and thus you may find difficulty locating what you want. The forum tends to be a place where people sound off with their feelings about the government – which isn't what you need to be a successful investor.

But I'm quibbling. Thisismoney has a fine portfolio service, using which you can set up a dummy portfolio that keeps you up to date with events (free registration required). Always worth a look.

### iii

Interactive Investor, normally known in Britain as iii, is different from the *FT* in that it wants to sell you financial services instead of merely telling you about them. The website (www.iii.co.uk) currently has approximately 1.6 million registered subscribers, probably only a small proportion of whom are actually buying services from the company. Most other site visitors are attracted instead by the market information (www.iii.co.uk/markets), the share price information, and the discussion forums. You can find all the RNS announcements here, too.

I especially like the 'Broker Forecasts' information at iii, which I find more informative and easier to get at than the info on the *FT*'s website. (You'll find a tab for the Broker Forecasts information near the top of the screen when-ever you've homed in on any particular share, for instance by inserting its name or TIDM identifying code into the Search facility.) And if you're in the mood to buy an ISA, a unit trust, or a Self Invested Personal Pension (SIPP), you've come to one of the right places. That's why, of course, the people at iii have put so much work into developing the site.

### *Hemmington Scott*

Hemmington Scott (or Hemscott, as it likes to be known; www.hemscott.com) is a free service that provides financial information on more than 2,350 UK and Irish listed companies, as well as all the companies listed on the S&P 500. (The Standard & Poor's 500 Industrial index is one of the most popular measures of the American stock market.) Unlike some of the other financial websites, Hemscott compiles its own company information instead of simply downloading what others are saying, so it's useful as a back-up resource if you need to corroborate something surprising you've heard.

The forward calendar of events feature is especially useful; click on 'News', then 'The Week Ahead'. And one section is devoted to mergers, which is also useful. But you'll need to register to get some of these services, and some information's only available to premium-rate subscribers, who pay between £50 and £150 per year.

The company share price information (including trading statistics) is crisp and accessible, and Hemscott doesn't attempt to force its own financial services down your throat like some of its competitors do. As before, you do need to register at Hemscott for this service, but this time it's free.

### Trustnet

Trustnet (www.trustnet.com) is the best online information source for anyone interested in managed funds of any type. And it's free! Chapter 14 talks about Trustnet's virtues at some length, and the website covers an exhausting array of funds, including thousands of products. The trade reads it, and you can use and enjoy its facilities as well.

Trustnet provides information on:

✔ Investment trusts

✔ Unit trusts

✔ Warrants

✔ Pension funds

✔ Insurance bonds

✔ Offshore funds

✔ Structured products (such as guaranteed equity bonds)

✔ Venture capital trusts and tax shelters

One of the things I especially like about Trustnet is that it's a very visual site. It uses graphics, brief information sheets, historical information, and a simply amazing range of ways to rank funds and reveal which ones are doing best.

You want to know whether technology unit trusts have outpaced East European investment trusts? Trustnet can tell you. You want to know which funds have done best (and worst) over the last year, or the last five years? You want to know whether Artemis's funds consistently outperform Foreign & Colonial's? You've come to the right place.

Even more, once you've found a fund you're interested in, you can home in on it in ever-greater detail. You can start by looking at how an investment trust's share price performance compares with the market as a whole, and also with its net asset value – see Figure 16-1.

**Figure 16-1:**
Share price
comparison
chart from
Trustnet.

You can then find out what companies it invests in – as Figure 16-2 shows.

**Figure 16-2:**
Summary of
companies
in which a
sample trust
invests.

| Largest holdings, 29-Aug-08 | | | | | | | |
|---|---|---|---|---|---|---|---|
| Holding | (%) | Rank | Prev | Holding | (%) | Rank | Prev |
| ARTEMIS INVESTMENT MANAGEMENT | 13.2 | 1 | (1) | REVUS ENERGY ASA | 4.1 | 6 | (9) |
| VOSTOK ENERGY | 10.6 | 2 | (2) | ARICOM PLC | 3.3 | 7 | (7) |
| SALAMANDER ENERGY PLC | 6.6 | 3 | (4) | GEOPARK HLDGS | 3.0 | 8 | (10) |
| NEW BRITAIN PALM OIL LTD | 6.4 | 4 | (3) | R.E.A.HLDGS PLC | 2.7 | 9 | (8) |
| HURRICANE EXPLORATION | 4.1 | 5 | (6) | TSI | 2.5 | 10 | - |

Then you can ask which parts of the world it invests in – as Figure 16-3 demonstrates.

**Figure 16-3:**
Summary
of different
geographi-
cal areas
in which
a trust
invests.

| Regional weightings, 29-Aug-08 | | | |
|---|---|---|---|
| Region | (%) | Prev | |
| UK | 74.4 | (1) | |
| Pacific Basin | 6.4 | (3) | |
| Norway | 4.1 | (4) | |
| Bermuda | 3.0 | (5) | |
| Canada | 2.7 | (2) | |
| Others | 2.7 | (6) | |
| USA | 2.1 | (7) | |
| Denmark | 1.8 | (8) | |
| Indonesia | 1.5 | (9) | |
| Cyprus | 1.3 | (10) | |
| **Total** | **100.0** | | |

And finally, you can ask what industry sectors the unit trust's most heavily committed to – as Figure 16-4 illustrates.

**Figure 16-4:**
Summary
of industry
sectors in
which a
sample trust
invests.

| Sector weightings, 29-Aug-08 | | | |
|---|---|---|---|
| **Sector** | **(%)** | **Prev** | |
| Oil & Gas | 35.6 | (1) | |
| General Financial | 24.3 | (2) | |
| Others | 10.0 | (3) | |
| Food Producers | 9.1 | (4) | |
| Mining | 6.9 | (5) | |
| Aerospace & Defence | 3.7 | (6) | |
| Electronic & Electrical Equipment | 3.5 | (7) | |
| Pharmaceuticals & Biotechnology | 2.4 | (9) | |
| Software & Computer Services | 2.3 | (10) | |
| Travel & Leisure | 2.2 | (8) | |
| **Total** | **100.0** | | |

If you're interested in managed funds, don't invest without consulting Trustnet first.

### Oanda

If you want to know anything about currencies, or coins and money in general, a Swiss website called Oanda (www.oanda.com) can tell you. At very few places do you get such an incredibly detailed run-down on comparative exchange rates, both present and historical. (X-rates at www.x-rates.com comes close for the recent past, and has some very nice charts, but it doesn't have the long-term stuff in such detail.)

The reason is that Oanda's also a currency-trading site, where you may be tempted to get involved in forward currency trades, options, and all kinds of stuff that's a bit more advanced than I really advise a beginner to tangle with. Use Oanda as a resource by all means, but don't say I haven't warned you about the risks of going any deeper.

### Kitco

If you're looking for information on gold, precious metals, or raw materials, Kitco (www.kitco.com) is a fantastic resource. Its round-the-clock bullion price charts are exemplary.

However, you also find excellent research materials at www.basemetals.com or TFC (http://tfc-charts.w2d.com). If you're interested in commodities, all of these web sites should be on your list of favourites.

### BBC

Loyalty to the good old BBC prompts me to include its website in this list. That and the fact that, if you use the BBC's news services at all, you're going to run into the website from time to time.

The BBC website (http://news.bbc.co.uk/1/hi/business) is nowhere near as good as its rivals. You only get a handful of major stock markets, and the share coverage is so-so. But where the BBC site does score is in the way it focuses on stories that affect the ordinary consumer – tax, pensions, and so forth. The archive contains a decent stock of 'how to' stories that's worth a look.

The BBC site does, however, score in two departments. First, its annual coverage of the Budget speech invariably contains links to the official sites where you can download copies of the full document. And secondly, its foreign country surveys (`http://news.bbc.co.uk/1/hi/country_profiles`) give you a quick and reasonably up-to-date 'thumbnail' view of what's happening in nearly 200 countries worldwide.

# Discussion Forums, and Why You Need Them

I want to start this section with a warning. Discussion forums can be scurrilous, hilarious, and often informative and thought provoking. Then again, they can sometimes be boorish, intimidating places where those who don't hold the consensus views are quickly bullied into going elsewhere.

Yes, I'm sorry to tell you that the City has a high proportion of professional traders whose normal modes of expression aren't suitable for your maiden aunt's ears – or for your children's either. A few discussion forums I've seen in Britain take profanity to new levels. (For some reason, American forums tend to be more civilised.) And others are so vague and woolly that I doubt whether very much useful information ever gets exchanged.

That said, I can't do without the financial discussion forums. At their best, they can give you the support and information you need to make a flying start in the investment business. An open secret is that some of the contributors hiding behind their aliases in the Motley Fool discussion forums are eminent City figures in their own right. And the mere fact that they're unselfishly sharing their wisdom with the likes of you and me speaks volumes about the trust and respect with which they're treated.

Good discussion forums are more or less self-policing.

### The Motley Fool

The Fool (as its fans generally know it) is the UK arm of an institution that's been running in America for 20 years or so. It's located at `www.fool.co.uk` (as distinct from the US parent company at `www.fool.com`), and unlike the parent it's still free of charge at the time of writing.

The Fool's everything the likes of Thisismoney want to be. With thousands of articles and a wide range of financial products for sale (the Fool happily sells you an ISA or an insurance policy), the website has sprawled its way into its present shape. Not everybody likes the way it's organised, but I find it ticks all the right boxes when I want to find out more on a subject I don't know much about.

The company information at The Motley Fool is obtained mainly from a company called Digitallook, which has an annoying transatlantic bias that sometimes stops it from coping with London's EPIC share identifier codes (nowadays more correctly known as TIDM codes). Digitallook also prefers to do everything through the international ISIN codes, which are rather more cumbersome than TIDMs, and which can cause confusion. I talk about ISINs, TIDMs and so forth in Chapters 2 and 3. ) But I can forgive it all of that for the Fool's discussion forums, which are the most varied, stimulating, and informative on the Internet as far as I'm concerned.

'To educate, amuse and enrich' has been the Fool's slogan since it was founded in Virginia in 1993. Its UK incarnation has been running since 1997 and is in a virtually unassailable position at the epicentre of UK investment discussion. (At least, as far as private investors are concerned. Professionals have their own places to go.)

The discussion boards now cover more than 200 companies, investment sectors, and favourite investing methodologies, and they're still growing. Perhaps 100 forums are devoted to off-topic subjects such as motoring, health matters, religion, and TV. Indeed, many posters find that posting on the Fool distracts them badly from getting on with their day jobs. You've been warned.

As you may expect, all of the company discussion boards include forward links to relevant statistical information and other company stuff. The Fool's other activities include personal dummy portfolios.

If The Motley Fool's success is down to any secret, that's surely that it avoids being strident. Although bitter arguments do sometimes develop, the boards are generally well policed and moderated so that the general level of mutual respect is high.

### ADVFN

ADVFN's website (www.advfn.co.uk) resembles the Blackpool Illuminations. A welter of flashing adverts in lurid reds and yellows leaves you in no doubt that people are trying to sell you stuff.

ADVFN's discussion forums are every bit as lurid, but perhaps none the worse for that. The banter's somewhat more robust than on the Fool (see 'The Motley Fool', earlier in this chapter). ADVFN welcomes technical analysts, who look for clues in the patterns their share charts make, more warmly than at The Motley Fool, where people like their views to be based on company fundamentals. Short-sellers (investors who borrow shares in order to buy them back, in the hope of getting them back more cheaply later) get a better reception on ADVFN, too.

## Forum etiquette

Unlike blogs, which are completely unregulated, the vast majority of discussion forums for the private investor are tightly controlled and carefully moderated by an adjudicator whose job is to stop anything illegal, unnecessarily offensive, or off-topic from getting on to the public record, or to pull something off the board if it does get through. The moderators aren't doing this just for your benefit – the forums' organisers can be prosecuted if their contributors post anything libellous, defamatory, or deliberately misleading, or anything that reeks of illegal insider trading or share ramping.

The usual rule of thumb with libel or defamation on a discussion forum is that the moderator gets off the legal hook if she removes any post that's given rise to a complaint, without delay and without quibbling. The post may, of course, be reinstated later if the moderator thinks it stands up to close scrutiny, but that's another story. And the moderators can (and do) ban forum members who misbehave. One favourite bugbear for a moderator is a person who has two separate online 'identities' and spends her whole time agreeing with herself!

Pretty well everyone who contributes to a discussion forum does so under a false name that protects her real identity. But in practice the moderators always know their contributors' true identities, because they need to be able to trace posters if they say or do something unacceptable.

These rules are important because they underpin the whole basis of trust that readers place in online forums. Don't ever believe anything that's said on a forum where you don't feel safe and confident.

ADVFN has some other notable strengths. One of them is the system of *stock screening filters*, through which you can select stocks depending on which criteria you feel are most important. You can, for instance, select the companies that have the highest dividend yields combined with market capitalisations (i.e. total company sizes) of more than £1 billion, and the filters deliver you the list of investment candidates you want. Or you can ask for the lowest price/earnings ratios among companies between (say) £100 million and £300 million, and the site will provide that as well.

And ADVFN's free of charge, though you do have to register to access the filters and research facilities.

## Blogs

Blogs are fun, irreverent, and an excellent source of juicy gossip. And, every so often, you find a real gem that someone who knows her stuff is writing. Other experts with knowledge and expertise don't take long to locate these gold-standard blogs. And once you've found one, you're likely to keep coming back for more.

Unfortunately, the vast majority of blogs are drivel. Not only are they tendentious, unbalanced, and badly researched, they're totally unregulated.

I talk about this point briefly in Chapter 8, but the main problem I want to make here is actually slightly different. The big problem with blogs is that people are conditioned to believe that anything they find in neatly printed type, properly set out and nicely worded, is authoritative and reliable. Only the younger generation seems to be aware that it ain't necessarily so. And almost any kind of poorly argued stuff looks better than it ought to when it's set out on the printed page.

So a fair proportion of very odd people write on blogs: dreamers, pathologically angry people, and those with an axe to grind. Harder to spot, however, are the intelligent people trying to persuade you that this or that stock's going to be the next big thing, when what they mean is that they're hoping to sell their holdings just as soon as they've talked the price up a bit.

Or as soon as they've talked it down. Short-sellers absolutely love the blogosphere. Cooking up a damaging story that isn't true is so much easier than inventing a positive one that requires a bit more proof. Everybody loves a good scandal, and a blog's just the place to spread one.

Blogs, unlike magazines or other news services, aren't subject to regulations. Their authors don't have to prove everything they say to a sceptical editor who 's going to give them a hard time if they get something wrong. They won't be hauled over the coals by the regulators if they commit some really serious sin. Blogs are just the place for a dedicated *pump-and-dumper* – someone who talks a share up and then sells it.

Some honourable exceptions prove the rule, of course. They come and they go, and they acquire their own learned circles. Many of the *Financial Times*' journalists run their own blogs, which are co-sponsored by the *FT*, as do many on the *Guardian* and *The Times*. So do many of the country's best economists, though you have to search for them because they tend to be elusive. Try Googling 'top UK investment blogs' for a representative sample of what's available at the moment.

# Investment Magazines

Investment magazines are having a hard time these days. They're finding difficulty competing with the wealth of lively and constantly updated information on your computer screen, often at zero cost to you.

And advertising's also a problem. Many of the country's biggest magazine publishers are having a tough time selling the ad space that ultimately pays for your monthly ration of dead tree. (The cover price you pay for the magazine just about hires the staff, but doesn't pay for the printing and distribution. That's down to the advertisers.)

But before you run away with the idea that investment magazines are strictly for middle-aged men with slippers and pipes and armchairs, I want to persuade you to take a closer look at their advantages.

## *Discovering the charm of a monthly read*

One thing that reading a magazine can do for you that a computer screen never can is relax you and take your mind to a different place. A place where nobody requires you to do anything but read. No feedback, no responsibility, no pressure. You can drink a glass of wine while reading a magazine without looking as if you're attending some sort of sad online party for loners.

But perhaps just as important is the simple fact that a magazine has corners and pages, and the stories have defined lengths that you can see at a glance before you start to read. One of the reasons electronic books haven't caught on yet is that having a physical shape in front of you is simply more reassuring than an endless stream of electrons that may go on for thousands of words or end after the next two sentences.

The psychology of the situation is less confusing and less stressful. You can read your magazine on the train, in the doctor's waiting room, or in the garden, and you have nothing to distract you from its arguments.

That's why I don't think investment magazines are ever going to go out of print. When you're giving an article your full, uninterrupted attention, you're more amenable to serious and challenging ideas. That's where the weeklies (*Time, Forbes, Business* and the monthlies (*What Investment?, Shares, Investors Chronicle*) have the chance to put a few deeper themes past you.

You get thought-provoking articles from senior fund managers and rare interviews with eminent economists who don't expound their thoughts very frequently on the Web. Maybe they feel that the less pressured atmosphere of these publications is a more 'appropriate' context for expressing their opinions. And of course, they know that a bunch of know-nothings aren't going to jump up immediately to attack them, the way they may on an online forum. Their thoughts, in other words, are 'framed' with more dignity on the printed page, because an editor's in charge.

Some magazines, including *Investors Chronicle*, publish hard-to-find information about directors' dealings in their own companies' shares – often a useful barometer of how well or how badly a company's doing. And finally, of course, investment magazines invariably have some of the best league tables for fund performances. Sure, they can't ever be as up-to-date as the info you get from Trustnet (www.trustnet.com), because after all you need a week or ten days to get a magazine through the printers, and that can be a long time in the wild and wacky world of investing. But the monthly magazines have the best relationships with the fund management industry – and, one way and another, you're likely to find a depth of collaborative knowledge that doesn't often happen on the Web.

## Valuing independent reportage

Don't believe that the investment magazines are 'in the pockets' of fund managers whose employers book the adverts and therefore call all the shots. While working as an investment hack on these magazines, I've often had to be pretty savage towards some of these people, and I can honestly say that they don't bear grudges. Indeed, some of them quite like the occasional attack from the press, because it helps to dispel any suspicion that journalists are crawling to them. I can't think of many publishing spheres where dissent from the press is welcomed in the same way.

I've mentioned some of the leading print publications that cater for the private investor. But I'm going to say once again that I don't regard my personal information system as complete unless I'm also reading politically oriented publications like *Time* or *The Economist*. The figures alone don't ever give you enough information when the politics are dictating the way things are decided. Enough said?

## The Foreign Press

Can you gain clues to how the investment markets are moving from reading the foreign press? Absolutely, if you've got the time. By reading articles written in the country you're interested in, you're cutting out the middleman and maybe getting a different perspective on things.

And if you're using an online service you don't need to be able to read foreign languages, because the majority of the really serious papers with financial sections tend to publish English-language editions. That's the joy of the Internet for you.

The problem you face is that you may not know in advance where the political sympathies of a foreign publisher lie. And this always risks colouring the quality of the information you get – consider how differently the *Guardian* and the *Daily Mail* cover the same news story.

Sadly, not all countries provide online news services for free. A fair proportion of the online news sources I mention charge between £20 and £250 a year for at least some of their services. Whether you're prepared to pay those sorts of sums for your information depends on how much you intend to invest in those countries. As someone once said: 'If you think business information is expensive, try ignorance.'

These foreign publications and websites are amongst the best for the investor:

- *BusinessWeek* (`www.businessweek.com`) offers a useful, wide-ranging review of American business issues.

- *Forbes* (`www.forbes.com`) is aimed solidly at the affluent private investor, and its personal financial advice probably doesn't suit a UK investor because of the national differences in tax systems. But its current news analysis is fine.

- *Harvard Business Review* (`http://harvardbusinessonline.hbsp.harvard.edu`) is probably a little deeper than you normally want to go, but its coverage of current business issues is top-notch.

- *The New York Times* (`www.nyt.com`) is often decried as a Democrat-only mouthpiece, but it really deserves more cross-party respect despite the occasionally strident tone of its editorials. It carries useful business stories, and its daily markets coverage is well laid out. You need to register (for free) for some services.

- The *Wall Street Journal* (`www.wsj.com`) is still the best American business paper, with by far the most extensive coverage of the financial markets. Like many large American papers, however, it tends to buy in its foreign news stories from agencies rather than running its own reporting teams in other countries. And most of its foreign coverage is subscription only: you only get the tasters and the teasers if you click on the links.

- *Der Spiegel* (`www.spiegel.de/international`) offers a European's-eye view of current affairs, in Europe and worldwide. Gently left of centre, and frequently controversial, but generally a good read. The current issue is free.

- For another European view, you may like to look at EUBusiness.com (`www.eubusiness.com`), an independent online publication that scores close to a million page views per month. Free registration's required.

- ✔ For East European affairs, consider a subscription to *European Investment News* (www.einnews.com), which costs an eye-watering $40 a month (around £20 at 2008 rates). But which provides en equally eye-opening volume of research that you won't find anywhere else.

- ✔ *South China Morning Post* (www.scmp.com) is the original Chinese business paper, and still the best. Its coverage extends to the majority of southeast Asian countries. But it costs a subscription of around HK$400 (about £25 sterling) per annum if you want to access all areas. This is seriously worth considering for some investors – not least because many of the free Chinese business papers are tightly controlled by the Chinese authorities and don't offer a very balanced editorial view, despite appearances.

- ✔ Nikkei Net Interactive (www.nni.nikkei.co.jp) is one of a relatively small number of Japanese news services that cater for English-language subscribers. A six-monthly subscription costs around ¥6,000 (roughly £30 at mid-2008 prices).

- ✔ News.com.au (www.news.com.au) is an Australian site owned by the Fox Group, with free daily coverage of business and general stories relating to Australia. But many investors prefer the paid-for services of Western Australia Business News (www.wabusinessnews.com), which costs A$280 (about £120) a year.

- ✔ A useful online resource is a website called World Newspapers www.world-newspapers.com, which publishes a pretty extensive list of online publications.

# *Reports, Tipsheets, and Newsletters*

Moving on a little, there's always a place in an any investor's armoury for at least some of the reports, tipsheets and investment newsletters that assail us from all sides. While some of them are available for free, usually from firms of stockbrokers who want you to think well of them, many more are paid-for services which tend to have one particularl thing thing in common – they all promise to give you the 'inside track' on the market, the secret trick that only the professionals know, or the confidential nudge that some highly-regarded investor has passed on to them recently over a breakfast of champagne and oysters.

Needless to say, most of these reports and tipsheets need to be taken with a goodly pinch of salt. But, that said, I tend to take the view that even the silliest-looking ideas can be worth examining just in case there's a grain of commonsense hiding in there somewhere. (There often is.) So I try to read as many as I have time for.

# *Analysing brokers' analyst reports*

I admit that I don't normally spend too much time worrying about what the stockbrokers' and investment bankers' analysts think of a share I'm considering buying. I prefer to make up my own mind, based on my own research. But for a beginner, knowing that Goldman Sachs, or one of the other big investment banks, thinks kindly of the company that's currently under your lens can be a big comfort. That's why I suggest that you take these analysts' reports seriously – at least until you've got enough experience under your belt to treat them with a little more healthy scepticism.

Most of the time, 'analyst report' is a rather glamorous way of describing the reports that the research desks of these investment banks put out at irregular intervals. 'Self-promotion exercise' comes closer to the mark. The major investment banks know perfectly well that newspaper editors are permanently searching for things to put in their publications. And the research desk doesn't take too long to bash out something that enables the papers to run a story headlined 'Deutsche Bank downgrades British Airways'. Without, perhaps, asking how much DB really knows about the airline in question, or indeed about airlines at all. What the heck, DB's name has got its name into the newspapers. And this time next month it may achieve that again by upgrading the same company.

Okay, so now you know I'm a dyed-in-the-wool sceptic. It's not that I'm a contrarian (an investor who does the opposite of what he's told most of the time – although there are plenty of those around.) Rather,I have my doubts about the depth of research that goes into these reports in the first place. But, leaving such scepticism aside, consider what an analyst looks for when she examines a company. Essentially, she asks the same questions you do:

✔ What are the prospects for this company, and for its whole business sector?

✔ How are its profits? Are they growing or shrinking?

✔ Is its debt level becoming uncomfortable? If so, is the bank lending environment getting tougher?

✔ Is the company big, or small, or somewhere in between? How does the stock market feel about big/small/in-between companies right now?

✔ Is this a cyclical share whose share price is likely to rise and fall in line with a predictable rhythm? (I discuss business cycles in Chapter 13, and they can apply to many types of industry.)

✔ Does any prospect of takeover activity exist, either for this share or for other companies in its particular sector?

> ✔ What's the general state of the financial market at the moment? Are people going to be tempted to risk their hard-earned cash on a good share right now, or are they all going to hunker down and wait for better times?

Magazines, too, enjoy putting buy and sell recommendations on shares, with results that are often pretty unimpressive. One British magazine was statistically shown to have got its predictions upside down over quite a long period. On balance, its buy recommendations had lost money and its sell recommendations had gone on to make good profits. Which was not the idea at all! But it wouldn't be right for me to single out any one publication, because a good many of the more expensive tipsheets don't do much better.

But, getting back to the brokers' analysts, one reason you can't afford to ignore these forecasts completely is that the things they say are going to hit the papers, regardless of whether they happen to be right or wrong. That means that millions of other people are likely to take their predictions seriously, and buy or sell accordingly. Many City experts feel that the nasty tendency is for these flaky analyses to become self-fulfilling prophecies.

So getting a sell rating from a big investment bank is very bad news! That is, unless you're the kind of investor who likes to rummage through sell recommendations for discarded diamonds.

---

# The sliding scale of approval

When giving a quick verdict, different publications have different ways of setting out the scale of urgency with which they think you should respond to a given share. But as a rule the categories offered for your delectation will be chosen from the following fairly standard options. In order of approval, they are:

✔ Strong Buy

✔ Buy

✔ Outperform

✔ Hold

✔ Underperform

✔ Sell

(Plus, of course, No Opinion)

Any publication worth its salt tells you how many analysts are in its 'representative sample'. Seven or eight analysts are capable between them of giving you a good idea of how the spectrum looks; one analyst isn't. Generally speaking, the bigger the company, the more analysts who have opinions about its prospects.

Fortunately, there's a shorthand way of understanding what the various analysts think of various companies, which works by comparing the views of large numbers of analysts in one place and then simply performing a head count. Figure 16-5 provides an excellent example, drawn from the *FT*'s website.

**CONSENSUS RECOMMENDATION**

| BUY | OUTPERFORM | HOLD | UNDERPERFORM | SELL | NO OPINION |
|-----|------------|------|--------------|------|------------|

This is the consensus forecast amongst 22 polled investment analysts.

| Analyst Detail | BUY | OUTPERFORM | HOLD | UNDERPERFORM | SELL | NO OPINION |
|----------------|-----|------------|------|--------------|------|------------|
| Latest | 1 | 1 | 7 | 6 | 7 | 0 |
| 4 weeks ago | 2 | 1 | 6 | 6 | 6 | 0 |
| 2 months ago | 0 | 2 | 7 | 5 | 9 | 0 |
| 3 months ago | 1 | 2 | 7 | 5 | 8 | 0 |
| Last year | 0 | 4 | 16 | 3 | 1 | 0 |

**Figure 16-5:** Consensus recommendation from the FT.

As you can see, just one table tells you a lot of information. Not just what the analysts currently think, but what they thought four weeks ago, and two months ago, and three months ago. Now, that information's helpful!

## Assessing tipsheets and newsletters

Any number of subscription tipsheets and newsletters are published, but only a few of them manage to deliver all the results they promise. However, that doesn't mean you shouldn't consider spending the £50–£100 a year they typically cost you.

Why not? Because they suggest new ideas. Because many of them are staffed by incredibly hard-working people who go to the ends of the earth to dig up opportunities that may not be obvious to everyone. And because their sometimes hard-nosed approach helps to keep the market sharp and efficient.

Some newsletters certainly irritate with their aggressively punchy style. Others try to tempt you into chancing your luck with tax loopholes and the like, and not everyone feels comfortable with that sort of approach. (Although, in their defence, British law is soundly behind the idea that if something's allowed, you should be entitled to do it. A landmark High Court decision from the 1930s is still in force that defends an individual's right to use any legal means at her disposal in order to reduce her tax burden.)

But for every tipsheet that strays too far from the beaten track, quite a few manage to stay on the right side of good taste and deliver a valuable service to their readers. Some specialise in particular investing approaches: income investing, for instance, or financial planning, or shorting, or long term buy and hold (known as LTBH to its supporters). Other newsletters focus on particular sectors: gold, pharmaceuticals, emerging markets, or technology. You get the idea.

On the whole, a particular type of investor reads newsletters. She's the person who's certain that she can gain more from the stock markets than the mainstream media like people to believe. And that's a viewpoint I can hardly disagree with.

# Chapter 17

# Understanding Company Accounts

. . . . . . . . . . . . . . . . . . . . . . . . . . . . . . . . . . . . . . . . . . .

## *In This Chapter*

▶ Working out how much you actually need to know

▶ Going through the profit and loss statement, the balance sheet, and the cash flow statement

▶ Introducing shortcuts that can save you time and improve your view

. . . . . . . . . . . . . . . . . . . . . . . . . . . . . . . . . . . . . . . . . . .

*I*f you want to know what a company's really doing, get your information straight from the horse's mouth. Instead of relying on what the morning papers say, or on what you've been told on the Internet, just get yourself a copy of the company's latest accounts and make up your own mind about what sort of state it's in and what its prospects are.

Well, that's the theory anyway. And in principle I can't disagree with it. The snag is that company accounts can be pretty daunting when you get up close and personal with them. The annual report may contain 20 pages of solid statistics, bristling with complications and footnotes and extra columns that really don't seem to mean anything obvious. Absolutely terrifying.

Okay, the chairman's report probably gives you the general gist of the situation, and if you're really lucky you may get a few pie charts and other graphics that give you a feel for the way things are going. But surely, that's just the company trying to put the best possible gloss on its performance? Aren't you trying to do a bit better than that? How much expertise do you really need?

## *Introducing Company Accounts*

The fundamentals of company accounts are really very straightforward, because they conform to a completely standardised format that's essentially the same for every company, from your local corner shop all the way up to BT. It's the add-on documents and all the supplementary twiddly bits that seem to make it so complicated.

A company's accounts actually contain only three basic items:

- ✔ The profit and loss statement
- ✔ The balance sheet
- ✔ The cash flow statement

If you're reading the accounts in the annual report document, then the directors' report at the start contains details of any forthcoming dividends (see Chapter 2 on dividends). And 98 per cent of people who read the accounts probably ignore the couple of pages of notes at the end. Everything else is just additional detail that the company may or may not decide to tell you about.

Now, don't get the impression that I'm instructing you to ignore the small print, because I really don't want something terrible buried in that small print to catch you out. But you can generally get along just fine by focusing on the three statements I've just mentioned: *the profit and loss statement*, the *balance sheet*, and the *cash flow statement*.

## Getting hold of the accounts

You can obtain a copy of the accounts from the company's registrar, or from the RNS (Regulatory News Service), the stock market regulator's official channel for distributing news information to the market. (I mention in Chapter 8 that you can get RNS reports from the London Stock Exchange itself (www. londonstockexchange.com/en-gb/pricesnews/marketnews/) or from all kinds of other online sources such as Citywire (www.citywire.co.uk). The *Financial Times* has a free annual reports service that allows you to order printed copies of many thousands of reports by mail.

Finally, if you look up your target company's own website, you're practically certain to be able to download a copy of the accounts, and perhaps the annual report in an attractive Acrobat PDF format, complete with mission statements and people management targets and pictures of smiling directors.

You should also be able to get hold of interim reports that tell you how the company's been doing in the last three months, or maybe the last six months. These reports probably haven't been audited to the same exacting standards as the annual accounts, so you do need to treat them with slightly more caution. But remember, if they've been released via the RNS system, you can be sure that they've been vetted to the $n$th degree. In my past career as an RNS report writer I got a good idea of just how tough regulatory supervision really is – and the RNS doesn't suffer mistakes gladly.

## *Working out how much you really need to know*

Millions of perfectly successful investors almost never look closely at the accounts of the companies they're investing in. And they may not know where to start looking even if they try.

Subject to the above caveats, you can probably get along fine with only a fairly rudimentary understanding of accounting principles. More important is to listen to what other people who are accounting experts have to say about a particular company's accounts, and to avoid dismissing their opinions just because they don't chime with your own views.

We do, after all, live in the age of the internet. We have online discussion forums in which people with brains the size of small planets talk about things that go right over our poor little heads. And you can also rely on the pretty comprehensive system of stock market regulation that also scrutinises every pronouncement, trading statement, and formal deposition for errors – and severely sanctions offenders for any it finds.

Most of all, the advanced global stock market system punishes transgressors even more sharply than the regulators do, by hammering the prices of companies they don't think they can trust. In short, the vast majority of references you're likely to come across to a company's accounts are sufficiently accurate to be good enough for you and me. Errors hardly happen, at least in the established media – although misinterpretations are another matter entirely.

That's quite fortunate really, because the deeper you go into a company's accounts, the more likely you are to find something you really don't understand. Or something that frightens you silly. Or – worst of all – something you think you understand when you actually don't.

Not for nothing do reference book publishers make small fortunes out of teaching people about the intricate workings of the accounts department. And not for nothing do consultancies charge thousands of pounds for ten-day courses on subjects that would make your head swim.

But then, accounts can be confusing places at the best of times. When two companies merge, or even just when one company buys a big new struc-tural division from somebody else, you get an accounting headache that takes us into the murkier realms of calculating 'like-for-like' sales (when one year's results have to be 'adjusted' to make sense against the previous year's sales, perhaps because the size of the company's operations have changed substantially in the interim period). And if the two merging operations have been working to different financial years from each other, the scope for 'creative accounting' becomes quite broad.

There's also the dangerous fact that accounting rules can be like shifting sands in the right accountants' hands – sometimes because the laws have changed, and sometimes because being opaque simply suits their purposes.

- ✔ The FRS-17 pension regulations have changed the shape of company balance sheets for ever – and made the balance sheets a good deal less useful for an investor.

- ✔ Company accountants exercise surprising latitude when valuing their property portfolios, or deciding the rate at which to write off capital assets like property or equipment. Goodwill items such as patents or brand loyalty can also be almost impossible to value on the balance sheet with any kind of precision.

- ✔ Some companies try to conceal just how much cash they owe! They might issue options that dilute their equity in the future, or in extreme situations they might move entire chunks of debt 'off-balance sheet' – for example, into their pension funds or their partly-owned foreign subsidiaries, or into corporate bonds that they can then sell to the banking market. In the aftermath of the Enron scandal this sort of thing really ought not to be able to happen any more – but you can bet your life that it does.

Chapter 8 covers all of these issues.

So those are the things you need to wary of. But we won't get anywhere if we allow ourselves to get paralysed by worry. So, instead, I'm going to try and cut through all these hidden dimensions, complications and angers, and focus instead on the most important things that you need to know.

If you think I've missed anything in this chapter, or if there's anything you don't understand, then I apologise in advance for having been less than clear. And if you're still puzzled after doing some additional research, then perhaps it would be as well to seek some professional advice, perhaps from a qualified accountant or financial adviser.

# *Reading a Profit and Loss Account*

The accounts you're about to read are based loosely on the trading results of a major British company with operations that extend throughout Western Europe. The company's multinational structure means that it isn't really just one company, but rather a whole group of companies under a single umbrella. And, like many companies of a similar size, it has been busy changing its shape in recent years, buying new divisions and selling off old ones. And, as you can imagine, this process of change plays havoc with a company's accounts.) I'm going to run you through the basic calculations here, focusing particularly on the parts of the accounts that are highlighted in grey.

Table 17-1 presents the Group Income Statement (that is, the profit and loss statement) for the whole organisation.

| Table 17-1 | Group Income Statement for the Year Ended 31 December 2007. | |
| --- | --- | --- |
| | *2007* | *2006* |
| | *£m* | *£m* |
| **Continuing operations** | | |
| **Revenue** | 900.32 | 605.15 |
| Net operating expenses | (830.00) | (555.00) |
| **Group operating profit** | 70.32 | 50.15 |
| Share of post-tax profits from associates | 1.94 | 0.67 |
| Net finance costs | (7.43) | (4.06) |
| **Profit on ordinary activities before taxation** | 64.83 | 46.76 |
| | (11.61) | (8.82) |
| **Profit for the year from continuing operations** | 53.22 | 37.94 |
| **Discontinued operations** | | |
| Profit for the year from discontinued operations | 0.00 | 7.04 |
| **Profit for the year** | 53.22 | 44.97 |
| Attributable to: | | |
| Equity holders of the parent | 45.98 | 38.85 |
| Minority interests | 7.24 | 6.12 |
| | 53.22 | 44.97 |
| **Dividends per ordinary share (p)** | 10.19 | 7.29 |

*(continued)*

### Table 17-1 *(continued)*

|  | 2007 | 2006 |
|---|---|---|
|  | £m | £m |
| **Discontinued operations** |  |  |
| Basic earnings per share | 25.72 | 22.25 |
| Diluted earnings per share | 25.66 | 22.07 |
| **Earnings per share from continuing operations** |  |  |
| Basic earnings per share | 25.72 | 17.87 |
| Diluted earnings per share | 25.66 | 17.61 |

The first item on the profit and loss sheet is the *Revenue*, otherwise known as *Income* (or, more prosaically, *Turnover*). As the name suggests, it's all the money that came in from operating the business during the year, and it was a bit more than £900 million in 2007.

Next comes the *Net operating expenses*, which basically tells us the cost to the company of running its operations during the year. The figure is £830 million, on the second line, written in parentheses to show that it's a negative number (a standard accounting tradition).

Next comes a *Group operating profit* of £70.3 million, arrived at by deducting the Net operating expenses from the Revenue. But sadly, you need more than staff and equipment to run a transport empire: £7.43 million of finance costs also have to be paid, representing loan interest and so on. Even the fact that the company has another £1.94 million of revenues from various other places can't stop the *Profit on ordinary activities before taxation* (that is, pre-tax profit) from dropping to £64.83 million.

Take away £11.61 million in tax, and you've got a *Profit for the year from continuing operations* of £53.22 million. Or post-tax profits, as you probably call them. These post-tax profits can then be distributed to the shareholders as *Dividends per ordinary share* – or the company can partially withhold them if it wants to build up its cash reserves.

In 2007 no activities were discontinued (that is, the company didn't sell anything off or close anything down), so the figures are nice and simple. In 2006, however, it sold off one of its divisions that was bringing in £7.04 million of profits. For the sake of clarity, I've left these discontinued operations in the table so you don't waste your time scratching your head and wondering why the end-of-year profits went up only marginally from £44.97 million to £53.22 million. In practice, of course, the fact that the figure's left in allows you to see very easily that the effective profit comparison has in fact risen from £37.94 million to £53.22 million.

If you skip now to the second-to-last item, *Earnings per share from continuing operations*, you see that the company's made what amounts to a 25.72p profit for every share it's issued. *Diluted earnings per share*, however, equals a marginally smaller 25.66p. That's a fancy way of describing a mathematical allowance for all the stock options, warrants, employee savings schemes, and other convertible gubbins that the company's already issued, all of which might one day get converted into shares. (But equally, they might not.) The 'diluted' figure gives you an idea of how things may look if they all get converted. The exercise of preparing such a 'worst-case scenario' may seem slightly absurd, but if it calms the investors' worries, why not?

In practice, Arriva's decided not to distribute all of that 43.5p cash to its shareholders: instead, it's declared a dividend of 22.65p for 2007, probably paid in two six-monthly instalments. The rest of the money goes back into the coffers to fund future growth.

# Understanding the Balance Sheet

The balance sheet's probably the trickiest part of the whole annual accounts system – see Chapter 8. Rarely do you find such a motley collection of overdrafts, debtors, creditors, tax bills, and pension liabilities, all bundled together in one place for the purposes of computing what the accountants rather optimistically describe as the 'value' of a company.

Table 17-2 presents the group balance sheet for our company.

Notice that on a balance sheet accountants don't try to say what's been going on during the year, the way they would with the profit and loss account. Instead, they just take a snapshot of how things looked at the very end of the period, and freeze-frame that snapshot for posterity, in all its transient glory.

| Table 17-2 | Group Balance Sheet at 31 December 2007 | |
| --- | --- | --- |
| | 2007 | 2006 |
| | £m | £m |
| **Non-current assets** | | |
| Goodwill | 147.69 | 100.24 |
| Other intangible assets | 19.44 | 12.22 |
| Property, plant, and equipment | 523.98 | 343.88 |
| Investments | 28.62 | 17.99 |
| Derivative financial instruments | 17.82 | 1.37 |
| | **737.55** | **475.69** |

*(continued)*

### Table 17-2 *(continued)*

| | 2007 | 2006 |
|---|---|---|
| | £m | £m |
| **Current assets** | | |
| Inventories | 18.50 | 12.22 |
| Trade and other receivables | 162.14 | 77.39 |
| Cash and cash equivalents | 43.07 | 30.66 |
| Derivative financial instruments | 9.81 | 3.29 |
| | **233.51** | **123.55** |
| **Total assets** | **971.06** | **599.24** |
| **Current liabilities** | | |
| Trade and other payables | 245.93 | 129.36 |
| Tax liabilities | 15.53 | 5.78 |
| Obligations under finance leases | 4.73 | 8.68 |
| Bank overdrafts and loans | 53.06 | 46.03 |
| Derivative financial instruments | 4.68 | 4.76 |
| | **323.91** | **194.60** |
| **Non-current liabilities** | | |
| Bank loans | 91.44 | 38.05 |
| Other loans | 55.49 | 51.59 |
| Retirement benefit obligations | 33.17 | 60.83 |
| Deferred tax liabilities | 39.42 | 15.86 |
| Obligations under finance leases | 40.19 | 18.76 |
| Other non-current liabilities | 51.44 | 23.56 |
| Derivative financial instruments | 5.72 | 0.42 |
| | 316.85 | 209.06 |
| **Total liabilities** | **640.76** | **403.66** |
| **Net assets** | **330.30** | **195.58** |
| **Equity** | | |
| Share capital | 4.46 | 3.47 |
| Share premium account | 10.89 | 7.84 |
| Other reserves | 47.25 | 20.30 |
| Retained earnings | 257.00 | 158.27 |
| Total shareholders' equity | 319.59 | 189.88 |
| Minority interest in equity | 10.71 | 5.71 |
| Total equity | 330.30 | 195.58 |

The purpose of the balance sheet is to set out what the company owns (its assets) and what it owes (its liabilities). Assets are divided into *fixed* (or non-current) assets – buildings, plant and equipment, goodwill, investments, and so forth – and *current assets*, such as inventories of stock or cash in the bank that has a more transient value.

The largest part of the current asset section, however, is the one that always makes me laugh. *Trade and other receivables*, as mentioned here, is the term that describes the debts other people owe to the company. Many small businesspeople somehow fail to think of their debtors as assets when they'd really rather have the debtors' money in their pockets instead. But for accounting purposes, that's the description. The money that people owe you is part of what makes your business more valuable. Counter-intuitive but true.

So our company had total assets of £971.06 million at the end of December 2007. Against that, it had £640.76 million of *Total liabilities*, comprising both *Current liabilities* and *Non-current liabilities*, leaving the company with *Net assets* of £330.30 million on the final day of its financial year.

The net asset value is one of the most important things investors want to know – and in the case of an investment trust, which does nothing but own other investments, it's the *only* thing they want to know! By comparing net asset value with the *market capitalisation* of the company (that's the share price multiplied by the number of shares in circulation), you can get a rough measure of just how much over the odds the stock market's prepared to pay for the company's shares, in anticipation of the profits it's going to make in the future. This is not quite the same as the *price to book value* (see Chapter 8), which subtracts all the current liabilities and current debts from the company's total assets, to give a slightly sharper view of its true valuation if the worst ever came to the worst.

To go back to our company, let's look now at the composition of those liabilities. £245.93 million was the sum the company owed to its trade creditors – rather more than the amount other people owed it. (It happens to be a largely cash-in-hand sort of business.) It owed £53.06 million to the bank in short-term loans and another £91.44 million in 'non-current' loans, which would normally mean mortgages, bond issues, and long-term borrowing commitments.

You may want to compare the Current assets with the *Current liabilities*. By dividing the two into each other, you arrive at a ratio called the *liquidity ratio*, which can give you some useful clues as to whether the company's facing solvency troubles. This particular company obviously has no problem, because the value of its assets outweighs its liabilities by more than 51 per cent (that is, the ratio's 1:1.51). But if it's below 1 you'd be entitled to think that only a miracle can save the company – or a buyer who didn't mind taking a very big gamble on sorting it out and bringing the company round! These are the kinds of situations in which banks are liable to pull the rug on a company's loans. Indeed, it can actually be an offence for a company to carry on trading in this position.

Some people like to refine the liquidity ratio still further by discounting the value of all stock from the current assets, on the reasoning that stock's worthless if people won't buy it, or if the company isn't around to sell it. The so-called *acid test ratio* can be quite a problem for retailers in hard times when the markets have gone quiet. But once again, our company isn't bothered because its stock inventory of £18.50 million is really very small in relation to its turnover.

The final part of Table 17-2 shows *Total equity*, which was worth £330.3 million at the end of 2007 – and, by no coincidence at all, that's exactly the same as the £330.3 million figure logged for the company's net assets. There'd be something seriously wrong with the calculations if the two figures didn't tally.

Where does this equity account come from? Well, the greater part of it – some £319.59 million – comes from *Shareholders' equity* and another £257 from *Retained earnings* (that is, cash in the bank).

A lot of other items are in the mix, but I'd be going in way too deep if I tried to analyse them here. For the moment, let's just focus on the key elements and save the complications for another day.

The company doesn't own itself – the shareholders do. So whatever the company's worth, that's what the shareholders own.

# *Interpreting the Cash Flow Statement*

For some reason the cash flow statement seems to be the Cinderella of the accounts business. And that's a pity, because it can reveal a lot. You may get so involved with the profit and loss account, and with the state of the company's assets, that you forget to ask which parts of the business are generating money and which ones aren't.

Each company's cash flow statement is slightly different, because each does something slightly different from all the others to earn its money. So making generalisations is quite hard. But in principle, the stock market wants to know:

- ✔ What money the company's operating activities have brought in, in both gross terms and net terms (after making allowance for interest and financing charges).

- ✔ What the company has spent on business acquisitions, and what has come in from disposals.

✔ How much the company's various loans and overdrafts have increased or decreased during the year.

✔ How much, if anything, the company has raised through floating shares or bonds, etc, during the year.

Look at Table 17-3. Notice that, for our sample company, in 2007 at least, the end-of-year position was really pretty much the same as in 2006. A £2.5 million decrease in the cash situation was small beer compared with the sheer scale of the £900 million turnover – but in fact there were some big transactions going on behind the scenes.

| Table 17-3 | Group Cash Flow Statement for the Year Ended 31 December 2007. | |
|---|---|---|
| | *2007* | *2006* |
| | *£m* | *£m* |
| **Cash flows from operating activities** | | |
| Cash generated from operations | 111.69 | 56.00 |
| Interest and finance charges paid | (7.43) | (4.24) |
| Tax paid | (2.43) | (8.72) |
| Net cash inflow from operating activities | 101.84 | 43.05 |
| **Cash flows from investing activities** | | |
| Acquisitions of businesses | (15.98) | (7.32) |
| Net cash assumed on acquisitions | 5.54 | 0.67 |
| Investment in associates | (1.26) | (14.63) |
| Disposal of business | 0.00 | 45.57 |
| Purchase of property, plant, and equipment | (104.67) | (59.92) |
| Disposal of property, plant, and equipment | 39.33 | 27.55 |
| Net cash used in investing activities | (65.34) | (23.10) |
| **Cash flows from financing activities** | | |
| Proceeds from issuing ordinary share capital | 0.59 | 0.42 |
| Decrease in loans due within one year | (17.73) | (2.31) |
| Increase/(decrease) in loans due after one year | 16.20 | (16.07) |
| Decrease in finance lease obligations | (6.84) | (2.77) |
| Dividends paid to the company's shareholders | (18.86) | (13.86) |
| Dividends paid to minority interests | (0.45) | (0.32) |

*(continued)*

**Table 17-3** *(continued)*

|  | 2007 | 2006 |
|---|---|---|
|  | £m | £m |
| **Cash flows from financing activities** |  |  |
| Net cash used in financing activities | (27.09) | (34.90) |
| **Net (decrease)/increase in cash, cash equivalents, and overdrafts** | **(2.30)** | **0.07** |
| Cash, cash equivalents, and overdrafts at the beginning of the year | 32.00 | 25.06 |
| Exchange losses on cash, cash equivalents, and overdrafts | (1.62) | (0.25( |
| **Cash, cash equivalents, and overdrafts at the end of the year** | **28.08** | **24.89** |

For instance, you see that the cash generated by operational activities rose by pretty well 100 per cent during the year, largely due to expansions of the business. And after tax, the *Net cash inflow* more than doubled. But the company stepped up its purchases of property, plant, and equipment from £59.92million to £104.67 million even though its revenues from selling things off rose by only £12 million, from £27.55 million to £39.33 million.

Although the volume of short-term loans decreased by around £18 million, it was effectively outweighed by a £32 million rise in longer-dated debts. And the amount paid out in dividends went up substantially from £13.9 million to £18.9 million.

This all looks rather boring. So where's the excitement?

Well, the statement is stable, on the whole, and it paints a reassuring picture of the company. But if the finance director of a company is playing fast and loose with his shareholders' cash, wheeling and dealing and constantly shifting the debts from one place to another, you can see it in the cash flow statement.

If too much activity is going on, or too many changes are happening at once, the cash flow statement is one of the first places you notice it.

Many bargain-hunters get really turned on by a big cash balance in the bank, especially in a small company, and they'll always tell you to pay special attention to how much money's in the coffers. They're not wrong, either.

Situations do sometimes arise where small companies' share prices fall to the point where their market capitalisations are quite literally smaller than their liquid cash assets. Barring major disasters, these situations are about as close to a no-brainer as you can get. Either the company's in the process of dissolving itself and has stopped trading – something that sometimes happens to investment trusts (see Chapter 14 on trusts) – or else a predator will soon be along to scoop up the company for its cash pile and the shareholders will be well rewarded. Either way, the point's worth remembering.

You can generally expect a company to produce several reams of supplementary information intended to support the three key tables: the profit and loss account, the balance sheet, and the cash flow statement. Much of this extra information's incomprehensible unless you've been following the company's fortunes in some detail – and some of it takes you to places that are too dark and confusing to fall within the parameters of this book!

# Understanding What Can Go Wrong

Just a reminder of something I say at various points throughout this book.. Accountants and auditors have a surprising amount of leeway in deciding how to set down fixed assets like property in a company's accounts. They can use wide discretion in calculating the value of intangibles such as brand names and patents. And, as many investors have found to their cost, some of them never quite seem to run out of enterprising ways to cloud the issue where debts are concerned. Chapter 9 covers the many fascinating tricks and manoeuvres surrounding asset declarations.

Be thankful for the Internet. Somebody on a forum's always gone into the accounts in more depth than either you or I want to go. And, although he may not always be right when he claims to smell a rat – or identify a hidden opportunity – taking a look's always worth your while.

# Looking at Five-year Summaries

The statutory accounts that companies normally provide to the regulators cover only the last two complete financial years. That's all that the rules require them to provide, and it gives the stock market enough information to be able to compute all the things they need – things like 'trailing averages' (which give you average performance levels over a period of time), or 'historic dividend yields', which often involve such incredibly complicated maths that no two press sources ever seem to be able to come up with the same figures.

But, for the really diligent investor, it's also worth looking out for tables that present a longer-term view of a company's financial background. It's all very well knowing that last year's turnover was better than the year before, but don't you think it would be helpful to know that the year before /that/ was an even better year – and therefore, that the low year in the middle was probably just an exception to the usual trend?

That's why many companies will helpfully supply you with five-year statistical summaries that can help you to get a better long-term view of how your company has been getting on. The chances are that the company's website will have such a table tucked away somewhere on its 'investor relations' page. But you can also find similar five-year company summaries listed on third-party websites such as Digitallook, which supplies the statistical material for the Motley Fool in the UK.

The website at `http://fool.digitallook.com` will get you started.

A word of warning, though. Although these independent websites try their best to keep their information up to date, they don't generally accept any responsibility for having got things wrong or perhaps out of date. Remember, they're dealing with vast amounts of data for vast numbers of companies, and it's quite easy to get small details wrong, or simply not to notice that some figure has been retrospectively 'adjusted' in a way that might change our perception of it.

What sort of 'adjustments' are those? Well, it's not entirely unknown for a company to have to restate its last year's trading figures if the financial regulators are at all unhappy with them. Very occasionally, a company will be required to rejig its results for several years going backward!

More probably, complications will result from a recent merger or acquisition which obliges the company to combine the results from two different operations – each of which might be using a different accounting system as well as different financial year-ends! The resulting figures will inevitably be an untidy collision of estimates, occasional obfuscation and sometimes blind guesswork, especially where intangible factors like brand names and trademarks have to be valued.

And those very approximate figures will need to be reworked backwards into the last five years' accounts as well if we're to get any idea of 'like-for-like' performance.

Then there are share splits (otherwise known as scrip issues) that might make it look to the superficial eye as though your company's shares are worth less than they used to be – whereas a closer look would reveal that the investors had actually been issued with free shares that effectively compensated them for the apparent 'loss'. (I talk about scrip issues in Chapter 9.) An information provider who's really on the ball will have reverse-calculated the effects of the scrip issue into his back figures – but accidents will happen, and they sometimes forget.

Enough of this – I think you've got the idea by now. Five-year statistical views are a really great tool to have in your investor's armoury, and they can often alert you to a long-term trend that you might not have noticed if you were just looking at the last year's figures. But do treat them with a large pinch of salt. And if you ever find anything that looks too good to be true, then remember, it probably is. Go off and check the company's historical charts for corroboration, or do some in-depth research before you lay down your money on something that might turn out to be a misunderstanding.

Used sensibly, five-year charts and tables can enhance your understanding of pretty well any kind of investment. Remember, you're investing to make money over a period of years that might extend for many decades. So at least take the trouble to make sure that you really know how the last five years have shaped up. You can never do too much research. Good luck!

# Part VI
# The Part of Tens

## In this part . . .

**T**his is where you'll find a set of easy-to-read checklists that will help you focus your attentions where they really matter.

What do you really need to know about a share before you buy it? Does your investment portfolio reflect your personality and your position in life? What are the unmistakeable signs of a company that's on the up and up? And what are the giveaway clues that tell you it's on the way down? You'll find short, pithy answers here.

# Chapter 18

# Ten Things to Know about a Share

∙∙∙∙∙∙∙∙∙∙∙∙∙∙∙∙∙∙∙∙∙∙∙∙∙∙∙∙∙∙∙∙∙∙∙∙∙∙∙∙∙∙∙∙∙∙∙∙∙∙∙∙∙∙

*T*he investing business involves more than just getting a tip from some-where and then looking up the price to see that it's okay. If you're going to protect yourself properly against making the wrong decision, you need to ensure that you've done most of the following.

## Knowing What the Share Price Has Done During the Last Five Years

Forget about how the share has soared in the last six months. Take a look instead at how the price curve has shaped up over a five-year period, or maybe even longer, because your company may be experiencing only a brief upturn during a period of long-term price decline.

Many of the online share price-charting facilities have a button that lets you specify 'all available data', or something similar. (On the FT online site, you access this through an 'Interactive Charting' option that's rather easy to miss.) In practice you'll probably get a chart that goes back to 1986 or there-abouts, because not many electronic records go back farther than that. But that timescale ought to be more than good enough for your purposes.

Lots of share price charts also have a section that records the volume of shares traded over a period of time. Was the buying and selling activity par-ticularly vigorous in any periods? Try to find out why.

Lastly, don't forget that most share price charts have been corrected to allow for any scrip issues (which happen when the company issues new free shares to its shareholders that effectively dilute the price per share without affect-ing the total stock market capitalisation). So if you see a chart suggesting that the share price in October 2003 was 200p when the historical records say 400p, the chances are that the company's had a one-for-one scrip issue since then, and the chart has backdated its effect on the share price. Finding out the details of any scrip issues shouldn't take long.

Chapter 5 has more on shares.

# Knowing the Company's Stock Market Size

You calculate the stock market size of a company (that is, its market capitalisation) by multiplying today's share price by the number of shares in issue. So if a company's shares are 200p and it's issued 100 million shares, you know that its market capitalisation is £200 million.

The number of shares in circulation is often growing, albeit by small amounts each time. This is because the company needs to issue new shares whenever one of its options holders redeems one of her options. The same goes for warrants, which are usually equivalent to 'virtual' shares until the day somebody decides to 'exercise' them, thus forcing the creation of a small amount of new equity to honour the warrants.

Companies may also decide to issue shares to put into their pension funds or their employee share ownership schemes. While this practice is very annoying for you, because it really does dilute the value of the shares you hold, it probably doesn't amount to a massive dilution.

Occasionally, technical glitches can get into the computer databases that manage online information sources' share information. For example, a website may accidentally overlook the fact that a company has another lot of shares listed in Australia, where it hasn't looked, and the result can be a wrong market capitalisation figure. If in doubt about a suspicious figure, check out the true situation.

Chapter 2 has more on company size.

# Knowing the Price/Earnings Ratio

The price/earnings ratio is probably the best analytical tool you have at your disposal. Comparing the company's pre-tax earnings with the current market capitalisation gives you a useful measure of just how keen the stock market is on the company's shares.

The trouble is, different information sources use different p/e calculations, and finding out which parameters they're using can often be alarmingly hard. The best p/e is the historical figure, which compares today's share price with the last year's earnings per share – the so-called trailing twelve-month (TTM) measurement. But some analysts insist on using forward p/es, which compare today's share price with the projected earnings in the coming year. Whose earnings estimates are these anyway? I think we should be told.

See Chapter 5 for the lowdown on p/e ratios.

# Looking at the Dividend, and Deciding Whether Current Profits Can Cover It

Dividends are a lifeline for some investors and a curse for others. Your decision's likely to depend on whether you're an income investor who wants a steady income stream, or a red-blooded growth investor who prefers the company to keep its profits and reinvest them, rather than handing them out willy-nilly to shareholders and impoverishing itself.

The camp you belong in doesn't matter – what you need to know is the dividend cover ratio. This tells you, very succinctly, the ratio between the profits the company's making and the dividends it's paying out. If the company's paying out all its profits as dividends, the ratio is 1. If it distributes half of its profits as dividends and keeps the rest for a rainy day, the ratio is 2.

A company with a dividend cover ratio of less than 1 is living on borrowed money, because it's handing out dividends faster than it can make profits. This is a portent of doom in many situations.

Chapters 2 and 5 tell you more about dividends.

# Finding Out When the Next Dividend Payment Is Due

An incredible number of investors fall into the ex-dividend elephant trap because they don't bother to check the qualifying date for the dividend. As soon as a company's shareholders have held a share for long enough to be entitled to the dividend, some of them will sell up immediately and disappear off into the wide blue yonder, leaving a sharply diminished share price behind them. (All things being equal, you can expect the market to mark down the share price by something close to the dividend yield figure on ex-dividend day.)

If you're unaware of all this, you might look in the paper and notice that the share price has plummeted by 5% in a day (or whatever), and you might die of shock. Conversely, however, if you can buy a share just before the ex-dividend date and the price doesn't drop by much even after you've qualified for the divi, that's a sign that the market likes your share. Either that, or all the other shareholders are stupider than they look.

# *Reading the Profit and Loss Statement*

I won't labour this point, because Chapter 17 explains everything. The majority of investors never really look at a company's profit and loss sheet closely enough, because they trust the rest of the investing world sufficiently to be confident that somebody, somewhere, is going to sniff out any rats among the figures.

That's okay right up to the point where you discover that two different information sources are giving you two different figures for the company's profits. Some of them talk about operating profits (the turnover, or revenue, minus the normal cost of running the business), while others look at the pre-tax earnings (which allow for the costs of servicing debts and depreciating assets, and so on). Still others quote 'like-for-like profits'), which are what you get when you rebalance your profit figures to strip out the effects of any expansion of the business during the year. (A store than that has 200 stores this year but only 100 last year is going to be showing some seriously skewed profit growth figures unless you stick with like-for-like figures.)

You aren't in a position to query any of these anomalies unless you know at least a bit about how to read the profit and loss statement for yourself. Doing so's optional, but you're a better investor for having the skills.

# *Looking at the Balance Sheet*

The average company's balance sheet is a can of worms.

There, I've said it. It contains an untidy agglomeration of figures, a lot of which have been put there either by choice or by chance. Okay, you'll have gathered that I'm not very keen on reading too much into the balance sheet.

Unlike the company's profit and loss account, the balance sheet isn't a record of what the company's done during the year.

Instead, it's a flash photograph of what the balance between assets and liabilities happened to look like on the last day of the trading year. That figure will have been distorted by random factors, such as how many creditors happened to have paid their bills by the year-end, and by not-so-random factors like the accountants' decisions to accelerate the capital write-downs on this or that piece of equipment, or to restate the value of assets that the company already held.

And then there's the effect of the pensions legislation, which also requires companies to include a figure for how much their pension assets or liabilities were might have been at the end of the trading year. In volatile times these pension asset figures swing up and down violently. And the results, for better or worse, go into the balance sheet at the end of the year when the photographer fires heris flashbulb and freezes the moment for posterity. Insane.

Chapter 17 goes through a company's accounts section by section.

# Knowing What Other Debts the Company Has

Okay, so you think you know all about your company. Its market capitalisation looks fine, its share price is moving ahead sharply, and goodness, its assets are growing magnificently. But are you quite sure that you know how they were obtained?

All companies have debts, which may be 'current liabilities' (payable in the next year or so, such as bank overdrafts) or 'non-current liabilities' (payable over longer than that, such as mortgages). Many companies have also issued corporate bonds (see Chapter 6 for the lowdown on bonds), and all of them will need to be honoured one day. Some companies have issued preference shares, which are interest-bearing shares that carry special privileges but probably aren't counted in the calculations that give the market capitalisation. And an awful lot of companies have issued smallish numbers of warrants and options that will one day need to be honoured when the holders exercise them.

You don't need to be an Enron investigator to realise that a company has more ways than one to take on a debt and tuck it away in a place where a naive investor might not notice it. Don't be a naive investor. Most companies are absolutely spotless in this respect, but the best way to be sure is to know your way around the annual report, and the balance sheet in particular – Chapter 17 shows you how.

# *Looking at the Directors' Statements*

Directorspeak, as this kind of jargon's often known (in homage to George Orwell's 'Newspeak' in his novel *1984*), is one of the dark arts of the business world, and you can learn a lot by sharpening your awareness of it.

The board won't want to say right out loud that the last six months' trading figures were absolutely dreadful – instead, it'll say that 'conditions are c hallenging' but that 'the company's projections are currently in line with what it said during its October interim statement'. It won't say that its latest venture has bombed – instead, it'll say that it's 'looking forward to developing a vibrant new business relationship' with whatever venture capital company is willing to take it off its hands.

Am I being too negative? Possibly so. There are many boards whose clarity and obvious sincerity marks them out among their peers, and I would follow these boards and their companies to the ends of the earth because I know they won't deceive me. But there are others whose companies would have to be really deep-value bargains before I would risk my cash in their hands.

Chapter 8 has more on directors' statements.

# *Checking the Buzz on Online Forums*

Online discussion forums are often a good place to listen to other people's perceptions of Directorspeak, and much else besides. Comparing your own perceptions of a company's prospects with what the old hands who've held its shares for years are saying is never a bad idea.

Some of them will be wrong, of course. And others will either be in denial about a situation that's going badly wrong, or else so madly in love with their shares that they're not seeing straight any more. But all these people are worth listening to, for the simple reason that their experience is greater than yours. Ignore them by all means, but at least make sure you know what they're saying first.

# Chapter 19

# Ten Ways to Make Your Asset Allocation Fit

• • • • • • • • • • • • • • • • • • • • • • • • • • • • • • • • • • • • • • • • • •

*T*he phrase 'one person's meat is another person's poison' is spot on when we're talking about investing. A young person with no dependants can afford to take all kinds of wild and exciting risks on small companies and recovery stocks that a middle-aged person contemplating retirement really shouldn't touch with a disinfected bargepole. And tax issues can mean that one sort of investment really doesn't suit some people at all.

So it's horses for courses.

Professional investment advisers talk about 'asset allocation' – which is just a fancy way of saying that you need to get the right balance between your dead-safe investments and your wild-ride, get-rich-quick schemes. Often, that means taking a long, cool look at your life and figuring out where you are and where you want to be in ten years' time.

## Assessing Your Life Situation

Take a good look at yourself in the mirror. How long do you intend to carry on working before you retire? Ten, twenty, forty years? Are you at your earnings peak right now, or is your income likely to fall away? How's your health?

And how about your liabilities? Are you footloose and fancy-free, or do you have young children you need to support through school and then perhaps university?

At a more immediate level, are you likely to want to get at your cash in the next five years? If so, how much of it? If you need to replace your car tomorrow or move to a new area because of your job, how easily can you afford it?

Chapter 4 helps you answer these questions and decide on an investing strategy to match your lifestyle.

# Adjusting the Balance

Are the investment patterns that were right for you five years ago still right for you now?

Do you need to increase the proportion of cash in your investment portfolio? Doing so is user-friendly, safe (subject to certain provisos, as Chapter 7 describes), and also surprisingly flexible.

Do you perhaps need to transfer some of your shares into bonds that provide you with a reliable fixed income for as long as you hold them? If you're intending to keep your bonds indefinitely, price volatility won't apply to you: a 6 per cent yield on the money you invested when you bought them is a 6 per cent yield for life (or at least, so long as the bonds run until their redemption date). Financial advisers often tell their fifty-something clients to look for a suitable moment to buy bonds, maybe five years before their planned retirement, and lock into the slower pace at a time when they can have the bonds cheaply. That sounds like good advice to me. Chapter 6 covers everything you need to know about bonds.

But for everyone else, shares and other equity-type investments are still the way to go in the long term. Fast-and-loose, high-risk shares tend to be more suitable for young people and for forty-somethings with cash to spare than for parents in their thirties or older people. For these people, a safer approach tends to fit their needs more closely. But hey, I'm making a big generalisation, and your priorities may be completely different. Who am I to tell you how to live your life? See Chapter 4 on matching your investment strategy to your responsibilities.

# Considering Whose Money You're Managing

Never, never take big risks if you're managing money for someone else who doesn't know much about investing. If you've got a nest-egg that's going to see your kids through school, you're insane if you blow it on something that may deprive them of part of their future. The same goes for Aunt Edith's inheritance that you're intending to pass on to the children when they reach 18. For these sorts of situations you want mainly cash (Chapter 7 covers cash investing), with perhaps a handful of large and solid ('blue-chip') companies to provide income and a reasonable hope of capital growth.

But even if you're not in this situation, don't automatically assume that your own money's all your own. Sole breadwinners whose spouse is completely dependent on them for income bear a responsibility to the spouse as well, and the duty of care's just as important.

I once had an acquaintance who was forced to admit to his wife that he'd just gambled away the family home on the futures markets, and that they were going to have to sell up. She is, of course, now his ex-wife. The fact that he was a financial adviser by trade and ought to have known better didn't make things any easier for him. (In fact, I suppose his trouble was that he thought he *did* know better.) But he's broke now, and probably selling double glazing. Being reckless is so very easy, and coping with the consequences so very hard.

# Deciding Between Capital Gains and Income for Tax Purposes

An investor who's paying maximum rate tax won't welcome the big income yields from some sorts of shares if 40 per cent of everything he earns is going to go to the taxman. Especially when he could be putting it into capital growth stocks instead, that wouldn't attract any taxes at all if he ran them through an Individual Savings Account (ISA).

# Deciding How Long You Can Afford to Lock in Your Money if Everything Goes Wrong

This is one of the most important decisions of all. If your money's in a guaranteed income bond (or a guaranteed equity bond, as they're sometimes known – see Chapter 6) from a bank or a building society, you aren't usually able to unlock the door at all until the five- or six-year term is up. Even in the few exceptional cases that are allowed, you'd suffer such big financial penalties on your withdrawal that you'd be wondering why you ever bothered.

But not just guaranteed income bonds lock up your money. If your cash is invested in small company stocks, whose fortunes tend to rise and fall with the economic cycle, you may have to wait a long time before you get the right price for them, because these stocks can be pretty illiquid sometimes. If in doubt, stick with larger companies where you know that at least your shares will be tradeable if you need to sell at short notice.

Most people's answer is that they can manage without some of the money but not all of it. So the right way forward is to have the right amount in a no-notice account, the right amount at 30 days' notice (say), and the right amount tied up for longer.

How much cash do you want to have available at a month's notice? Probably the equivalent of six months' income, but that's a strictly personal choice.

Chapter 4 covers the issues that help you make this decision.

# Figuring Out Your Attitude to Debt

Okay, here's something a bit radical. Throughout this book, I've tried to dissuade you from being tempted to borrow money in order to invest it in the financial markets. And a good thing too. Borrowing money in order to try and make more money (or 'leveraging', to give it its proper name) is a mug's game, because if you make the wrong call and your investments go down you might end up losing more than your original stake. That's what went wrong with my friend who had to tell his wife that their home was no longer their own, because he'd gambled and lost with money he didn't really have.

But even a moment's consideration will remind you that we all borrow to invest, whether we realise it or not. If you have a £100,000 mortgage on your home and also £40,000 worth of investments in the stock market – or even just in a pension plan – then strictly speaking you're in more debt than you really need to be. You're effectively borrowing £40,000 in order to feed your speculation habit, when in theory you could pay it all off and have less debt. Shock, horror.

Logic, of course, is a fool. You can only get so far in life by reducing your debts to the minimum and refusing to invest (or even to start to save!) until they've all been paid off. Instead, if you want your financial security to grow, then you need to take at least some risks in the financial markets – even if it's just the risk of the British government defaulting on your granny bonds, which isn't very likely. Didn't the parable of the talents in the Bible tell us that the son who earned the most praise was the one who invested his money actively, rather than simply burying it in the ground? (Although I'll have to agree that in this case the son got the money as a gift, and not as a loan.)

But the principle still holds well enough. Investing is considered to be a good and desirable thing by society in general, not least because it helps to create wealth. (How many jobs would there be if nobody took the risk of investing?) So it follows that it's okay to have a balance between your total debts and your investments, providing that you're personally happy with the balance.

People handle this balance in different ways. At the most cautious extreme are the people who hold all their savings and their debts in something like the Virgin One account, where your savings effectively go into a pot that offsets the outstanding mortgage balance, so as to give you an overall debt balance that's less than your mortgage. Slightly further up the risk scale are the people who take out mortgages to buy second homes, in the hope of making a profit. (Yes, that's another way of leveraging up your investments.)

At the far extreme of the risk spectrum are the adventurous types who borrow quite openly in order to invest directly in shares and bonds – something that your bank manager won't knowingly let you do unless you've got a proven track record of successful investing – and the real flying trapeze artists who speculate on derivatives with money they don't necessarily have at all. (I talk more bout derivatives in Chapter 12.)

And somewhere in the middle are the rest of us, who have one mortgage and a couple of pension plans, plus a little bit invested in the stock market. We don't like to think of ourselves as gambling with borrowed money, but to some extent that's effectively what we're doing. Are you happy with that? If not, then you need to sit down and do some serious thinking about whether you're really destined to be an investor or a 100 per cent safety player instead.

## Asking Whether You Enjoy the Investment Game for Its Own Sake

Lots of people really don't enjoy investing at all. That's absolutely fine. Most of us have more important things to do with our time than spend it poring over company accounts, and only the exceptions really get the buzz that makes everything worthwhile.

Here's another way of putting the question. If you were charging yourself £30 an hour for the time you spent on your investments, would you still be making a profit? If not, perhaps you're better off employing a professional to do your investing for you. The most obvious way of doing this is to buy unit trusts and investment trusts (see Chapter 14 on trusts). Or, if you want just a bit more control over things, exchange traded funds or other investments that you can buy and sell at short notice.

I haven't got much doubt that almost anybody with an ounce of common sense can beat the market professionals with a little application. No, make that 'with a *lot* of application'. Either way, if you don't enjoy the thrill of the chase, then you're only going to make yourself miserable.

## Figuring Out Whether You're a Herd Follower or a Maverick

Imagine yourself in a cowboy movie. Are you the silent loner who rides into town with a radical scheme that's going to shake up the locals a little bit? Or are you the wise old doctor who tries to dissuade the new arrival from pushing his scheme, because he's stirring things up too much and the locals prefer the attractions of safety in numbers?

An odd question, perhaps, but maybe it deserves some thought. The trouble with sticking to the well-trodden path and just following the herd is that you always end up with a merely average result. When the market goes up, your fortunes go up by an average amount. And when they go down, you feel every bit of the pain. That's herd behaviour for you.

The maverick has other ideas. He's always looking for opportunities to break loose from the pack. He may identify a cyclical trend that's moving upward, and rather than trying to persuade everybody else that he's right, he puts his own money in. Or he may decide to try shorting a stock, by selling shares he doesn't actually own (see Chapter 9 on this tactic) because he feels it's going to go down soon and shorting is the only way to make a profit out of the situation. Either way, he's pitting himself against the consensus and generally living off his wits.

All well and good. Do remember, though, that the mavericks in the cowboy movies have a tendency to end up face down in the dust. Shorting is a very risky business, and even the best investors get wiped out sometimes. And cyclical trends can be a lot less logical than you may suppose. Just ask anyone who's tried to fathom out the commodity markets in the last few years.

But I've set out some rather extreme positions here and fortunately a middle course can mitigate the risk. By keeping your wits about you and by knowing your stuff, you can certainly gain an edge on everyone else. But does it suit your temperament? And have you got the time to do the research?

# Making Sure You Know How Important This Money Is to You

Would your approach to investing be different if you were gambling with a future nest egg or if the money were just a little windfall that you could playing with for fun, on the off-chance you may strike it lucky? If the answer's yes, consider investing safely in the first scenario and setting up a different account to allow yourself a flutter on something frivolous and speculative every now and then.

I keep a small part of my share portfolio in a completely separate trading account, which I never, ever top up with fresh money. Capital growth (i.e. a rising share price) is the only way my money's ever going to grow! And it's growing just fine, so I suppose I must be doing something right. But if it ever crashed, I'd be out of my mind to try to rescue it with fresh funds. Don't pour good money after bad. Grandmother said that, and it's as true as ever.

Chapter 4 covers different investing strategies to suit different types of people.

# *Asking Whether You Can Get Over a Mistake*

This is the crunch question, really, and it comes right down to how well you know yourself. What do you do when you make a mistake and lose money? Do you go into denial and give the dice another spin, in the hope that you can break your run of bad luck before it's had a chance to start? Or are you racked by the torment of having deliberately put yourself in a losing position because you're too stupid to listen to good advice from people who know what they're talking about?

I want to encourage you to take a calmer, kinder approach to yourself. Every investor makes mistakes. I certainly do. And so does Warren Buffett, the world's most successful investor. He bought 7 per cent of the Coca-Cola Company in 1988 when its stocks were worth around $5, watched them rise to nearly $40 . . . and then held them while they went right down to $15 again! Buffett also missed out on the entire technology boom of the late 1990s, because he didn't trust companies he didn't understand. And yet he's still the world's greatest investor, and the world's richest investor.

The right approach when you make a mistake is to sit down and force yourself to learn something from your errors, instead of hoping you can leave your 'bad luck' behind. That sounds simple, but you may be surprised how many people are temperamentally unfit for the task. No pain, no gain. Are you ready?

# Chapter 20

# Ten Warning Signs that a Company May Be on the Ropes

• • • • • • • • • • • • • • • • • • • • • • • • • • • • • • • • • • • • • • • • • • • • • • •

*1*t's all very well being able to pick a stock that's about to go through the roof – and sometimes, to be honest, it isn't all that difficult as long as you use the tools I've been showing you in this book. But there's more to the art of investing than simply picking winners. You also have to be able to tell which shares are going to be losers – and, no less so, which of your former winners are about to turn into losers.

I'm going to confess that I've sometimes lost profits that I thought were safely in the bag, because I was too slow to recognise the signs that a company's fortunes were on the turn. Sometimes that happened because I simply failed to notice something important that was going to affect the company in an adverse way. But sometimes it was because my pig-headed pride stopped me from acknowledging that I'd been holding on too long, and that it was going to be all downhill from here.

For instance, I might say to myself: 'Look, the stupid market's got this share all wrong. Its price has been hammered beyond all rhyme or reason, but it was a good share when I bought it and it's still a good share now. All I've got to do is hold tight for a while and wait for the rest of the world to recognise its true value.'

Or: 'Yes, I do realise that the good times are over for this company, but yesterday's price fall was really a bit overdone. I think I'll wait a few days, and maybe it'll have bounced a bit so that I can sell out at a better price.' Famous last words!

How can you avoid these pitfalls? By staying alert, and by trying not to kid yourself that you always know best. Some of the following warning signs will turn out to be false alarms. But others will serve you well. Either way, looking out for bad news is a good habit that will always stand you in good stead.

# Profits Are Stagnant or Falling

Often you look at a company's results and notice that sales and/or profits have gone down sharply. Something isn't necessarily wrong here, although things certainly look that way. For instance, the company may have sold off some of its divisions, in which case the fact that turnover has dropped isn't very surprising. Conversely, of course, buying up a competitor or expanding rapidly may have boosted its headline profits.

Shop chains are especially vulnerable to these sorts of distortions, because retailers are continually adding and subtracting premises from their businesses.

But the situation is different if like-for-like profits have fallen. This means that, when the accounts have been adjusted to take account of the changes in activity, they're still showing a drop in activity. That's bad news, and you shouldn't dismiss it lightly.

# The Dividend Cover Is Looking Stretched

Often, a company that isn't doing particularly well issues an improbably large dividend to its shareholders, pretty much as an incentive to stay aboard the sinking ship and not dump the shares. Indeed, this may happen even if the company's making losses and not profits at all. Now that's a pretty urgent sign that you need to take a closer look.

Of course, good reasons may exist for the dividend being so large. The company may have a lot of cash in the bank, perhaps because it's sold something off, or it may have decided simply to treat its shareholders.

At times like these, the dividend cover figure's a really good way to check the soundness of a company's ability to pay its dividends. The figure tells you the multiple between its pre-tax profits and its dividend. A ratio of two (at least) is generally healthy; a figure of one denotes that the company isn't keeping any cash back for developing the business; and anything less than one's simply going to be unsustainable if it continues for very many years at a time.

Chapter 2 describes dividends in detail.

# The Share Price Is Below Its 200-day Moving Average

Chapter 10 talks about charts, and why some people don't like them very much. Forget about all those pretty patterns on a piece of paper, they say, and focus your attention instead on the fundamentals that make the company what it is. Profits, losses, balance sheets, and business performance – that's what everyone really wants to hear about. None of this faffing about with charts, please.

Well, up to a point I tend to agree. But one of the places a chart can really score is when it tells you how the stock market's current valuation of a share compares with its average valuation over a longish period. The long-term 'moving average' figure helps you to screen out all the little ups and downs and focus your attention on the underlying picture instead. And a chart that shows how this moving average has behaved over an even longer period is better still.

For instance, if your shares have averaged 200p over the last nine months but they're 180p now, you know that they're cheaper than their recent historical average (obviously). But that may simply be due to a short-term statistical bump in today's price. You have a much better picture of things if you can see on a chart that two months ago, the 200-day average was still only 200p. In that case today's price probably isn't much to worry about. But if the 200-day average shows a curve that's been going up from, say, 150p and your share price has just lurched downwards, then you've got a different situation on your hands, and you at least need to stop and find out why this is happening.

Of course, the whole market may just be going downhill, in which case you may not have much to gain by jumping ship unless you're going to sell out into cash. But seeing these things always helps.

You can choose how long you want your moving average period to be, but 200 days is a popular choice. That's 200 trading days, of course, excluding weekends and bank holidays, so it's roughly 42 weeks in 'real money'.

# Directors Are Selling Their Shares

A company director selling a big batch of shares in her own company always looks bad. If she's one of the company's insiders, what nasty secrets does she know that are encouraging her to get out?

That's being a bit negative, of course, and a perfectly valid reason may exist. If a company's founder has put everything she's got into building up a business, why shouldn't she sell off a bit once she's turned it into a success and buy herself a well-earned new home or a Caribbean island with the proceeds? People forget too easily that the business itself is a very large part of what many business people own, and often they can't enjoy the fruits of their labours (or even retire) without cashing in some of their shareholdings.

But the stock market is rightly suspicious of director dealings. That's why every such sale or purchase is published in an official Stock Exchange Regulatory New Service statement, so that everybody can examine the evidence and make up their own mind.

A sale that happens just before the company goes into its annual 'closed period' is doubly suspicious. That's the month or so before the company's due to present its annual accounts and silence descends on the PR machine. If a director chooses the day before the closed period to make a big sale, then she's a fool because the stock market always suspects the worst and the share price is likely to plummet.

# The Sector Is Troubled, with No Obvious Upturn in Sight

Consider the pub trade in Britain, which got into bad trouble in mid-2007 after England and Wales introduced a ban on smoking in licensed premises. The nation's nicotine addicts were quickly persuaded to start buying their booze at Tesco and drink it at home instead of paying a landlord to pour it for them. Clear statistical evidence existed from Ireland and Scotland, which had already taken this step, that non-smoky pubs were good for families but bad for beer sales, but for some reason nobody saw the problem coming. Those who did, and who sold out of pub chains, saved themselves a 75 per cent fall in their shareholdings, and sometimes more.

Or consider the British steel industry, which is now effectively a subsidiary of the Indian steel industry. By the time that Tata Steel had bought up the Anglo-Dutch steel company known as Corus in 2007, the last vestiges of Britain's former steel operator, British Steel, which formed the main part of Coruis, were already struggling with a welter of problems. Not only were Corus's steel plants in Wales and the north of England getting rather long in the tooth, especially compared with leaner and more recently-equipped rivals in Poland, India, South Korea and China, they were also in the wrong part of the world to take advantage of the emerging-market boom in a material which was, after all, rather heavy and costly to transport. In 2009, with raw steel prices still falling, the prospects for British steel manufacturing plants was looking bleaker than ever.

Thus, it was mainly geography rather than politics which decided the fate of Britain's steel heritage in the 21st century. In America, however, the steel mills were just as antiquated (in fact they were worse), but they benefited from preferential government treatment that kept them viable for much longer than their European counterparts. There's no justice.

# The Company Depends Heavily on a Client Who's in Trouble

If your company depends heavily on selling stuff to another company that's in trouble of its own, or to a country that's experiencing an economic crisis, the stable door may have been open for too long for you to make a satisfactory exit – in which case you may have to sit tight and wait for a recovery. But if you can anticipate the problem in advance, then you're on the way to becoming a skilled and successful investor.

What about national markets that get holed below the waterline? Well, you could probably see in advance that cars weren't going to sell well once the oil price had trebled in 2007/2008. And by the time the stock market crisis of 2008 had kicked in, nobody was buying cars because people were simply trying to hold onto their savings! But unexpected scares and other temporary factors are harder to anticipate. Political factors can make conditions suddenly hard for an exporter to do its stuff.

How do you arm yourself with the materials you need to fight this problem? By reading as much as you can, as often as you can. The review sections in financial newspapers, the television news, and magazines such as *Time* or *The Economist* help to keep you abreast of current macro trends.

Chapter 3 has the lowdown on relating what you read to market realities.

# A Merger Approach Looks like Falling Through

Mergers are generally good news for investors, unless they're trying to make income from their investments rather than capital gains. You don't often find a merger going through for less money than the company's worth at the time (as measured by its market capitalisation, the stock market's favourite measure of company size. You calculate the market capitalisation by multiplying the share price by the number of shares in issue.). That's because the merger deal requires approval by a large majority of shareholders, and they're not likely to settle for anything less than they've already got.

But a share's price rising quite dramatically during the run-up to a takeover is common, especially if several bidders are competing with each other for the honour of acquiring the target company. Things can really get a bit overheated in these situations, and you often find that some investors (very sensibly) sell out to one of the bidders while the battle's still going on. In this way they can lock in their gains, just in case the whole situation comes unstuck.

Which it does, quite frequently. The collapse of a merger approach can do terrible damage to a share price, and the price is not unknown to fall below its level before the bidding war started. If you feel that the talks are going nowhere – or (horrors) if one of the bidders discovers something it doesn't like in the company's accounts (which it can scrutinise once the takeover process is under way) – then you may want to get out while the going's good.

I mentioned just now that mergers can be bad news for some income investors. Here's why. If you're already using all of your annual capital gains allowances but you're not earning enough to pay income tax, you're one of those people who prefers a steady income stream to a series of capital gains. An unwelcome takeover of your company dumps a pile of cash into your account, which attracts capital gains tax at the highest rate you personally qualify for. (At the time of writing this was 18 per cent, which was slightly less than basic-rate income tax.)

I talk more about merger approaches in Chapter 8.

# New Reporting Regulations Have Exposed a Pensions 'Black Hole'

Chapter 8 takes a look at the way recent legislation has changed how people look at company pension valuations. Generally, companies now have to post details about the state of their pension funds in their annual accounts, because the pensions they're running for their employees' futures represent a real liability for the future. They need to have made proper pension provisions in advance if they're not to be swamped by a massive surge of pension claims that they haven't got the cash to deliver when the time comes.

These days, for all the reasons I mention in Chapter 8, companies' pension pots are much more visible than they used to be. But because the pension plans include an awful lot of shares and other volatile investments, their values can rise and fall pretty dramatically from one year's end to the next. And that's where the 'black holes' come in. Many large and profitable corporations have found themselves with alarmingly large commitments of cash that they simply haven't got. Either they have to make up that cash somehow, or they find their share prices being driven down by bearish investors who figure that the pension shortfalls are going to erode their standing, and even their stability, in the future.

Not very surprisingly, companies are now fighting back by trying to reduce the numbers of their employees who qualify for 'defined benefit' pension plans (where the company owes them a certain amount of money in retirement, no matter what the situation is) and switching to 'defined contribution' pension systems, in which future pensioners have to take their chances and accept whatever the market happens to give them when they leave the company.

What can you do if you see a big black hole appearing? Well, first of all don't ignore it. Find out whether the problem's being caused simply by the temporary state of the stock market. Figure out whether the company's taking steps to restrict the growth of the problem, for example by shifting its workforce across to 'defined contribution' pensions that carry less risk.

Then, if you decide to sell, choose your moment carefully. Unlike a stock market shock, a pension shock probably emerges only very slowly, so the chances are you have plenty of time.

# A Recent Merger Doesn't Seem to Have Produced any Useful Synergies

Mergers are expensive, inconvenient, and sometimes divisive, and companies need to have pretty good reasons for going into them. The most important reason is that they can make some cost savings by combining two operations. So a paper manufacturing company may well save money by buying a forestry firm.

But in the 1970s and early 1980s a veritable flood of mergers took place that really didn't make much sense at all. The brick manufacturer Hanson bought up clothing retailers like United Drapery Stores, cigarette manufacturers like Imperial Tobacco, and even a couple of health supplement manufacturers. When Hanson tried (and failed) to buy Imperial Chemical Industries in 1991, people began to realise that this strategy showed no sense , and soon Hanson's share price crashed to the point where the group was quite lucky to survive at all. The era of conglomerates was over.

Except that it wasn't. In 1998 Germany's Daimler motor company bought America's Chrysler car maker, with fairly disastrous consequences for both companies. Whereas Daimler's focus had always been on up-market excellence at premium prices, Chrysler's model range was decidedly mass market, with relatively poor manufacturing standards. Most Chrysler cars were effectively unsellable in Europe, and this quickly became apparent. The synergies between the two companies were almost non-existent. Meanwhile Daimler's attempts to enforce German-style management methods on the somewhat more entrenched Chrysler workforce led to a series of industrial conflicts, which Daimler eventually resolved by selling Chrysler to a private equity company in 2007.

The DaimlerChrysler experience proved bruising and financially damaging for both companies. If you ever see two unlikely companies being forced together – a bank and an insurance company, a food manufacturer and a chain of chemists' stores, or an airport operator and an oil producer – think very hard about whether the marriage is likely to prove harmonious. And if you can see the glue coming unstuck in a company you already own, run.

# The Auditors Have Qualified the Company's Accounts

Problems don't get much worse than this. You might think it sounds like a good thing for the accounts to be qualified, but take my word for it, it means pretty much the opposite.

When the auditors qualify the accounts, it means at the very least that they haven't been able to substantiate every transaction the company claims to have made. And at the very worst, they want to distance themselves from what may turn out to be an iffy situation. When you hear that a major company has changed its auditors, you may want to do a little digging to see whether the auditor or the company was unhappy with the situation.

Corrections can happen at a lower level too. The regulators can occasionally insist that a company 'restates' its results, perhaps for a number of years going backwards. One British company was caught 'padding' its sales figures a few years back by encouraging its wholesalers to buy much more than they needed at the end of every trading year, – thus giving the impression that turnover was much healthier than it actually was. In that case, the results were backdated, the chief executive and the finance director resigned, and no further action was taken. But the stock market exacted a cruel revenge: the company's shares plummeted because everybody had lost confidence in its figures. Only after nearly five years and a big corporate restructuring did the company find its way back into favour.

Chapters 8 and 9 look at interpreting auditors' and regulators' reports and knowing how to respond.

# Chapter 21

# Ten Red-Hot Clues to an Opportunity

● ● ● ● ● ● ● ● ● ● ● ● ● ● ● ● ● ● ● ● ● ● ● ● ● ● ● ● ● ● ● ● ● ● ● ● ● ● ● ● ● ●

*A*lthough it's often hard to generalise about what makes a share a red-hot opportunity, there are certain signs that you really shouldn't ignore. Stop and examine them carefully, because although some of them will turn out to be red herrings, others will turn out to be the real deal.

Of course, some people insist that you can never find a truly undiscovered red-hot opportunity, because if it's genuine the market will already have spotted it and the bargain will have evaporated as soon as some 'expert' has bought into it ahead of you. I don't believe that, actually. Indeed, it puts me in mind of an old joke.

Two economists are walking down the street when one of them spots a £50 note lying on the pavement. 'Look,' says one of them. 'Somebody's dropped a £50 note!' 'Don't touch it,' says the other one, 'it's bound to be some sort of a scam. If it had been a genuine £50 note, somebody else would have picked it up already.' And so the two of them walk on up the road, leaving the banknote blowing around in the breeze.

And the moral? Somebody has always got to be the first to spot an opportunity. Who says it can't be you? Just be careful, though, that you keep your wits about you. And always be prepared to walk away if you're not completely happy.

# The Price/Earnings Ratio Is Below the Sector Average, but Rising

Having a high price/earnings ratio is very flattering for a company, of course, because the fact tells us that the market has a lot of faith in the company's prospects for the future. So much faith, in fact, that it's prepared to pay a higher-than-usual multiple of the present annual earnings when the investors buy their shares. (For a description of how the p/e earnings are calculated, see Chapter 5 or consult the glossary.) But a high p/e has a downside for you too, because a high p/e figure suggests that you have to wait longer than other investors before you see the fruits of your labours.

Much nicer to find a share that isn't commanding such a high p/e as its fellows in the market sector, but seems to be catching up fast.

You need to do a little extra research, of course. The stock market may not be efficient but it isn't often completely stupid, so something in the accounts may be limiting your company's potential. I'd want to find out what sort of debts the company was carrying and whether anything else that doesn't appear on the trading statements was overburdening it. Maybe it's issued a large number of options or warrants that may dilute its equity in future years. Or it may be relying particularly strongly on one particular customer, or one area of the market, for most of its business.

As long as the growth looks set to continue, and as long as you can say confidently that no booby-traps exist like the ones I've mentioned, a share with a low p/e ratio relative to its peers is always worth looking at. Try checking out the chat forums on the Internet to see whether anything's going on that you aren't aware of. And if you have any kind of paid-for Internet news access that may give you an edge, this is the time to use it.

# Like-For-Like Sales Are Up Strongly

If the company has bought up one of its competitors or started a whole new business division from scratch, then comparing this year's figure directly with last year's isn't either fair or realistic. Like-for-like figures strip out these distortions, and you can usually get them from the company's postings on the Stock Exchange Regulated News Service (the official news board). Interim trading statements also draw attention to them.

Did I say 'like for like sales', incidentally? What you really want are like-for-like profits, of course. But then again, a new acquisition can sometimes take a while to bed in, and the same for a new operation to turn profitable, so the profit line not following the sales line exactly isn't necessarily a problem. The company is bound to incur transitional expenses and teething troubles that delay the curve a little.

A big rise in like-for-like profits doesn't protect you from disappointment if your company's operating in a particularly fashion-conscious area where things are likely to change dramatically from one year's end to the next – computer games, for example – or in a sector like oil or mining where prices can be very volatile. But taken in conjunction with other considerations, such a rise can point you in the right direction.

# Brokers' Recommendations Improve

If you have access to a set of brokers' reports for each share you're interested in, then you probably find that they're set out in an onscreen format that tells you how many brokers think the share is a buy this month, how many think it's a strong sell, and how many are declaring it a hold. Plus, with a bit of luck, you have a similar set of tables from last month, and two months before that, and six months before that. In effect, you're getting a stop-motion animation picture that tells you the whole story about how the share's perceived prospects are changing.

Do the brokers ever get things wrong? Of course they do. They're only human, and sometimes they get a bit carried away by each other's enthusiasm. But generally speaking, the more brokers you're looking at, the less likely they are overall to be out by a very big margin. A website that compares the opinions of 15 brokers is much more reliable than one that only has one or two. And if your company's very small – for instance if it's listed on the Alternative Investment Market (AIM) rather than the main stock market – you may find that the only broker available is the company's 'house broker', which is hardly unbiased when it gives you its opinions.

Do rest assured, though, that for larger companies you have a good deal of statutory protection from false or deliberately misleading assessments by brokers. They'd be in big trouble if they tried to get you all excited about a share that they didn't think much of – but needed you to buy, because they had lots to get rid of. People have gone to jail for less than that.

All things being equal, the availability of online brokers' analyst reports is one of the greatest contributions the Internet has made to personal investing so far. You always need to do your own research too, but as long as you regard the reports as a shorthand set of pointers towards possible investment decisions, they're useful.

# The Company Is about to Be Promoted into the FTSE-100

Talk about self-fulfilling prophecies! You probably already know that the FTSE-100 index is composed of the 100 largest companies in the stock market, measured in terms of their market capitalisation. But something rather weird tends to happen in the twilight zone between, say, the 99th position and the 102nd position. As soon as the company in 101st position gets 'into the zone', its shares start to put on value, so that with a bit of luck it overtakes Number 100 and makes it into the index. There it stays until the new Number 101 fights back and overtakes it again. The jockeying and jostling within what I call the zone is continuous, and the battle's often viciously fought.

Why does this happen? A company in the FTSE-100 is massively more attractive to the stock market than a company that's sitting just outside it. Loads of funds are only allowed to invest in FTSE-100 companies, for a start, and they all want to have a piece of anything that enters the magic century at the top of the market. (By the same token, they're all forced to sell as soon as the company drops out again.)

Then you have so-called FTSE tracker funds, whose managers don't even have a choice about whether to buy the company's shares. Instead, they're literally forced to buy in as soon as a company enters the select Footsie club. So as soon as a company gets close to the magic 100th position they're all getting their chequebooks out.

As you may expect, this situation causes quite a lot of disruption to the market. If every fund manager tried to buy the new entrant's shares on the day it actually entered the FTSE-100 index, chaos would ensue and not enough shares would be available. The prices would be all over the place.

So the stock market does something rather sensible. It issues an advance report, at regular intervals, that tells everyone which companies are due to be promoted to the FTSE-100 and which ones demoted. You can find these advance warnings on the FTSE's website (www.ftse.com); go to 'Indices', then 'Index Changes'. Always worth a look.

# *The Economic Cycle Is Moving to Favour Companies like Your Target*

Here the trick is not so much to buy the shares, but to figure out which sectors are going up in the world and which ones are about to come down.

I talk in Chapter 3 about the importance of business cycles, which are one of the most important factors that determine how an industry's fortunes are likely to change. (For instance, smaller companies suffer disproportionately during recessions because interest rates go up at the same time as their markets are shrinking. But by the same token, they tend to shoot ahead once the recovery gets established.) And Chapters 3 and 13 explain, commodity prices tend to move in long-term cycles that move entire market sectors in pretty predictable ways.

You can't necessarily time the market to perfection, of course. Buying and selling shares (or other investments) at exactly the right moments in history is something that's best left to other people with finely honed instincts, iron constitutions, and bottomless wallets.

Consider a 'top-down' approach to investing. Look at the macro-environment – the politics, the business atmosphere, the general state of the economy – and then pick your market sectors accordingly. Only when you've done that do you set about selecting the companies you're actually going to invest in. Or, if you prefer, you can simply buy an investment trust or an exchange-traded fund (ETF; see Chapter 14) that shadows a whole market sector on your behalf. Task accomplished.

Assuming you're not going for a fund, how do you select the companies to buy from within your chosen sector? I'm inclined to use the price/earnings ratios and the dividend covers as my starting point (Chapter 5 covers both). But others prefer to look at the details of how their businesses are running and make much more finely tuned, business-oriented decisions about which companies to buy and which ones to leave waiting on the short list for another day. The decision's up to you.

# The Underlying Macro-environment Is Improving

Having an improving economic climate isn't always a guaranteed recipe for making a successful investment, but that situation certainly helps. If other share buyers are feeling less worried about credit squeezes and stay-at-home consumers, less chance exists of you being unable to get the quantities of shares you want at the price you want them. And less worry that you're not able to sell them easily at the right price when you eventually decide to.

Generally, smaller companies tend to enjoy recoveries the most. Consumer products, especially 'discretionary items' like sofas, televisions, and home improvements, also tend to pick up strongly.

One group of people who don't welcome a better economic environment are bond buyers. In theory at least, an economic recovery tends to suck money out of the 'low-risk' bond market by encouraging investors to sell up and switch their cash into equities instead – something that's bound to be bad for bond prices in general. You also have the problem that an economic recovery's often accompanied by a slight increase in inflation, which is the bond investor's enemy. As I explain in Chapter 6, bond investors worry that the fixed interest yields on their bonds may not amount to a hill of beans if the inflation rate ever gets too high – and so the capital value of their bonds (the actual price they can get by selling them) is likely to suffer because other investors don't want to buy them either.

But, providing that the economic recovery can remain free of higher inflation, both sides of the investment game can win.

# The Share Price Has Been Unfairly Devastated

Nothing's better than finding a share that doesn't deserve to be lying in the gutter, but it's there anyway and it's going cheap. Three or four times in the last ten years, I've come across healthy companies that have been smashed down in this way, mainly because they've been lumped together with other companies in the same sectors that have been punished for very genuine offences. Sometimes you can make 50 per cent in a few months by simply waiting for the market to come to its senses – sometimes even more.

Why do these things happen? Partly because fund managers are busy people who don't always have the time to stop and examine the fine details of a situation as closely as they may. So the babies get thrown out with the bathwater when the whole sector is sold out. This is especially true with index tracker funds (see Chapter 14), which often lop 20 per cent off the price of everything in a market sector because that's simpler than differentiating finely between different companies.

At other times, a company makes a genuine misjudgement that elicits a vast over-reaction from a panicky market. I remember seeing one company that had almost £2 billion taken off its market capitalisation because it very foolishly bought a useless, deadbeat subsidiary worth about £500 million. It could have written off four subsidiaries like that, closed them down, and simply walked right away from them all before its actions justified a £2 billion markdown. In practice, it sold off the troublesome subsidiary for a £300 million loss and its share price instantly rocketed back to normal levels.

These situations don't happen very often, but when they do they're very profitable indeed for canny investors. Chapter 5 covers investing in shares.

# *Predators Are Circling the Company*

In practice, by the time you hear about a bid battle for a company, the chances are you're too late because everybody else has heard the same story and the share price has been marked up accordingly to the point where you may not make very much of a profit. But you can improve your chances of getting a takeover windfall just by keeping your antennae sharply tuned.

Oddly enough, some times do occur when great waves of takeover activity hit an entire market sector, and when you're in with a chance of a takeover windfall every time you buy any share in that sector. Some area of the business world always has too many of a particular kind of company, and a bit of market consolidation doesn't go amiss.

A few years ago, banking takeovers were making all the news. Then the water and electricity companies were swallowing each other up. By 2008 the focus had switched to small mining companies, which were being snapped up by larger miners who didn't have the time to dig new mines of their own. By 2015 it may be airlines or motor manufacturers or computer makers in the frame. If you can figure out first which sectors they are, you can get rich.

# The Company Has Announced a Technical Breakthrough

You may never experience anything better than the feeling of getting in on the ground floor when a company announces some amazing new discovery that's going to change the world and make its shareholders a lot of money. Unless, that is, you happen to have bought the shares the week before! In that case you've probably got yourself a bargain.

Technical discoveries are great for companies, because they attract media interest and get the company's name in the public domain. But be a bit careful with those industries where technical innovations tend to leapfrog each other and leave their rivals completely superseded. You may be laughing while your own company remains in the lead, but you're holding your head and moaning when somebody else announces something that leaves your company's products in the dust. If these sorts of industries interest you, think seriously about spreading your risks by buying a tracker fund or an investment trust that backs a whole group of these companies rather than just one. You often find that a discovery by one company attracts attention to its whole sector, so you may not surrender quite so much growth as you expect.

For pharmaceutical companies, the distance between developing a new product and actually getting it onto the market can be long and frustrating. Drug products are often forced to undergo years of testing before they're approved for use in many major markets, and you may easily find that some adverse effect nobody was expecting stops a promising drug in its tracks. If in doubt, hedge your bets by buying several contenders, because these sorts of products only rarely leapfrog each other in the way I've just described: even second-best drugs still sell well.

# The Company Earns Its Money in a Currency that's Set to Strengthen

You can get into trouble with some people by insisting that you can forecast big currency movements, even approximately. But all the evidence suggests that's true. If you're thinking of investing in a company that always benefits from selling to one other currency group somewhere in the world, then you've got a good reason for taking the state of the currency markets into account when you try to price up that company's shares.

For example, the US dollar lost almost 40 per cent of its value against the euro during the mid to late 2000s, mainly because the financial markets didn't have much faith in the way the US economy was being run. And, more specifically, because the trade deficit and the government budget deficit were both being allowed to run more or less out of control.

That meant, among other things, that German companies had a terrible time trying to sell European-manufactured cars and other machines to the Americans during those mid-decade years. US consumers just couldn't afford the exorbitant number of dollars that were now required to buy 10,000 euros' worth of European car. So they didn't. Instead, German companies had to set up their own manufacturing plants in the United States if they wanted to benefit from America's low manufacturing costs and sell the resulting products to other Americans.

If you were a British investor who bought shares in a German company during the same period, you'd have been laughing all the way to the bank – £1,000 worth of Siemens shares would have made you an additional £300 or so in sterling terms, even if Siemens' share price in euros hadn't budged an inch during that time.

China's vast exporting companies have done well in the last decade because their currency has been loosely 'pegged' to a basket of other currencies, which has made it unusually cheap. (That's to say, it's been kept within a limited range of divergence from the average of those other currencies.) But by the later years of the decade the signs were that the renminbi yuan would be allowed to strengthen by maybe 10–20 per cent. If you're invested in a company that buys things from China you'd probably worry about this, because the goods would soon cost 10–20 per cent more, and that isn't good for business. But if you bought shares in a Chinese company, you'd see all your capital returns boosted by 10–20 per cent instead. (Unless, that is, the appreciation of the currency completely flattened its export prospects.)

Either way, you can see why I encourage you in this book to take a wider view of the investing environment, and to think hard about buying some foreign stocks. Doing so is easy these days thanks to a better international trading environment, and it's flexible and safe too. ETFs (exchange-traded funds) and investment trusts give you some excellent ways of riding the macro-economic waves up and down. With a little luck, and a little skill, and a lot of newspaper reading, you can stay positioned correctly at all times to exploit the shifts in the global currency environment. Chapter 11 covers international investing.

# Appendix

# Glossary

• • • • • • • • • • • • • • • • • • • • • • • • • • • • • • • • • • • • • • • • • •

*T*he financial pages are a minefield of jargon: you need to have a working knowledge of the lingo to get you through to the other side unscathed. This glossary gives you explanations for over 100 terms you'll come across along the way.

**AIM:** The Alternative Investment Market, a more lightly-regulated division with the London Stock Exchange which is designed for smaller and growing companies.

**Annuity:** A permanent return from a one-off cash investment. Annuities often form the main payout mechanisms for pension funds after retirement.

**AER (Annual Equivalent Rate):** A tightly-defined representation of the true interest rate that you can expect to receive on a cash investment. Because all AERs are calculated in the same way, they make it easier to compare the various rates on offer.

**APR (Annual Percentage Rate):** Similar in spirit to AERs, but directed toward borrowers rather than investors A tightly-defined representation of the true interest rate that you can expect to pay on a loan, etc. As with AERs, APRs make it easier to compare the rates on offer.

**Arbitrage**: The practice of buying stocks, bonds, currencies etc in one kind of market and then selling them another market, in the hope of exploiting a difference between the prices quoted in those markets.

**Balance Sheet:** One of the three main parts of a company's financial statements. The balance sheet shows the company's assets and sets them against its liabilities to produce a figure known as the Net Asset Value.

**Bear:** Strictly speaking, an investor who sells a security today in the hope of buying it back more cheaply later on. But the term is more generally used to mean an investor who thinks the markets are headed downwards.

**Bid-Offer Spread:** The difference between the bid and offer prices of a share or a trust. That is to say, between the price which you'd pay if you were buying it and the price you'd get if you were selling it instead.

**Blue Chip:** A large and solid company which is generally chosen for its stable earnings and its consistent performance. Many investment trusts seek out blue-chip companies in preference to smaller and more volatile ones.

**Bonds:** Debt securities (i.e. loan instruments) which are issued by governments and large companies as a way of raising capital. Traditionally, most bonds have entitled their holders to a fixed rate of interest for a fixed number of years, at the end of which they are redeemed at face value by the borrower. Modern bonds can be much more varied and complex, however.

**Book Value:** The value of the company's assets, as set out in its accounts – but the term is often used to exclude intangibles like brands or patents. This is useful because it gives the stock market an idea of what the company's assets would fetch if they had to be sold off in a hurry.

**Broker (see Stockbroker):** The intermediary who buys and sell your shares on your behalf, and who may then manage your portfolio for an additional fee. Some brokers offer full advice services, while others restrict themselves to merely buying and selling and charge cheaper prices.

**Bull:** Generally, an investor who buys a security in the hope of selling it later on at a higher price. More generally, the term is used to mean a stock market optimist.

**Bullion:** Gold, in all its forms. But mostly in its physical form. The term is sometimes stretched to include silver and platinum. (But not gemstones.)

**Call Option:** An option certificate which gives you the right to buy a security at a later date, at a given price. The opposite of a Put Option, which entitles you to sell.

**Capital Gains Tax (CGT):** A government tax which is charged on the capital gains (appreciation profits) which you make by trading a share or a mutual fund. The tax is usually paid only when you 'realise' your profits by selling up, and it falls in respect of the same financial year. At the time of writing, the first £10,000 or so of capital gains was normally exempt from CGT – as were all gains achieved through an Individual Savings Account.

**Capitalisation Issue:** Normally a rights issue, which aims to bolster a company's balance sheet by offering new shares in addition to the company's existing shares.

**Chinese Wall:** An artificial division that stops two departments of a big investment company from comparing notes in a way that might give them an unfair advantage over outsiders. By stopping one side of the business from knowing what the other side is up to, the Chinese Wall prevents malpractice and manipulation.

**Closed Period:** The period just before the publication of a company's results, during which its investors are not allowed to trade their shares and no significant financial information is released to the public.

**Closed-Ended Fund:** A managed fund which has a fixed number of shares that cannot be varied once they've all been sold. This means that the only way the fund can grow is by investing its money well. Unit trusts, on the other hand, are 'open-ended' and can issue any number of new units as required to meet demand.

**Commodity:** Strictly speaking, any basic product where the price of one lorryload of goods will be the same as another lorryload of the same type of goods. They are all regarded as being functionally identical, and therefore as having the same value. In practice, the term is usually used to describe minerals, metals, some types of farm produce and precious metals.

**Consolidation:** A consolidation is the process by which one company takes over another, so as to reduce the number of players in the market and improve efficiency. A consolidation issue, however, is when a company replaces a large number of shares with low values for a smaller number of shares with bigger values.

**Corporate Bonds:** Bonds which are issued by companies rather than by governments. Unlike government bonds, most of which are unlikely to go bust, the issuers of corporate bonds are regarded as fallible. So they generally have to pay higher interest rates to compensate their investors for this possibility.

**Coupon:** A commitment which the issuer of a bond makes, whereby it promises to pay its owners a regular fixed annual payment throughout the fixed lifetime of the bond. The coupon rate is expressed as a percentage of the face value of the bond.

**Day Trading:** The practice of sitting at a computer screen and making short-term speculative trades throughout the day, in the hope of turning a modest but reliable profit. Old-style day traders cash in their entire holdings every evening; however, this tradition is now dying out.

**Dead Cat Bounce:** The phenomenon whereby even the most fatally wounded share will probably bounce back a little bit once it eventually stops falling, for technical reasons. A dead cat bounce should not be confused with a sign that the share is still alive!

**Derivatives:** Strictly speaking, a derivative is any investment instrument whereby the value of the investment is determined by the performance of some other asset – perhaps a commodity, or maybe a financial instrument like a share or even a whole stock market index. Futures, options, warrants and swaps are all types of derivatives.

**Discount:** The amount by which the amount you pay for an investment trust undershoots the actual value of its underlying asset values. An overshoot, by comparison, would be called a premium. Most investment trusts carry discounts rather than premiums, because the market needs to deduct the likely cost of a quick liquidation from the assets if it is to properly value the fund.

**Dividend:** Part of a company's after-tax profits which it distributes to its shareholders as a thank-you for their loyalty, usually once or twice a year. Some companies don't issue dividends, preferring to keep the cash within the company in order to grow the business instead. Occasionally, if there's been a cash windfall, the company may also declare a special dividend.

**EBITDA:** Earnings Before Interest, Taxes, Debts and Amortisation. A rough-and-ready formula that shows you how the company's day-to-day operations are performing if you strip out all the irksome costs of buying and maintaining assets or paying taxes. Treat with caution.

**EPIC:** Short for Exchange Price Input Computer. The term is still widely used to describe the unique identifier code that every listed equity investment has. Nowadays, however, that term should really be replaced with the term Tradable Instrument Display Mnemonic (TIDM), which effectively means exactly the same thing.

**Equity:** The part of a company's capital that consists of shares, usually ordinary shares, as distinct from the bonds, bank loans and other debts that it might also be using to fund its growth. To all intents and purposes. The term 'equities' means the same thing as 'stocks' and 'shares'.

**Ex-Dividend:** A company has gone 'ex-dividend' when the day arrives on which its investors have become entitled to receive their yearly or half-yearly dividends. It is not unknown for share prices to fall on ex-dividend day, because the value of the dividend has effectively been 'stripped out' by the grateful shareholders, leaving only a divi-less share for others to buy. Until the next ex-dividend day, that is.

**Execution-Only:** The cheapest and most frill-free way to buy or sell a share. An execution-only broker will trade your shares but won't offer any advice or other value-added facilities.

**Exposure:** The total amount that you stand to lose if everything goes belly-up. Especially important to 'highly geared' or 'highly leveraged' investors. If you've bought £1,000 worth of futures contracts on a 10 per cent margin, it doesn't matter that you've only had to lay down £100 in advance: the £1,000 is still what you'll owe if the worst-case scenario should arise.

Fund managers also use the term in the positive sense of 'getting exposure' to a certain range of market risk – perhaps by buying a number of different shares within a sector so as adjust the balance of a collective portfolio in one direction or another.

**Financial Services Authority (FSA):** The independent official body which regulates the entire financial services industry in Britain. Its responsibilities range from setting out the rules for companies' public announcements to enforcing order among the market professionals. It also manages the ombudsman's offices which deal with complaints.

**Flotation:** The process by which a company gets onto the stock market. This will generally mean that is issues news shares which it makes available to the public. Sometimes, however, the shares are 'privately placed' instead to a small group of professional backers.

**Free Float:** A company's 'free float' is an approximate estimate of how many of its shares are genuinely available to the public – as distinct from shares that are held by long-term investors and other interested parties who are unlikely ever to sell. The smaller the free float, the more likely it is that the shares may turn volatile when large numbers of investors scramble for a deceptively small number of available shares.

**FTSE™ 100:** The UK's most commonly-quoted index of London-listed shares. Essentially, it is calculated from the share prices of the exchange's 100 largest companies, in terms of their market capitalisation. There are literally hundreds of other FTSE indices, however.

**Fund:** A collective investment where many different people pool their money to buy a portfolio of shares, bonds or other securities. The fund will be managed by a professional.

**Futures:** An agreement whereby you undertake to buy (or sell) a given product, at a specified future date and at a pre-determined price. Futures are often said to be 'geared', because you don't put down all your money until the last moment.

**Gearing ('Leveraging'):** Some investments, such as futures, covered warrants, and options, allow you to multiply your chances of striking it rich by requiring you to put down only a small part of the amount you want to invest up-front. If all goes well, you can then sell your investments at their full price even though you've only paid for part of them, leaving you heavily in profit. But this multiplier effect goes into reverse if your investments should make a loss rather than a gain.

Many investors also talk about 'gearing' or 'leveraging' their investments by borrowing money which they then invest in the financial markets. For this kind of gearing to work, they have to make a better cash profit from their investments than their loans are costing them.

**Gilts or Gilt-Edged Securities**: Bonds that have been issued by the British Government. Gilts and a UK-only phenomenon: in America they'd be called treasury bonds.

**Growth Stock:** A stock that's been bought because it's expected to grow especially fast, albeit at higher than usual levels of risk.

**Guaranteed Equity Bond:** Actually a misnomer. These products aren't bonds at all but investment funds, which invest your cash in stock market-related instruments, and which promise to pay you a return that relates to the growth of the stock market during a fixed period of time. The usual deal is that you'll get 100 per cent of your money back if the market should fall instead of rise; however, there have been some notoriously devious exceptions in the past.

**Hedge:** A hedge is a manoeuvre by which an investor seeks to offset the risk that he's taking in one direction with a counterbalanced risk in the other direction. If he's bought a lot of a company's shares, he might insure himself against a sharp downturn in their price by taking out a put option which will pay out handsomely if his worst fears should come true. Responsibly handled hedging strategies create stability.

**Hedge Funds:** Hedge funds are similar to other managed funds, except that their managers are completely free agents who are not subject to any of the normal rules as to what classes of investments they may pursue (cash, bonds, bullion, currencies, etc).

The other important point about hedge funds is that they seek to obtain an 'absolute return' – by which they mean that they aim to make money regardless of which way the market moves. They achieve this largely through the use of derivatives, and by 'shorting' (selling investments that they do not yet own, in the hope of being able to buy them back more cheaply later on).

**Index:** A performance measure for an entire stock market, or perhaps for a subset of that market. Frequently used as the basis for derivative contracts.

**Individual Savings Account:** A tax-efficient form of investment that is available only to UK-resident investors. Individuals may make in-payments up to a certain specified cash limit in any year, and their investments are then protected in perpetuity from capital gains tax while also enjoying certain concessions against income tax.

**Insider Trading:** The practice of buying or selling an investment while in possession of market-sensitive' information that has not been released to the wider public. Insider trading is a serious offence which commonly carries a jail sentence.

**Interbank Lending Rates:** The interest rates that banks charge each other when they lend each other money. This will normally be less than they would charge to private individuals, but probably more than the Bank of England's own MPC lending rate.

**Investment Trust:** A type of collective investment fund, whereby a listed company is set up especially to own a portfolio of securities which are then bought and sold on behalf of its shareholders. Unlike a unit trust, an IT is 'closed-ended', meaning that it can issue no more shares once it's been fully subscribed: instead, its shares rise and fall like those of any other company, in accordance with the level of market demand.

**Junk Bonds (see High-Yield Bonds):** Junk bonds were originally issued in the 1970s and 1980s to fund speculative hostile takeovers and other high-risk ventures – the deal being that if the ventures succeeded, the investors would get improbably large returns on their money. But they if the ventures failed, the junk bonds would become almost worthless.

These days the term has shifted so that it describes any corporate bond that doesn't make so-called 'investment-grade' status. (Meaning that the issuing company or government isn't considered to be even reasonably close to offering the level of investor protection that a solid western government or blue-chip company would provide.) These junk bonds have to pay substantially bigger 'spreads' of interest over other, more creditworthy borrowers.

**Keynesian Economics:** Expressed extremely simply, the defining quality of the Keynesian theory is that a government can sometimes stimulate economic activity by increasing the money supply – perhaps by initiating large employment-generating projects, even if it means borrowing too much money for comfort. And that the resulting stimulus to business will make the probable inflationary risks that result seem worthwhile.

Keynesians are more or less diametrically opposed in their views to monetarists, who believe that careful metering of the money supply is paramount to the stability of economic growth, and that all economic policy should proceed from that principle.

**Leverage:** See 'Gearing'

**Limit Order:** Investors can set limit orders with their stockbrokers, whereby the brokers receive the authority to buy or sell shares on their behalf as soon as the market prices move within a certain band. Thus, if I want 1,000 Marks & Spencer shares but I'm not prepared to pay more than 500p each for them, I can instruct him to buy them if (and when) the piece ever reaches that level. I can also instruct him to sell my Lloyds TSB shares as soon as the market price moves higher than, say, 450p.

**Liquidity:** Liquidity is a term used by the financial markets to describe the ease with which you can trade a security on the market. If you want to sell a share but there aren't many people interested in buying it, we say that its liquidity is low and that you might have to accept a lower price for it. But if you've got shares in a blue chip company it's practically certain that you'll be able to unload them to somebody without difficulty, because the pool of potential investors is so much bigger.

**Listed Company:** A listed company is any company whose securities have been formally approved to be traded on the Stock Exchange. To achieve this approval, it must have released at least some of its shares to the public, and it has to abide by strict rules that govern its conduct.

**London International Financial Futures and Options Exchange (LIFFE):** London's foremost exchange for trading in futures, options and so forth. LIFFE is a subsidiary of the EuroNext European stock exchange group, which in turn is linked to the NYSE Group – the owner of the New York Stock Exchange.

**Long:** Going long on a share is when you're buying it with a view to holding it – as distinct from going short, which is when you merely borrow the share from somebody else in order to sell it quickly and hopefully buy it back later at a cheaper price, thus making a profit. Generally, a long investor expects the share to rise. A short investor, by comparison, is sure that it will fall.

**Margin:** You're buying shares (or futures contracts, or whatever) 'on margin' when you're only paying a small fraction of the proper price up front. The deal is that you will be required to settle up in full at a later date when the transaction is completed. Margin investing is a key form of geared investing, and it's not recommended for beginners because of the abnormally high risk. See 'Gearing'.

**Market Capitalisation:** Market capitalisation is generally accepted as the most reliable measure of a company's size, even though it relates only to the stock market's perceived value of the company and is not actually based on any firm computation involving the company's business record or its assets. You calculate the market capitalisation figure by multiplying the current share price by the number of shares that are currently in issue.

**Market Maker:** A market maker provides a supply of available shares in a company, which will be made available to your broker if he wants to buy them on your behalf. In practice, there are very few independent market makers left – nearly all of them are subsidiaries of broking firms. In principle, market makers are competing against each other on price through the Stock exchange's automated online bidding system; however, with very small companies in the AIM market there might be only one market maker trading in the shares.

**Monetarism:** Essentially, monetarists hold that the only sound way to grow an economy is to control the money supply so that it stays closely related to the underlying rate of economic growth. In this, they differ radically from Keynesians, who believe that it is sometimes desirable for a government to pour new money into a stagnating economy for the sake of stimulating growth.

**Monetary Policy Committee (MPC):** The panel of independent experts at the Bank of England who meet for two days every month to determine the interest rates available to British banks. In so doing, they effectively control the supply of credit in the UK – an essential element of their work toward their fiscal objective of reconciling Britain's inflationary risks with its economic growth.

**Mutual Fund:** This used to be an American-only term, but these days it's being heard more frequently on this side of the Atlantic. A mutual fund is any kind of collective investment scheme that pools investors' money so that it can then be invested in stocks, bonds or other securities. The fund will be professionally managed. Examples include investment trusts, unit trusts and pension funds.

**Net Asset Value (NAV):** The Net Asset Value of a company (or a mutual fund) is the total value of its assets, less the total of its liabilities. Many trusts, especially unit trusts, publish their NAV figures every day.

**Nominee Account:** A nominee account is any investment account where somebody else holds and administers the shares on your behalf. Although, strictly speaking, it's the nominee whose name is on the share certificate, and who may exercise any votes on your behalf, the law is clear that the 'beneficial rights' still belong to you and cannot be removed.

**OEICs:** Open-Ended Investment Companies. OEICs are a modern form of mutual funds, developed on the initiative of the European Union, which combine the qualities of both unit trusts and investment trusts. They are 'open-ended', which means that they can expand and contract according to demand – whereas a conventional investment trust is 'closed-ended' and can't change the number of shares it has issued.

**Offer Price:** The price that the seller is asking for the shares he wants to sell you (or the units, in the case of a unit trust). As distinct from the bid price, which is the price that you will offer him. The 'bid-offer spread' between the two can sometimes be quite large.

**Open-Ended Fund:** Open-ended funds can issue as many units (or shares) as they like at any time. Instead of being dictated by the laws of supply and demand, like the price of an ordinary share, the price of these units (or shares) will always remain close to the Net Asset Value.

**Option:** An option is a derivative which allows you the guaranteed right to buy or sell a security at a fixed price, usually within a specified period of time. It does not actually oblige you to buy the security – you can walk away and write off the option if the price is wrong when the time comes.

**Ordinary Shares:** The most common form of share in the UK. Ordinary shareholders have equal voting rights for each share they hold, and they may also be entitled to dividends, which are their share of the company's profits. The parity rules might be slightly different for some non-UK companies.

**Over the Counter (OTC) Market:** The OTC is an informal market for trading shares in companies that aren't listed on the London Stock Exchange. As such, it's hardly regulated at all, and it should be considered high-risk.

**Penny Shares:** Generally, penny shares are shares in companies with very low market capitalisations, so that their shares quite literally cost only pennies to own. Often they'll be companies that have fallen from grace in the past and which still hold out the tempting possibility of surging back, thus making their shareholders rich. The vast majority of penny shares will never recover; however, a few will always buck the trend in spectacular fashion. Suitable for hobbyists and gamblers, but not really an investment strategy for the long term.

**Pound Cost Averaging:** When share prices fall, most investors either sell them or sit tight and do nothing. Pound cost averaging, however, is where you undertake to invest a fixed amount every month whatever happens. So when prices fall, your fixed monthly investment simply buys you more shares for your money. Conversely, when prices rise it will get you fewer shares. Mathematical studies show that a disciplined policy of pound cost averaging beats the market by 1 per cent-2 per cent a year over the long term. If you have a pension fund where you pay in a fixed amount of cash every month, you are already an expert in pound cost averaging.

**Preference Shares:** Preference shares are very different from ordinary shares. They are effectively a kind of loan to the company, whereby you are entitled to a fixed rate of income which will typically be much bigger than the dividends that ordinary share investors get. Plus, if the company goes bust you get preferential treatment in the distribution of its remaining assets.

**Premium:** (See also 'Discount' for the converse definition.) An investment trust's shares are said to be trading at a premium if the price per share is greater than the Net Asset Value per share.

**Price/Earnings Ratio (P/E ratio):** A measurement of how much confidence the market has in a company's shares, which is calculated by dividing its share price by its earnings per share. In effect, it's telling you how many years' worth of pre-tax profits (at current levels) you're paying for each share that you buy.

A high p/e ratio generally suggests that investors think the company's prospects are good. A low p/e, however, may mean either that its prospects are poor or else that this year's profits have fallen but the share price hasn't! Be careful.

**Put Option:** A put option is a document which entitles its holder to sell an underlying asset at a future date, at a specified price. Put options tend to be favoured by bears who think that prices are likely to fall, thus making their guaranteed prices look attractive.

**Rating Agencies:** Rating agencies are specialised companies which earn their money by assessing the creditworthiness of governments or other companies (especially ones which issue corporate bonds). The bond markets are heavily dependent on their assessments when they decide how to price these bonds. The marjet-leading agencies include Standard & Poor's, Moody's and Fitch IBCA.

**Redemption Date:** The date on which a bond is due to be redeemed in full at its original face value. This is the day when the entitlement to a fixed annual income also stops. Generally, the closer a bond gets to its redemption date, the closer its price will get to the face value. (See also 'Yield Curve')

**Rights Issue:** A company that needs to raise more cash may decide to declare a rights issue, in which it invites its existing shareholders to buy additional shares in the company, usually at a discount to their normal value. Rights issues tend to be unpopular with shareholders, because they feel that they're being strong-armed into investing more cash in the company than they might perhaps want. If the rights issue doesn't attract enough buyers, the shares will be left with the issue's underwriters, probably at a heavy discount. This is bad for publicity.

**RNS:** The Exchange's Regulatory Information Service, which regulates the way that information from listed companies gets disseminated to the market. The RNS officials make sure that all such information is fair and accurate; that nothing is omitted that the market might need to know; and that everybody gets the information at the exact same instant, so that nobody is at a disadvantage.

**S&P 500:** Standard & Poor's leading share index, which comprises the shares of 500 of America's largest US companies. Unlike the Dow Jones Industrial Average, which is a rather representative sample of only 30 giant companies, the S&P 500 can reasonably claim to reflect the industrial marketplace. Unlike the DJIA, it is also a 'weighted' index, in which the biggest companies count for more than the smaller ones.

**Scrip Issue:** A Scrip Issue ("capitalisation issue") is declared when a company wants to reduce the price of its shares so as to make them seem more affordable. By handing out, for instance, one free share for every two shares that its shareholders already own, it effectively cuts its share price by a third because the market automatically compensates for the dilution. Except that it often rises above that level! Exactly why is one of life's enduring mysteries. People just like buying cheap shares.

**Securities:** A general name for stocks, shares, bonds, funds and derivatives of all types.

**SEDOL:** The Stock Exchange Daily Official List code, a 7-digit reference that denotes a listed security. Sometimes a fund that doesn't have an EPIC (qv) or a TIDM denominator of its own will be known by its SEDOL number.

Settlement: When you buy or sell a stock, it takes a few days for the market to get the paperwork done and to complete the financial transactions. This is known as the settlement period.

**Share:** Any company's 'authorised share capital' (a rather nominal term) is divided up into a number of equal parts, which are known as shares. By owning one, you obtain statutory rights to an portion of the company's value, whatever that might be, and to an equal share of any proceeds that might come from its eventual dissolution. You also get a guaranteed right to an equal distribution of any dividends that it might decide to pay out.

That, at least, is true of ordinary shares. Preference shareholders receive bigger annual payouts which are permanently fixed, and they have a better claim on the proceeds of any winding-up process.

**Short:** A short position is what an investor takes when he or she expects a stock or a market to fall. Short investors might sell a warrant or take out a put option, or they may simply 'short' the stock by borrowing it and selling it in the fervent hope of being able to buy it back more cheaply later on.

**Stamp Duty:** A tax which the government levies on all share purchases (including investment trusts) – although not, at present, on share sales. There are many anomalies, especially with regard to Exchange Traded Funds, many of which are exempt from stamp duty even though they resemble shares.

**Stop-Loss:** A disciplined investing approach where you decide in advance that you'll sell if a share should ever fall below a certain level in relation to its best price during the time you've owned it. Thus, if you have a 20 per cent stop-loss and the price has doubled from 100p to 200p, you'll promise yourself to sell it if it ever drops back to 160p. In so doing you are 'locking in' most of your gains.

**Structured Products:** A mysterious name for a complex kind of tracker fund. Instead of investing your cash directly in the underlying securities, a structured product's manager uses the derivatives markets (mainly futures and options) to achieve a similar result through hedging, while also keeping his risks tightly contained. Most guaranteed equity bonds and exchange traded funds are structured products.

**Technical Analysis:** The rather controversial practice of trying to determining future market trends by looking at share performance charts. Technical analysts focus on the market's psychology, rather than on the underlying qualities of the share itself – in contrast to fundamental analysts, who focus solely on the figures and the corporate details.

**TIDM:** A method of identifying companies by three or four letter names. Has now taken over from the old EPIC system (qv).

**Tracker fund:** A mutual fund that aims to exactly equal the performance of a share index – or, occasionally, a commodity. The fund might do this by investing a carefully-proportioned amount of cash in each share within the index, but nowadays the fund managers prefer to hedge through the futures markets in order to achieve the same result (see 'Structured Products'). Management fees tend to be low, because there are no active decisions being taken – instead, the computers decide everything.

**Trust:** An arrangement whereby one or more people (trustees) are empowered to run the investments belonging to somebody else. Trusts are a binding legal arrangement with heavy responsibilities on the trustees.

**Underwriting:** When new shares are first issued, the issuer needs to know what will happen if they aren't fully taken up by the market. An underwriter is paid to guarantee that it will buy anything that's left over after the sale – usually at a discounted price.

**Unit Trust:** Unit trusts are 'open-ended funds' (qv), where investors pool their cash so that it can be invested in a portfolio of securities by a manager. The trust will then issue so-called units to its investors, instead of shares. The advantage of an open-ended arrangement is that the manager can constantly adjust the number of units to the level of investor demand. This means, in effect, that the unit price is always tied closely to the Net asset value (NAV) of the fund. (There is no tension between supply and demand.)

**Value Investing:** A value investor is someone who looks out for shares that have been priced unreasonably cheaply, in relation to their 'intrinsic worth' (as defined by their fundamentals). He then buys them up in the hope that their prices will revert to the historical norm. There are many styles of value investing, and fashions tend to come and go: for instance, some people prefer to back large companies, which will often pay hefty dividends, while others seek their fortunes in smaller companies with greater growth potential. Famous value investors have included Benjamin Graham (who is normally credited with inventing the concept) and more recently Warren Buffett, the owner of Berkshire Hathaway and the world's richest man.

**Volatility:** Investors can learn a lot about a share by measuring its volatility – the amount by which its price jumps about in response to daily events. A highly volatile share is probably unsuitable for long-term investors but perfect for day traders and hedge fund managers who can profit from every twitch in the price. The world's most prominent volatility index is the VIX in Chicago, which aims to track the market's expectations of volatility on the American S&P 500 stock market over the next 30 days. For obvious reasons, this is also known as the Fear Index.

**Warrants:** Warrants are documents which give their holders the right to buy a share or a bond at a fixed price, and from a certain date onwards. If the security's daily price goes higher than the warrant's fixed price, it will be worth buying at the fixed price. If not, the warrant holder can simply walk away or sell his warrant to another investor.

**Yield:** The yield from a share is the effective return that you could reckon to earn from its dividends if you were to buy it at today's share price. Well, almost. It's usually calculated by dividing the historical dividend into the current share price – which is an odd mis-match, if you think about it. Some people choose to base their calculations on the anticipated dividend during the current year, which probably gives a more useful figure.

**Yield Curve:** During the early years of a bond's life, its yield (as reflected in the price that it commands) will probably vary quite a lot from the 'coupon' – the fixed-rate interest payment that it promises to pay to its investors each year. But as the bond gets closer to its redemption date, its yield will always revert back toward the coupon return. The yield curve is a graphic representation of how the returns look at any given time for bonds of different maturities.

# Index

## • A •

'absolute return' policy, 257
ADVFN
  debt breakdowns from, 105
  discussion forum, 69
  overview, 280–281
  share-filtering system, 69
  for valuing companies without
    profits, 159
Alternative Investment Market (AIM)
  defined, 341
  free float in, 181
  oil drillers, explorers, and producers
    in, 233
  online resources, 69
  value investing in, 68–69
amortisation effect, 137–138
announcement date for dividends, 174
Annual Equivalent Rate (AER), 138, 341
Annual Percentage Rate (APR),
    137–138, 341
annual reports, 291–292. *See also*
    company accounts
annuity, defined, 341
arbitrage, 341
Arthur Anderson (Enron accounting
    firm), 182
asset allocation
  adjusting the balance, 316
  assessing your life situation for,
    315–316
  for bonds, 109
  capital gains versus taxes, 317
  debt considerations, 318
  defined, 315
  for foreign shares, 200–201
  herd follower versus maverick
    approach, 320–321
  liquidity considerations, 318
  managing for another, 317
  professional help for, 320
  for retirement versus fun, 321
  risk tolerance issues, 80, 322
  for trusts, 320
assets. *See also* market capitalisation
  on balance sheet, 299
  current versus long-term, 102
  debt ratio to, 102
  debtors as, 299
  depreciation, 165
  fixed asset valuations, 165–169
  intangibles, 161–162
  with licensed trade, 168–169
  property valuation, 165–167

## • B •

'B' shares, 43
balance sheet
  defined, 341
  example, 297–298
  interpreting, 299–300, 312–313
  liabilities on, 299
  liquidity ratio figured from, 299–300
  market capitalisation not related to, 97
  pension liabilities in, 169–171, 294
  purpose of, 299
  retained earnings on, 300
  rights issues reflected in, 104
  shareholders' equity on, 300
  as snapshot, 297
  total equity on, 300
  trade and other receivables on, 299

banks. *See also* cash investments;
  financial institutions; investment
  banks
 dividend yields from, 99–100
 fines and fees by, 138–140
 Payment Protection Insurance on
  loans, 139
 p/e ratios for, 27, 83
 safety of deposits in, 134
 shopping around for, 139–140
*Barclays Capital Equity Gilt Study*, 106
base metal commodities, 241
basket warrants, 217
BBC website
 international news from, 44
 oil price information from, 231
 overview, 278–279
bear raids, 185
bears
 bulls versus, 64
 defined, 64, 341
 Elliott Wave theory on, 194
 macro-economic influences for, 64
 shorting by, 63
 synergy with bulls, 62
benchmark bonds, 113, 119–120
bid price, 24
bid-offer spread, 341
Big Bang revolution (1986), 15, 38, 39, 67
Bigcharts website, 50
bit-of-everything investing, 73
'blind' trusts, 76
blogs
 cautions about using, 13, 156, 282
 Data Explorers shorting blog, 186
 Motley Fool blog style, 136
 overview, 281–282
Bloomberg website, 50, 230
blue chip company, 342
bonds. *See also specific kinds*
 *Barclays Capital Equity Gilt Study* on, 106
 benchmark, 113, 119–120
 buying, 113–114, 116–117

 capital gains on, 111
 cash investments versus, 111, 133
 corporate, 121–124, 343
 defined, 109
 described, 12, 342
 direct ownership of, 74–75
 *Financial Times* price listing, 117–119
 foreign, 114–115
 gilts, 345
 government, 114–121
 guaranteed income, 259–264, 346
 interest rate considerations, 133
 inverted yield curve, 112
 junk (high-yield), 124–127, 347
 National Savings and Investments,
  114, 132
 nominee accounts for, 75–76
 price fluctuations of, 110, 111, 113
 ratio in your portfolio, 109
 reasons for investing in, 108–109
 redemption date, 109, 110, 351
 relationship between yield and price,
  117, 119
 reliability of, 107–108, 109, 113
 stocks compared to, 106, 107–108
 variable meanings for, 133
 yield curve of, 112, 354
 yield interest taxed for, 115
 yield of, 110–113, 121–122
bonus share distributions, 176–177
book value
 defined, 342
 price to book value (PTBV), 97, 160, 299
BP Statistical Review of World
  Energy, 229
brand names, valuing, 162, 294
breakouts, 191–192
Brent Blend, 232
brokers. *See* stockbrokers
broker's analysts
 changes since the 1980s, 14, 15
 reports, 287–289
broker's reports, 333

Buffett, Warren (investment expert), 51, 56, 71–73, 95, 182
bullion, 342
bulls
  bears versus, 64
  defined, 62, 342
  Elliott Wave theory on, 194
  macro-economic influences for, 62
  market timers versus, 64
  optimists versus, 62
  synergy with bears, 62
Bush, George (US president), 55
business cycle
  in developing countries, 56–58
  importance of, 56
  using to your advantage, 58, 335
_BusinessWeek_, 285
buying shares. _See also_ share prices
  checking five-year period before, 309
  dummy portfolios for learning about, 87–88
  free float concerns, 180
  information to check before, 87
  opportunities, clues for, 331–339
  before takeovers, 164
  unfairly devastated, 336–337
  warning signs of trouble, 323–330
buy-outs. _See_ takeover
buzzwords, 58–60

## • C •

call options, 218, 342. _See also_ options
call warrants, 217
Canadian Oil Sands project, 228
capital gains considerations for asset allocation, 317
capital gains tax (CGT)
  defined, 342
  investment decisions based on, 86
  ISA considerations, 86, 131

capitalisation issues
  defined, 342
  rights issues, 42, 103–104, 351
  scrip issues, 177–178, 305, 309, 351
cash flow statement
  differences among companies, 300
  example, 301–302
  information generally included in, 300–301
  insolvency or takeover indications in, 303
  interpreting, 302–303
  too much activity in, 302
cash investments
  Annual Equivalent Rate (AER), 138
  Annual Percentage Rate (APR), 137–138
  bank fines and fees on, 138–140
  bonds compared to, 111, 133
  child trust funds for, 132
  finding price information for, 135–136
  FSA rules for, 134
  fund rules for, 130
  inflation issues, 133, 135
  interest rate considerations, 133, 135, 139
  ISAs for, 132
  liquidity of, 129
  need for, 129–130
  notice or term accounts for, 132
  NS&J bonds for, 132
  reasons for, 130, 132–133
  safety of, 134
  Shari'a law issues, 131
  shopping around for banks, 139–140
  stocks compared to, 105–106
  tax considerations, 130–131
Ceefax website, 44
ceilings, 192–193
CGT. _See_ capital gains tax
chairman's report, 291
channels of investment. _See_ investment channels

Chard website, 241
charts. *See also* technical analysis
  checking decisions using, 194–196
  comparison, for foreign investments, 203, 204, 205
  online resources for, 50, 71, 195
  for share price performance, 87
Chicago Board of Trade, 225
Chinese Walls, 15, 342
Citywire website, 145, 292
closed period, 343
closed-ended fund, 343
closing price, 25
CMC spread-betting service, 70
Comex, 225
commodities. *See also* futures; *specific kinds*
  American dominance in, 225, 227
  base metals, 241
  defined, 343
  exceptions to the cyclical process, 222–223
  finding information on, 224
  finding price information for, 224–228
  food, 223, 233–235
  forward pricing for, 225
  grading systems for, 220
  knowledge needed for investing in, 223–224
  long-term price cycles for, 221–223
  oil, 228–233
  precious metals and diamonds, 223, 235–241
  spot price for, 227
  supercycle theory for, 223–224
  tracker investments, 220
  uranium, 242
  US dollar prices for, 227
commoditisation, 220
companies
  blue chip, 342
  defined, 16

dependent on client in trouble, 327
foreign, finding information on, 203, 205
insolvency issues, 17–18, 101, 303
large, limits on power of, 97–98
listed, 348
overview, 16–18
profit-and-loss calculations for, 26
responsibility and bottom line, 54
warning signs of trouble, 303, 323–330
without earnings, valuing, 94–95, 157–160
company accounts. *See also specific statements*
  balance sheet, 297–300
  cash flow statement, 300–303
  current liabilities, 17
  EBITDA use in, 181–183
  fine points not requiring understanding, 2
  five-year summaries, 303–305
  insolvency issues, 17–18
  issues to be wary of, 294, 303
  knowledge needed for, 293–294
  non-current liabilities, 17
  obtaining, 292
  professional advice for, 294
  profit and loss statement, 295–297
  qualified by auditor, 330
  standardised format for, 291–292
comparison charts, 203, 204, 205
competition
  profit point affected by, 158
  property bought to prevent, 98
  takeover scenarios, 163
compound interest, power of, 65, 66
consolidation
  defined, 343
  takeover scenario, 163
consolidation issues, 178, 343
contrarian investing, 71–73
controlling shareholdings, 152, 153

corporate bonds. *See also* bonds
  default risk with, 121–122
  defined, 343
  financial pages information on, 122–124
  online resources, 124
  risk premium with, 122
  yield of, 121–122
covered warrants, 217
credit cards, 136
crisis of 2007/2008, 28, 255–256
currency
  charts, 195
  in developing countries, 58
  economic trends, 56
  for market capitalisation, 97
  risks with foreign investments, 206–207
  stock market sensitivity to movements of, 53
  stock opportunities related to, 338–339
  strong versus weak, 53, 56
current liabilities, 17
cyclical process of commodities, 221–223

*Daily Mail*
  cash investment information from, 135
  information offered by, 44
*Daily Telegraph*
  cash investment information from, 135
  commodities information in, 224
  pharmaceuticals prices example, 23
Data Explorers
  newsletter, 63
  shorting volume information from, 186
day trading, 70–71, 343
dead cat bounce, 179, 343
debt. *See also* debt ratio
  asset allocation considerations, 318–319
  on balance sheet, 299
  disguised, 104

effects on stock market, 54
finding information on, 104–105
foreign economic dependence on, 55
hidden, spotting, 183–184, 294
importance of, 104–105
insolvency issues, 17–18, 101, 303
need for, 100
Payment Protection Insurance on loans, 139
pension liabilities, 54, 169–171, 183–184, 328–329
researching for company, 313
rights issues for capitalisation, 42, 103–104, 351
debt ratio
  as debt/equity ratio or gearing ratio, 102
  defined, 102
  minus numbers for, 103
  percentage expressing, 102–103
deflation, 53–54
deposit account interest rate considerations, 133
depreciation, valuing, 165
*Der Spiegel*, 285
derivatives. *See also* options
  cautions about investing in, 209
  defined, 209, 343
  futures, 210–216, 345
  guaranteed income bonds' use of, 260
  for oil investing, 229
  warrants, 104, 105, 216–217, 354
diamonds. *See* precious metals and diamonds
direct ownership, 74–75
directors of companies
  responsibilities and liabilities of, 16–17
  shares sold by, 325–326
director's report, 292, 313
discount, defined, 344

discussion forums. *See also specific forums*
  cautions about using, 13, 279, 314
  etiquette, 281
  recommended forums, 279–281
  usefulness of, 279, 314
dividend cover, 100–101, 311, 324
dividend yields
  calculation of, 33
  defined, 31
  from mature industries, 99–101
  for sectors, 83–84, 99–100
dividends
  announcement date, 174
  compound interest on, 65
  defined, 17, 31, 344
  dividend cover, 100–101, 311, 324
  equality principle of, 42
  ex-dividend dates, 174–177, 311, 344
  high-dividend stocks, 99–101
  as indications of company health, 32
  lacking for tracker funds, 48
  not important for value investing, 68
  overview, 31–33
  payment date, 174
  payment of, 31–32
  p/e ratio related to, 83, 98
  process stages, 174
  in profit and loss statement, 296, 297
  record date, 174
  special, 176
  tax considerations, 99
  in UK versus other countries, 32
DJ-AIG commodity indices, 234, 235
double bottom pattern, 192
double top pattern, 190–191
dummy portfolios online, 87–88, 160

• E •

Earnings Before Interest, Taxes, Debts and Amortisation (EBITDA)
  dangers of, 182–183
  defined, 182, 344
  Enron fraud using, 181–182
economic growth
  business cycle for, 56–58
  debt-based, 55
  effects on stock market, 52
  sustainable long-term rate of, 52
*The Economist*, 201, 224
effective monthly interest rate, 137
Einstein, Albert (physicist), 65
Elliott Wave theory, 194
emerging markets, 202
energy, long-term information on, 229
Enron fraud, 181–182
equity
  on balance sheet, 300
  defined, 344
  scheduled exit by backers, 163
ETF Stock Encyclopedia, 264
ETFs. *See* exchange-traded funds
EUBusiness.com, 285
eurobonds, 121
EuroNext exchange, 38–39, 40
*European Investment News*, 286
European Islamic Investment Bank plc, 131
Exchange Price Input Computer (EPIC), 344
exchange-traded funds (ETFs)
  for base metals, 241
  for commodities, 220–221
  defined, 220
  described, 12, 220
  ease of buying and selling, 201
  finding information on, 264
  finding price information for, 266
  for food commodities, 234–235

how they work, 264–265
indices tracked by, 16
for international investments, 199,
200–201, 266
for oil investing, 229–230
operators, 200
for precious metals, 237–238, 240
transaction costs, 201
ex-dividend date
caveats for share price limits, 175
defined, 174, 344
finding information on, 176
for foreign investments, 176
price fall on, 174–175, 311
execution-only trading. *See also* nominee
accounts
defined, 14, 344
for foreign investments, 200
low costs of, 75
exercising
options, 218
warrants, 216–217
exposure, 212, 344

### • F •

falling knives, 179
Fibonacci numbers, 194
financial advisers
buying bonds through, 114
for help with company accounts, 294
financial institutions
crisis of 2007/2008, 28
defined, 18
financial assets controlled by, 18
overview, 18–19
stock market under-performed by, 19
financial pages. *See also specific*
*newspapers*
buzzwords, 58–60
commodities information in, 224
corporate bond information in, 122–124

government bond information in, 113,
116–118
information offered by, 33–34, 44
for international news, 44
making purchase decisions using, 87–88
making sales decisions using, 88–89
online resources versus, 85–86
reading information correctly, 86
relating numbers to context, 22, 33–36,
43–44
risk indicators in, 81–84
rules governing journalists, 154–156
sectors allocated differently among, 45
share price examples, 22–24
shares overview, 41–43
statistics overview, 22–33
widened scale of news in, 37
Financial Services Authority (FSA)
cash investment rules of, 134
defined, 345
financial markets' regulation by,
154–156
*Financial Times. See also FT*.com
Actuaries Share indices, 81–82
Aerospace and Defence section, 24
AIM listings, 233
annual reports service, 292
bond price listing example, 117–119
cash investment information from, 135
commodities price information in,
225–227
detailed breakdown in, 84
information offered by, 44
Level 2 searches, 205
managed funds in, 245
market capitalisation in, 96
p/e ratios in, 28–29
regulatory announcements from, 145
sector indices, 82–84
symbols in second column, 25
unit trust price information from, 250

Fitch IBCA bond ratings, 115–116, 126–127

five-year summaries, 303–305

fixed asset valuations
  depreciation, 165
  licensed trade, 168–169
  property, 165–167

flotation, 345

food commodities. *See also* commodities
  challenges involved in, 233–234
  DJ-AIG indices, 234, 235
  as exceptions to the cyclical process, 223
  exchange-traded funds for, 234–235
  finding price information for, 235

*Forbes*, 285

foreign investments. *See* international investments

foreign trade surplus, effects on stock market, 52

forward or prospective p/e ratio, 29, 95

forward pricing for commodities, 225

free float
  of AIM-listed companies, 181
  bottlenecks from lack of, 180
  in Britain versus foreign markets, 180–181
  defined, 154, 345
  finding information on, 181
  takeover considerations, 154

FRS-17 requirements, 169–171, 294

FSA. *See* Financial Services Authority

*FT.com. See also Financial Times*
  bond price listings, 117
  comparison charts, 203, 204, 205
  dummy portfolios, 87
  ex-dividend date information from, 176
  free float information from, 181
  managed funds on, 246
  oil price information from, 230
  overview, 273–274

FTSE
  actuary indices, 29 April 2008, 82–83, 100–101
  advance reports on index changes, 334
  computers' impact on, 48
  dividend cover figures, 100–101
  free float accounted for, 181
  indices, 40
  overview, 40–41
  p/e ratios for indices, 81–82
  sector adjustments by, 46
  UK index series values, 81

FTSE AIM indices, 49, 82

FTSE-100 index
  company about to be promoted into, 334
  defined, 345
  overview, 49–50
  p/e ratio for, 82
  shares moved by, 49
  tracker funds, 49, 334

FTSE-250 index, 82

fully hedged, defined, 215

fundamental analysis, 189, 191

funds. *See also* managed funds; trusts; *specific kinds*
  cash investment rules for, 130
  defined, 345

futures. *See also* commodities; derivatives
  cautions about speculative use of, 210, 214
  defined, 210, 345
  expiration date and uncertainty of, 216
  exposure, 212
  finding information on, 215
  guaranteed income bonds' use of, 260
  in hedge funds, 214
  for hedging prices, 215
  margin call on, 212
  oil market, 231–232
  origins of, 213

ticket analogy for, 210–214
trading on margin, 211, 213
usefulness of, 210

## • *G* •

GalMarley website, 241
gearing or leveraging
  asset allocation considerations,
    318–319
  defined, 318, 345
  by hedge funds, 257
  trading on margin, 213
gearing ratio. *See* debt ratio
GIBs. *See* guaranteed income bonds
gilts or gilt-edged securities, 345. *See
    also* government bonds
glossary, 341–354
gold. *See* precious metals and diamonds
golden shares, 180
goodwill, valuing, 161–162, 294
Google, managed funds on, 246
government bonds
  *Barclays Capital Equity Gilt Study* on, 106
  benchmark, 113, 119–120
  buying, 113–114, 116–117
  capital gains on, 111, 115
  cash investments versus, 111
  defined, 109
  eurobonds, 121
  *Financial Times* price listing, 117–119
  foreign, 114–115, 119–121
  inverted yield curve, 112
  National Savings and Investments,
    114, 132
  price fluctuations of, 110, 111, 113
  rating systems, 115–116
  ratio in your portfolio, 109
  reasons for investing in, 108–109
  redemption date, 109, 110
  relationship between yield and price,
    117, 119
  reliability of, 107–108, 109, 113, 116
  stocks compared to, 105–106, 107–108
  yield curve of, 112
  yield of, 110, 111, 112, 113
Graham, Benjamin (investment
    theorist), 51
greed/fear mass psychology, 188–189
Group Income Statement, 295. *See also*
    profit and loss statement
group operating profit, 296
growth stocks
  defined, 346
  Far East sectors, 46
  high-tech sectors, 47
guaranteed equity bonds. *See*
    guaranteed income bonds (GIBs)
guaranteed income bonds (GIBs)
  defined, 346
  derivatives used by, 260
  described, 259
  fixed term for, 260
  marketing claims untrustworthy for,
    260–262
  precipice bond clauses, 262–263
  reading the contract, 264
  stock investments versus, 261
  tax liabilities, 262
*Guardian*
  information offered by, 44
  Top 100 shares example, 23

## • *H* •

Hargreaves Lansdown share-filtering
    system, 69
*Harvard Business Review*, 285
head and shoulders pattern, 191–192
hedge funds
  'absolute return' policy of, 257
  crisis of 2007/2008 blamed on managers
    of, 255–256
  defined, 346

hedge funds *(continued)*
  fees, 257
  futures in, 214
  lack of information about, 255, 256
  leveraging by, 257
  ordinary managed funds versus, 256–258
  regulatory issues, 258
  shorting by, 186, 257
hedging, defined, 346
hedging prices, 215
Hemmington Scott website, 153, 275–276
hidden debts, spotting, 183–184, 294
HiFX charts, 195
high beta stocks, 60
high-tech sectors
  growth stocks in, 47
  options issued in late 1990s, 104
  p/e ratios for, 83
  valuing companies without earnings, 94–95, 157–160
high-yield bonds. *See* junk bonds
historical or trailing p/e ratio, 29, 90–91
holidays' effect on effect on stock market, 34
Hoovers website, 153

**• I •**

icons in this book, 7–8
iii (Interactive Investor website), 135–136, 275
IMF website, 201
income. *See* revenue; turnover
income investing, 65–67
indices. *See also* FTSE; tracker funds; *specific indices*
  American, 41
  defined, 346
  exchange-traded funds tracking, 16
  finding information on, 50
  for food commodities, 234

overview, 48–50
p/e ratios for, 81–82
shares moved by, 49
usefulness of, 48
volatility created by, 49
Individual Savings Accounts (ISAs)
  AIM companies ineligible for, 69
  capital gains tax considerations, 86, 131
  for cash investments, 132
  declining use of, 66–67
  defined, 346
  dividends reported by, 32
  further information, 67
  swapping money in and out of, 135
industry sectors. *See* sectors
inflation
  bond yield fluctuation from, 110, 113
  in business cycle, 57–58
  cash investment issues, 133, 135
  in developing countries, 58
  effects on stock market, 53–54
  negative real interest rate due to, 133
Infomine website, 242
insider trading
  defined, 346
  FSA concerns about, 154–155
  prevalence of, 155
  rules governing journalists, 154–156
insolvency of company
  warning signs of trouble, 303, 323–330
  who gets paid first, 17–18, 101
intangible assets, 161–162
Interactive Investor website, 135–136, 275
interest rates
  Annual Equivalent Rate (AER), 138, 341
  Annual Percentage Rate (APR), 137–138, 341
  in business cycle, 57–58
  cash investment issues, 133, 135, 139
  negative real interest rate, 133
interim reports, 292

*International Crude Oil Market Handbook*, 232
*International Herald Tribune*, 44
international investments
  bonds, 114–115, 119–121
  company information for, 203, 205
  comparison charts for, 203, 204, 205
  currency risks with, 206–207
  in emerging markets, 202
  exchange-traded funds for, 199, 200–201, 266
  ex-dividend date information for, 176
  with execution-only firms, 200
  finding information on, 201–206
  foreign publications and websites, 284–286
  free float concerns, 180–181
  ignoring structural differences, 206
  language skills not needed for, 199
  LIFFE for, 40, 348
  managed funds for, 199, 200–201, 244
  need for, 200–201
  transaction costs, 200
  UK strictures escaped by, 201
International Petroleum Exchange, 225
Internet resources. *See* online resources
inverted yield curve, 112
Investigate website, 145
investing approaches
  bit-of-everything investing, 73
  contrarian investing, 71–73
  day trading, 70–71
  deciding on yours, 3
  income investing, 65–67
  long-term buy-and-hold (LTBH), 67–68
  preparation needed for, 64–65
  value investing, 68–69
*Investing For Dummies*, 67, 79
*Investing in Shares For Dummies*, 67, 79

investment banks
  changes since the 1980s, 14, 15
  Chinese Walls in, 15, 342
  crisis of 2007/2008, 28
investment channels. *See also specific kinds*
  direct ownership, 74–75
  nominee accounts, 75–76
  trusts, 76
investment magazines
  current challenges for, 282–283
  foreign, 284–286
  independent reportage from, 284
  monthly, 283–284
  UK, 282–284
investment trusts (ITs)
  asset allocation for, 320
  defined, 347
  described, 16
  discounts and premiums, 252–253
  finding information on, 253
  net asset value, 252–253, 254
  unit trusts versus, 248, 252, 254
  volatility of, 254
investor profiles. *See* investing approaches
*Investors Chronicle*, 246
Investorwords website, 59
ISAs. *See* Individual Savings Accounts
iShares ETF operator, 200
ISIN, using, 245–246

## • J •

junk bonds (high-yield bonds). *See also* bonds
  for companies needing money, 126
  defined, 124, 347
  ratings for, 126–127
  risk with, 124–125, 126–127
  for takeover activities, 125
Jupiter Merlin Growth Portfolio, 249, 250

## • K •

'Key World Energy Statistics', 229
Keynesian economics, 55, 347
Kitco website
  base metals site, 242
  commodities information from, 195,
    225, 228, 241, 278

## • L •

land banks, 98, 165–167
leveraging. *See* gearing or leveraging
liabilities. *See* debt
licensed trade, property value
    disappearing for, 168–169
LIFFE. *See* London International Financial
    Futures and Options Exchange
like-for-like sales, 293–294, 332–333
limit orders. *See also* stop-loss
  defined, 347
  ex-dividend date issues, 175
limited liability companies, 17–18
liquidity
  asset allocation considerations, 318
  balance sheet for figuring company's,
    299–300
  of cash investments, 129
  defined, 347
  difficulties in measuring, 59–60
listed companies, defined, 348
LiveCharts website, 71
*Lloyd's List*, 227
loans. *See* debt
London Bullion Market, 225
London International Financial Futures
    and Options Exchange (LIFFE)
  commodities price information
    from, 225
  defined, 348
  EuroNext ownership of, 40
London Metal Exchange, 225

London South East website, 274
London Stock Exchange (LSE)
  AIM listings, 233
  Big Bang revolution (1986), 15, 38,
    39, 67
  changes since the 1980s, 13–15
  company accounts from, 292
  dummy portfolios online, 87
  exchange-traded fund information
    online, 264
  food product price listings, 235
  foreign company information
    online, 205
  market capitalisation online, 96
  Regulatory News Service, 145–146, 351
  website, 270–271
long, defined, 348
long-term buy-and-hold (LTBH), 67–68
low beta stocks, 60
Lyxor ETF operator, 200

## • M •

macro-economic influences
  assumptions about, 51–54
  bearish, 64
  bullish, 62
  business cycle, 56–58
  economic trends, 54–56
  using to your advantage, 58, 335–336
magazines
  foreign, 284–286
  UK, 282–284
*Mail on Sunday*, 135
managed funds. *See also* exchange-
    traded funds (ETFs); tracker funds
  benefits of, 244–245
  codes for, 245–246
  for emerging market investments, 202
  hedge funds versus ordinary funds,
    256–258

for international investments, 199,
    200–201, 244
need for, 244
watching the fund manager, 246, 248
wealth of information on, 245
management buy-out (MBO), 162
margin
  defined, 348
  trading futures on, 211, 213
margin call, 212
market capitalisation. *See also*
    capitalisation issues
  assets not appearing as, 157
  'B' shares for, 43
  balance sheet not related to, 97
  comparing net asset value to, 299
  currency used for, 97
  defined, 29, 95–96, 97, 157, 348
  finding quotations of, 96, 97
  hidden debts, 183–184
  importance of, 30, 96, 310
  as imprecise figure, 96–97
  limits placed on big companies, 97–98
  overview, 29–30
  preference shares for, 43
  price to book value for, 97, 160
market makers
  activities after market closes, 25
  changes since the 1980s, 14, 15
  defined, 348
market psychology. *See* technical
    analysis
market sectors. *See* sectors
mass psychology, 188–189. *See also*
    technical analysis
mature industries
  benefits in periods of downturn, 84
  declining industries versus, 46
  dividends from, 99–101
  stability of, 46
MBO (management buy-out), 162

mergers. *See also* takeover
  company accounts complicated by,
      293–294
  likely to fall through, 327–328
  synergy not working after, 329–330
mining. *See also* commodities; precious
    metals and diamonds
  dividend yields from, 99–100
  finding price information for, 224–228
  foreign shares in, 200
  fractional share prices for, 24
  futures for hedging, 215
  long-term price cycles for, 221–223
momentum, defined, 59
monetarism, 348
Monetary Policy Committee (MPC), 349
*Money* magazine, 246
Moody bond ratings, 115–116, 126–127
Morrisons
  limits on power of, 98
  property owned by, 98, 165
Motley Fool
  cash investment information from, 136
  five-year summaries from, 304
  overview, 279–280
  regulatory announcements from, 145
  value investing information from, 69
  for valuing companies without
      profits, 159
  Your Money tutorials on, 136
multi-agency firms, 15
Muslims, Shari'a law issues for, 76, 131
mutual funds
  defined, 349
  structured products, 352
  tracker funds, 353

National Savings and Investments
    (NS&I), 114, 132
negative real interest rate, 133

net asset value (NAV)
  defined, 349
  importance of, 299
  of investment trusts, 252–253, 254
net operating expenses, 296
New Paradigm (1990s), 54–55
New York Commodities Exchange, 225
*New York Times*, 285
News.com.au, 286
newsletters and tipsheets, 289–290
Nikkei Net Interactive, 286
nominee accounts
  defined, 15, 32, 349
  dividend payment into, 32
  overview, 75–76
  reliability of, 75–76
  share certificates with, 15, 349
  trade-offs with, 75
non-current liabilities, 17
notice or term accounts, 132
Nybot, 225

• *O* •

Oanda website, 278
OEICs (Open-Ended Investment
  Companies), 251, 349
offer price, 24, 349
Office of Fair Trading, 136
oil
  Canadian Oil Sands project, 228
  drillers, explorers, and producers, 233
  exchange-traded funds for, 229–230
  finding price information for, 230–231
  futures market, 231–232
  investing approaches, 229–230
  long-term energy information, 229
  petroleum grades, 232
online resources. *See also FT*.com
  BBC, 44, 231, 278–279
  blogs, 281–282
  Buffett's shareholder addresses, 73
  cash investment information, 135–136
  Ceefax, 44
  charts, 50, 71, 195

child trust funds, 132
commodities price information, 225,
  227–228
company accounts, 292
controlling shareholdings
  information, 153
conventions for URLs, 4
corporate bond information, 124
day trading, 70–71
debt information, 105
discussion forums, 279–281
dummy portfolios, 87–88, 160
European Islamic Investment Bank
  plc, 131
exchange-traded fund information, 264
ex-dividend date information, 176
financial pages versus, 85–86
food commodities price
  information, 235
foreign company information, 205
foreign versus UK, 19–20
foreign websites, 285–286
free float information, 181
Hemmington Scott, 153, 275–276
index information, 50
Interactive Investor (iii), 135–136, 275
*International Herald Tribune*, 44
international investment information,
  201–202, 285–286
Investorwords site, 59
Kitco, 195, 225, 228, 241, 242, 278
London South East, 274
London Stock Exchange, 270–271
long-term energy information, 229
for managed funds, 246
market capitalisation, 96
Oanda, 278
official websites, 270–272
oil drillers, explorers, and producers,
  233
oil price information, 230–231
overwhelming volume of, 269
precious metals price information,
  236, 241
regulatory announcements, 145

RNS statutory announcements, 271–272
share-filtering systems, 69
shorting volumes, 185–186
Stockcharts forum, 189, 194
takeover indications, 164
Thisismoney, 274–275
Trustnet, 276–278
unit trust price information, 250
unofficial websites, 272–279
uranium price information, 242
value investing information, 69
for valuing companies without
    profits, 159
OPEC basket price, 232
open-ended funds, 349
Open-Ended Investment Companies
    (OEICs), 251, 349
options. *See also* derivatives
call, 218, 342
debt disguised by, 104, 183
defined, 218, 349
exercising, 218
historical perspective on, 209–210
investors short-changed by, 105
need for understanding, 209–210, 217
put, 218, 351
ordinary shares
defined, 41, 350
fixed number of, 41
nominal value of, 42
over-the-counter (OTC) market
defined, 350
value investing in, 68–69
warrants on, 217

● *P* ●

Paddypower spread-betting service, 70
palladium, 239. *See also* precious metals
    and diamonds
patents, valuing, 161, 294
payment date for dividends, 174
Payment Protection Insurance (PPI), 139
p/e ratio. *See* price/earnings ratio

penny shares, 350
pension fund liabilities
checking, 169–171
dangers of, 54
as hidden debts, 183–184
warning signs of trouble, 328–329
pension plans
breaching covenants, 170
capital gains tax considerations, 86
FRS-17 requirements, 169–171, 294
takeover issues for, 153
Personal Equity Plans (PEPs), 32, 69
petroleum. *See* oil
platinum, 238–239. *See also* precious
    metals and diamonds
Platts, 227
points, defined, 60
portfolio allocation. *See* asset allocation
portfolios online, dummy, 87–88, 160
pound cost averaging, 350
PPI (Payment Protection Insurance), 139
precious metals and diamonds. *See also*
    commodities
as exceptions to the cyclical
    process, 223
exchange-traded funds for, 237–238, 240
finding price information for,
    236–237, 241
gold certificates, 237
gold collectable coins, 240–241
silver, platinum, and palladium,
    238–240
unpredictability of gold's value,
    235–236
precipice bond clauses, 262–263
preference shares
debt disguised by, 104, 183
defined, 43, 350
investors short-changed by, 105
premium, defined, 350
Premium Bonds, 109
pre-tax profits, 27
price alerts, 175
price to book value (PTBV), 97, 160, 299

price/earnings ratio (p/e ratio)
  average, 28
  avoiding traps, 91–92, 94
  below sector average, but rising, 332
  in comparison charts, 203, 204, 205
  defined, 27, 350
  dividends related to, 83, 98
  errors and distortions in, 90–91
  for ex-growth companies, 27
  historical or trailing, 29, 90–91
  importance of, 310
  investor confidence shown by, 27
  prospective or forward, 29, 95
  researching reasons for, 92–94
  as risk indicator, 81–82
  for sectors, 82–83
  too good to be true rule for, 91
  transport company examples, 92–94
  valuing companies without earnings,
    94–95
profit and loss statement
  dividend earnings per share on, 297
  dividends per ordinary share on, 296
  earnings per share from continuing
    operations on, 297
  example, 295–296
  Group Income Statement, 295–296
  group operating profit on, 296
  need for understanding, 312
  net operating expenses on, 296
  profit for the year for continuing
    operations on, 296
  revenue, income, or turnover on, 295
profit point, 158
profits. *See also* dividends
  defined, 25
  investing in companies lacking, 26
  pre-tax, 27
  stagnant or falling, 324
  valuing companies lacking, 94–95,
    157–160

property
  bought to prevent competition, 98
  land banks, 165–167
  with licensed trade, 168–169
  valuing, 165–167
prospective or forward p/e ratio, 29, 95
psychology, mass, 188–189. *See also*
    technical analysis
PTBV (price to book value), 97, 160, 299
pub properties, 168–169
public limited companies (plcs), 17–18
put options, 218, 351. *See also* options
put warrants, 217

## • *Q* •

qualified accounts, 330

## • *R* •

rating agencies, 351
rating systems for bonds, 115–116,
    126–127
Reagan, Ronald (US president), 55
real estate. *See* property
Real Estate Investment Trusts (REITs),
    168–169
record date for dividends, 174
redemption date, 109, 110, 351
regulatory announcements
  amusing content in, 151
  Appointment of Administrator example,
    147–148
  auditor changes, 330
  for changes to controlling
    shareholdings, 152
  finding RNS reports, 145
  FSA safeguards for, 154–156
  Holdings in Company example, 146
  importance of, 271–272
  Issue of Debt example, 146
  journalists' responsibilities, 154–156

online resources, 272
policing and enforcement of, 144, 145
RNS regulations for, 145
situations requiring, 144
from Subsea Resources, 147–148
Suspension of Shares example, 147
takeover indications in, 164
typical RNS announcements, 145–146
using to your advantage, 150–152
Regulatory News Service (RNS). *See also*
    regulatory announcements
company accounts from, 292
defined, 351
statements not required made through,
    149–152
statutory announcements online,
    271–272
takeover indications in
    announcements, 164
typical announcements, 145–146
website, 145
REITs (Real Estate Investment Trusts),
    168–169
Remember icon, 7
resistance levels, 190, 191, 192–193
retained earnings, 300
Reuters, debt breakdowns from, 105
revenue. *See also* turnover
income types affecting, 26
in profit and loss statement, 295
rights issues
balance sheet reflecting, 104
defined, 42, 103, 351
overview, 103–104
rising floors, 192–193
risk
benefits of mature industries, 84
with corporate bonds, 121–122
currency, with foreign investments,
    206–207
finding stocks to fit your profile, 84

with government bonds, 107–108,
    109, 113
with junk bonds, 124–127
p/e ratio as indicator, 81–83
tailoring to your circumstance, 80, 322
with takeovers, 163
RNS. *See* Regulatory News Service
Rules Governing the Substantial
    Acquisition of Shares, 153

• **S** •

Sainsbury
limits on power of, 98
property owned by, 98, 165, 166
S&P 500, 351
scrip issues, 177–178, 305, 309, 351
sectors
allocation of shares to, 45–46
consolidation in, 163
dividend yields for, 83–84, 99–100
Far East, 46
for growth industries, 46–47
high-tech, 47
for mature industries, 46
methods of defining, 45
for middle-ground industries, 47
overview, 45–47
p/e ratio for share below average, but
    rising, 332
p/e ratios for, 82–83
troubled, 326–327
unit trusts for, 250
variations for companies within, 84
securities, defined, 352
SEDOL, 245–246, 352
selling shares. *See also* share prices
challenges involved in, 88–89
after takeover offers, 164
trailing stop-loss for, 89
warning signs of trouble, 323–330

sentiment, defined, 59

settlement, defined, 352

share certificates

changes since the 1980s, 14, 15

with nominee accounts, 15, 349

share prices

below 200-day moving average, 325

bid price, 24

checking five-year period for, 309

closing price, 25

consolidation issues raising, 178, 343

daily price movement, 24–25

dead cat bounce, 179, 343

ex-dividend price fall, 174–175, 311

falling knives, 179

fractions in, 24

highest and lowest, 25

holidays' effect on, 34

information offered by newspapers,
33–34

limitations of, 34–36

offer price, 24, 349

opportunities, clues for, 331–339

overview, 22–24

performance charts for, 87

reasons for fluctuations, 34–35

as reliable indicators, 79

scrip issues lowering, 177–178, 309, 351

trade price, 24

unfairly devastated, 336–337

usefulness of, 36

warning signs of trouble, 323–330

share-filtering systems, 69

shareholders

equity on balance sheet, 300

of insolvent companies, 17–18, 101

*Shares* magazine, 246

shares or stocks. *See also* share prices;
technical analysis

avoiding emotional ties to, 89

'B' shares, 43

bonds compared to, 106, 107–108

bonus share distributions, 176–177

buying, 87–88

cash compared to, 105–106

certificates for, 14, 15, 349

common mistakes to avoid, 173–183

currency-related opportunities,
338–339

debt ratio considerations, 101–105

defined, 41, 352

direct ownership of, 74–75

dividend considerations, 98–101

financial pages information on, 85–86

free float, 154, 180–181, 345

fundamental analysis, 189, 191

further information, 79

guaranteed income bonds versus, 261

market capitalisation issues, 95–98

nominee accounts for, 75–76

opportunities, clues for, 331–339

ordinary, 41–42, 350

overview, 41–43

p/e ratio considerations, 89–95

pension fund investment in, 169–171

power of company ownership, 41

preference shares, 43, 104, 183, 350

rights issue, 42, 103–104, 351

risk issues, 80–84

scale of approval for, 288

selling, 88–89

warning signs of trouble, 323–330

Shari'a law issues, 76, 131

Shaw, George Bernard (playwright), 19

shorting

asset allocation considerations, 321

bear raids, 185

dangers of, 184–185, 321

defined, 184, 352

finding information on, 185–186

by hedge funds, 186, 257

impact on stock behaviour, 63, 185

overview, 63

rationalisation for, 184

silver, 238, 239. *See also* precious metals and diamonds
soft commodities. *See* food commodities
*South China Morning Post*, 286
special dividends, 176
splits (scrip issues), 177–178, 305, 309, 351
spot price for commodities, 227
stamp duty, 352
Standard & Poor bond ratings, 115–116, 126–127
statistics. *See also specific kinds*
  daily price movement, 24–25
  dividends overview, 31–33
  limitations of, 34–36, 80, 86
  market capitalisation overview, 29–30
  price/earnings ratio overview, 27–29
  profits, 25–27
  relating to the context, 22, 33–36
  risk indicators, 81–84
  share prices overview, 22–24
  too good to be true rule for, 22, 91, 178
statutory announcements. *See* regulatory announcements
Stock Exchange Daily Official List code (SEDOL), 245–246, 352
stock market
  Big Bang revolution (1986), 15, 38, 39, 67
  business cycle's effect on, 56–58
  buzzwords, 58–60
  common mistakes to avoid, 173–183
  complexity of, 37, 38–39
  crisis of 2007/2008, 28, 255–256
  electronic exchanges, 38–39
  emerging markets, 202
  EuroNext exchange, 38–39
  financial institutions out-performed by, 19–20
  FTSE indicators, 40–41
  holidays' effect on, 34
  macro-economic influences, 51–56

  panic of October 1987, 34
  reasons for fluctuations, 34–35
  regulatory bodies, 38, 40
  relating numbers to context, 43–44
  shorting's impact on, 63
  thinking ahead of the curve, 51
stock splits (scrip issues), 177–178, 305, 309, 351
stockbrokers
  activities after market closes, 25
  buying bonds through, 114
  changes since the 1980s, 13–15
  defined, 342
  improved recommendations from, 333
stockbroker's analysts
  changes since the 1980s, 14, 15
  reports, 287–289
Stockcharts forum, 189, 194
stocks. *See* shares or stocks
stoozing, 136
stop-loss
  defined, 352
  ex-dividend date issues, 175
  trailing, 89, 175
structured products, 352
Subsea Resources, 147–148
*Sun*, 44
*Sunday Telegraph*, 135
supercycle theory for commodities, 223–224
supermarkets
  limits on power of, 98
  property owned by, 98, 165–166
support levels, 192–193
swaps. *See also* derivatives

• *T* •

takeover
  cash flow statement indications of, 303
  finding information about possibilities, 164

takeover *(continued)*
  kinds of, 162–163
  regulatory announcements prior to,
    150–152
  risks with, 163
  rules for, 152–154
  Rules Governing the Substantial
    Acquisition of Shares, 153
  weighing the potential for, 162–164, 337
taxes
  asset allocation considerations, 317
  on capital gains, 86, 115, 342
  cash investment issues, 130–131
  depreciation issues, 165
  with direct ownership, 74
  dividend considerations, 99
  on GIB returns, 262
  on gilts, 115
  investment decisions based on, 86
technical analysis
  breakouts, 191–192
  ceilings, 192–193
  charting share price performance, 87
  checking decisions using charts,
    194–196
  chiropractic compared to, 187–188
  defined, 353
  double bottom pattern, 192
  double top pattern, 190–191
  Elliott Wave theory, 194
  greed/fear mass psychology in, 188–189
  head and shoulders pattern, 191–192
  online resources for charts, 50, 71, 195
  resistance levels, 190, 191, 192–193
  rising floors, 192–193
  Stockcharts forum, 189, 194
  support levels, 192–193
  triangle pattern, 193–194
  viewing charts realistically, 189
technical breakthrough by company, 338
Technical Stuff icon, 7

technology sectors. *See* high-tech
    sectors
television, financial news on, 44
term or notice accounts, 132
Tesco
  free float, 181
  limits on power of, 98
  property owned by, 98, 165, 166
TFC Charts, 195, 228, 242
Thisismoney website, 274–275
TIDM, 245–246, 353
*Times*
  cash investment information from, 135
  commodities information in, 224
Tip icon, 7
tipsheets and newsletters, 289–290
too good to be true rule, 22, 91, 178
tracker funds. *See also* exchange-traded
    funds (ETFs)
  benefits of, 245
  for commodities, 220–221
  defined, 48, 353
  dividends lacking for, 48
  for FTSE-100 index, 49, 334
  management charges low for, 48
  overview, 48–49
  structured products, 352
trade price, 24
trading on margin, 211, 213
trailing or historical p/e ratio, 29, 90–91
trailing stop-loss, 89, 175
transaction costs
  changes since the 1980s, 14
  for exchange-traded funds, 201
  for international investments, 200
  LTBH strategy affected by, 67
triangle pattern, 193–194
Trustnet website
  corporate bond information on, 124
  Fund Manager News section, 248
  managed funds on, 246

overview, 276–278
unit trust information on, 249, 250
trusts
asset allocation for, 320
'blind', 76
child trust funds, 132
defined, 76, 353
investment trusts, 16, 252–254, 347
OEICs, 251
for Shari'a law compliance, 76
UCITs, 251
unit trusts, 248–250, 353
uses for, 76
turnover. *See also* revenue
defined, 25
in profit and loss statement, 295
for valuing companies without
profits, 158
TV, financial news on, 44

## • *U* •

UCITs (Undertakings for Collective
Investment in Transferable
Securities), 251
UK Coal, property owned by, 166–167
underwriting, 353
unemployment, in business cycle, 57–58
unit trusts
asset allocation for, 320
defined, 353
fees, 249
finding price information for, 250
idea behind, 248
investment trusts versus, 248, 252, 254
prices typical for, 249
for sectors, 250
United Nations Conference on Trade and
Development (Unctad), 225
uranium, 242

utility companies
changes since the 1990s, 47
dividends from, 73
low p/e ratios for, 27
share price fluctuations for, 87

## • *V* •

value investing
defined, 353
importance of debt in, 104–105
overview, 68–69
valuing companies. *See also* market
capitalisation
accepting the market value, 156, 157
checking pension liabilities, 169–171
fixed asset valuations, 165–169
guesswork involved in, 156
intangible assets, 161–162, 294
opportunities, clues for, 331–339
price to book value (PTBV), 97, 160
spotting hidden debts, 183–184
unfairly devastated share prices,
336–337
weighing takeover potential,
162–164, 337
without earnings, 94–95, 157–160
Virtual Trader website, 87
volatility. *See also* risk
defined, 354
indices as creators of, 49
of investment trusts, 254

## • *W* •

*Wall Street Journal*, 50, 285
War Loan bonds, 109
Warning! icon, 8
warrants. *See also* derivatives
debt disguised by, 104
defined, 216, 354
exercising, 216–217

warrants *(continued)*
  expiration date, 216
  finding, 217
  investors short-changed by, 105, 217
  kinds of, 217
  overview, 216–217
Web resources. *See* online resources
West Texas Intermediate (WTI), 232
*What Investment?* magazine, 246
World Gold Council, 224–225
World Newspapers website, 286

X-Rates charts, 195

Yahoo! website
  corporate bond information on, 124
  dummy portfolios using, 87
  foreign company information on, 205
  index information on, 50
yield. *See also* dividend yields
  of bonds, 110, 111, 112, 113, 121–122
  defined, 354
  high-yield bonds (junk bonds),
    124–127, 347
yield curve, 112, 354

# Notes

# Notes

# FOR DUMMIES®

## Do Anything. Just Add Dummies

# UK editions

## BUSINESS

978-0-470-51806-9

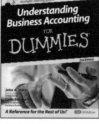

978-0-470-99245-6

978-0-470-75626-3

## FINANCE

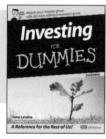

978-0-470-99280-7

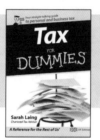

978-0-470-99811-3

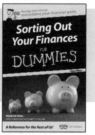

978-0-470-69515-9

## PROPERTY

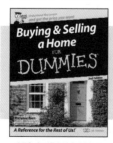

978-0-470-99448-1

978-0-470-75872-4

978-0-7645-7054-4

Backgammon For Dummies
978-0-470-77085-6

Body Language For Dummies
978-0-470-51291-3

British Sign Language
For Dummies
978-0-470-69477-0

Business NLP For Dummies
978-0-470-69757-3

Children's Health For Dummies
978-0-470-02735-6

Cognitive Behavioural Coaching
For Dummies
978-0-470-71379-2

Counselling Skills For Dummies
978-0-470-51190-9

Digital Marketing For Dummies
978-0-470-05793-3

eBay.co.uk For Dummies,
2nd Edition
978-0-470-51807-6

English Grammar For Dummies
978-0-470-05752-0

Fertility & Infertility For Dummies
978-0-470-05750-6

Genealogy Online For Dummies
978-0-7645-7061-2

Golf For Dummies
978-0-470-01811-8

Green Living For Dummies
978-0-470-06038-4

Hypnotherapy For Dummies
978-0-470-01930-6

13902_p1

# FOR DUMMIES®

## A world of resources to help you grow

## UK editions

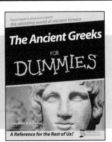

# FOR DUMMIES®

## The easy way to get more done and have more fun

## LANGUAGES

978-0-7645-5194-9

978-0-7645-5193-2

978-0-471-77270-5

## MUSIC

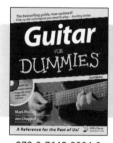

978-0-7645-9904-0

978-0-470-03275-6
UK Edition

978-0-7645-5105-5

## SCIENCE & MATHS

978-0-7645-5326-4

978-0-7645-5430-8

978-0-7645-5325-7

Art For Dummies
978-0-7645-5104-8

Baby & Toddler Sleep Solutions For
Dummies
978-0-470-11794-1

Bass Guitar For Dummies
978-0-7645-2487-5

Brain Games For Dummies
978-0-470-37378-1

Christianity For Dummies
978-0-7645-4482-8

Filmmaking For Dummies, 2nd
Edition
978-0-470-38694-1

Forensics For Dummies
978-0-7645-5580-0

German For Dummies
978-0-7645-5195-6

Hobby Farming For Dummies
978-0-470-28172-7

Jewelry Making & Beading For
Dummies
978-0-7645-2571-1

Knitting for Dummies, 2nd Edition
978-0-470-28747-7

Music Composition For Dummies
978-0-470-22421-2

Physics For Dummies
978-0-7645-5433-9

Sex For Dummies, 3rd Edition
978-0-470-04523-7

Solar Power Your Home For Dummies
978-0-470-17569-9

Tennis For Dummies
978-0-7645-5087-4

The Koran For Dummies
978-0-7645-5581-7

U.S. History For Dummies
978-0-7645-5249-6

Wine For Dummies, 4th Edition
978-0-470-04579-4

**Available wherever books are sold. For more information or to order direct go to
www.wiley.com or call +44 (0) 1243 843291**

13902_p3

# FOR DUMMIES®

## Helping you expand your horizons and achieve your potential

## COMPUTER BASICS

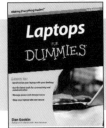 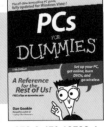 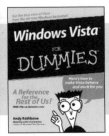

978-0-470-27759-1    978-0-470-13728-4    978-0-471-75421-3

## DIGITAL LIFESTYLE

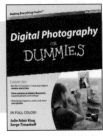  

978-0-470-25074-7    978-0-470-39062-7    978-0-470-17469-2

## WEB & DESIGN

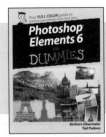  

978-0-470-19238-2    978-0-470-32725-8    978-0-470-34502-3

Access 2007 For Dummies
978-0-470-04612-8

Adobe Creative Suite 3 Design Premium
All-in-One Desk Reference For Dummies
978-0-470-11724-8

AutoCAD 2009 For Dummies
978-0-470-22977-4

C++ For Dummies, 5th Edition
978-0-7645-6852-7

Computers For Seniors For Dummies
978-0-470-24055-7

Excel 2007 All-In-One Desk Reference F
or Dummies
978-0-470-03738-6

Flash CS3 For Dummies
978-0-470-12100-9

Mac OS X Leopard For Dummies
978-0-470-05433-8

Macs For Dummies, 10th Edition
978-0-470-27817-8

Networking All-in-One Desk Reference
For Dummies, 3rd Edition
978-0-470-17915-4

Office 2007 All-in-One Desk Reference
For Dummies
978-0-471-78279-7

Search Engine Optimization For
Dummies, 2nd Edition
978-0-471-97998-2

Second Life For Dummies
978-0-470-18025-9

The Internet For Dummies, 11th Edition
978-0-470-12174-0

Visual Studio 2008 All-In-One Desk
Reference For Dummies
978-0-470-19108-8

Web Analytics For Dummies
978-0-470-09824-0

Windows XP For Dummies, 2nd Edition
978-0-7645-7326-2